Good
Clean
Humor

Collected and Narrated by
George C. Debnam, M.D.

A retired physician after fifty years and six months of dedicated Christian medical service and twenty-six years as deacon in a Protestant church.

February 2008

Raleigh, North Carolina

Good Clean Humor
Collected and Narrated by
George C. Debnam, M.D.

© Copyright 2008, Debnam Publishing Company

ISBN 13: 978-0-9815665-0-4
ISBN 10: 0-9815665-0-2

Library of Congress Control Number: 2008901676

All rights reserved

First printing, 2008

Debnam Publishing Company
P.O. Box 25997
Raleigh, NC 27611-5997

for more information, please contact us at:
www.debnampublishing.com
info@debnampublishing.com

Design & Publishing Services by Publications Unltd • Raleigh, North Carolina
WWW.PUBLICATIONSUNLTD.COM

Good Clean Humor

True humor springs not more from the head than from the heart. It is not contempt, its essence is love. It issues not in laughter, but in still smiles which lie far deeper. —*Thomas Carlyle*

Humor is an affirmation of dignity, a declaration of man's superiority to all that befalls him. —*Romain Gary*

A man isn't poor if he can still laugh. —*Raymond Hitchcock*

Good humor is goodness and wisdom combined. —*Owen Meredith*

With the fearful strain that is on me night and day, if I did not laugh, I should die. —*Abraham Lincoln*

Good humor isn't a trait of character, it is an art which requires practice. —*David Seabury*

Humor is the other side of tragedy. Humor is serious. I like to think of it as one of our greatest and earliest national resources which must be preserved at all costs. It came over on the Mayflower and we should have it, all of it. —*James Grover Thurber*

For health and the constant enjoyment of life, give me a keen and ever present sense of humor, it is the next best thing to an abiding faith in providence. —*George Barrell Cheever*

FOREWORD

The following is a collection of humorous vignettes, fables and stories designed to entertain and to inform. These stories were heard by Dr. Debnam around the open fireplace in his home on a farm in Franklin County, North Carolina, by his mother and family members during his years in elementary and high school in Franklin County; during his years as a college student at Shaw University in Raleigh, North Carolina, and in his years at Meharry Medical College in Nashville, Tennessee, from sermons and speeches he has heard in churches and from doctors and patients whom he has met during his fifty years and six months tenure as a family physician. The author's catch has also included the fare at the barbershops, service stations and on the many jobs Dr. Debnam held while working his way through college and medical school.

Webster's dictionary states that a smile is (1) "to look pleased or amused, show pleasure, favor, amusement and kindness by a curve of the mouth." (2) "to look pleasant; be agreeable; look with favor." It is written in the Holy Writ: A merry heart doeth good like a medicine: but a broken spirit drieth the bones. (Proverbs 17:22)

The Value of a Smile

A smile costs nothing, but creates much good. It enriches those who receive it without impoverishing those who give it away. A smile happens in a flash but the memory of it can last forever. No one is so rich that he can get along without a smile. No one is too poor to feel rich when receiving a smile. Smiles create happiness in the home, foster goodwill in business and are the countersigns of friends. A smile is rest to the weary, daylight to the discouraged, sunshine to the sad and nature's best antidote for trouble. Yet smiles cannot be bought, begged, borrowed, or stolen for they are of no earthly good to anybody until they are given away willingly.
—Anonymous

CONTENTS

Foreword 5

I Laughs About Animals
The Talking Parrot 14
The Sleeping Dogs 15
The Bird In Cold and Warm Weather 16
The Talking Mule 17
The Talking Skull 18
The Flying Turtle 19
The Copperhead 20
The Moonshiner and the Rattlesnake 21
Eating Farther Down the Hog 22
The Man in the Moon 23
Rabbit-hunting and the Pig 24
The Rabbit, the Fox and the Mule 25
The Rabbit and the Fox 26
The Wise Mule 27

II Laughs About the Church
The Silver Dollar and the Brown Cent 30
Money Goes to Church 31
I Am Money 32
The Chandelier 33
Length Versus Brevity 34
The Deacon and the Beggar 35
The Lord's Prayer 36
The Blind Man on a Moonlit Night 37
Top Ten Hymns for People
  Beyond the Age of 65 38

Not Taking a Chance	39
Signs	40
Still Water	40
All Dressed Up and Nowhere to Go	41
If the Shoe Fits, Wear It!	42
Billy and the Last Supper	44
The Plus Sign	45
A Second Opinion	46
How to Build Up the Cause of Christ	47
Why People Go to Church	48
A Church Garden	49
Space Talk for Churches	50

III *Laughs About College*

The Books of the Bible	52
Shakespeare	53
"The Shadow Do"	54
The Doughnut	55
πr^2	56
$\pi = 3\,^1/_7$ or 3.14	56
B.T.U.	57
Rock and Roll Guitar	58
Big Words	59
A Smart Small Boy	60
Crisis at the Bus Station and the Street Corner	60
Memory Versus Knowledge	61
He Who Works	62
Train Wreck	62
Dick Tracy	63
A Certain Father and His Son	64

	George Washington	64
	The Boy and His Father	65
	George Washington and the Cherry Tree	66
	Who Is Asking the Questions	67
IV	**Laughs About Marriage**	
	The Drunk Man In the Cemetery	70
	Chewing Tobacco	71
	A Needle in the Lamp Post	72
	Nursing the Baby	72
	Beef-stew Couple	73
	Future Occupations	74
	The Quadruplets	75
	A Powerful Son	76
	The Cost of Marriage	76
	Santa Claus	77
	Billy and his Father	77
	50th Wedding Anniversary	78
	The Father of the Bride	79
	The Old Maid and the Burglar	80
V	**Laughs About Clergy and Ministers**	
	The Minister and My Grandmother	84
	The Minister and the Peach Brandy	85
	The Three Ministers and the Bats	86
	Let It Walk!!! Let It Walk!!!	87
	Beware of Leftovers	88
	They Came to Pass; They Did Not Come to Stay	89
	Do Not Give Him My Drumstick	90
	The Four Year Old Grandson	91

	The Minister, the Little Boy and Heaven	92
	The Preacher and the Cow	93
	A Bellyfull	94
	The Minister and the Car Repairs	95
	The Calendar	96
	How to Get Rid of a Minister	97
VI	*Laughs About Physicians and Medical Professionals*	
	The Wrong Diagnosis	100
	The Doctor and the Rash	101
	Weight Loss	102
	Get the Right Directions	103
	Dying Between Two Thieves	104
	The Doctor and the Organs	105
	Difficult for Them, But Not for Me	106
VII	*Laughs About Ghosts*	
	The White Dog and the Wake	108
	On the Cooling Board	109
	James and the Potato	110
VIII	*Miscellaneous Laughs*	
	Working Together	112
	Explanation	113
	Pipe in Mouth	114
	Disappointing Rewards	114
	The Lady and the Mountains	115
	I'm Sopping My Own Gravy Now	116
	The Bootlegger	118
	The Little Man Waving the Stick	119
	What Day of the Week Were You Born?	120

The Way You Look at It	120
Friendship	121
Little Things Are Important	121
No Self Pats	122
Success	122
Whose Job Is It?	123
I Am Not Lost	124
The Horseshoe Nail	125
Bibliography	127
George C. Debnam, M.D.	128

I.
LAUGHS ABOUT ANIMALS

- *The Talking Parrot*
- *The Sleeping Dogs*
- *The Birds in Cold and Warm Weather*
- *The Talking Mule*
- *The Talking Skull*
- *The Flying Turtle*
- *The Copperhead*
- *The Moonshiner and the Rattlesnake*
- *Eating Farther Down the Hog*
- *The Man in the Moon*
- *Rabbit Hunting and the Pig*
- *The Rabbit, the Fox -and the Mule*
- *The Rabbit and the Fox*
- *The Wise Mule*

THE TALKING PARROT

The owner of a parrot took his parrot to the ABC store (or Alcoholic Beverage Control Store) on Saturday. The parrot asked his owner, "Where is this, where is this?"

The owner replied, "This is a whiskey store, whiskey store."

The next day the owner took the parrot to church, and the parrot was quite loquacious. He began to yell, "Whiskey store, whiskey store," as the choir began to sing and the deacon tried to pray.

The owner became irate and scolded, "Hush you fool. This is no whiskey store, this is the church."

The parrot replied, "Same crowd! Same crowd!"

—Anonymous

Moral:

1. Watch where you go. Parrot may be watching you.
2. Does the world know whether you are a Christian or not? They should.

THE SLEEPING DOGS

A young couple always brought their two golden retrievers to church on Sunday. The new pastor changed the rule and stated that the dogs had to stay at home. He said that the Lord wanted people in the pews, not dogs.

The young couple dutifully took their dogs home as their pastor requested and returned to church.

As the pastor stood at the door, shaking hands at the close of services, the husband came and shook his hand remarking, "Pastor, thank you for having us to take our dogs home. My wife and I have always trained our dogs to stay awake in church. However, if they had been here today, they would have definitely gone to sleep."

—Anonymous

Moral:

1. Do not let sleeping dogs lie. It may be a bad example for the Congregation.
2. There should be enough enthusiasm in the sermon to keep the dogs awake — as well as the parishioners.

THE BIRD IN COLD AND WARM WEATHER

There was a bird that was spending the winter in the far North with all of its ice and snow; life was severe and grim, indeed. The bird had heard that weather conditions were much better in the South, so the bird flew south.

In the South the bird noticed a cow grazing in a pasture and crept up behind the cow to get warm. The cow had a movement that covered the bird and made him very warm, indeed. In fact, he became so warm that he began to chirp and sing. A cat heard him singing and crept up behind the bird and ate him. There are several morals to this story:

—Anonymous

Moral:

1. If you have some business, keep quiet about it because you don't want everyone to know your business.
2. Everyone that puts you in a pickle is not necessarily your enemy and;
3. Everyone who gets you out is not necessarily your friend.
4. Stay alert and focused
5. The Good Book says to watch as well as pray.

—Anonymous

THE TALKING MULE

A worker was stealing corn from a barn. A mule was nearby in a pasture. There was a ventriloquist nearby who could see the mule, as well as the worker stealing the corn, but the worker could not see him. The ventriloquist threw his voice into the mule. This is what the mule said, "Fella, fella, you had better stop stealing the boss's corn."

The fella looked around and only saw the mule and he replied to the mule, "Mule, I am tending to my business and you had better be tending to your own business."

The mule repeated himself, "Fella, fella, you had better stop stealing from the boss's corn."

The fella replied, "Mule, how many times have I got to tell you to tend to your business and leave mine alone?"

The ventriloquist picked up an ear of corn, threw it and it hit the mule. The mule galloped up toward the boss's house. The fella dropped the sack of com and ran behind yelling, "Boss! Boss! This mule is getting ready to tell you a big lie!"

—Anonymous

Moral:

- Please listen to sound advice: don't steal corn or anything else.

THE TALKING SKULL

A man was walking through the woods one day and he discovered a skull. He said out loud to himself, "What in the world is this skull doing here and whose skull is it?"

He was very amazed when the skull spoke to him and said, "My mouth brought me here and if you don't watch out, your mouth is going to bring you here, also."

The worker went back and told his boss that there was a skull down in the woods that could talk. The boss responded incredulously, "That is impossible."

The worker insisted, "If you don't believe me, come and go with me down into the woods and I will show you."

The boss submitted, "It is a long way down there; but my friends and I will go and that skull had better talk, or you are going to be in serious trouble."

So down into the woods they went. Both the worker and the boss spoke to the skull, and the skull said not a word. The boss became angry. He and his friends dispatched the worker for lying, and left him down in the woods with the skull.

As soon as they left, the skull said, "I told you that my mouth got me here and your mouth would get you here — and here you are."

—*Anonymous*

Moral:

- It pays to listen to good advice.

THE FLYING TURTLE

There was a turtle in the far North who had two geese as friends. Every fall the geese would fly south to Florida to escape the cold. The turtle asked his geese friends to let him fly south with them. They said, "How are we going to do that? You have no wings!"

The turtle thought and thought and he came up with this idea. "Get a stick and each one you take an end of the stick in your mouth and I will bite the stick in the middle between you and we can fly to Florida." The geese thought it was a brilliant idea and so off they went. Everything was fine until they passed over a field where people were working. The people looked up and said with much amazement, "My goodness! Look at that turtle flying! Wonder who thought up that brilliant idea."

The turtle opened his mouth and said, "I did!"

—*Anonymous*

Moral:

1. You do not have to answer all questions that are asked.

2. Sometimes it is wise to keep one's mouth shut.

THE COPPERHEAD

Two fellows from a foreign country were walking down a rural road when they saw a snake with broad chestnut red bands between coppery red ones crossing the road. One fellow ran up to the snake and stomped its head. The snake bit him on the leg. He stomped the head of the snake a second time, and the snake bit him again. He stomped on the head of the snake for the third time, and the snake bit him again.

He turned to his buddy and said to him, "Why don't you stomp him some, I am getting weak and dizzy."

—*Anonymous*

Moral:

1. You do not get close enough to a copperhead to stomp him unless he is already dead.

2. Stomping snakes is not good exercise any way.

3. Killing a snake requires a hoe with a long handle.

THE MOONSHINER AND THE RATTLESNAKE

In the western mountains of North Carolina, there was a gentleman engaged in the manufacturing business. He manufactured white lightning, or moonshine. This night he had been up on the mountain all night long and had partaken very liberally of his manufactured product. On the way down, he suddenly found himself within the coils of a rattlesnake. It was already too late to jump, so he said to the rattlesnake, "Come on and bite me, old fellow. I am in better shape now than I will ever be again."

—*Anonymous*

Moral:

1. Be ye also ready for ye know not the minute nor the hour.
2. Alcohol is a good remedy for snake poison.

EATING FARTHER DOWN THE HOG

There was a man named John Ashe who cut wood for a living. He usually would accept for pay just a hog's head raised in a part of the country where they grew hogs. So one day someone gave him a piece of shoulder, which tasted very good to him since he had never tasted it before. He passed by one of his old friends, who had killed a couple of hogs. The children called out, "Mama, here comes Uncle John."

She called out, "Children, tell Uncle John I will give him a hog's head to cut a load of wood." He just threw up the back of his hand and wouldn't stop. Finally, their mother came out and called, "John, John, I will give you two hog heads for one load of wood."

He kept on going and said, "Children, tell your mama I'm eating farther down the hog now."

—*Anonymous*

Moral:

- Hog heads are good, but shoulders, hams and pork chops are better.

THE MAN IN THE MOON

There was a wolf who loved cheese. One night during the full moon, he caught a fox and was going to eat him. The fox said, "Please, Mr. Wolf, do not eat me and I will show you where a large cheese is."

The wolf said, "You had better not be kidding." So the fox led the wolf to a large well. The full moon was shining over the well and its reflection was upon the water in the well and it looked just like a cheese.

The fox said, "Mr. Wolf, there is the cheese in the bottom of the well." The well was a two-bucket well that was operated by a pulley. One bucket went down while the other bucket was coming up. The wolf said, "Get in a bucket, go down and get it and bring it up to me."

The fox got in the bucket and went down into the well. Once down, he began to yell, "Mr. Wolf, it is so heavy that I can't lift it. Please get in the other bucket and come down to help me." The wolf, with thoughts of big cheese in his mouth, jumped into the other bucket and started down. The wolf was larger and heavier than the fox. As he went down, the fox came up. As they passed each other in the middle of the well, the fox said, "Good-bye, Brother Wolf. You will get there soon and feast on cheese with the man in the moon."

—*Anonymous*

Moral:

1. Greediness has its drawbacks.

2. The greedy serve the devil without receiving his wages.

—*Charles Calele Colton*

3. Greediness in the process of getting more, deprives itself of the true end of getting; it loses the enjoyment of what it had got.

—*Thomas Sprat*

RABBIT-HUNTING AND THE PIG

I went to rabbit-hunting
I killed a rabbit dead
My pig, he came a-grunting
I hit him in the head.
That pig, he laid and wallowed
As if he was trying to die
Then my daddy hollered
Boy, I tried to fly.
I slipped back home that night
And sat down by the fire
I could not rest alright
I was watching my daddy's eye.
Mother sent me out to fetch a pail of taters
I walked out in the dew
My daddy grabbed his gaiters
I'll tell you those taters flew.
We had a race across the field,
and went up toward Aunt Mattie's
My daddy was whipping me step by step
You all should have seen my daddy.

—*Anonymous*

Moral:

1. A good run is better than a bad stand.
2. Always be prepared to run.

THE RABBIT, THE FOX AND THE MULE

The rabbit had a mule and his friend the fox asked, "B'rer Rabbit, will this mule kick?"

The rabbit said, "No, B'rer Fox, you can lie down behind that mule all day and he won't kick." The fox lay down behind the mule and went to sleep.

The rabbit slipped and tied the fox's tail to the mule's tail and hit the mule with a switch. The mule took off down through the fields. The little fox was going up and down. The rabbit yelled "Hold him, B'rer Fox!!!"

The fox yelled back, "How can I hold him when I don't have a single foot on the ground?"

—*Anonymous*

Moral:

1. Keep your feet on the ground and keep your head straight.
2. Watch what you go to sleep behind and what you go to sleep around.

THE RABBIT AND THE FOX

The rabbit and the fox set out to courting. They knew where some girls were, but someone had to go up and call the girls out. The girls had a very jealous daddy. The rabbit said, "Brer Fox, if you will stay here, I will go and call the girls."

The fox said, "OK."

The rabbit said, "Brer Fox, I don't believe you will stay until I get back."

The fox replied, "Just tie me to a tree, Brer Rabbit, and you will know that I will still be here."

So the rabbit tied the fox to the tree and went off to call the girls. The farmer had recently bought some new dogs, which the rabbit and fox did not know about, and these dogs jumped the rabbit as he neared the house. The rabbit headed back toward the fox, who could hear the barking of dogs getting nearer and nearer. The fox yelled, "Bear around, Brer Rabbit! Bear around Brer Rabbit!"

The rabbit yelled back, "Sorry, but I have got to come straight through."

—*Anonymous*

Moral:

1. Always pick loyal and faithful friends.

2. Don't let anyone tie you up.

3. A good run is better than a bad stand.

THE WISE MULE

A farmer loaded a wagon high with wood. A mule grazed nearby, but every once in a while he would cast a glance at the farmer loading the wagon. Finally, the farmer hitched the mule to the wagon and said, "Bob, Bill, Jim, Red, Spud, get up." The mule pulled off with the load of wood. A neighbor who was close by asked the farmer how many names did he call the mule. The farmer said, "Five names."

The neighbor said, "I have never seen a mule with five names. What is the mule's real name?"

The farmer replied that his name was Spud, the last name that he had called. The neighbor asked, "Why in the world are you calling him all of those other names?"

The farmer replied, "This mule is a wise mule and he would not pull this load by himself. He has to have some help."

—*Anonymous*

Moral:

1. That mule knew his limitations.
2. That is why blinders are put on mules' bridles. He does not need to see what is behind him or beside him. He needs only to look in front of him.
3. All of us need some help at times.
4. Even the Lone Ranger had Tonto.

II.
LAUGHS ABOUT THE CHURCH

- The Silver Dollar and the Brown Cent
- Money Goes to Church
- I Am Money
- The Chandelier
- Length Versus Brevity
- The Deacon and the Beggar
- The Lord's Prayer
- The Blind Man on a Moonlit Night
- Top Ten Hymns for People Beyond the Age of 65
- Not Taking a Chance
- Signs
- Still Water
- All Dressed Up and Nowhere to Go
- If the Shoe Fits, Wear It!
- Billy and the Last Supper
- The Plus Sign
- A Second Opinion
- How to Build Up the Cause of Christ
- Why People Go to Church
- A Church Garden
- Space Talk for Churches

THE SILVER DOLLAR AND THE BROWN CENT

A big silver dollar and a little brown cent

Rolling along together they went,

When the dollar remarked, for the dollar can talk

"You poor little cent, you cheap little mite

I am bigger and more than twice as bright

"I'm worth more than you a hundred-fold

And written on me in letters bold

"Is the motto drawn from the pious creed?

'In God we trust' which all can read."

"Yes, I know," said the cent. "I'm a cheap little mite

And I know I'm not big nor good, nor bright

"And yet," said the cent, with a meek little sigh

"You don't go to church as often as I."

—*Anonymous*

Moral:

+ It is not what you can do, but it is what you really do.

MONEY GOES TO CHURCH

A well worn one-dollar and a similarly distressed twenty dollar bill arrived at a Federal Reserve Bank to be retired. As they moved along the conveyor belt to be burned, they struck up a conversation.

The twenty-dollar bill reminisced about its travels all over the country. "I've had a pretty good life," the twenty proclaimed. "Why I've been to Las Vegas and Atlantic City, the finest restaurants in New York, performances on Broadway, and even a cruise to the Caribbean."

"Wow!" said the one-dollar bill. "You've had an exciting life!"

"So tell me," says the twenty, "where have you been throughout your lifetime?"

The one-dollar bill replied, "Oh, I've been to the Methodist Church, the Baptist Church, the Lutheran Church..."

The twenty-dollar bill interrupts, "What's a church?"

—*Anonymous*

I AM MONEY

Dug from the mountainside, washed

In the glen

Servant am I or master of men.

Steal me, I curse you;

Grasp me and hoard me.

A friend shall possess me,

Lie for me, die for me

Covet me, take me.

Angel or devil, I am what you make me.

—*Anonymous*

Moral:

- Money is neither good nor bad, but it can be used for good or bad purposes.

THE CHANDELIER

A young minister went to his first church conference in his new assignment and noted that the sanctuary was not well lighted, as it should have been. He announced to his parishioners that this church needed a chandelier. The Chairman of the Deacon Board replied — "Pastor, this church does not need a chandelier. In the first place, no one here knows how to play it. In the second place, we have no hymn books for the choir to sing with it. In the third place, we don't have enough money to buy one. In the fourth place, all this church needs is more light."

—*Anonymous*

Moral:

- Be careful with your choice of words. Stay as simple and down to earth as much as possible. Do not run the risk of being misunderstood.

LENGTH VERSUS BREVITY

Two men were sitting quietly in the congregation on Sunday morning while the minister was preaching. He was doing an excellent job so they said that they were going to give $20.00 each in the plate when it was passed. They had hoped for a short sermon because they had another engagement. The minister continued to preach, so they said that they were only going to give him $15.00 each. He continued to preach and they cut him down to $10.00 each. He continued to preach, and they cut him down to $5.00 each; and he continued to preach. They cut him down to $0.00, and he continued to preach. So when the plate was passed, they reached in and took out $10.00 each, saying, "When he started, we owed him, but now he has made us miss our engagement, so he owes us."

—Anonymous

Moral:

1. Quit while you are ahead.

2. When you have finished, please quit.

3. Length has its benefits, but brevity has its merit also.

THE DEACON AND THE BEGGAR

The deacon was on his way to teach Sunday School one morning. As he stepped out on the street, there was a beggar at his door. The beggar said, "Mister, please give me some bread. I have not eaten for three days."

The deacon said, "Get out of my way, I am on my way to teach Sunday School."

The beggar pleaded, "Please Mister, please."

The deacon cut a slice of bread so thin that one could read a newspaper through it and gave it to the beggar. As the beggar raised the piece of bread to his lips, the deacon said, "But you have not said the blessing. You can't eat my bread unless you say the blessing."

The beggar said, " Sir, I do not know one."

The deacon said, "Then I will teach you one. Repeat after me. Our Father, which art in heaven."

The beggar said, "Wait a minute, didn't you say, 'Our Father'?"

The deacon said, "Yes."

The beggar said, "Then if he is our Father, then we are brothers aren't we?"

The deacon said, "Yes, we are brothers in Christ."

The beggar said, "Then if we are brothers, cut that slice of bread like you would cut it for your brother and add some meat to it."

—*Anonymous*

Moral:

1. We are our brother's keeper.
2. Church is what one does from 1:00 P.M. on Sunday until 11:00 A.M. on the next Sunday.
3. The beggar got the best of the deacon who did not know who his brother was.

THE LORD'S PRAYER

Two gold miners struck it rich in Wyoming when they discovered a gold mine. However, the gold vein was not enough to satisfy the both of them, so they decided to give the mine to one of them and the other one would move on and find another mine in Montana, where gold had been recently discovered. They made a bet. He who knew the Lord's Prayer would get the mine. The first miner said:

"Now I lay me down to sleep.

I pray the Lord my soul to keep.

If I should die before I wake,

I pray the Lord my soul to take."

The second miner said, "You did know the Lord's Prayer. The mine is yours, and I am heading to Montana."

—Anonymous

Moral:

1. Neither one knew the Lord's Prayer.

2. The blind can lead the blind.

3. Sometimes, the blind leads those who can see.

4. The gold mine was doomed in the hands of people who did not know the Lord's Prayer.

THE BLIND MAN ON A MOONLIT NIGHT

Two young men on a moonlit night went to choir practice and noticed that all women in a certain family were there. The only person they had left at the house was the father who was completely blind. Said one to the other, "Let's go and steal some chickens. No one is home but the father and he is blind and can't do anything." So they went to the house, which was about a mile away from the church. The chickens were making a lot of noise. One fellow was in the chicken house putting them in a bag and the other one stood on watch at the door. He saw the blind man coming with his big hickory stick and yelled, "Here comes the blind man!" and ran away. The fellow in the chicken house did not hear the warning and continued putting chickens in the bags. When he finished, he saw the blind man poised just outside the door with his hickory stick drawn back. The fellow threw down the bag of chickens, tore off the top of the chicken house and escaped through the top. He did not dare go past the blind man with the hickory stick.

—Anonymous

Moral:

1. A blind man with a hickory stick is no push over.

2. Stealing is bad anyway.

3. Thou shall not steal.

TOP TEN HYMNS FOR PEOPLE BEYOND THE AGE OF 65

10. "It is Well with My Soul (But My Back Aches a Lot)"
9. "Nobody Knows the Trouble I Have Seeing"
8. "Amazing Grace (Consider My Age)"
7. "Just a Slower Walk with Thee"
6. "Count Your Many Birthdays, (Name Them One by One)"
5. "Go Tell It on the Mountain, (And For Goodness Sake, Speak Up!!)"
4. "Give Me That Old Timer's Religion"
3. "Blessed Insurance"
2. "Guide Me, O Thou Great Jehovah" "(I Have Forgotten Where I Parked My Car)"
1. "Nearer, My God to Thee"

—Anonymous

NOT TAKING A CHANCE

George went on a vacation to the Middle East with most of his family, including his mother-in-law. While they were visiting Jerusalem, George's mother-in-law died. With the death certificate in hand, George went to the American Consulate's Office to make arrangements to send the body back to the States for proper burial.

The Consul, after hearing of the death of the mother-in-law, told George that sending the body back to the States for burial was very, very expensive. It could cost as much as $5,000.00. The Consul continued, "In most cases, the person responsible for the remains normally decides to bury the body here. This would only cost $150.00."

George thought for some time and answered, "I don't care how much it will cost to send the body back; that's what I want to do."

The Consul, after hearing this, said, "You must have loved your mother-in-law very much considering the difference in cost."

"No, it's not that," said George. "You see, I know the story of a person buried in Jerusalem many years ago. On the third day he arose from the dead! I just can't take that chance ... my mother-in-law has to go back to New York. They do not arise from the dead in New York.

—*Anonymous*

SIGNS

A sign in front of a church in rural Wake County, North Carolina reads:

"WALMART IS NOT THE ONLY SAVING PLACE."

A sign in front of a church in rural North Carolina reads:

"VISITORS WELCOME;

MEMBERS EXPECTED."

STILL WATER

A young lady was discussing her wedding plans with her pastor at one of the conservative and strait-laced Baptist churches. The young bride-to-be did not want to march in on Lohengrin's "Here Comes the Bride." She wanted to march in on a Rhythm and Blues song titled "Still Water Runs Deep."

The old pastor stated, "Sister, it may run deep at some churches, but it will not run deep at this one." The bride-to-be changed her church. The marriage lasted only three months.

—*Anonymous*

Moral:
- It ran deep, but it did not run long.

ALL DRESSED UP AND NOWHERE TO GO

As I grew up in rural North Carolina, there was a family of a father, a mother, and seven girls. All were members of the church except the father. In those days, the churches in the area held their revivals during the months of July and August. There were no air conditioners in the churches at the time.

The father would go to church each night of the five nights that church was in revival. These were the days of the mourner's bench. Prior to the sermon, the minister would ask all Christians to raise their hands. Then he would ask all sinners to raise their hands. The sinners would then be invited to the mourner's bench to get religion. The father would always raise his hand with the sinners, but would refuse to go to the mourner's bench in spite of much begging and pleading by the minister.

The father did this year after year, going to the church, sitting on the back bench, raising his hand with the sinners and refusing to go to the mourner's bench. After many years, the father finally died. The daughters and the wife dressed him up so nicely after he was taken to the funeral home and was embalmed. They arrayed him in a handsome black suit, white shirt and black bow tie. He lay in state in the parlor of the home for visitation and viewing for three days prior to burial.

An old minister who knew him well and whose church he had visited many times came by to visit and to view him. As he was leaving, he met several other viewers and visitors in the yard. He said to them, "That man is all dressed up, but has nowhere to go."

—*Anonymous*

Moral:

- Be sure you know your destination.

IF THE SHOE FITS, WEAR IT!

In order to take care of all the excuses for not attending church, the following information was placed in a local newspaper:

1. Beds will be placed in the fellowship hall for those who say, "Sunday is my only day to rest."
2. Eye drops will be available for those with tired eyes from watching TV too late on Saturday night.
3. Steel helmets will be provided for those who say, "The roof would cave in if I ever went to church."
4. Blankets will be furnished for those who think that church is too cold and air-conditioning for those who say it is too hot.
5. We will reserve the front pews for those who like the pastor's sermons and the back pews with earplugs for those who dislike his sermons.
6. Scorecards will be available for those who list the hypocrites present.
7. TV dinners will be available for those who can't go to church and cook the noon meal for the family.
8. We will have a selection of trees and shrubs for those who like to see God in nature.

—Anonymous

Every church has, in addition to the brakeman, a construction crew and a wrecking crew. To which do you belong? One of them for sure.

Every church has three types of members: the workers, the jerkers, and the shirkers.

There are four classes of church members: the tired, the retired, the tiresome, and the tireless.

It seems that some church members have been starched and ironed, but too few have been washed.

Church member — No matter how you nurse a grudge, it won't get better.

BILLY AND THE LAST SUPPER

My nephew Billy, at the age of four years, was being shown a picture of The Last Supper by his father. Billy was a young fellow who had problems with his eating. His parents had to close their eyes and count until he had drunk his orange juice. They also had to threaten to coerce him into eating his bacon and eggs, drinking his milk, and eating other foods at the table. Billy had found out early that he could command the attention of both parents at the table by raising their concerns about his not eating. He enjoyed this attention immensely.

The father explained the great story of The Last Supper and said this to Billy, "The Lord is serving His disciples the Last Supper, and He is talking to His disciples. What do you think He is saying to them?"

Billy, remembering his many experiences at the table, replied quickly, "He is saying, eat up now, boys, this is the last meal that you are going to get."

—*Anonymous*

THE PLUS SIGN

Whatever Works ...

Little David, who was Jewish, was failing math. His parents tried everything tutors, mentors, flashcards, special learning centers — and nothing helped.

As a last resort, someone told them to try a Catholic school. "Those nuns are tough," they said. David was soon enrolled at St. Mary's.

After school on the first day, David ran through the door and straight up to his room, without even kissing his mother hello. He started studying furiously. Books and papers were spread out all over his room. Right after dinner he ran back upstairs without mentioning TV, and hit the books harder than before. His parents were amazed; a miracle was in the making.

This behavior continued for weeks, until report card day arrived. David quietly laid the envelope on the table, and went up to his room. With great fear and trepidation, his mother slowly opened the report card; David had gotten an "A" in math!

She ran up to his room, threw her arms around him and asked, "David, honey, how did you do it? Was it the nuns?"

"No," said David, "On the first day of school when I saw that guy nailed to the plus sign I knew they weren't fooling around!"

—*Anonymous*

A SECOND OPINION

A mountain climber fell from a high mountain but was able to catch a small tree and break his fall. While hanging there in midair, he called to Heaven for help. The voice from Heaven said, "Turn loose the tree, I will take care of you." The climber called Heaven again for help and said, "Lord, I need a second opinion. Is there anyone else up there?"

Moral:

- The faith of a mustard seed is enough to move a mountain.

—Anonymous

HOW TO BUILD UP THE CAUSE OF CHRIST

Christians need to:

    Wake up

    Sing up

    Preach up

    Pray up

    Stay up

    Pay up

    But never give up

    Let up

    Back up

    Shut up

Until the cause of Christ and the Church in the world is built up.

    —*"Church Bulletins Bits"*

WHY PEOPLE GO TO CHURCH

Some go to church to take a walk;
Some go there to laugh and talk.
Some go there to meet a friend;
Some go there their time to spend.
Some go there to meet a lover;
Some go there a fault to cover.
Some go there for speculation;
Some go there for observation.
Some go there to doze and nod;
The wise go there to Worship God.

—*"Church Bulletins Bits"*

A CHURCH GARDEN

First, plant five rows of peas:
- Presence.
- Promptness.
- Preparation.
- Purity.
- Perseverance.

Next to these, plant three rows of squash:
- Squash gossip.
- Squash criticism.
- Squash indifference.

No garden is complete without turnips:
- Turn up for the meetings.
- Turn up with a smile.
- Turn up with new ideas.
- Turn up with determination to make everything count for something good and worthwhile.

—*"Church Bulletins Bits"*

SPACE TALK FOR CHURCHES

All systems go — the Sunday morning service is about to begin.

Age of space — the auditorium on Sunday night.

Artificial gravity — the look on everyone's face, when the pastor announces he's going to preach on tithing.

Burned-out-booster — the preacher a about 10:00 P.M. on Sunday night.

Did you read me? — what the discarded church bulletin might say if it were alive.

Echo 1, Echo 2 — the preacher's jokes.

Escape velocity — the speed at which people leave the church on Sunday morning.

Extra-vehicular activity — errands the pastor runs for church members.

G force — the pressure exerted by a soloist who wants to sing.

Ground zero — the pulpit.

Joint cooperation in space — congregational singing.

Parent craft — learning to get along with the parents of your Sunday school children.

Return to earth — the preacher standing at the door after the service.

Scrubbed — visitation called off due to lack of interest.

Surveyor — pulpit committee.

Ten-minute hold — the invitation.

Walking in space — what some church members think the preacher ought to do — all the time!

—Bernie Rhodes

III.
LAUGHS ABOUT COLLEGE

- *The Books of the Bible*
- *Shakespeare*
- *"The Shadow Do"*
- *The Doughnut*
- *πr2*
- *π = 3 1/7 or 3.14*
- *B.T.U.*
- *Rock and Roll Guitar*
- *Big Words*
- *A Smart Small Boy*
- *Crisis at the Bus Station and the Street Corner*
- *Memory Versus Knowledge*
- *He Who Works*
- *Train Wreck*
- *Dick Tracy*
- *A Certain Father and His Son*
- *George Washington*
- *The Boy and His Father*
- *George Washington and the Cherry Tree*
- *Who Is Asking the Questions*

THE BOOKS OF THE BIBLE

Long ago, the church-related colleges required students to go to chapel two or three times during the week and on Sunday afternoons. In addition, the colleges also had courses called Introduction to the Bible 101 and Introduction to the Bible 102.

At one of these church-related colleges, an old minister taught Bible 101 and 102. Every year for thirty years, his final exam question was to name the Books of the Bible.

The students would study their math, biology, and English, and would learn the names of the Books of the Bible, all 66 of them and they would get an "A" in the course.

In his thirty-first year of teaching the course, he changed the final examination question to "Trace Paul's second journey through Asia Minor." Pandemonium gripped the class. One male student spent two hours trying to remember some cities in Asia Minor. Finally, he gave up and wrote this on his final examination paper: "Reverend Smith, of Paul's journey through Asia Minor, I know nothing, but if you want the books of the Bible, here they are." The compassionate old minister gave the young man a "c" with the explanation that he had indeed learned something about the Bible.

—Anonymous

Moral:

1. Nothing beats a trial but a failure.

2. One must try.

3. Effort is worth something.

SHAKESPEARE

An English professor asked one of his students the following question: "Mr. Easterling, why did the ghost in The Merchant of Venice speak in Latin?"

The student replied, "Dr. Brawley, Mr. Shakespeare had the ghost to speak in Latin, because Latin is a dead language."

Dr. Brawley, retorted, "Mr. Easterling, I knew that you knew nothing about the man when you called him Mr. Shakespeare. I have studied Shakespeare's works in six languages, and nowhere was he addressed as Mr. Shakespeare. It was always Shakespeare, no mister about it."

—*Anonymous*

Moral:

- Be careful what you say and to whom you say it.

"THE SHADOW DO"

There was a radio program in the early years of my life that came on NBC and was known as the "SHADOW." The Shadow went about correcting wrongs and punishing lawbreakers and offenders.

The show always came on the radio with a very deep resonant, ominous and menacing voice and said these words: "Who knows what evil lurks in the hearts of men? The Shadow knows. Ha! Ha! Ha! Ha!"

There was a worker in the NBC Headquarters in New York who listened to this introit and would practice it and go all over town — in the barbershops, on the streets and everywhere — with the famous opening. There were people all over town who were saying, "John Jones can say that statement better than the star of the show. They ought to let him say it sometimes."

One Sunday night the star of the show suddenly became ill and could not do the show, so they rushed the fellow in who was doing it all over town to take his place. This was his great moment in time.

As the lights went on and he was to make the great statement, which would have made him famous forever, this is what he said: "Who knows what evil lurks in the hearts of men. The Shadow do."

Moral:

1. Somewhere along the line, he had forgotten the statement.
2. Moreover, he had split a verb, which was unforgivable in those days.
3. He was just not ready after many rehearsals.
4. Get it right, or leave it alone.

—Anonymous

THE DOUGHNUT

There was a young man who was a very fine football prospect. He was an all-state performer, highly recruited across the country. He had only one major drawback; he was a very poor student and had difficulty with his classes.

A college coach succeeded in recruiting the young man to come to his college. He spoke with the teachers, and they devised a plan to keep the young man in school and let him star on the football team. Here was the plan. He was to go to class and ask no questions. He was to be perfectly quiet and he would be given a "C" and pass on to the next class.

On the very first day in biology class, the teacher drew a large circle and then a smaller circle inside the larger circle. This was supposed to be a cell with a nucleus. The teacher asked the class to identify the structure. No one said anything and the young football player held up his hand. The professor ignored him because he was aware of the deal.

The young football player became adamant and told the teacher, "Sir, can't you see that my hand is up, why don't you recognize me?" The teacher, faced with this set of circumstances, asked him the question, and he replied very boldly and confidently, "Teacher, everybody knows that is a doughnut and I want to eat one at this very moment."

—*Anonymous*

Morals:

1. Sometimes it is better to be seen and not heard.

2. It is better to be quiet and thought a fool than to speak and remove all doubt.

—*President Abraham Lincoln*

πr^2

A teacher asked a young male student the following question:

"George, how much is πr^2?"

The young man replied, "Teacher, pies are not square. They are round."

— *Anonymous*

Moral:

- One must understand the question.

$$\pi = 3\,{}^1/_7 \text{ or } 3.14$$

B.T.U.

At a Baptist university, the physics teacher asked a student the following question: "What is a B.T.U.?"

The student replied that a B.T.U. is a Baptist Training Union. The physics professor stated that it may be true at a Divinity School, but in physics it is a British Thermal Unit — the amount of heat required to raise one pound of water 1° Fahrenheit.

—Anonymous

Moral:

1. It all depends on where you are. In England, you are in a lift. In America, you are in an elevator.
2. In England, you are in a hack. In America, you are in a taxi-cab.

ROCK AND ROLL GUITAR

A mother who was trying to enroll her son in college asked the admissions officer, "Won't it help his admissions exams to know that he is so good on the rock and roll guitar?"

"It might have helped ten years ago," the admission officer replied, "but now we are looking for good listeners, because they have to listen to the professors to learn in college."

—*Anonymous*

Moral:

1. Let us think about a good thing.

2. Let us search for a good thing.

3. Let us find a good thing.

4. Let us keep and appreciate a good thing.

5. Above all, please recognize a good thing.

BIG WORDS

A young ministerial student went up to his professor one Friday afternoon and asked the professor to help him pronounce these three words.

1. Omnipotent

2. Omnipresent

3. Omniscient

The professor gave him the proper pronunciations, but he then asked the young student why he needed this information. The young ministerial student stuck out his chest and said, "I am going to preach at a rural church on Sunday, and I want to describe God to that rural congregation."

The wise old professor told the student, "Son, those people will run you away from there with those big words. Please remember what Jesus said about God. He said, 'Our Father which art in Heaven.' Just tell them that God is a good and great father. That will take care of everything."

—*Dr. John W. Fleming*

Moral:

- Again, keep it sweet and simple. Do not use a baseball bat to swat a fly. A fly swatter will do.

A SMART SMALL BOY

A small boy brought home his report card. His father was disturbed about the grades, "Your teacher must think you are very stupid."

"Well daddy, no wonder he thinks I am stupid. I am only in the fifth grade and he is a college graduate."

—*Anonymous*

CRISIS AT THE BUS STATION AND THE STREET CORNER

A student arrived at the bus station in a city where he was supposed to enroll in college at the late hour of 11:00 P.M. He did not have a sufficient amount of money to take a taxi, so he called the college and got the President on the phone. The President said, "We have both Greyhound and Trailways stations here. I will be glad to come and get you if you will only tell me at which bus station?" The young man said, "Sir, I do not know."

The President advised the student to go to the nearest corner and obtain the names of the intersecting streets and he would hold on in the meantime. The student came back and said, "Mr. President, I am on the corner of Walk and Don't Walk."

Moral:
- Some need to go to college and some need to go to work.

—*Anonymous*

MEMORY VERSUS KNOWLEDGE

On the first day of school, the teacher asked six-year-old James whether or not he knew the alphabet. "Yes," said James and he proceeded to say them:

A	J	S
B	K	T
C	L	U
D	M	V
E	N	W
F	O	X
G	P	Y
H	Q	Z
I	R	…and so forth

The teacher went to the blackboard where the alphabet was listed at the top — written both in print and in cursive. With a pointer, she asked James to identify each one. He could not identify a single one. The teacher said, "James you know how to say your ABC's, but you don't know them."

—*Anonymous*

Moral:

- A lot of us say things that we do not know.

HE WHO WORKS

1. He who works with his hands is a laborer.
2. He who works with his hands and his head is a craftsman.
3. He who works with his hands, his head, and his heart is an artist.
4. He who works with his hands, his head, his heart, and his feet is a salesman.

—Anonymous

TRAIN WRECK

A teacher was teaching a class and wrote a problem on the black board. Train A and Train B were 100 miles apart. They were traveling toward one another. Train A was traveling 40 miles per hour and Train B was traveling 25 miles per hour. The question was — at what point would they meet? The problem was presented to Sylvester. Sylvester said, "Teacher, I do not know the answer, but I am going to get my brother Leroy."

When asked by the teacher why he was going to get Leroy, Sylvester replied, "Leroy has never seen a train wreck and these trains are going to wreck if they continue to travel toward one another."

—Anonymous

Moral:

1. Interpretation is a part of the test.
2. Leroy was not going to help answer the problem as given by the teacher.

DICK TRACY

In my freshman year of medical school, Gross Anatomy was an awesome subject. Every five students had a cadaver to dissect and identify the structures.

There was one professor with a foreign accent. He pronounced his R's as W's. His favorite pastime was to walk up to a student and ask a question in orthopedics, which we were supposed to have in our third year, not our first year. When we could not answer, and did not know the answer to the question, his routine was to pull out a grade book and write a grade beside our names. He would say, "You do not know. I give you *zewo*. What have you been *weading*, Dick *Twacy?*"

—*Dr. A.A. Williams*

Moral:

- A zero is not funny.

A CERTAIN FATHER AND HIS SON

A certain father one day asked the president of a college if it would be possible for his son to take a short course, not spending so much time in school. To this the President replied, "Yes, he can take a short course. It all depends on what you want to make out of him. When God wants to make an oak, He takes a hundred years; but, He takes only a few months to make some other small plants. It takes time to build a man or a tree, and it takes all kinds of weather."

—*Anonymous*

Moral:

- A plant or a tree, to be or not to be. That is the question.

GEORGE WASHINGTON

A father was looking at his son's report card and said, "Son, this report card is terrible! Did you know that George Washington was at the head of his class when he was your age?"

The son replied, "Yes dad, but did you know that he was the President of the United States when he was your age?"

—*Anonymous*

Moral:

- A smart son.

THE BOY AND HIS FATHER

A very prosperous farmer had an eight-year-old son. He also had ten barns of corn and ten barns of wheat. When needy neighbors stopped by to ask him for some of his wheat and corn, he would always say, "Sorry, I have none to spare." The little boy heard these requests and he heard his father's answers.

Each morning at the breakfast table, the father would bless the food and add these words, "Lord bless the needy and the hungry. Please give them food and shelter and administer to their needs."

One morning when he had finished saying this blessing, the little eight-year old son said, "Father, I wish I had your wheat and your corn." The father said, "What would you do with it, son?" The little boy said, "I would answer that prayer that you made about the poor and the needy."

Moral:

1. Little pitchers have large ears.

2. And a little child shall lead them.

GEORGE WASHINGTON AND THE CHERRY TREE

In the western mountains of North Carolina, two boys rolled a boulder down the mountain striking the outdoor toilet and knocking it one mile down the mountain into the valley. Later that day, their father asked, "Who rolled the big rock down the mountain striking the toilet?"

The boys said, "We did, father." The father gave them a severe whipping. The boys could not understand the whippings and said, "Father, we told the truth and we were whipped. George Washington's father did not whip him when he admitted cutting down the cherry tree." The father replied, "George Washington's father was not in the Cherry tree when he cut it down."

—Anonymous

Moral:

- Know where your father is, please!!!

WHO IS ASKING THE QUESTIONS

A seven-year old lad was in elementary school, and there was some concern that he was academically challenged and that the curriculum was too much for him. A testing expert was called in to test him. The expert asked these questions:

1. Spell dog?
2. Spell cat?
3. Spell man?
4. Spell cow?
5. Spell pony?
6. Spell rat?
7. Spell ball?
8. Spell bat?
9. Spell hand?
10. Spell foot?

The young lad looked at the tester and said nothing, so a report was written up finding that the young lad was challenged. So the school sent a letter to his father advising him that the pupil would receive modified curriculum-special education at another school.

The father could not believe this. He called the pupil into the house from the playground, asked him to spell the same words and these were his responses:

1. Dog "D O G – daddy"
2. Cat "C A T – daddy"
3. Man "M A N – daddy"
4. Cow "C O W – daddy"
5. Pony "P O N Y – daddy"
6. Rat "R A T – daddy"
7. Ball "B A L L – daddy"
8. Bat "B A T – daddy"
9. Hand "H A N D – daddy"
10. Foot "F O O T – daddy"

"Well, son, why did you not spell these words during the tests at school today since you know how?"

The little boy replied, "Daddy, a grown man asked me how to spell those words. If he is grown and can't spell them, I am not about to tell him. Any grown man ought to be able to spell those words himself."

—*Anonymous*

Moral:

1. It all depends upon who is asking the questions.

2. And a little child shall lead them.

IV.
LAUGHS ABOUT MARRIAGE

- *The Drunk Man In the Cemetery*
- *Chewing Tobacco*
- *A Needle in the Lamp Post*
- *Nursing the Baby*
- *Beef-stew Couple*
- *Future Occupations*
- *The Quadruplets*
- *A Powerful Son*
- *The Cost of Marriage*
- *Santa Claus*
- *Billy and his Father*
- *50th Wedding Anniversary*
- *The Father of the Bride*
- *The Old Maid and the Burglar*

THE DRUNK MAN IN THE CEMETERY

There was a lady who had a husband who came home drunk every night with no money. She and her two brothers worked out a schedule to rid him of his bad habit. He had to pass through the cemetery to get home. So the brothers dug a deep hole in the path trough the cemetery and covered it with straw. When the drunken man came through one night, he fell into the hole. The brothers, hiding behind the tombstones, said in a deep base voice, "What are you doing in my grave?"

The drunken man replied with these words. "What in the world are you doing out of it?" He crawled out of the hole and went home, but he continued to drink every night. His mind was unchanged.

Moral:

- Sometimes the best laid plans of men, women and mice come to naught.

—Anonymous

CHEWING TOBACCO

There was a lady who was a great housekeeper who kept her hearth pretty and white with lime. Her husband chewed Brown Mule chewing tobacco and spat tobacco juice everywhere, trying to get it into the open fireplace. His wife begged and begged him to quit chewing, and after about a year, he quit.

But six months later she noticed another plug of Brown Mule chewing tobacco in the breast pocket of his bib overalls. She was indignant and said, "Honey, you promised me that you were going to stop chewing tobacco."

He answered, "I have stopped chewing tobacco."

She replied, "If you have stopped chewing, why is that big plug of Brown Mule up there in your bib pocket?"

He replied, "Honey, I just like to smell it every now and then." She said, "Honey, please get rid of it because if you keep smelling it, you are going to start back chewing it after a while."

Moral:

- Bad habits are hard to break.

—Anonymous

A NEEDLE IN THE LAMP POST

A little old lady was courting, and she wanted to get married. To impress her boyfriend with how young she was, she hid a needle in the lamp post some distance from the house. When she and the boyfriend were swinging in the swing one afternoon, she asked the boyfriend if that was a needle that she was seeing in the lamp post. The boyfriend went out to check, and indeed there was a needle in the lamp post. He was so impressed that he married her the next day. At the wedding reception the little old lady slapped the wedding cake off the table saying, "Scat you cat!"

Moral:

- What some people won't do to get married.

—*Anonymous*

NURSING THE BABY

A young couple went to see the doctor about their new baby. The baby was breast-feeding. The baby was complaining with the "tummy ache," and the doctor diagnosed the baby as having "colic."

He gave the mother a long list of things not to eat for they may also produce "colic."

The father of the baby asked the doctor, "Should I change my diet, and will my diet give the baby colic?"

The doctor said, "No, not unless you are nursing the baby."

—*George and Mary Lou Glover*

Moral:

It all depends upon who is doing what.

BEEF-STEW COUPLE

A man and his wife had been married for fifty years. They were a "beef-stew" couple. He was always beefing about something and she was always stewing. One day their children persuaded them to go to a psychologist. They were having one of their very worst arguments at the time. When they were ushered into the doctor's office, the woman kept talking as fast as she could for fifteen minutes.

After trying several times to get her attention, the doctor got up from his chair and went to her side. He kissed her thoroughly. She stopped talking.

"Now, husband, she should have that treatment about three times a week," the doctor told him.

"Right, doctor, if you say so. I'll bring her back to you three times a week. Please give her the treatment."

—*Anonymous*

Moral:

+ Things often are not as simple as they seem to be.

FUTURE OCCUPATIONS

The teacher was teaching in a one-teacher school where she taught all seven classes of an elementary school. Every Friday afternoon, before dismissal, she would have a program in which the children gave speeches and recitals.

She called on John to say his speech.

John: "When I grow up to be a man, I want to take a trip to Japan, if I can, and I think I can."

Then she called on Mary.

Mary: "When I grow up to be a lady, I want to be the mother of a fine baby, if I can, and I think I can."

Then she called on James.

James: "When I grow up to be a man, I do not want to go to Japan. I want to stay here and help Mary with her plan, if I can, and I think I can."

—Anonymous

Moral:

Everyone has plans. Some are good and some are not so good.

THE QUADRUPLETS

A wife went to the doctor and came home and reported to her husband. Her husband inquired as to what the doctor had to say. She reported that he said, "I have good news and bad news."

The husband asked her, "What is the good news?"

She replied, "I am pregnant."

The husband then asked, "What is the bad news?"

The wife replied, "He said that I have four heartbeats, and I am going to have quadruplets."

The husband said, "Gee whiz, that is indeed bad news because we already have twelve children."

The wife said, "I have been thinking very seriously about this news ever since I left the doctor's office and I already have four good names for them."

The husband said, "What are the names?"

She said, "They are Randolph, Rudolph, Get-oph and Stay-oph."

—*Anonymous*

Moral:

- These are appropriate names for the last four of sixteen children. They also send a message.

A POWERFUL SON

"My son," said Themistocles, "you are the most powerful man in all Greece. The Athenians rule the Hellenes, I rule the Athenians, your mother rules me, and you rule your mother."

—*The Speaker's Desk Book of Quips, Quotes, and Anecdotes*

THE COST OF MARRIAGE

A young man who was deeply in love and wanting to get married went to his father and informed the father of his situation. He then asked the father, "Sir, how much does it cost to get married?"

The father replied, "Son, I married your mother thirty years ago and I am still paying, so I really do not know how much it costs."

—*Anonymous*

Moral:

1. Some things cannot be valued in terms of money.

2. Marriage is coming — high cost or low cost.

3. Do like the father — keep on paying.

BILLY AND HIS FATHER

Billy came home from school one evening with the evidence of disobedience plainly visible upon him. To escape the merited chastisement, he crawled under the bed from which refuge his mother could not dislodge him. When Billy's father arrived, the situation was explained to him and he took the matter in hand. Getting down on the floor, he started to crawl under the bed after his wayward son. "Gee whiz," exclaimed Billy moving over, "Dad, is she after you too?"

—*Dr. Miller W. Boyd, Jr.*

Moral:

- Billy knew who wore the pants in the household.

SANTA CLAUS

One of our present troubles seems to be that too many adults, and not enough children, believe in Santa Claus.

—*Anonymous*

50th WEDDING ANNIVERSARY

A couple was enjoying their 50th wedding anniversary. They slept in twin beds in one room. The wife feeling very romantic on their 50th wedding anniversary night, went over and woke her husband up at 8:00 P.M. and said, "This is our 50th anniversary night. Can you recall what we were doing at 8:00 P.M. fifty years ago?"

The husband said, "No. What were we doing?" She said, "You were tickling my toes." The old gentleman got up and tickled her toes for twenty minutes and went back to sleep.

At 9:00 P.M., she got up and went over and woke him up again and posed the question, "Honey this is our 50th wedding anniversary night. Can you remember what we were doing fifty years ago at 9:00 P.M.?"

He said, "No. What were we doing?"

She said, "You were stroking my hair." So he got up and went over to her bed and stroked her hair for twenty minutes laid back down and went to sleep. She said, "I will not bother him again at 10:00 P.M., but I will try him again at 11:00 P.M. At 11:00 P.M. she went over to his bed again and posed the question, "Honey this is our 50th wedding anniversary. Do you remember what we were doing fifty years ago at 11:00 P.M.?"

He said, "No. What were we doing?" "Honey, you were biting me on my neck." Immediately, the husband jumped out of bed and started toward the kitchen. She said, "Honey, where are you going?"

He said, "You know that every night after I eat supper, I place my teeth in a dish of baking soda water until the next morning. If I am going to bite you, I had better go and get my teeth."

—Anonymous

Moral:

1. It is not by the gray of the hair that one knows the age of the heart.

   —*Baron Lytton*

2. If wrinkles must be written upon our brows, let them not be written upon the heart. The spirit should never grow old.

   —*James A. Garfield*

3. Youth is a blunder

   Manhood is a struggle

   Old age is a regret

   —*Benjamin Disraeli,*
   Queen Victoria's favorite Prime Minister

THE FATHER OF THE BRIDE

The father of a recent bride was asked by his friends to give them the names of his daughter's china, silver and crystal patterns. He replied, "I do not know them. Please ask my daughter or my wife. I was told only to 'dress up,' 'show up,' 'shut up' and 'pay up.' I have done all of these. The rest is up to them."

—*Dr. Clarence G. Newsome*

Moral:

1. Obedience is better than sacrifice.

2. A good soldier carries out his orders.

THE OLD MAID AND THE BURGLAR

A story I'll tell of a burglar bold
Who started to rob a house.
He opened the window and then crept in
As quiet as any mouse.

He looked around for a place to hide
As the folk were all asleep,
And then he said to himself,
"I'll make a price to keep."

So under the bed the burglar crept,
Close up to the wall.
He didn't know it was an Old Maid's room,
Or he wouldn't have had the gall.

He thought of all the money he would steal
As under the bed he lay;
But what he saw at 9:00 P.M.
Made his hair turn gray.

The old maid came in at 9:00.
"I am so tired," she said.
She thought that all was well that night.
She didn't look under the bed.

She had big teeth
And a big glass eye,
And on the bed she lay.
The burglar had 40 fits and knew he could not stay.

From under the bed, the burglar crept.
He was a total wreck.
The old maid wasn't asleep at all.
She grabbed him by the neck.

She didn't holler, scream, shout and talk.
She was as cool as a clam.
She only said, "My saints be blessed!
At last, I got me a man."

From under the pillow, a gun she drew
And took the burglar by the neck firmly and said,
"Young man, you had better marry me,
Or I will blow off the top of your head."

She held him so firmly
That he hadn't a chance to scoot.
He looked at her big teeth and big glass eye and said,
"Madam, for Pete's sake,
Go ahead and shoot."

—*Mrs. Almeter Glascoe*
USED BY PERMISSION

V.
LAUGHS ABOUT CLERGY AND MINISTERS

- *The Minister and My Grandmother*
- *The Minister and the Peach Brandy*
- *The Three Ministers and the Bats*
- *Let It Walk!!! Let It Walk!!!*
- *Beware of Leftovers*
- *They Came to Pass; They Did Not Come to Stay*
- *Do Not Give Him My Drumstick*
- *The Four Year Old Grandson*
- *The Minister, the Little Boy and Heaven*
- *The Preacher and the Cow*
- *A Bellyfull*
- *The Minister and the Car Repairs*
- *The Calendar*
- *How to Get Rid of a Minister*

THE MINISTER AND MY GRANDMOTHER

In the rural South of my boyhood, it was customary to eat dinner by the courses, based upon the Old English style. One would eat his salad, then eat his meat, then eat his vegetables one by one and then eat his dessert. This sequence of events was based on the several course meal, an old English custom.

A certain minister mixed all of the courses except the dessert on his plate at the same time. My grandmother was quite perturbed at this breach of etiquette. She asked him, "Reverend, why are you mixing all of those foods?"

He replied, "Sister Smith, they are all going to the same place."

—Mrs. Cherrie Debnam, my Mother

Moral:

1. People going to the same place may sometime ride together.
2. If the food is going to fight, it is better for it to do so in the plate or the mouth.

THE MINISTER AND THE PEACH BRANDY

There was a minister who was fond of peach brandy and one of his parishioners was bringing some to him. The parishioner became alarmed and told the minister that unless he notified the church about the peach brandy, he would have to stop bringing it to him.

At the next church conference, the minister stood up before the congregation and said, "Brother Jones, I appreciate the peaches that you have been bringing me and I especially enjoy the spirits in which you have done so." The Church gave Brother Jones a standing ovation for looking after the minister by bringing him peaches and being very nice about it.

—Anonymous

Moral:

- It is sometimes how you describe a situation that will get you that desired result.

THE THREE MINISTERS AND THE BATS

Three rural ministers were dining and there ensued a discussion of church problems.

Minister A: "We have bats in our church and we have had difficulty getting rid of them. We put out a great deal of D.D.T. and those bats thrived on it."

Minster B: "We had bats also and we put cats in the church. Those bats whipped those cats and ran them out of the church in one week."

Minister C: "We had bats in our church also. We handled ours just a bit differently than you two did yours. We had each one of them to join the church, be baptized and we told them what their monthly dues and tithes were and we have not seen them since that time."

—*Anonymous*

Moral:

1. When it is time to put up or shut up, many church disciples, or members, will choose to shut up.

2. The bats wanted a free church. They did not want to pay rent.

3. Many church disciples have followed the trail blazed by the last bats.

LET IT WALK!!! LET IT WALK!!!

A young minister took over the pastoral charge of an old dilapidated church, which had not had the best care in years gone by. The congregation was disenchanted and disheartened and down in the "dumps" about their church.

At the first church conference, the young minister sought to energize and inspire his congregation to do better. He started off by saying to the congregation:

"Brothers and sisters, the Lord wants this church to rise up and walk!!!"

The congregation replied, "Let it walk, Pastor!!! Let it walk!!!"

Encouraged by their response, the young minister continued. "Brothers and sisters, the Lord wants this church to run!!!"

The congregation responded, "Let it run, Pastor!!! Let it run!!!"

"Brothers and sisters, the Lord wants this church to fly!!!"

The congregation responded, "Let it fly, Pastor!!! Let it fly!!!"

"But if it flies, brothers and sisters, we have to have more money!!!"

The congregation responded, "Let it walk, Pastor!!! Let it walk!!!"

—*Anonymous*

Moral:

1. Bring all of your tithes into the storehouse so that there may be meat in mine house. (Malachi 3: 10)

2. On the first day of the week, let each of you lay by himself in store as the Lord has prospered him. (1 Corinthians 16:2)

3. Too many churches are walking rather than flying, and God is not pleased.

BEWARE OF LEFTOVERS

A young minister preaching his first sermon at a new church got his message a little off track. He stated in his sermon that Jesus took 5,000 barley loaves and 2,000 fish and fed five people, and he marveled at the miracle.

One of the deacons said, "Pastor, that was no miracle. I could take 5,000 barley loaves and 2,000 fish and feed five people."

The next Sunday, the pastor got the message right. Jesus took five barley loaves and two fish and fed 5,000 people and had twelve baskets left over.

The Pastor asked the same question, "Deacon, could you do that?" The deacon said, "Yes, Pastor." The pastor returned, "Where would you get the food?"

The deacon quietly replied, "Pastor, we had enough left over from last Sunday that we could feed them all today."

—*Anonymous*

Moral:

- Beware of leftovers. Be sure that the refrigeration is good.

THEY CAME TO PASS; THEY DID NOT COME TO STAY

A young minister was the pastor of a church, and he had an old and trusted black yardman who seemed to have a biblical quotation to fit every difficult situation that the young minister found himself in at the church and there were indeed many. The minister grew to love and respect this old gentleman because he was always wise and a "shelter in a time of storm."

One day the young minister asked him, "Jacob, you have given me so many wise and fitting quotations from the Bible. What is your favorite quotation?"

The old man looked at him and said, "Pastor, I have many favorite quotations from the Bible." But the minister persisted and Jacob finally said, "Pastor, I reckon my favorite quotation is 'And it came to pass.'"

The young minister was very perplexed and said, "How can that be? 'It came to pass' is present in the Bible hundreds of times."

Old Jacob replied, "Pastor, I have had a lot of troubles, trials, disappointments and tribulations in this world. They came to pass; they did not come to stay."

—*The Daily Bread*

Moral:

- The syntax here would not pass muster in English 101 or English 102, but in this world it is right on time. It came to pass: it did not come to stay.

—*Anonymous*

DO NOT GIVE HIM MY DRUMSTICK

In the rural South, it was customary for a family to invite the minister and his family by for Sunday dinner. Usually, the children were fed at another table or at the same table after the minister and his family had eaten.

The minister's favorite food was southern fried chicken and they ate very liberally of that portion of the dinner. On this particular occasion, the father of the house was president of a college and his Presiding Bishop and employer were having dinner. The president made the mistake of permitting his four-year-old daughter to eat with the Bishop. The father served everyone's plate, including the Bishop's. As he piled the fried chicken high on the Bishop's plate, the four-year-old girl yelled out, "Daddy, don't give him my drumstick!"

—Dr. Marjorie Boyd Debnam, my wife

Moral:

1. Children will speak their minds, Bishop or no bishop, preacher or no preacher.
2. That drumstick was the best part of the chicken and the four-year old daughter was well aware of the fact.

THE FOUR YEAR OLD GRANDSON

A minister was preaching during a Sunday morning 11:00 A.M. service when he noticed that the Chairman of the Deacon Board was sitting in the Amen Corner with his four-year-old grandson in his lap. The deacon was fast asleep.

The irate minister yelled to the four-year-old grandson to "Wake your grandfather up. Can't you see that he is asleep?" The little boy replied, "Reverend, please wake him up yourself. After all, you are the one that put him to sleep."

—*Anonymous*

Moral:

1. A quiet, calm word to the deacon after the service would have been far better than for 800 people to know that he was asleep.

2. The little four-year-old grandson stole the show from the minister.

THE MINISTER, THE LITTLE BOY AND HEAVEN

A minister was walking down the street searching in vain for the Post Office when he saw a little boy playing with marbles in a yard.

"Little fellow," asked the minister, "can you tell me how to get to the post office?" The little boy gave him the correct directions. After the minister had walked up the street a few feet, he remembered that he had said nothing to the little boy about Jesus, so he returned to the little boy and said, "Son, do you know anything about Jesus?"

The little boy said, "Yes."

The next question was, "Son, do you want to go to Heaven?"

The little boy quietly replied, "Mister, what are you doing talking about Heaven? They tell me that it is way up yonder beyond the sky. You do not know the way to the post office, and you are right down here in the city with it. How do you know the way to Heaven?"

—*Anonymous*

Moral:

- Please consider the answers that you may get from the questions that you ask.

THE PREACHER AND THE COW

A minister was making visitation calls to his parishioners. This was in the old days, and he was traveling by horse and buggy. He drove up to a parishioner's house and saw a cow grazing on a hill. The cow was so skinny that one could count all of her ribs. He said to himself, "That old cow in not long for this world." He tied his horse in the backyard and started for the kitchen door. The father of the house, who was also a deacon in the church, had brought a half gallon jar of white lightning to the house that morning and it was sitting on the kitchen table. One of the daughters looked out of the window and said, "Mother, here comes Reverend Jones."

The mother said, "Get rid of that moonshine at once. Throw it out the back door."

"Mother, we can't do that because he is coming in the back door."

The mother said, "There is a pan of buttermilk there on the table, put it in the buttermilk and we will throw it out later."

This was done and the minister entered the house. He read from the Bible, he prayed, and they sang a hymn. The mother offered the pastor a cup of coffee. He said that it was too late for coffee. Then she offered him some tea, and he said that he always drank tea at 12:00 noon but it was now only 11:00 A.M. He asked her, "Sister, isn't that buttermilk over there in that pan? I always love buttermilk. Please give me a glass of buttermilk."

Reluctantly, she gave him a fruit juice glass of buttermilk. He said, "Sister, you drink milk out of a big glass not a fruit juice glass." So she gave him a big glass. He drank it down and asked for a second glass and began to sweat. His heart began to race, and he began to preach for a few minutes. He left and went to his horse and buggy. He looked up on the hill, and the cow was still there grazing. As he looked upward toward Heaven, he prayed, "Lord, please give me a cow like that."

—*Dr. Clifton Jones*

Moral:

- Watch the buttermilk and the goat milk.

A BELLYFULL

In the old days when revivals were held in the rural South services were held twice a day from Monday through Friday nights. The services were held from 2:00 P.M. to 3:30 P.M. and then from 7:30 P.M. to 9:00 P.M. There was a mourner's bench where the unsaved would sit until they had a conversion.

At one particular church, a lady and her seven-year old son attended Monday, Tuesday, Wednesday, Thursday and Friday, all of them twice a day. On Friday night, prior to the final service the minister went through the congregation asking everyone how much they had enjoyed the service. When he reached the mother and the little boy, he asked them how much had they enjoyed the service. The mother said, "Reverend, I can't answer you right now, because I am full. I will talk to you later." So the minister asked the little boy how he had enjoyed the week of services. The little boy answered and said, "Reverend, I am just like my mother. I have had a bellyful. I am full up to here. I don't want no more. I have had enough."

—*Mr. Rex Powell*

Moral:

- Art Linkletter has taught us to be careful what we ask children because they will tell you the truth.

—*Anonymous*

THE MINISTER AND THE CAR REPAIRS

There was a minister who had three sons, James, Leroy and Luther. They lived on a big farm. James and Leroy were the older ones and Luther was the youngest. James and Leroy delighted in putting their car up on some blocks and working on it for a whole week or more. One day the father said, "I am going over to Cranford's Garage to have my car worked on.

Little Luther said, "Father, why don't you let James and Leroy work on your car? They are always working on theirs."

The father said nothing. Sometime thereafter, James and Leroy put their car up on some blocks and worked on it for three weeks. Then they took it down at 3:00 P.M. on Saturday and drove to town for a night of joy and fun. His father said, "Luther, come here a minute." He went with his father to the site where the car had been sitting. There was a hubcap there with seventy-five bolts and nuts in it, and the car had already gone to town. The father said, "You asked me six months ago why I did not let James and Leroy work on my car? I did not say anything because I was waiting to show you. Those people in Detroit would not have put all of these nuts and bolts in the car unless they were necessary. Something bad is going to happen to that car. This is why I don't let them work on my car."

Moral:

1. There is only one way to do a thing. Do it the right way.

2. Accept no bribe in lieu of the truth.

—*The Reverend Luther Coppedge*
USED BY PERMISSION

THE CALENDAR

A minister in a rural church had been preaching for some time. He tried to glance at his watch only to discover he had left it at home. There was no clock on the wall, so he inquired of his congregation, "Does anyone here have a watch? I have left mine at home."

The chairman of the deacon board stood up and said, "Reverend, you have been preaching so long, you do not need a watch. You need a calendar, and I have one right here in my billfold."

—*Anonymous*

Moral:

1. Tempus fugit.

2. There are two kinds of time—chronos and kairos. Be sure that they don't coincide.

HOW TO GET RID OF A MINISTER

1. Look him straight in the eye when he is preaching and say, "Amen," once in a while. He'll preach himself to death in a few weeks.
2. Pat him on the back and brag on his good points. He'll work himself to death.
3. Start paying him a living wage. He's probably been on starvation wages so long he'll eat himself to death.
4. Rededicate your own life to Christ and ask the preacher to give you a job to do. He'll probably die of heart failure.
5. Get the church to unite in prayer for the preacher. He'll become so effective some larger church will take him off your hands.

—The Zondervan 1980 Pastor's Annual

VI.
LAUGHS ABOUT PHYSICIANS AND MEDICAL PROFESSIONALS

- *The Wrong Diagnosis*
- *The Doctor and the Rash*
- *Weight Loss*
- *Get the Right Directions*
- *Dying Between Two Thieves*
- *The Doctor and the Organs*
- *Difficult for Them, But Not for Me*

THE WRONG DIAGNOSIS

Two men were walking through the woods engaged in a very loud and vituperative argument. There was one man in front and one man following the other.

The man in front grabbed a large tree limb, carried it forward with him, and then turned it loose. The limb returned to its original place and knocked the second man down. The second man got up and thanked the first man who had brought the limb forward saying, "Thank you for holding that limb, because if you hadn't held it, it would have killed me. Thank you for saving my life."

—Anonymous

Moral:

- With a friend like this, one does not need an enemy.

THE DOCTOR AND THE RASH

A doctor was just opening his office for the first time. His first patient had broken out in a rash from head to feet. The good doctor looked him over and excused himself for a moment. Going into the back room, he opened his medical book and began to look for a name to put on the rash. Failing to find one, he went back to his patient. In a very professional voice he asked, "Have you ever had this before?"

"Oh yes, three times," the patient replied.

"Well you've got it again," the doctor told him.

—Anonymous

Moral:

- Still no name for the condition, but it was very reassuring to the patient that he would be no sicker than he was the other three times.

WEIGHT LOSS

An obese patient went to the doctor to lose weight. She was given a diet to follow and exercises to do.

At her next visit one month later the patient had gained ten pounds. The doctor was very perturbed and began to ask questions.

"Are you on your diet?"

"Yes sir."

"Are you eating anything else?"

"Yes sir."

"I am eating my regular food plus your diet."

—*Anonymous*

Moral:

Be sure that all minds and hearts are clear.

GET THE RIGHT DIRECTIONS

When I was in medical school, a professor shared the following scenario with the class of medical students.

You are in your third month of medical practice in a rural setting. You are called to make a house call. Here are your directions.

1. Leave town going east on Road 101 and go twenty miles to Williams' Crossroads.
2. Turn right onto Road 102 and go twenty miles to Blalock's Crossroads.
3. Turn left on Road 103 and go fifteen miles and you will see a fat lady standing by the road waving you down. You have traveled fifty-five miles. The lady says, "Doctor, my husband is over yonder in the field laying down in the furrow behind the mule and the plow. Please go over there and see about him."
4. We were instructed to go over into the field and check his right overall hip pocket. If this man has a box of Arm & Hammer Baking Soda in that pocket, he has had a ruptured peptic ulcer.

—Anonymous

Moral:

1. Do not miss the diagnosis, please!!!
2. Keep looking until you find the patient.
3. Do not take all day to do so.
4. Keep good tires on your car.
5. You had to travel to be a doctor in the old days.

DYING BETWEEN TWO THIEVES

A nice little elderly Christian lady went to see her doctor. The doctor examined her and said, "Mrs. Sally, I have saved your life five times in the past, but your new condition is bad, and I can't save you this time."

The little old lady said, "Is that right, doctor?"

He said, "Yes."

She said, "Dr. Jones, please send someone across the street and tell Lawyer Brown to come over here at once!" Lawyer Brown came very quickly. She said, "Dr. Jones, please stand on one side of me and, Lawyer Brown, please stand on the other side of me." After they were in position, she folded her hands and looked up to heaven and said, "Jesus, come on and get me now. I am dying just like you did. I am dying between two thieves. This doctor and this lawyer have cleaned me out."

—*Anonymous*

Moral:

The truth shall make you free, although sometimes it hurts.

THE DOCTOR AND THE ORGANS

A middle-aged medical doctor of very humble origins was on vacation in Canada when he was surprised to see something very familiar in a museum there. There was a grand pipe organ from the late 1880's that stretched to the ceiling, and the doctor instantly recognized it. "We had two of these organs at home on our farm — some rich church left them there after the Civil War."

The curator told him, "Sir, please see if they are still there. We will pay you $140,000 for just one organ and $280,000 for both!"

The doctor called his sharecropper siblings on the home place in North Carolina and told them of the family's windfall in excited terms. He demanded to know the whereabouts of these organs, only to hear his stoic sister explain the organs' fate. "Well, you know, we had some people who farmed with us in the 60's, Brother George, and you know how poor they had to be, so they done chopped those things up for firewood years ago!"

The doctor was shocked and mentioned the devil's home in a one-word sentence. His sister said, "No brother, it wasn't hell, it was North Carolina in 1961, and it was plumb cold!"

—*Marjorie L. Debnam, M.D.*

DIFFICULT FOR THEM, BUT NOT FOR ME

A professor of surgery at Howard University was operating on one of his patients for an enlarged thyroid gland, or goiter, in her neck. He was performing his procedure under local anesthesia and the patient was fully awake. He was also performing it in the presence of a class of students, very carefully going over the anatomical structures, dangers, and risks as he performed the surgery. He said to the students, "This is a very difficult operation. If you cut here, you will cut the superior thyroid artery and may cause the tissues of half of the thyroid gland to die. If you cut down here, you may cut the recurrent laryngeal nerve, and the patient will not be able to talk or sing because this will paralyze her vocal cords. It is very, very difficult, and you have to be very, very careful."

The patient said, "Doctor! Doctor! You did not tell me that this operation was going to be all that difficult. Maybe we should not proceed with it."

The doctor replied, "Madame, it is difficult for them. It is not difficult for me." He proceeded to finish the surgery without further discussion or elaboration.

—Anonymous

Moral:

- Do not tell all that you know.

VIII.
LAUGHS ABOUT GHOSTS

- *The White Dog and the Wake*
- *On the Cooling Board*
- *James and the Potato*

THE WHITE DOG AND THE WAKE

There was a family who maintained a nice home and had a large white Spitz dog to guard it. The dog had one flaw, which was that he liked to roam around away from home for a few days and then return. This dog was about 50 pounds in weight and was almost the height of a man on his hind legs. Whenever he returned from his wandering, he would jump on his hind legs on the front screen door.

Following one such absence, the dog returned to his home to find numerous cars and evidence of a party going on inside. The family had just buried a brother of the master and there were people sitting around telling inappropriate jokes, laughing over owing the deceased money, not helping the family with cleaning up, and other offenses long into the night. The dog was confused and did not do his usual ritual at first but sat and waited.

Well, after 1:00 A.M., one loud-mouthed kin of the deceased stated, "I wonder what Johnny would say about us sitting up and talking? You know the dead can't come back."

The master began, "I know what he would say — "but before he could finish, the dog, hearing his master, jumped up on the door and slammed it loudly!

The assembled mourners fled to all corners of the house in fear of the white-tailed ghost at the door. The man cried out, "Whoa, Johnny, don't come back here!" The master shocked everyone by laughing and opening the door, to the horror of all present. "Johnny can't come back, but this here dog sure did," he chuckled. As everyone ran from the premises, the master gave the dog a chicken leg in thanks.

—Marjorie L. Debnam, M.D.

ON THE COOLING BOARD

It was at the church at a wake. In the old days they would have prayer meeting with the body lying in state all night long. Big John was considered the best praying man for miles around, and he was the last one to pray that night. No one could beat Big John praying.

"O Lord, have mercy tonight." Big John, when he was praying, kept his eyes shut all of the time. "O Lord, bless the relatives of the bereaved family."

Big John heard a rumble, but he thought it was shouting. So after a while he heard a door open. He opened his eyes. The corpse was sitting up on the cooling board, and everybody else had done gone.

Big John said, "Don't you move! If you ain't dead now, you will die some day!" and kept moving toward the door. And when he went out the door, he split the wind and vamoosed all at the same time.

—*Anonymous*

Moral:

1. The Good Book says, "One should watch as well as pray."

2. Every shut eye is not asleep.

3. Every goodbye is not gone.

JAMES AND THE POTATO

James was a young man who always fell asleep when he sat down for a while. So one night at a wake, he went to sleep. His friends sat the corpse up in the casket and put a piece of potato in his mouth. Then they went outside and rattled the windows, waking up the sleeping James. When he saw the corpse with the potato in his mouth, he said, "You may eat with some folks, but you won't eat with me. Bye-bye!"

—Anonymous

Moral:

1. Be careful where you go to sleep.

2. Watch your friends; your enemies can't get to you.

3. Sleep with one eye open.

VIII.
MISCELLANEOUS LAUGHS

- *Working Together*
- *Explanation*
- *Pipe in Mouth*
- *Disappointing Rewards*
- *The Lady and the Mountains*
- *I'm Sopping My Own Gravy Now*
- *The Bootlegger*
- *The Little Man Waving the Stick*
- *What Day of the Week Were You Born?*
- *The Way You Look at It*
- *Friendship*
- *Little Things Are Important*
- *No Self Pats*
- *Success*
- *Whose Job Is It?*
- *I Am Not Lost*
- *The Horseshoe Nail*

WORKING TOGETHER

In the olden days, a new rubber-tire buggy was a much-desired vehicle, just as Lexus or Mercedes Benz, Town Cars, Chryslers and Jaguars are today.

A young man was taking his girlfriend for her first ride in his new rubber-tire buggy. He also had a new whip that he had become adept in using. The buggy was, of course, pulled by a very fine horse.

As they drove along, the young man was demonstrating his prowess with the whip. He saw a squirrel climbing a tree and — POW! — he took the squirrel down with the whip. He saw a rabbit darting across the road and — POW! — he took the rabbit down with the whip. He saw a frog sitting on the side of the road and took him down with the whip. And then they rounded a curve in the road and there was a huge hornet's nest hanging from a tree with many hornets crawling all over it. The young man did not take it down with his whip. His girlfriend reminded him of what he had done to the squirrel, the rabbit, and the frog, and she wanted to know why he had not done it to the hornet's nest. His reply to her was "Honey, those hornets work together. You had better not bother things that work together."

—Anonymous

Moral:

1. Together we stand; divided we fall.

2. A house divided against itself cannot stand.

3. Behold, how good and how pleasant it is for brethren and sisters to dwell together in unity!!! (Psalms 133:1)

EXPLANATION

A company was in the process of obtaining group insurance for its employees. There was one who worked there who refused to sign because his father had signed a paper forty years ago and had lost twenty acres of land. He had taught his children not to sign papers. For six months, the worker refused to sign.

One day the owner sent for him and asked him to sign the papers. He said, "Boss, I am telling you the same as I told the rest of them. I am not signing."

The boss asked, "How many years have you worked here?"

He replied, "Twenty-eight years."

"Were you not our Employee of the Year for last year and the year before that?"

He replied, "Yes, sir."

The boss said, "Please go back downstairs, clean out your locker, and go by and tell your co-workers of twenty-eight years goodbye. By that time, Miss Becky, our payroll lady will have your check ready for you to pick up. This company must have group insurance."

The worker said, "Boss, give me that old paper. I will sign it." He signed the paper and started out the door.

The boss said, "Wait a minute. What made you change your mind?"

The worker said, "Boss, the rest of them did not explain it to me the way that you did."

—*Anonymous*

Moral:

A good explanation is very important.

PIPE IN MOUTH

A man was riding on a train with his pipe in his mouth. A lady told him that if he was a gentleman, he would not be smoking in the presence of ladies.

The man protested and said, "Lady, I am not smoking."

She said, "I see your pipe right there in your mouth."

The man said, "Yes, my feet are in my shoes, but I am not kicking."

—Anonymous

Moral:

1. To be rather than to seem — *Esse Quam Videre* (North Carolina's Motto)

2. Do not rush to judgment too quickly.

3. Do not jump to conclusions.

DISAPPOINTING REWARDS

Sometimes, we do not get the reward that we are expecting and working for. I had a friend named Joe who had a rich aunt. He spent years of his life pretending he was fond of his aunt and her twenty cats. When she died, all of her money went to charity, and all of her cats went to Joe.

Moral:

- Joe was very disappointed. The plans of mice and men often come to naught.

—Anonymous

THE LADY AND THE MOUNTAINS

An 85-year-old lady from Wake County encountered mountains for the first time in her life as she traveled with her son and daughter-in-law to Camp Campbell, Kentucky, just outside of Nashville, Tennessee. This was prior to the existence of Interstate 40, and one had to travel U.S. 70 to reach Nashville. The mountains were formidable and to an 85-year-old grandmother who had never seen one mountain, it was sheer horror. She was a back seat driver who whooped, yelled, hollered and cried all of the way through the mountains. When she reached Camp Campbell, where they were to stay for a week, she did not enjoy it at all. Her constant question was, "Buddy," as she called her son, "do we have to go back through those mountains?"

He said, "Mama, we can go up through Indiana, Ohio, Pennsylvania, Maryland and Washington, D.C., but it is twice as far that way. Mama, how is your money? It will require a lot of gas."

"Buddy, you know that I don't have any money."

"Mama, we can go through Tennessee, Georgia and South Carolina, but the distance is still the problem, and money is still the big problem."

So after a week, they made the trip back through the Smokies and other mountains. The same calisthenics happened as on the trip to Camp Campbell. Around Hickory, N.C., the grandmother looked back through the rear view window and saw the Blue Ridge and Smokies getting lower on the horizon. Then she looked through the front windshield and could see no mountains or even hills in front of her, she said to her son, "Buddy, it looks like we are out of those mountains now. You don't have to play with it no more, just take me on to Wake County and there I will be until my dying day." —*Mrs. Lannie McCullers*

Moral:

1. Do not get too old before you see some of the wonders of God's handiwork.
2. Thank God for a careful driver.
3. Thank God for Interstate Highways 40, 77, 85, 95, 26, 440, 540 & 81.

I'M SOPPING MY OWN GRAVY NOW

A fellow worked for a doctor. The doctor would leave home before breakfast every morning and the fellow would carry breakfast to the doctor's office. One morning the doctor down the street was sitting and looking out of the window from his upstairs office. He saw the worker coming down the street with his breakfast. The worker took a biscuit from the plate, sopped the biscuit in the doctor's gravy and ate it. When he reached the office the doctor gave him a few licks and told him he was fired. The doctor said, "I don't allow anybody to sop out of my gravy. Get out, and get some gravy of your own to sop!"

The worker left and moved over to Arkansas from Mississippi where he had worked for the doctor. The first year that he was in Arkansas, farming was good. He made money and bought a pair of mules and some plow tools. The next year farming was good and he started buying forty acres of land, paid for his mules, bought a horse and buggy and some nice clothes. The next year he went back home to see his mother in Mississippi. He went by to see the doctor he had worked for when he lived in Mississippi. The doctor wanted to know who he was driving for, when he saw him in the new buggy with the nice horse.

He said, "I'm driving for myself."

The doctor said, "What are you doing now, John?"

He said, "I'm farming."

The doctor said, "Who for John?"

He said, "Myself."

The doctor said, "And you are farming for yourself?"

He said, "Yes, sir."

The doctor said, "Own your own mules?"

He said, "Yes, sir."

The doctor said, "Own your own land?"

He said, "Yes sir."

The doctor said, "Well John, tell me just what are you doing in Arkansas?"

He said, "Sir, I'm sopping my own gravy now."

—*Anonymous*

Moral:

1. The gravy is better when you are sopping your own.
2. James Brown said, "I don't want anyone to give me nothing. Just get out of my way and I will get it for myself."

THE BOOTLEGGER

The revenue man in the days of prohibition was out trying to catch a bootlegger. A fellow by the name of Sam was coming down Lawton Street, and the revenue agent was standing on the corner looking shabby. "Say, boy," the agent called out to Sam, "come here." Sam went over to him and the agent flashed a ten-dollar bill. He says, "I'll give you this ten-dollar bill if you get me a quart of whiskey."

Sam said, "Yes sir, but a quart will cost you forty dollars."

So he gave Sam forty dollars. Sam had a shoe box under his arm. He asked the agent, "Will you hold this shoe box till I go around the corner? I'll be right back." So the agent took the box and held it for Sam while he went to get the whiskey.

Sam stayed so long he said, "I'm going to see what's in this box." So there was his quart of whiskey. He had his quart of whiskey, Sam had his forty dollars, but the bootlegger is still loose. He has not been found yet.

—*Anonymous*

Moral:

1. What you see is what you get.

2. You fool me, and then I will fool you.

THE LITTLE MAN WAVING THE STICK

The 280-piece symphony was being put through its paces by the maestro. The symphony was practicing at its home base in the Memorial Auditorium, Raleigh, North Carolina. A young man sitting in the seats was thoroughly enjoying the exercise. He suddenly decided that he wanted to become a member of this great musical aggregation. He went to the front office and told the secretary, "I want to be a part of the North Carolina Symphony Orchestra."

The secretary said, "Good, let us fill out an application." She took down his name and address and other valuable personal information. She got to the last question and asked him politely, "Sir, what instrument do you play?"

He said, "Ma'am, I don't play any instrument, but there is a little man standing in front of them waving a stick. I know that I can wave that stick better than he can." Incidentally, the maestro waving the baton wrote the score, knew every note and key and could identify each of the 280 instruments that were playing.

—*Anonymous*

Moral:

1. He who knows, but knows not that he knows — teach him.
2. He who knows not, and knows that he knows not is asleep — awake him.
3. He who knows not and thinks that he knows is a fool — shun him.
4. He who knows and knows that he knows is wise — follow him.

WHAT DAY OF THE WEEK WERE YOU BORN?

What was your greatly-blessed and highly-favored day of the week?

Monday's child is fair of face;

Tuesday's child is full of God's grace;

Born on Wednesday, sour and sad;

Born on Thursday, merry and glad;

Born on Friday, worthily given;

Born on Saturday, work hard for your living;

Born on Sunday, you will never know want.

—Anonymous

THE WAY YOU LOOK AT IT

A man was driving in the country one day, and he saw an old man sitting on a fence rail, watching the automobiles go by. Stopping to pass the time of day, the traveler said, "I never could stand living out here. You don't see anything, and I'm sure you don't travel like I do. I'm on the go all the time."

The old man on the fence looked down at the stranger and drawled, "I can't see much difference in what I'm doing and what you're doing. I sit on the fence and watch the autos go by, and you sit in your auto and watch the fences go by. It's just the way you look at things."

—Anonymous

FRIENDSHIP

A good friend is like good chocolate:

Quality ingredients,

Nothing artificial,

Always appreciated.

—*Anonymous*

LITTLE THINGS ARE IMPORTANT

Please Do Not Overlook Them.

NO SELF PATS

Nature knows best. She hasn't arranged your anatomy so as to make it easy for you to pat yourself on the back.

— *Anonymous*

SUCCESS

The world is not interested in the storms you have encountered, but whether you brought the ship in safely to port.

— *Anonymous*

WHOSE JOB IS IT?

This is a story about four people named **Everybody, Somebody, Anybody,** and **Nobody.** There was an important job to be done and **Everybody** was asked to do it. **Everybody** was sure **Somebody** would do it. **Anybody** could have done it, but Nobody did it.

Somebody got angry about that because it was **Everybody's** job. **Everybody** thought **Anybody** could do it, but **Nobody** realized that **Everybody** wouldn't do it. It ended up that **Everybody** blamed **Somebody** when **Nobody** did what **Anybody** could have done.

—*Anonymous*

I AM NOT LOST

There was once a young man in Raleigh who had a baby carriage and some drums and danced for the passersby. He became a permanent fixture on Fayetteville Street, the main street of Raleigh, the capital city of the State of North Carolina. This young man, whom everybody considered to be retarded, was at times, quick on his feet and quick with his thinking and his wit.

One day, a gentleman stopped his car and asked this young man, "John, please give me directions to the Seaboard Train Station."

The young man replied by saying, "How did you know my name was John?"

The driver said, "Oh, I just guessed it." The young man, whose name was Woodrow, said, "Well, since you are such a good guesser, just guess your way to the train station."

The driver told the passenger that was riding with him, "That fellow is crazy."

Woodrow said, "I may be crazy but I am not lost: you are."

—*Woodrow Montague*

Moral:

1. If he had not called him John, Woodrow would have told him the way to the train station.

2. He compounded his error by saying that Woodrow was crazy.

3. Woodrow, though retarded, got the best of both arguments.

THE HORSESHOE NAIL

For lack of a nail,
A shoe was lost.
For lack of a shoe
A horse was lost.
For the lack of a horse,
A rider who was a knight was lost.
For lack of that knight, a battle was lost.
For loss of that battle, an entire kingdom and people were lost.
All for the lack of one little horseshoe nail.

—*Anonymous*

Moral:

+ Be careful about small things. They are important.

Bibliography

1. Anonymous
2. "Church Bulletin Bits"
3. George C. Debnam, M.D.
4. Reverend Dr. John Wilson Fleming
5. Dr. A. A. Williams
6. George and Mary Lou Glover
7. Dr. Miller W. Boyd, Jr.
8. Dr. Clarence G. Newsome
9. Mrs. Almeter Glascoe
10. Mrs. Cherrie L. Debnam
11. *The Daily Bread*
12. Dr. Marjorie Boyd Debnam
13. Dr. Clifton Jones
14. Mr. Rex Powell
15. Reverend Dr. Luther Coppedge
16. *The Zondervan 1980 Pastor's Annual*
17. Marjorie L. Debnam, M. D.
18. Mrs. Lannie McCullers
19. Woodrow Montague
20. Many others whose names cannot be recalled by me over the years.

GEORGE C. DEBNAM, M.D.

A Biographical Sketch

George C. Debnam was born in Youngsville Township of Franklin County, North Carolina. He is the son of the late James Otis Debnam and Cherrie Smith Debnam.

He received his early education in the public schools of Franklin County. In 1947, he received a B.S. Degree from Shaw University, Raleigh, NC with a major in mathematics and minors in Biology, Chemistry, Physics and Pre-medical education. Entering Meharry Medical College in Nashville, Tennessee in 1947, he received an M.D. Degree in 1951. He did his internship and residency in surgery and family practice at Saint Agnes Hospital in Raleigh, NC 1951-1954. His first practice was in the Town of Fuquay-Varina, 1954-1955. He entered military service in October 1955 and served for two years in San Antonio, Texas, at Fort Sam Houston, Texas, Japan, Korea and Womack General Hospital at Fort Bragg, North Carolina. He served with the rank of Captain as the Commander of the 44th M.A.S. Hospital and at the 121st Evacuation Hospital at ASCOM City, Korea, from 1955-1957 where he was a member of the Thirty-eighth Parallel Medical Society and served with honor and distinction.

Dr. Debnam delivered 11,500 babies and performed more than 5,000 surgical operations before ceasing these phases of his medical career in 1993. His practice was one in which he followed his patients from the cradle to the grave. He remained with them in their times of sorrow. The families very often requested that he give tributes at the funerals. His name and that of the Debnam Clinic, P.A. are listed with thanks on many obituaries for dedicated services rendered.

He was honored in the Wake County Physician magazine in its "Profile of the Month" for December 1998. In the article, he was highlighted by members of the Wake County Medical Society for commendable medical and community service rendered. In addition, Dr. Debnam was an awardee of the National Black Alumni Hall of Fame Foundation, Inc., inducted into its category of medicine; nominated by the Shaw University National Alumni Association, and installed in the NBCAA Hall of Fame, September 24, 1999. He was recipient of the "1999 Michael Weeks Humanitarian Award," presented by Wake Medical Hospital medical staff of 850 doctors yearly to an outstanding and humanitarian physician on that staff.

Dr. Debnam was married to the late Marjorie Boyd Debnam, a community activist and humanitarian recognized in the Raleigh Hall of Fame for her community work in social concerns and in medical programs. Mrs. Debnam was a member of a great family of African-American educators, clerics, physicians and was a native of Morristown, Tennessee. She was a Sociologist by training, with a B.A. Degree in Sociology from Fisk University in Nashville, Tennessee. She was office manager for the Debnam Clinic and office and together they founded The Friends of Distinction, a group of 700 young African-American males from junior year in high school to the end of their study in college.

Dr. and Mrs. Debnam were the proud parents of three daughters; Mrs. Gwendolyn Debnam Morgan, an Assistant Professor of English at Clark-Atlanta University in Atlanta, Georgia, and has a B.A. Degree from Fisk University in Nashville, Tennessee and a M.A. Degree in English from Atlanta University and has also studied at Oxford University in England. The twins, Marie Georgette Debnam, M.D. and Marjorie Lynnette Debnam, M.D. also received their Bachelor Degrees from Fisk University and their M.D. Degrees from Meharry Medical College, also in Nashville, Tennessee and then did their Internal Medicine training at

Cambridge Hospital, Harvard Medical School in Boston, Massachusetts. They served as Chief Medical Residents of this program prior to returning to Raleigh in 1995 to join their father, George C. Debnam, in his practice. The three practiced together until December 31, 2001, when Dr. George Debnam retired after 50 years and 6 months of dedicated medical service to thousands of North Carolina residents.

On November 21, 1997, Shaw University renamed the Shaw Administration Building the "George C. Debnam Building." This honor was afforded him for his many contributions to Shaw University as a past Board Chair and a continuing hard-working member of the Shaw University Board of Trustees.

Dr. Debnam currently serves as Director of Public Relations for the Debnam Clinic, Membership Chairperson and Field Representative of the Old North State Medical Society.

Dr. Debnam is a member of the Shaw University Board of Trustees and was Vice Chairperson of the Board of Trustees from 1975-1983. He was Chairperson of the Board of Directors of the Estey Hall Foundation, Inc. and led in its $6 million historic restoration. Estey Hall, built on the Shaw University campus 1870-1874 and known as Estey Seminary, is the oldest building for the college of black women in the world. Wherever the black college woman is found, it all started at Estey Hall and Seminary in 1870.

Dr. Debnam is a Trustee Emeritus of North Carolina Central University, where he was Vice Chairman of the Board from 1975-1983. He served as a member of the Board of Management of Raleigh Branches of Mechanics and Farmers Bank from 1970-1993 and was Board Chairman from 1980-1991. For many years, he served as a member of the Board of the Raleigh Salvation Army, Inc.

Dr. Debnam is a 32nd degree Mason and is a member of Eta Sigma Chapter of Phi Beta Sigma Fraternity, Inc. He is a member of Widow Son Lodge #4, Boyer Consistory #219 and the Kabala Temple #177 in Raleigh, North Carolina. He was initiated and confirmed in the Iota Chapter, Phi Beta Sigma Fraternity, Shaw University in 1947. He was honored as Man of the Year from that fraternity and seven other fraternities and sororities in the Raleigh area. He is a charter member of Gamma Sigma Chapter of

Sigma Pi Phi Fraternity, Inc. and is also a member of many other service organizations.

Dr. Debnam was the senior attending physician in family practice at Wake Medical Center, which is a major, 750-bed general hospital and trauma center serving the 850,000 citizens of Wake County and nine surrounding counties. He served three, two-year terms on the hospital's executive committee.

Dr. Debnam is currently Vice President of the L.A. Scruggs Medical Society of Raleigh and Wake County, North Carolina. Having been founded in 1888, L.A. Scruggs is the oldest organized black medical society in America and is older than the Old North State Medical Society, and the National Medical Association, the state and national African-American medical associations. He was President of the Old North State Medical Society and was honored by that society in 1977 and 1997 as its "Doctor of the Year." On June 3, 2000, he was among thirty-four Healthcare Professionals honored with the Old North State Trailblazer Award.

In 1977, Dr. Debnam was named Doctor of the Year by the National Medical Association, which represents 23,000 African-American physicians in the United States and its territories. He has represented The Old North State Medical in the NMA House of Delegates for over thirty years and has served as Chairman of the NMA Credentials Committee in 1986 and 1987; 1989-1991; and 1993-2000. He was elected as a member of the Nominating Committee for the National Medical Association each year from 1981-2000. Beginning in Washington, D.C., in 1964, Dr. Debnam has attended thirty-seven consecutive annual Conventions and Scientific Assemblies of the National Medical Association. He has also represented the Wake County Medical Society at its yearly Conventions in Pinehurst, North Carolina.

Dr. Debnam has been the recipient of many honors and awards during more than fifty years as a physician and community servant. His motto is recorded in the Shaw University Bear, the yearbook for the graduating class of 1947. It reads "The elevator to success is broken, take the stairs."

Dr. Debnam believes that hard work and dedication can accomplish much if we would only try them. He believes that one should "accentuate the positive, eliminate the negative and latch on to the affirmative" for success. He believes that his medical gifts are not only appointed but have also been anointed. He praises God for what He has done for him, and God is first in his life. Dr. Debnam wants to be remembered as "An old soldier in the Army of the Lord." He states that, "I hope to be able to say, like the Apostle Paul, when my head is pressing a dying pillow, 'I have fought the good fight, I have kept the faith and I have stayed on God's course.' I have not been perfect; I did not dot every 'i' and cross every 't,' but I hope to have done enough that I will be welcomed up there where the wicked shall cease from troubling and a weary soul shall be at rest."

consulting | design | rentals

Your Complete Event Solution

Sales Meetings
Conventions

Award Banquets
Trade Shows

Product Launches
Grand Openings

Customer Appreciation
Employee Recognition

Lighting • A/V & Sound • Special Effects • Technical Support
Tents & Canopies • Tables & Chairs • Custom Linen • Catering Equipment
Staging & Dance Floors • Lounges • Theme Décor • Trade Show Booths

1400 NW 15th Avenue, Portland, OR 97209   (503) 294-0412
Bend, OR   Seattle, WA   Las Vegas, NV

www.wcep.com

Bravo!® Publications, Inc.
630 B. Avenue, Suite 205
Lake Oswego, Oregon 97034
p. 503.675.1380
f. 503.675.1204
www.BravoEvent.com

This resource guide is comprised of paid advertisements. Although advertisers must meet a quality level of standards to be featured in this guide, Bravo! Publications, Inc. cannot and does not guarantee or take responsibility for services provided by said advertisers. No affiliation exists between Bravo! Publications, Inc. and any advertiser featured. Every reasonable effort has been made to provide the most accurate and up-to-date information. The copyright of each individual vendor page is held by that vendor, and has been used with permission by that vendor. Any questions regarding content on the individual vendor pages should be directed to the vendor directly. We assume no responsibility for errors, inaccuracies, or misrepresentations by any of the vendors listed in this publication.

Copyrighted and registered © 2009 by Bravo!® Publications, Inc. All rights reserved. No part of this work may be reproduced or transmitted in any form or by any means, electronic or mechanical, including photocopying and recording, or by any information storage or retrieval system, without permission in writing from the publisher.

Printed in the United States of America
ISBN 978-1-884471-47-6

Acknowledgements

Publisher
Mary Lou Burton

Account Managers
Kate Henry
Jennifer Maust

General Manager
Denise Hall

Production & Design
Jodie Siljeg
Bryan Hoybook

Web Sites & Optimization
Subpixel, Inc. - Subpixel.com
Don Richardson - Digitalpopcorn.com

Trade Show Production
Tracy Martin
Jennifer Maust

Public Relations & Marketing
Heather Willig

Special Projects
Helen Kern
Michelle Clayton
Tina Monje

Intern
Adrienne Jarvis

Prepress & Printing
Consolidated Press

Cover Photo
AJ's Studio
Portland Classical Chinese Garden

Back Cover
Bryan Hoybook Photographer
Crater Lake National Park

Mary Lou Burton - Bravo! Founder & Publisher

All great things begin with only a single thought. On her honeymoon, with the planning of her huge Italian wedding still fresh in mind, she and John, relished in the thought of having a single resource to use when planning such an important event. Turning that into reality, Mary Lou and friend Marion Clifton crafted the first Bravo! Wedding Resource Guide in 1990 with an Apple IIe and a single-sheet bubble-jet printer. By 1994, the idea was taken a step further by publishing the first Event Resource Guide along with a meeting and hospitality trade show, Bravo! Live produced each October. In recent years, Bravo! has added the Bravo! Wedding Affairs in November and February and the Central Oregon Wedding Showcase in January.

Graced with her large Italian family and four children: Alex, Nick, Will and Greta, Mary Lou is no stranger to the need for an organized, simple way to entertain, educate, and care for her family. She dedicates her life to acting with intention: if it is going to bring a smile upon a sad face, light the fire within a soul, or illuminate a cloudy path, she will find the time and energy to accomplish it.

www.bravoevent.com

Table of Contents

Accommodations 11
Business Publications & Media 19
Casino & Theme Parties 25
Catering Services 29
    Beverage & Espresso 30
    Cakes & Desserts 35
    Full-Service 37
Entertainment 51
    Bands 52
    Consultants 58
    DJ's 60
    Entertainers & Performers 64
    Musicians 71
Event Design, Production & Décor 73
    Event Design 74
    Floral 78
    Floral & Balloon Décor 80
    Lighting 81
Event & Meeting Sites 83
    Boats 84
    Casinos 85
    Convention & Exhibition 88
    Event & Meeting Sites 93
Event Planners 209
Event Professional Organizations 215
Event Services 225
    Advertising & Signage 226
    Audiovisual 227
    Child Care 229
    Communications 230
    Convention & Trade Show 231

Event Services - Continued
    Lighting 232
    Rentals 234
    Staffing & Employment 239
Executive Gifts & Promotional Items 241
Golf Courses & Tournaments 247
Interactive Entertainment 257
Invitations & Calligraphy 267
Photography 271
    Photo Booth 272
    Photography 273
    Photography - Flip Book 276
Recreation, Attractions & Sports . 277
Resorts & Retreats 285
Speakers & Trainers 297
Team Building 307
Transportation & Valet 315
Videography 323
Wineries & Custom Labeling 329
Wine Tours 335

Regional Destinations

Central Oregon 341
Coastal Region 343
Mt. Hood & Columbia River Gorge 345
Southwest Washington 349
Willamette Valley 353
Yamhill Valley 355

Index 359

www.bravoevent.com

Web Sites

{ BravoWedding.com }

{ BravoCentralOregonWedding.com }

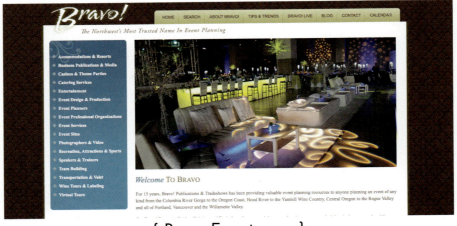

{ BravoEvent.com }

www.bravoevent.com

Get inspired by the latest trends and extraordinary services.

Since 1995, *Bravo!* has been bringing together the top area businesses in the event planning industry to one location to showcase their services.

Bravo! Publications **invites you to experience an event industry trade show like no other in the Pacific Northwest at** *Bravo! Live: A Showcase of the Hospitality & Meeting Industry* **every October.**

Go to *BravoEvent.com* for a schedule of events.

Bravo! VIPlanner Network:

Bravo! VIPlanners qualify for special benefits including:

- Social, educational and networking events
- Online VIPlanner Social Network
- Early entrance to the Bravo! Live
- Plus much more

For more information, visit our website
BravoEvent.com

www.bravoevent.com

Bravo!® Resource Guides

When you want information — you want Bravo!

Bravo! Publications is proud to offer regional Resource Guides for planning meetings, events and weddings. Each of the guides featured on this page is filled with important information and details about the area's finest businesses and service providers. Each page is presented in easy-to-read, resumé style format, alphabetically, by category. Designed to be user-friendly, each of these guides truly are your planning resource!

Oregon & S.W. Washington
Bravo! Wedding Resource Guide

Featuring more than 500 venues and services for planning your entire wedding in Oregon and Southwest Washington

Suggested Retail - $9.95

Greater Puget Sound
Event & Wedding Resource Guides

The 2009 Editions feature more than 560 pages of easy-to-read, resumé-style write-ups on area businesses and service providers, listings of area Banquet and Event Sites, how-to's, checklists, and all the helpful hints you've come to expect!

www.bravoevent.com

Bravo! Wedding Planner

Easy-to-use Wedding Planning System
$29.95

Included is everything from calendars and time schedules to contracts and lists for delegating duties, all which have been put into one easy-to-use, centralized system guaranteed to guide brides from engagement to their wedding day looking calm, cool and beautiful.

To purchase or for a complete list of retail locations, please visit *BravoWedding.com*.

www.bravoevent.com

The Bravo!® Wedding Planner
&
Wedding Resource Guide

IF YOU ARE PLANNING A WEDDING,
GETTING MARRIED OR KNOW SOMEONE WHO IS,
ORDER WHAT EVERY BRIDE NEEDS TO PLAN A PERFECT WEDDING!

- BRAVO! WEDDING PLANNER $29.95
- BRAVO! WEDDING RESOURCE GUIDE $9.95

PLEASE SELECT BRIDAL GUIDE EDITION:
- OREGON & S.W. WASHINGTON '09 EDITION
- PUGET SOUND '09 EDITION

SHIPPING AND HANDLING ADDITIONAL—$5 PER ITEM $ _____

TOTAL: $ _____

METHOD OF PAYMENT:

- CHECK OR MONEY ORDER ENCLOSED   · CHARGE TO: VISA OR MASTERCARD

NAME OF CARD HOLDER: _____

ACCOUNT NO: _____

EXP. DATE: _____ SIGNATURE: _____

PLEASE ALLOW 7 TO 10 DAYS FOR DELIVERY

NAME: _____
ADDRESS: _____ MAIL STOP: _____
CITY: _____ STATE: _____ ZIP: _____
PHONE: _____ FAX: _____ E-MAIL: _____
WEDDING DATE: _____

SEND ORDER TO: BRAVO! PUBLICATIONS, INC.
630 B. AVENUE · LAKE OSWEGO, OREGON 97034
503.675.1380, 800.988.9887; FAX 503.675.1204
WWW.BRAVOWEDDING.COM

Accommodations

A Majestic Mountain Retreat

Mailing Address
38250 Pioneer Boulevard #602
Sandy, Oregon 97055
o. 503.686.8080
h. 503.622.0413
f. 503.622.0474
e. becca1st@gmail.com
www.AMajesticMountainRetreat.com

About A Majestic Mountain Retreat

Serenity . . . This is your experience when you arrive at A Majestic Mountain Retreat - a handcrafted, three-story, luxury Log Home nestled in the forest of Mt. Hood, Oregon surrounded by towering trees, awe-inspiring mountains and a sea of blue skies. Every attention to detail has been made with your ultimate comfort and relaxation in mind.

This magical home is complete with pillow-top beds wrapped in 600 thread count linens, down comforters and Pendleton blankets. Melt into the deep-cushioned leather sofas and custom draperies surrounding you as you entertain your friends and family in the granite kitchen with top-of-the-line appliances and colorful china. The walls are graced with scenic photographs of the natural magic that is Oregon. The stairs are hand-carved from trees from the land and the second-story powder room's sink basin is carved from a local builder and the stand is a tree from the land.

Contact
Rebecca Niday

Price
$250 - $875 a night

Capacity
12 Guests

Quick Facts
- Pillow-top Beds with Wonderful 600 Thread Count Linens
- Luxurious Bath Towels & Robes
- Gourmet Kitchen with Granite Counters & Stainless Steel Appliances
- The Kitchen is Generously Equipped by a Professional Chef
- Pine log beds, table & chairs
- 2-Story Wood Burning Stone Fireplace
- Game Room with a Poker/Game Table, Foosball Table & Games
- TV with Satellite and DVD's
- Wireless Satellite Internet Service

WHAT'S NEW

The Cedar House: A Retreat space that sleeps 6!

Accommodations

"Easy to get to. Hard to leave."

3880 Westcliff Drive
PO Box 887
Hood River, Oregon 97031
p. 866.912.8366
p. 541.436.2660
e. info@columbiacliffvillas.com
www.columbiacliffvillas.com

Only One Hour East of Portland
On the sunny side of the Cascades the luxurious, Columbia Cliff Villas overlook the Columbia River Gorge with unforgettable views of the "The Hatchery" Windsurfing Beach, lush gardens and a 208' waterfall that has been the hallmark of the historic Columbia Gorge Hotel.

Luxury Accommodations
29 different rooms and suites can be configured as 1-3 bedroom interconnected units to set the perfect stage for business meetings, retreats, wine excursions, outdoor adventures and weddings. All rooms feature gorgeous woodwork and exquisite appointments. Many offer gourmet kitchens and garages.

Extraordinary Services
Event and meeting coordination. Private chef dining and catering can provide any type of fare. Nanny services. Room service and spa services in all suites.

Area Attractions
World famous for breathtaking views, windsurfing and outdoor adventure. The Columbia River Gorge (a National Scenic Area) now offers 40 wineries, five golf courses, endless hiking and biking, fishing and water sports, year-round skiing on Mt. Hood, art galleries and award winning restaurants to suite any palate.

Contact
Steve Tessmer
Owner & General Manager

Price
$169 - $895

Capacity
Meetings up to 30

Amenities
- Kitchens
- Fireplaces
- Private Spa Services
- Nanny services
- Private chef dining
- Catering available
- Pet friendly

Testimonials
John & Michelle - Camas, WA:
"Wow, we were absolutely blown away with this place. The entire experience was the best in the Gorge."

Seth - Portland, OR:
"Serenity, immediate discovery, Columbia Cliff Villas creates an immediate connection with the lifestyle and unmatched splendor."

TYPES OF EVENTS
Business meetings, retreats, team building, achievement awards, wine dinners and weddings.

www.bravoevent.com

PORTLAND CONVENTION CENTER

THE PLACE TO MEET.

1441 NE 2nd Avenue
Portland, Oregon 97232
p. 503.233.2401
f. 503.238.7016
e. sales@cpportland.com
www.cpportland.com

About Crowne Plaza Downtown/Convention Center

The Crowne Plaza-Downtown/Convention Center offers easy access from I-5 and I-84 and is just 20 minutes from Portland's International Airport. The hotel is just four blocks from the Oregon Convention Center and two blocks from the Rose Quarter and Memorial Coliseum. The Crowne Plaza is located in "Fareless Square" with access to the MAX Light Rail, where passengers can easily explore downtown Portland's incredible shopping, museums, galleries, and restaurants. The Lloyd Center Mall, Oregon's largest shopping mall, is located just seven blocks from the hotel and features an eight screen cinema and an indoor ice skating rink.

So Many Near-By Attractions

- Willamette River and the East Esplanade walking path – 4 blocks
- Oregon Museum of Science and Industry – 1 mile
- Chinese Gardens – 1 mile
- Saturday Market – 1 mile
- Oregon Zoo – 6 miles
- Japanese Gardens – 6 miles
- Multnomah Falls – 30 miles

Contact
Trisha Dirks
Executive Meetings & Events Manager

Price
Please inquire

Capacity
9,000+ square feet of meeting & banquet space; seating groups from 10 to 600

Quick Fact
- Recently completed a multi-million dollar renovation to become the new Crowne Plaza Portland.

WHAT'S NEW

241 newly remodeled, spacious guest rooms, featuring coffee makers, hairdryers, irons & ironing boards, deluxe-size work desks, microwaves and refrigerators and 42' flat screen TV's. All rooms include the Crowne Sleep Amenities.

See page 119 under Event & Meeting Sites

Bravo! Member Since 1998

Accommodations

Falcon's Crest Lodge
In Government Camp

Mt. Hood Vacations
38250 Pioneer Boulevard #607
Sandy, Oregon 97055
p. 503.686.8080
f. 503.622.0474
e. becca1st@gmail.com
www.FalconsCrestLodge.com

About Falcon's Crest Lodge

This amazing 5,700 sq. foot lodge, in the heart of Historic Government Camp, is walking distance to lifts, hiking trails and town. Craftsman style woodwork, granite counters and slate floors provide rustic charm and the luxury you desire. Falcon's Crest lets you relax in luxury and comfort.

Falcon's Crest sleeps 24 comfortably. There are 3 Deluxe King Master Suites with private baths and private decks and 1 Deluxe Family Suite that sleeps 4 with its own private sitting area and Jacuzzi tub. There are 2 bunk rooms, each sleeping 6, with full, private bathrooms. One even has its own 32-inch Satellite TV. Four families will feel right at home!

The Great Room has a custom Bar, the Dining Room a 15-foot log Family-Style table and your fully-equipped gourmet kitchen has a gas Viking 8-burner stove.

The Game Room has a Foosball Table, Air Hockey, Poker/Game Table and plenty of Board Games for the whole family.

Multiple large decks have great views of Mt. Hood and the night lights of Ski Bowl. At days end, relax in our new top-of-the-line 6-person Hot Tub. Falcon's Crest Lodge is how life is meant to be enjoyed!

Contact
Becca Niday

Price
$425 to $1,150 a night

Quick Facts
- Wireless Internet & Sirius Satellite Radio
- Big screen- HDTV with Satellite, DVD & VCR, X-Box
- Large laundry room with washer & two dryers
- Slate foyer with convenient storage for ski gear

Testimonials
"This house is Heavenly! It is amazingly well-equipped & I LOVED the kitchen. The beds were the most comfortable I have ever slept in. The kids enjoyed the games and we all had a fantastic time. Everything about this home is excellent."
– Jeannie C.

"I just wanted to thank you again for all your help in making our stay at Government Camp so wonderful. Falcon's Crest was a dream! Hope we'll be able to visit again."
– Cathy O.

See page 287 under Resorts & Retreats

www.bravoevent.com

Accommodations

Hilton Garden Inn
Portland Airport

12048 NE Airport Way
Portland, Oregon 97220
p. 503.255.8600
f. 503.255.8998
e. Terrie.Ward@hilton.com
www.portlandairport.hgi.com

Four Star Service At A Three Star Price

Hilton Garden Inn Portland Airport offers spacious guest rooms full of thoughtful amenities complemented by friendly service and a relaxed atmosphere.

By focusing precisely on what guests have said they need and want, and less on what they don't use, we deliver the highest degree of service and cost savings to both business and leisure travelers, without sacrificing the quality associated with the Hilton name.

Stellar Location

We are located just three miles east of the Portland International Airport, by car or via our 24-hour complimentary shuttle. The Hilton Garden Inn is easily accessible off Interstate-205 and is only 12 miles from the Oregon Convention Center, the Rose Garden Arena and downtown Portland.

Special Services

We offer a special group rate with a booking of 10 or more guest rooms per night.

This hotel is a 100% smoke free facility.

Contact
Terrie Ward

Price
$91 to $131

Capacity
Four meeting rooms totaling 2,100 square feet, accommodating 10 to 80

Amenities
- Tables & chairs provided
- Servers included in price
- Full beverage service available; provided by hotel only
- Wide selection of linens & napkins provided
- China & glassware provided
- Wireless Internet access; full range AV equipment available at additional cost
- Cleanup provided by staff
- Complimentary parking
- ADA – yes

AWARD-WINNING INN
Awarded the JD Power Award, two years in-a-row

See page 135 under Event & Meeting Sites

Green Seal Certified

Bravo! Member Since 1999

www.bravoevent.com

RED LION HOTEL
PORTLAND · CONVENTION CENTER

Accommodations

1021 NE Grand Avenue
Portland, Oregon 97232
p. 503.820.4156
f. 503.235.0396
e. janet.kearney@gaha.biz
www.redlion.com/conventioncenter

About Red Lion Hotel Portland Convention Center

Beautiful 173 room hotel, including three suites, centrally located across from the Oregon Convention Center, on the MAX light rail line in fareless square. Over 8,000 square feet of meeting/event space on the 6th floor with beautiful views of OCC, downtown and the west hills. Comfortable café for breakfast, lunch and dinner; room service; lounge with view; marketplace for sundries and snacks; guest laundry; fitness center.

Complete renovation of hotel rooms including bathrooms, meeting space, lobby, café and lounge. Finished in 2009.

Guest rooms include coffee maker, iron and ironing board, refrigerator, hairdryer, dataports, cable television with premium channels and Nintendo. All rooms have one king or two queen beds.

We are the pet-friendliest hotel around! Only $20.00 charge per stay, however, join the Red Lion R&R frequent guest program and your pet stays free!

Contact
Janet Kearney, CMP

Price
Varies according to event

Amenities
- Located adjacent to the Oregon Convention Center, near the Rose Garden. Five minutes to downtown Portland!
- Recent renovation includes a new bright, contemporary atmosphere in all meeting/event space; guest rooms; lobby & other public spaces.
- Beautiful Windows Skyroom event space with outdoor terrace overlooking the city for up to 250 people. Gorgeous!
- 4,000 square foot Grand Ballroom, completely renovated this year!
- Premier conference suite with executive style seating overlooking the city!
- Pet friendly! Red Lion is the pet-friendliest hotel chain around!

WHAT'S NEW
Renovation….the Red Lion is "brand new again"!

Bravo! Member Since 1997

www.bravoevent.com

Notes

Business Publications & Media

PORTLAND BUSINESS JOURNAL

www.portland.bizjournals.com

Established in 1984, The Portland Business Journal is a weekly newspaper that covers local business news. It is written for business executives and publishes stories about specific industries, trends and people. It is considered a "must read" by professionals, and its award-winning editorial makes The Portland Business Journal the best news source for local business in Greater Portland.

Editorial
The Portland Business Journal has dedicated coverage of the hospitality industry. Editorial sections specifically relating to events and meetings include:
- Meetings and Conferences Issue
- Hospitality, Tourism and Dining Issue
- Meetings and Conventions
- Best of the Holidays: Dining and Entertaining
- Top 25 Meeting Facilities list
- Top 25 Meeting Facilities-out of area list
- Top 25 Restaurants list
- Top 25 Resorts list
- Top 25 Hotels list

Subscriber Information
The Portland Business Journal subscribers are key decision-makers for their companies.
- 57% in top management
- 89% use off-site meeting facilities
- 70% use local hotels
- Dine out an average of four times a week
- 81% college graduates
- Average household income: $224,000
- 73% drink Oregon wine
- 54% drink Oregon microbrews

Contact
851 SW Sixth Avenue
Suite 500
Portland, Oregon 97204
p. 503.274.8733
f. 503.219.3450
www.protland.bizjournals.com

Rob Smith
Editor

Matt Kish
Managing Editor

Liby Waltemath
Marketing Manager

Rob Vaughn
Director of Sales

Audrey Smith &
Susan Greening
Hospitality Account Executives

CIRCULATION
- 12,000 total circulation
- 58,000 readers

READERSHIP
- 77% read four out of four issues
- 64% consider The Business Journal their primary source of local business news

Bravo! Member Since 2006

www.bravoevent.com

EVENT SOLUTIONS
For Successful Events, Meetings and Incentives

About Event Solutions

Event Solutions has a 14-year history of providing corporate event planners and producers with the news, strategies, trends and ideas they need to plan successful events, meetings and incentives. Our editorial mission is to inspire the events industry to share insights and best practices to help event planners grow their events and businesses.

Time-honored and pragmatic, Event Solutions offers the resources — in the magazine, online and at our award-winning annual Conference & Tradeshow — that corporate event directors, meeting planners, independent producers and senior-level event leaders rely on.

We're set apart by comprehensive coverage focusing on every aspect of event planning and production. From design to entertainment, marketing to budgeting, lighting to site selection, travel and production, we bring readers the real event solutions they need.

Add in tips and trends in columns like Event Savvy and It Report plus instantly available news online and in Solutions:eNews, and you've found the most trusted news source in the events industry.

Contact

Meredith McIlmoyle

PO Box 11660
Tempe, Arizona 85284

p. 408.831.5100 ext. 118
f. 408.777.2300
e. meredith@event-solutions.com

www.event-solutions.com

Quick Facts

- Event Solutions magazine is a monthly publication for event professionals.

- Event Solutions Conference & Tradeshow provides planners with comprehensive education, idea-generating events and a tradeshow floor with more than 600 suppliers to spark your imagination.

- Solutions:eNews, event-solutions.com, and our digital edition offer on-the-go solutions.

WHAT'S NEW?

Join us at the annual Event Solutions Conference & Tradeshow March 8 – 10, 2010 in Las Vegas. Conference registration information available at event-solutions.com.

Bravo! Member Since 2007

Meetings | west

550 Montgomery Street
Suite 750
San Francisco, California 94111
p. 800.358.0388
f. 415.788.1358
www.meetingsfocus.com

About Meetings West

Meetings West delivers news, features and the most thorough destination information on the Western US, Western Canada & Mexico meetings markets. Planning professionals who hold meetings in these regions read Meetings West for hotel, conference and convention facility updates, industry news, and planning insights.

Meetings West is published by Meetings Media, which also brings you a newly designed website, MeetingsFocus.com, designed for you to research destinations, read industry news, search property listings, and more. We also produce weekly western edition enewsletters, monthly educational videos, and weekly meeting Planner video tips.

Meetings West is a free monthly publication delivered to Meeting Professionals nationwide who confirm that they plan/hold meetings in the western states. To subscribe, please log on to: www.MeetingsFocus.com.

Contacts

For Advertising Information:

Shawne.Hightower@meetingsmedia.com
Advertising Director,
415-782-2248

Jay.Driscoll@meetingsmedia.com
Regional Sales Manager,
319-861-5028

For Editorial Information:

Tyler.Davidson@meetingsmedia.com
Editorial Director,
415-782-2250

For Subscriptions:

Heather.Bernhard@meetingsmedia.com
Audience Marketing Manager,
319-861-5014

Quick Facts

- 31,010* subscribers;
  *BPA June 2009
- Annual planning directory: Meetings West Guide
- Weekly enewsletter: Subscribe at www.MeetingsFocus.com

www.bravoevent.com

About Oregon Business Magazine

Oregon Business is the only statewide business magazine in Oregon. The 28-year-old magazine is an award-winning publication, and was named one of the top business publications in the nation in 2009 by the American Society of Business Publication Editors.

The magazine has a readership of more than 20,000 top-level civic, business and political leaders. It covers issues and news trends. Its signature project is the 100 Best Companies to Work for in Oregon, and this year launched the 100 Best Green Companies and the 100 Best Nonprofits. Oregon Business' website offers original reporting, blogs by its editors and columnists along with the day's news highlights.

Named one of the top 3 business publications in the country in 2009 by the American Society of Business Publication Editors.

Contact

Jason Garey

610 SW Broadway Suite 200
Portland, Oregon 97205

p. 503.445.8817
f. 503.221.6544
e. jasong@oregonbusiness.com

www.oregonbusiness.com

Quick Facts

The magazine has a readership of more than 20,000 top-level civic, business and political leaders.

WHAT'S NEW

OB launched two new projects this year: the 100 Best Green and the 100 Best Nonprofits to Work for in Oregon.

Bravo! Member Since 2008

Business Publications & Media

Smart Meetings Media is the premier information resource for national corporate and association meeting professionals who make purchase decisions for meetings and events planned in the Western U.S., Western Canada and Mexico.

Smart Meetings Media serves the meeting planning market with an integrated media approach, with its Smart Meetings magazine, Smart Meetings Action Kit, SmartMeetings.com and *The Smart Meeting*.

Target Audience
Qualified meeting planners and C-level executives responsible for planning association, corporate or incentive meetings.

Our Commitment:
- Connect qualified meeting planners with hotels and destinations in the West
- Invest in a higher standard of excellence with in-depth coverage of the West, breaking news and relevant content
- Feature a sophisticated, fresh, easy-to-use design
- Educate readers on current industry trends
- Reach a national audience of readers who plan in the West
- Include editorial coverage for partners within our comprehensive destination features
- Provide the best tools for lead-generation

"Whitetail Club & Resort has been and advertiser in *Smart Meetings* for several years. I have confirmed booked business from our advertising in *Smart Meetings* and even have a repeat customer, delivering ROI for our precious advertising dollars! As an Idaho meeting venue, we have always appreciated the in-depth editorial coverage of meetings in Idaho and their attention to our Mountain Resort. With the launch of their digital magazine in 2009, *Smart Meetings* will stay on the cutting edge for the foreseeable future!"

– Jocelyn Kidd
Shore Lodge (Formerly Whitetail Club & Resort), McCall, Idaho

Bravo! Member Since 2008

475 Gate Five Road, Suite 235
Sausalito, California 94965
p. 415.339.9355
f. 415.339.9361
e. colin@smartmeetings.com
www.smartmeetings.com

Contact
Colin Murphy

Readership Demographics:
- 96% rate the quality of Smart Meetings as Good, Very Good or Excellent
- 88% are involved in purchasing event and meeting products/services
- 47% approve and/or make the final decision on meetings
- 61% rate Smart Meetings as a "Must Read"

SMART EVENTS – YOUR SOURCE FOR FACE-TO-FACE SOLUTIONS

Smart Meetings' live events offer you three dynamic formats to connect with our qualified meeting planners in an intimate setting that allows you to establish solid relationships and generate group business. All of our custom-tailored events meld up-to-the-minute education and unparalleled networking experiences in a welcoming and fun ambience. Our exclusive events provide unmatched results—you won't find these opportunities anywhere else.

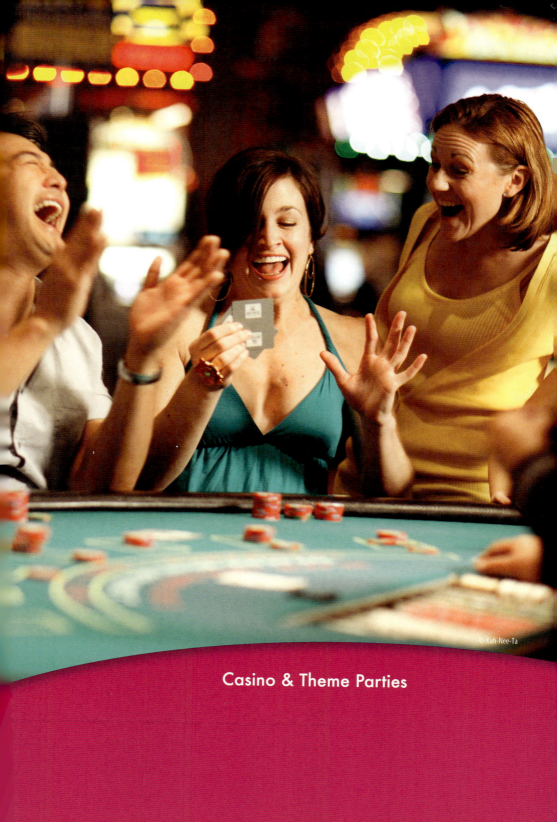

Casino & Theme Parties

All About Fun

When you think Casino Parties, think All About Fun! At All About Fun our main focus is FUN! We want your guests to leave your party with a smile, so we've put together a staff of dealers that will engage your guests, teach them the game and show them how to "WIN BIG" in a FUN way your guests will remember. Whether the game of choice is Black Jack, Craps, Roulette or Texas Hold 'Em Poker, we've got the right mix of casino games for you.

Need a Great Fundraising Idea? The Casino Fundraiser!

If you've seen a drop in donations and need a big boost, host a Casino Fundraiser designed for your organization. A Casino Fundraiser is a great way to bring your donors together and get them excited about supporting your non-profit. We'll show you how you can maximize your receivables and keep your costs down, to make your fundraising event is a huge success.

Casino Parties Are Great For

Corporate mixers, employee appreciation events, birthdays, graduation parties, fundraisers, and holiday parties.

A Casino "Holiday" Party?

You bet! A Casino Party is one of the most popular entertainment choices for large and small holiday events. Whether you're entertaining 70 or 700, All About Fun will put the FUN in your party.

Contact
Jason Hedges

p. 503.516.3878
www.allaboutfun.info

Price
Call for Quotes

Services
- Casino Parties.
- Inflatables & interactive games for company picnics.
- Live entertainment including game shows, comedy, hypnosis & magicians.
- Disc Jockeys & other music services.

CALL "ALL ABOUT FUN!"

We can take care of all your event planning and entertainment needs with our huge selection of entertainment and event planning services.

See page 258 & 259 under Interactive Entertainment

www.bravoevent.com

7901 SW Nimbus Avenue
Beaverton, Oregon 97008
p. 503.726.2121
f. 503.419.4494
e. sales@teamcasino.net
www.teamcasino.net

Team Casino – *Making Your Party a Winner!*

With Team Casino, you'll work with one experienced event planner from start to finish. We're always happy to meet and share ideas on creating a party your guests will talk about for years to come!

Team Casino's amazing personal service, tournament quality equipment & fun, friendly dealers really make the difference. We make the planning process easy for you, and produce a high-quality, professional atmosphere where anyone and everyone can have a good time!

Team Casino Parties Are Perfect For:

ANYTHING! Corporate events, Customer Appreciation, Conferences, Trade Shows, Company Picnics, Private Parties, Weddings, Birthdays, Anniversaries, Reunions, and of course:

Fundraisers!

Our Fundraising bookie works personally to create the BEST fundraiser you've ever had.

Contact
Kristina Griffith

Price
Varies by size, date & location. No party too big or small! Always a free & immediate quote.

Quick Facts
- Casino Parties with Custom Funny Money!
- Texas Hold'em Tournaments
- Night at the Derby Horseracing
- Giant Screen Wii Tournaments
- Arcade Games
- Sports Lounge Games
- DJ & Music Services
- Servicing locations in Oregon, Washington & Idaho

WHAT'S NEW
Always be in the know! Follow @Team_Casino on Twitter & Facebook!

See page 264 under Interactive Entertainment

Bravo! Member Since 2008

Casino & Theme Parties

13315 NE Airport Way
Portland, Oregon 97230
p. 503.224.0134
f. 503.224.0278
e. Shannon@wildbills.com
www.wildbills.com

About Wild Bill's

More than 26 years entertaining corporate and non-profit clients with our unique interactive events. Casino nights, poker parties, murder mysteries and game shows are some of the exciting entertainment options available for your group.

Whether your group is 30 or 5,000, our professional staff is there every step of the way of make sure your event exceeds all expectations!

Voted the most popular form of entertainment by event planners nationwide, casino parties are perfect for: Fundraisers, Company Parties, Reunions, Conventions, Grad Nights, Client Appreciation Parties, Holiday Parties, Picnics and Private Parties.

New Location

After many years in Northwest Portland, we have moved to a brand new 20,000-square-foot facility with a 2,000-square-foot event space on N.E. Airport Way. Whether you come to our venue or we go to yours, we'll make sure your event is the best ever!

Contact
Shannon Walker

Price
Custom packages, please call for quote

Quick Facts
- Casino Parties
- Poker Parties & Tournaments
- Murder Mystery Dinner Theatre
- Hollywood Style Game Shows
- The Turf Club, Video Horse Racing
- Gaming Equipment Sales & Rentals
- Full Service Event Space Now Available at our New Location
- Fully Insured

WHAT'S NEW
For more information please visit our website
www.wildbills.com

See page 203 under Event & Meeting Sites & 265 under Interactive Entertainment

Bravo! Member Since 1995

www.bravoevent.com

Catering Services

Beverage & Espresso
Cakes & Desserts
Full-Service

Beverage & Espresso

PO Box 10452
Portland, Oregon 97296
p. 503.222.5855
e. drinkbarevents@gmail.com
www.drinkbarevents.com

Drink Bar Events and Staffing is a professional bartending service that provides an incredible experience for your event. Unrivaled, Drink is the only company of its kind in Portland and uses professional, OLCC certified, seasoned bartenders, liquor aficionados and sommeliers for events.

As the wine, beer and cocktail culture is growing, so is the demand for a knowledgeable, superior bar staff for your event. We have expertly executed large corporate affairs for more than 2,000 and small, intimate in-home celebrations for less than 10. Drink can fill your needs for everything in between. We work independently and in conjunction with any caterer to provide the perfect party experience. We pride ourselves on the ability to let the host enjoy their party, while we handle the details. We look forward to working with you!

Drink Bar Events and Staffing offers:
- Custom wine & cocktail lists
- Seasoned bar & serving staff
- Sommeliers & Liquor Aficionados
- Vineyard & Brewery Tours
- On & Off-Site Events

Contact
Jessica Endsworth

Price
Starting at $10 per person

Quick Facts
- Custom drink menus, specialty cocktails & wine lists
- Large corporate & private events; on & off-site from 10 – 2000 people
- Weddings, birthdays, anniversaries, office & in-home parties
- Wine, beer & liquor classes or vineyard, brewery & distillery tours
- Access to a variety of event locations, caterers, photographers, rental companies, florists, & will refer accredited vendors for all event needs
- Arrange all bar equipment rentals, acquire all liquor, beer & wine, aid in obtaining OLCC permits / licenses

www.bravoevent.com

About Espresso Arts Catering

At Espresso Arts Catering, we have our beans custom roasted for you by Stumptown Coffee Roasters just before your event. Using organic milk or soy, we then lovingly craft our lattes, cappuccinos, and mochas. We also offer exquisite coffee alternatives like our hot chocolate with homemade whip cream and spicy chai lattes. From Foxfire Teas we offer a large assortment of fragrant loose leaf teas. Whether you have an office gathering of 50 or a large event of 1500, we have a package to fit every budget. We can accommodate small groups with our sleek, compact cart and be ready and rolling in minutes, while our large dual-machine package will efficiently serve large groups all day long.

"Their coffee is incredibly delicious, they serve it with a smile and love, they are the best."
— Pacific First Center tenant

"...this is a coffee cart like no other."
— Serena Davidson, Serena Davidson Photography

Bravo! Member Since 2007

Contact
Christine Herman-Russell

p. 503.475.3979
e. christine@espressoarts.com

www.espressoarts.com

Price
Affordable packages for any size event

Quick Facts
- Serving groups of any size in all of Oregon & Washington
- Espresso & French press services available
- Exclusively serving Stumptown Coffee Roasters, Foxfire Teas, & DragonFly Chai
- Please inquire about our current selection of Stumptown coffees
- Latest industry standard professional café equipment
- Iced espresso drinks, Italian sodas, orange juice, & pastries available upon request

"The Finest in Espresso Catering"

p. 1.877.281.8155
p. 206.282.8155
e. Holly@EspressoElegance.com
www.EspressoElegance.com

Full-Service Espresso

When you choose Espresso Elegance, you are selecting a high-class espresso catering company that strives to enhance your important occasion by bringing a signature taste of the Pacific Northwest right to your event. Your guests will enjoy unlimited espresso drinks served to them by professional and friendly baristas. You are encouraged to customize the service to match your taste preferences, including selecting your favorite brand of coffee to be served.

No Event is Too Large or Too Small

From intimate gatherings of 5 guests to events with over 5,000 guests, Espresso Elegance handles every detail. We are equipped to serve events of all sizes with over 18 state-of-the-art espresso carts. With every event, Espresso Elegance is committed to exceeding your expectations.

"We were so pleased, the process to reserve the event was easy & the service was excellent. I received such positive feedback from our employees!"
– Vernier Software

Bravo! Member Since 2008

Contact
Holly Patton

Price
Customized affordable pricing to fit your event & budget. Pricing is based on the number of guests & length of service.

Quick Facts
- Fully licensed & insured to serve events of all sizes in Washington & Oregon.
- Espresso Bars, Fruit Smoothie Bars, Italian Soda Bars & gourmet pastries are available to serve your guests.
- Eco-Friendly, Certified Kosher & Gluten Free packages available.
- Customizable service to fit your event & taste preferences from the brand of coffee to specialty menus.

WHAT'S NEW
Espresso Elegance is celebrating our 20th Anniversary of being the largest espresso caterer in the nation since 1989. To celebrate, we introduced our Eco-Friendly Espresso Catering package for events.

Espresso Volare

PO Box 6625
Portland, Oregon 97228
p. 503.246.3398
f. 503.245.0373
e. myra@espressovolare.com
www.espressovolare.com

About Espresso Volare

Our experience counts! Oregon's original espresso caterer, under continuous operation by Myra Furnish Lee. We are a full-time, professional catering service serving all of Oregon and SW Washington.

Having been involved in the catering and service industry since 1985, we have chosen to specialize exclusively in Espresso Catering since 1992.

Description of Service

Personal and professional espresso catering service for all groups of all sizes and events of all types, from morning meetings to evening occasions. You provide the 110v electrical service, we do all the rest.

Serving Cappuccino, Lattes, Mochas, Decaf or Regular, Hot or Iced; we bring 12 flavors, plus 4 sugar-free. Also serving Chai Lattes, Assorted Teas, Hot Chocolate and Steamers; Non-Fat, 1%, 2%, Whole and Soy Milk; Fresh Squeezed Orange Juice and Americanos.

Other additions can include Italian sodas, individual iced juices, artisan pastries, bagels and assorted flavored cream cheeses; fresh seasonal fruit salad; box lunches, amazing cookies and elegant desserts.

Contact
Myra Furnish Lee

Price
Call for pricing, we'll work with your budget

Quick Facts
- Oregon's premiere coffee & espresso catering & beverage service
- Includes something for everyone!
- Great coffee & great service are our business
- Please call for references
- Proudly featuring Longbottom Coffee
- Serving groups from 20 to 2,000
- We think and act green

PLANNERS TIP:
Please call for helpful suggestions to take your event to the next level, coffee and beyond. Think of us for any event when you want a non-alcoholic, fun, unique or elegant addition...the possibilities are endless... espresso and beyond. We will meet and exceed your expectations.

Bravo! Member Since 1997

About Maui Wowi Coffees and Smoothies

Maui Wowi Hawaiian Style Coffees and Smoothies provides its customers with the freshest products available from the islands. Additionally, we have the ability to add multiple options and products to meet your specific needs and criteria for your special day.

Additional Information

Our mobile Ka'anapali allows us to entertain your needs through a variety of applications including but not limited to: Wedding Rehearsal Events, Bachelor/ Bachelorette Parties, Holiday Events, Corporate Team Building, Employee Appreciation, Golf Outings, etc. If you can visualize an event we will work with you to make it happen!

What's New?

We now have a Kosher product available for Bat Mitzvahs and Bar Mitzvahs. Additionally, we can add your alcohol to any of our signature beverages to liven up any event.

Contact

Kendall & Tammy Thiemann

4001 NW 8th Circle
Camas, Washington 98607

p. 360.335.3180

e. kthiemann@comcast.net
e. tammythiemann@comcast.net

www.mauiwowiportland.com

Price

Call us!

We provide catering services as follows

The possibilities are endless...use your creativity or call us for ideas - we will work with you to make your event a memorable one.

- Social catering
- Corporate catering
- Sporting events
- Fairs & festivals
- Trade show/Convention Center catering
- Fundraisers
- Charitable organizations
- Graduation parties, Fraternity / Sorority events & Luaus
- And much more!

Bravo! Member Since 2008

www.bravoevent.com

Cakes & Desserts

Dippity Doodads
Chocolate Fountain Rentals

8205 NE 91st Street
Vancouver, Washington 98662
p. 360.798.7395
f. 360.885.2036
e. shirley@dippitydoodads.com
www.dippitydoodads.com

$ THE FONDUE FOUNTAIN FITS THE BILL $

In our new economy everyone is looking for the most value for every dollar. The Fondue Fountain is the perfect way to provide great visual impact & a variety of scrumptious foods while adhering to the strictest budget!

Nothing is more fun, more elegant and more economical than a Dippity DooDads fondue fountain. The fountain experience encompasses delicious dipping items, entertainment, guest participation, and is most certainly budget friendly.

The tried and true will never let you down…dipping juicy red strawberries or puffy marshmallows into Milk, Dark or White premium chocolate fondue is the ultimate treat! A popular & economical idea is the "dessert buffet", where a chocolate and/or caramel fountain take center stage & many delicious dippers flank the main attraction.

Versatility? We offer several fondue options; Nacho Cheese, Creamy Caramel, Tangy Ranch Dressing & our latest addition, Hot Chicken Wing Sauce!

Please invite us to your wedding reception, corporate gathering, holiday party, fundraiser, Bat/Bar Mitzvah, graduation, prom….we can do it all!

Call today to reserve your fountain for ANY OCCASION!

Contact
Shirley Easton

Price
$185 - $495

Quick Facts
- Four fountain sizes to accommodate any size group
- Serving the Portland/Vancouver area within 100 mile radius
- 10% Discount when renting two or more fountains
- Listed as a preferred vendor for many of the areas finest venues
- Price includes fondue, properly attired attendant, skewers, set-up, breakdown & clean-up of all fountains
- Proudly serving our area for 6 years

Bravo! Member Since 2007

WHAT'S NEW
Ask about our CHOCOLATE bullets, shot-gun shells and yes, hand grenades…really! Makes a great gift for your favorite sportsman.

www.bravoevent.com

The Party Scoop

A unique dessert experience for your special event!

About The Party Scoop

The Party Scoop, Inc. was formed to fill a niche in the dessert catering industry. Our service comes to you providing the best in freshly scooped premium ice cream and customized toppings.

Experience this new and unique way to cater your next party or meeting, whether at your office, wedding reception, picnic or personal party. It is our passion to help make your event a very memorable experience.

Event Types

- Corporate events
- Wedding receptions
- Company picnics
- Anniversaries
- Birthday parties
- Special occasions
- Bat/Bar Mitzvahs

Contact

Bea Thomas

PO Box 3623
Tualatin, Oregon 97062
p. 503.539.0011
e. thepartyscoop@verizon.net
www.thepartyscoop.com

Price

Customized quotes to fit your event and budget

Quick Facts

- A unique sundae bar service for any occasion
- We serve local Tillamook ice cream
- We bring our special service to you
- Locally owned, fully licensed and insured
- Set-up and clean-up is included

Bravo! Member Since 2008

Aarnegard's PREMIERE CATERING

Full-Service

2432 SE Umatilla Street
Portland, Oregon 97202
p. 503.235.0274
f. 503.235.8225
e. premierecatering@comcast.net
www.premierecatering.biz

About Aarnegard's Premiere Catering

Aarnegard's Premiere Catering offers fine dining in any location, customized to fit your style of entertaining, culinary tastes, and budget. We offer location catering at its finest...on the mountain top, at the beach, or in your garden... possibilities are endless.

Let Aarnegard's Premiere Catering make your event a true culinary success. We specialize in on-site cooking (ask for details). Nothing compares to freshly prepared foods for your event. Your guests will notice the fresh flavors and quality of your menu.

Aarnegard's Premiere Catering is a full-service caterer, providing everything needed for a successful event. Regardless of the type of event or service required, you can count on the reputation Aarnegard's Premiere Catering has earned, with over 20 years experience in the event business. With this experience, we are able to accommodate both large and small events. We will show you how experience pays off.

Contact
Michael Peters

Price
Please call for quote

Quick Facts
- Event planning & site selection
- Licensed to serve alcoholic beverages
- Rental coordination (china, glassware, silverware, tables, chairs, tents)
- Props & decorations
- Entertainment (bands, disc jockeys, musicians)

PROFESSIONAL & COURTEOUS

Premiere Catering prepares all entrees on-site to offer only the Finest and Freshest Entrees possible. Our professional & courteous service staff will assist in making your event successful. From set up to clean up, you will find our staff efficient and friendly.

Bravo! Member Since 2000

Busy Bee Catering

PO Box 295
Welches, Oregon 97067
p. 503.622.6743
f. 503.622.0167
e. busybeecatering@hotmail.com
www.busybeecatering.com

About Busy Bee Catering

Busy Bee Catering is located in beautiful Welches, Oregon, at the foothills of Mt. Hood. We provide service to many special local venues as well as service to the Metro Area, Hood River, Central Oregon and the Willamette Valley. We love the beauty and bounty that Oregon has to offer and like to showcase these aspects in the way we present our foods. We are available to provide a full array of services ranging from event planning and vendor coordination to delivery, set up or even drop off.

We have been busy catering weddings, corporate events, family picnics, and parties of every theme and type. We would love to work with you to create the kind of function that shows your personality and entertaining style. We have made lots of friends catering in the last 20 years and would be happy to provide a variety of references. Take the hassle out of your next ski trip or camp out with meals prepared in our local kitchen. Just stop by our convenient location on your way up the mountain. Whatever you are planning, please consider Busy Bee Catering...we love to cater and it shows!

Contact
Todd & Jan Ostrom

Price
Menus to accommodate all budgets

Quick Facts
- Over 20 years experience in corporate, social catering & event planning
- Long time relationships with local vendors to ensure freshest, high quality ingredients
- Creative presentation using clever props, fresh greens, flowers & herbs
- Caring, friendly & professional staff
- We are a fully licensed & insured off-site caterer
- Fresh delicious foods that make even a simple menu elegant
- On-site grilling & cooking
- Busy Bee Catering is a sustainable business
- Menu tasting available

Bravo! Member Since 2008

www.bravoevent.com

Full-Service

Catering At Its Best
special events & corporate catering

professional service ~ stylish presentation the food... speaks for itself

Since 1995 Catering At Its Best has been providing full service catering throughout the greater Portland area. Our catering services range from elaborate special events and corporate meetings, to in-home parties, barbecues, holiday parties and boxed lunches. You can select from one of our pre-printed menus or let one of our experienced Event Planners design a custom menu created to complement your event. We pride ourselves on using only the freshest and highest quality ingredients. In addition to outstanding food and service, Catering At Its Best can provide you with all the necessary "extras!"

We will work with you every step of the way to make sure your event is a complete success!

Excellent food and excellent service…
Anything else is unacceptable.

p. 503.238.8889
f. 503.238.8893
e. info@caibpdx.com
www.caibpdx.com

Contact
Toni Robinson

Price
Based on menu selection & type of service

Services
- Full-service catering & special event company
- Vegetarian & special dietary menus available upon request
- Customized event planning & site location
- On-site manager at every event
- Full-service bars, experienced professional servers & OLCC licensed bartenders
- Complete rental coordination (tents, tables, chairs, dance floors, etc.)

a proud participant

PORTLAND COMPOSTS!

a program of the city of Portland Office of Sustainable Development and Metro

Portland Composts! Participant
RecycleWorks Award Winner

Bravo! Member Since 1995

www.bravoevent.com

Full-Service

CRAVE Catering

1324 SE 8th Street
Portland, Oregon 97214
p. 503.224.0370
f. 503.224.3919
e. catering@cravepdx.com
www.cravepdx.com
http://twitter.com/CraveCatering

Chef Inspired Sustainable World Cuisine

Crave Catering gives you the confidence you need to make a good impression through creative, chef inspired cuisine. We take great care in our ingredients, hand-picking produce & other local products to foster community support for local farmers, fishermen, and artisans. Let this locally owned, sustainable caterer **MAKE** your next event. Our clients come back for more after telling us how everyone is **STILL** raving about the food! We are a Full Service Caterer that offers event set-up, equipment rental coordination, and full bar service.

Each year Crave Catering commits to becoming 10% more sustainable! From a hybrid delivery vehicle to real silverware & plateware. We've already decreased our impact on landfills by 70% over the last 3 years!

CORPORATE - Luncheons, Picnics, Holidays, Cocktail Parties.

PRIVATE - Birthdays, Weddings, Anniversaries, Bar/Bat Mitzvahs

NON-PROFIT - Auctions, Galas, Fundraisers

FILM PRODUCTION - TV Shows, Commercials, Movies

Contact
Catering Department

Price
Call or visit www.cravepdx.com for ordering, menus, and pricing

Quick Facts
- Locally owned business with more than 25 years of experience
- Founding Member of the Sustainable Catering Association
- We use local seasonal produce
- Naturally raised meats & poultry, and sustainable seafood
- Portland Compost Participant
- Portland RecycleWorks Award Recipient

CULINARY CRAVEings
Pacific Northwest
Rustic Italian
Traditional American
Asian Fusion
Caribbean Cuisine
Nuevo Latino
Old World French
Slow and low Barbecue
and much more!

RecycleWorks Award Winner, Portland Composts! Participant

Bravo! Member Since 1999

www.bravoevent.com

Full-Service

9037 SW Burnham Street
Tigard, Oregon 97223
p. 503.620.9020
f. 503.620.3964
www.cateringbydeangelos.com

DeAngelo's Catering

DeAngelo's Catering offers all types of menus from self- or full-service buffets to formal sit-down affairs. We offer the client the opportunity for full-service event planning including food, rental coordination, site evaluations, décor, and more. Our menus offer a wide range of food including Asian, Italian, Mexican, African, Caribbean, and Hawaiian; excellent service staff is available, attire is always appropriate.

Approved Caterer locations:
- Holy Names Heritage Center
- McLean House
- Wisteria Gardens in Brush Prairie
- The Party Room at Wild Bill's
- Pittock Mansion
- Museum of Oregon Territory
- World Forestry Center and Museum
- Marshall House
- Leach Botanical Gardens
- Oregon Square Courtyard
- Many more

Contact
DeAngelo's Catering

Price
Catering for any Budget Range!

Based on a per-person basis.

Catering...Just For You!
- Over 25 years experience ranging in all types of catering needs
- Food is scratch-prepared & exquisitely presented
- Custom Prepared Menus
- Corporate Packages
- Unique Venues
- Sustainable Events
- Fully licensed & insured to serve alcoholic beverages
- FREE consultations
- Complete flexibility to adapt to special needs & requests
- All full-service buffet décor at no-charge

NEED IDEAS?
Visit our website at
CateringByDeangelos.com

Bravo! Member Since 1996

ELEPHANTS DELICATESSEN

115 NW 22nd Avenue
Portland, Oregon 97210
p. 503.224.3955
f. 503.546.4495
www.elephantsdeli.com

About Elephants Delicatessen

Since 1979, Elephants Delicatessen has proudly served our community as Portland's premier catering company and specialty foods retailer. We make all of our great local foods from scratch every day for your eating enjoyment. We offer drop off catering, full service events and the option of holding your event in our lovely Private Garden Room.

Elephants Catering is committed to providing each of our clients with delicious foods, and friendly, knowledgeable service. We're working each day to exceed your expectations, and to engage and delight your senses.

Serving the Catering Needs of the Portland Metro area for 30 years!

We have the resources and expertise to manage any event, from small daily corporate meetings to large-scale extravaganzas. Elephants Catering is built upon the foundation of providing our clients with exceptional quality and service. As a corporate catering and event planning services company, we partner with clients and individuals to make their jobs easier, help them achieve their goals – and stay on budget!

Supporting our Community Responsibly

We are committed to sustainable business practices that improve our products, processes and facilities while reducing our environmental impact. Ask your sales associate how you can help by choosing our eco-friendly corporate products.

Contact
Catering Associates
e. cateringsales-csa@elephantsdeli.com

Price
Catering & Event options for any budget!

Quick Facts
- Corporate Catering
- Special Events
- Picnics & BBQ's
- Drop Off Catering
- Full Service Catering & Events
- Professional Event Planning Services
- Curbside Pick-up
- Sustainable "Green" Business Practices

Our Private Garden Room Features:
- Capacity: 55 Seated 75 Standing
- Retractable Roof
- Distinctive Open Fireplace
- Linen Service
- Fresh Flower Arrangements
- AV Equipment Available
- Full-service Beverage Selection
- On-Site Parking

Bravo! Member Since 2001

Full-Service

GOURMET PRODUCTIONS
It's a mouthful!

39 B. Avenue
Lake Oswego, Oregon 97034
p. 503.697.7355
www.gopro-lo.com

- **Sustainability**

We are a locally owned independent business. Every effort is made to reduce our impact on the environment by purchasing from local businesses, recycling, using biodegradable service ware, encouraging carpools and supporting mass transit.

Think global. Eat local.

- **Ingredients**

We learn your specific tastes, needs and desires. Custom menus are created just for you. We promise seasonally driven food with high emphasis on value and quality.

- **Services**

We are your friendly Portland caterer, a group of committed foodies serving food that tastes as good as it looks. From start to finish, we offer menu planning, preparation and site coordination for corporate events such as Open Houses, Launches, Project Wrap Ups, Box Lunches, Anniversaries, Holiday Parties, and BBQs.

Contact
Catering department or catering@gopro-lo.com

Price
Based on menu selection, guest count and service requests.

Inquire about a **free** consultation.

Premier Portland Caterer since 1993
- Local organic food is our passion!
- Large event specialists:
- Visit our web site for menu ideas & see our instructional videos on our YouTube channel.

What our customers say:

"Your food was superb, and we fully enjoyed ourselves as you made it easy to pull off a wonderful event."

– B.A.

SPECIAL OFFER

Mention this page when you call and receive four hours of complimentary bartending when you book a full service event with Gourmet Productions.

43

Bravo! Member Since 2007

Full-Service

Jake's CATERING
AT THE GOVERNOR HOTEL

614 SW 11th Avenue
Portland, Oregon 97205
p. 503.241.2125
f. 503.220.1849
www.jakescatering.com

A Historic Gem

Listed on the National Register of Historic Places, The Governor Hotel is an architectural beauty. Built in 1909, the hotel has been completely restored to its original grandeur. The recently completed renovation of the Heritage Ballroom unveils Portland's best-kept secret, resurrecting this one-of-a-kind grand space for events after a hiatus of more than 60 years. The classic design and ornate craftsmanship were preserved in the original Italian Renaissance styling. The room's high vaulted ceilings, marble floors and black-walnut woodwork and walls are truly unique.

Jake's Catering...A Tradition

Jake's Catering is part of the McCormick & Schmick's family of restaurants, including Jake's Famous Crawfish. Jake's is one of the oldest and most respected dining institutions in the Portland area, and Jake's Catering upholds this prestigious reputation.

Known for offering an extensive range of Pacific Northwest menu selections, including fresh seafood, pasta, poultry and prime cut steaks, Jake's Catering has the variety, flexibility and talent to cater to your needs.

Availability and Terms

Our Italian Renaissance-style rooms offer variety and flexibility for groups of 25 to 700. The newly renovated Heritage Ballroom, Renaissance Room, Fireside Room, Library and eight additional rooms gracefully complement the charm of The Governor Hotel. We require a 50% deposit to confirm your event and payment in full 72 hours prior to event for estimated charges.

Contact
Catering Director

Price
$25 to $55

Capacity
700 reception; 500 sit-down

Amenities
- Tables & chairs for up to 500
- Professional, uniformed servers
- Full-service bar & bartender
- Cloth napkins & linens in variety of colors
- Fine china & glassware provided
- A/V available upon request
- Ample parking

TYPES OF EVENTS

From stand-up cocktail and appetizer receptions to fabulous buffet presentations to complete sit-down dinners for groups and gatherings of all sizes.

See page 140 under Event & Meeting Sites

Bravo! Member Since 1994

Jo Foody

Full-Service

p. 360.607.3281
e. jodell@jofoody.com
www.jofoody.com

About Jo Foody's Catering

Jo Foody is a full service catering company located in Downtown Vancouver. Whether it is a private dinner party, wedding, a winemaker dinner, a child's birthday, or a corporate party, our goal is to make every client's vision come to life!

Jo Foody caters private and corporate events in the Portland/Vancouver area ranging in size from 10 to 300 or more. We have also provided concessions and backstage catering at venues such as the MicroBlues festival previously held in Esther Short Park, the Grand Opening of the new Battleground Skatepark, the Nautilus FitJam, Blues by the Sea in Garabaldi, Oregon, and many other such events.

Additionally, the owners have over 10 years experience in organizing Non-Profit Auction fundraisers.

Contact
Jodell Hinojosa

Price Range for service
Pricing depends on menu selection

Quick Facts
- Customized menus for each client
- Variety of cuisines for both formal & casual events
- Exclusive Foody Blues BBQ made with house rubs & sauces
- Event concessions available

Bravo! Member Since 2008

Full-Service

Pearl CATERING

206 NW 10th Avenue
Portland, Oregon 97209
p. 503.860.0203
f. 971.327.6688
e. carla@urban-restaurants.com
www.pearlcateringpdx.com

About Pearl Catering

Pearl Catering, delivers a menu of crowd pleasing favorites richly influenced by Northwest ingredients, beautifully presented and full of flavor! Whether you are looking to serve passed hors d'oeuvres or a buffet dinner, Pearl Catering offers a variety of creative menus for any budget. Have something special in mind? No problem, we are happy to customize a menu to meet your specific needs and budget.

Pearl Catering is the exclusive in-house full service caterer at Urban Studio, the Pearl District's quintessential event space. Ideal for weddings, receptions, private parties and corporate events, our experienced catering and event staff will make the planning process a pleasure and your event a success.

Price
Please call for quote

Quick Facts
- Full service & licensed caterer for both food & alcohol service
- Gourmet box lunch program
- China, silverware & basic linen
- Drop-off service, plated dinners, passed hors d'oeuvres or buffet
- Elegant or casual customized menus
- Setup & cleanup included
- Friendly & knowledgeable event & serving staff

WHAT'S NEW?
Rental cost of Urban Studio is waived with a minimum food and beverage purchase. Call for more information 503.860.0203

See page 201 under Event & Meeting Sites

www.bravoevent.com

7800 SW Durham Road
Portland, Oregon 97224
p. 503.620.8855
f. 503.620.3355
e. info@portlandcateringcompany.com
www.portlandcateringcompany.com

About Portland Catering Company

We offer thoughtful menus filled with dishes that are always fresh and well prepared and our gracious and attentive staff will take care of even the smallest details. Whether you're planning an intimate gathering for a family reception, an annual charity black-tie gala or a large, glittering holiday affair to celebrate with your corporate staff, Portland Catering Company will make your event a truly special occasion.

We will work with you to set the right tone, select the perfect menu and create an atmosphere that will make you and your guests feel pampered and completely at ease. From planning to perfect ending, let us help you every step of the way.

In addition to helping you plan your menu, we can assist you with so much more. Selecting a venue, handling the rentals, and coordinating with all of your vendors - we pride ourselves on making your event effortless - so you can relax and enjoy!

Contact
Erin Cutlip

Price
Based on menu selection, guest count & type of service

Services
- Full-service caterer
- Customized menus to fit within your budget
- Friendly & professional staff
- Menu items prepared fresh daily & from scratch
- Free menu tasting available

There's No Better Way to Impress, Except With the Best!

www.bravoevent.com

Full-Service

1410 SW Morrison
Suite 600
Portland, Oregon 97205-1930
p. 503.248.9305
f. 503.243.7147
e. rafatis@rafatiscatering.com
www.rafatiscatering.com

Our Cuisine

Unique, inspiring dishes that complement any theme or style. Specializing in Pacific Northwest, Pan Asian, South and Central American, Middle Eastern, Caribbean/Island - we are ready to create the perfect menu for your event. Consider fresh Heirloom Tomato Gazpacho with Tortilla Skewered Shrimp, Tangerine Scallop Martinis with Cashew Crumble, entrée or small plates like our popular Painted Hills Tenderloin with Gorgonzola Risotto and Maysara Pinot Noir Wine Reduction Sauce, Chef's exhibitions of our famous Seafood Paella, or Wok Stations of fabulous Pan Asian Stir Fry.

Our Services

From the simplicity of everyday luncheon meeting needs, the formalities of white glove dinner service, the complexities of seminars and conferences, to themed corporate receptions or the selection of the perfect event location site, you can count on Rafati's. Our event coordinators will be happy to prepare detailed plans based on theme, décor, budget and other specific goals, then produce them with savvy style and flair.

Event Locations

Rafati's is located in and the exclusive caterer for the historic Tiffany Center, exclusive caterer for the Chinese Gardens Tea House, and is preferred at the Lawrence Gallery and Chinese Gardens. Our clients also enjoy our signature catering and event services at a wide selection of locations, facilities and private residences throughout Oregon and Southwest Washington.

Contact

Jessica Rafati
Event Manager

Price

The cost is determined by the menu selection, level of desired service and number of guests

Quick Facts

- More than 25 years catering to Portland's metro community
- Concentration on locally produced foods & sustainable products
- Unique, sophisticated presentations & themes
- Full bar services, local wineries, breweries & distilleries
- Highly trained & credentialed professional service staff
- Event planning included with full-service catering

With innovative menus, passionate focus on fresh local ingredients, edgy presentations & unparalleled service, you can depend on Rafati's each & every time to help you achieve the "wow" factor for your event catering needs!

Bravo! Member Since 1994

2236 SE Belmont
Portland, Oregon 97214
p. 503.297.9635
f. 503.234.4051
e. cater@vibranttable.com
www.vibranttable.com

Catering
We prepare extraordinary food in the smallest of quantity and on the grandest of scales. From corporate gatherings to intimate parties, every event - small or grand - is within our capabilities.

Floral
Our floral design team is trained to see the perfect blend of form and color to complement your event's overall look. We are adept at using color, texture, scent and sound to highlight the unique attributes of every event.

Décor
Our staff skillfully combines flowers, candles, vases, trellises and other accessories that give the biggest impact to the smallest details.

Venue
Our exquisite cuisine and dynamic services have earned us an exclusive spot at these fine venues:

The Portland Art Museum, Zenith Vineyard, The Loft and The Treasury Ballroom. You will also find us on the preferred list at many other vibrant settings. Please visit our website for a complete list.

Contact
Kurt Beadell
Creative Director & Co-Owner

Price
Based on guest count, food selection & service requirements.

Please contact us for a free consultation.

Quick Facts
- Our services range from fine cuisine and innovative décor to floral artistry and event theme creation
- Portland Caterer of the Year 2007, 2008 and 2009 (Oregon Bride Magazine)
- We follow sustainable event practices
- Recycleworks Award recipient

THE LOFT ON BELMONT
Our one-of-a-kind urban event space is available for private events. Able to accommodate up to 100 guests, The Loft features large windows, a fireplace, lobby bar and striking, contemporary décor.

Bravo! Member Since 2000

www.bravoevent.com

800 NW 6th Avenue
Portland, Oregon 97209
p. 503.223.0070
f. 503.223.1386
e. candace@wilfsrestaurant.com
www.wilfsrestaurant.com

About Wilfs Restaurant & Bar

Wilfs Restaurant & Bar at Union Station, minutes from downtown, offers a unique, convenient location for all your events: lunch, dinner, meetings, wine tasting, family celebrations, to the perfect wedding! Our catering includes box lunches to a formal sit-down affair.

Easy as 1-2-3

Wilfs offers coordinating services to help unravel the complexities of event planning. Expert staff offers personal service and attention to the details, and Candace, our event coordinator, will create a seamless event. Our experience in asking the "right" questions from the start, assures you, your event for 10 to 1,000, will be effortless.

The Perfect Plan

Our packages are created for your moment. We offer reception-style, sit-down, or a cocktail party atmosphere; either at the restaurant or an event site. We source our ingredients from our NW backyard, creating contemporary cuisine with a classic touch for every palate.

Contact
Candace McDonald

Price
Starting at $15 per person

Quick Facts
- Capacity from 2 to 1,000
- Settings include Union Station Depot Lobby, Rose Garden, entire restaurant
- Outdoor urban roof top venue over looking the city
- Off-site catering services
- Event coordinator
- Easy parking
- A sustainable company
- Open warehouse setting for up to 800
- Vegan & vegetarian options

WILF'S RESTAURANT & BAR
- Unique location
- Outdoor urban roof top venue
- Locally grown products from the NW
- Open warehouse setting up to 800

See page 204 under Event & Meeting Sites

Bravo! Member Since 1992

www.bravoevent.com

© Patrick Lamb

Entertainment

Bands
Consultants
DJ's
Entertainers & Performers
Musicians

world. chamber. jazz.

PO Box 42502
Portland, Oregon 97242
p. 503.235.0355
f. 503.235.0355
e. jessica@3legtorso.com
www.3legtorso.com

Contact
Jessica Beer

Price
Call for quote

Quick Facts
- Diverse repertoire from stately background music to celebratory dance music.
- Flexible ensemble size suitable for all occasions & events: duo, trio or quintet.
- Original compositions and arrangements of traditional world music.
- Instrumentation includes violin, accordion, double bass, vibraphone, xylophone, glockenspiel, trumpet and various percussion & sound effects.

Offering a sophisticated blend of Klezmer, Latin, Eastern European gypsy, French musette, Chamber music and American jazz, 3 Leg Torso has long been regarded as one of the Northwest's premiere ensembles for special events. Their cosmopolitan musical style embraces wit and humor within thoughtful, uncommon and beautiful musical arrangements.

In addition to tastefully fulfilling the musical needs of private clients, the ensemble carries on an active concert and recording career, including licensing and composing music for film and television. Career highlights include:

~ Being profiled on NPR's "All Things Considered,"

~ Performing at the re-opening of the Hollywood Bowl (2004) and at the Getty Center (2008),

~ Scoring a short film that was admitted to the 2009 Cannes Film Festival,

~ Being commissioned by the Portland Institute of Contemporary Art (PICA) and the Metropolitan Youth Symphony (MYS) for new work,

~ Completing a residency at the 2006 San Luis Obispo Mozart Festival, and

~ Being the two-time winner of the Portland Music Award for "Outstanding Achievement in World Music"

Past clients include National Association of Secretaries of State (NASS), Oregon Consular Corps, Willamette Week, The City of Portland, American Institute of Architects (AIA), Oregon Music Educators Association (OMEA) & Standard Insurance Company.

"Responsible, punctual, respectful and charismatic, I know I can rely on [3 Leg Torso] for an enjoyable and effortless evening."
– Susan Edwards, Curatorial Associate, Seattle Art Museum

Bravo! Member Since 2008

WHAT'S NEW?
Now available as a duo (violin, accordion) or trio (violin, accordion, double bass) in addition to the full quintet!

The Brian Odell Band

Mixing the tried and true formula of the singer/songwriter with infectious drum rhythms, funky yet melodic bass lines, and the fresh flavor of turntableism puts The Brian Odell Band in a genre all its own.

Booking The Brian Odell Band will bring one of the most unique and sought after bands In Portland to your event. Their eclectic mix of classic and contemporary covers, along with their truly fresh and original sound, will ensure that your event will be remembered for years.

Our goal is to bring originality and showmanship to the private event world. A cheesy band can kill the party before it's even started. We are committed to making the day more than you thought it could be by simply doing what we do...to see for yourself, come see us live. Visit www.thebrianodellband.com for a list of our upcoming shows.

"Thank you so much for making our special day more than we dreamed it could be. Everyone was complimenting us on the band the whole night. You guys are the best!"

– Mark and Brittany

"Thank you so much Brian Odell Band. You guys did a fantastic job! Your mix of contemporary covers and original music was exactly what we were looking for. Thanks for making our wedding such a special day."

– Dave and Marie

Contact
Brian Odell

1053 Hallinan Street
Lake Oswego, Oregon 97034
p. 503.869.6766
f. 503.210.6768
e. admin@thebrianodellband.com
www.thebrianodellband.com

Price
Call for pricing

Quick Facts
- Not your ordinary cover band
- We can provide full-band, acoustic duo, solo or simply a DJ
- Years of experience playing private events including Dornbecher Children's Hospital fundraisers & the LIVESTRONG Challenge 2006–2008

Bands Covered
- Dave Matthews Band
- Tom Petty
- Johnny Cash
- John Mayer
- Jason Mraz
- The Doobie Brothers
- Jack Johnson

Bravo! Member Since 2008

Make Your Next Event A Hit

Blazing talent and onstage charm have made David Cooley and the David Cooley Band a premier event entertainment choice across the Northwest and around the world. The David Cooley Band delivers standout performances with swing, rhythm & blues, pop standards, and rock & roll classics.

The Band

From a quartet, five, six, seven, or eight-piece group, the David Cooley Band comes as you like it.

Entertainment That Delivers

Hired entertainment can make or break an event. The key to making everyone happy at your next event is the rockin', bluzin', swingin' sound of the David Cooley Band performing the best in 20th century American dance music – certain to keep everyone from the CEO to the newest employee smiling and dancing all night long.

Premier West Coast Entertainment

Leading organizations in the Pacific Northwest and across the U.S. routinely book the David Cooley Band for an exceptional entertainment experience.

Swingin' Hearts And Rockin' Souls At:

Conventions • Trade Shows • Holiday Parties
Grand Openings • Outdoor Events • Tributes
Receptions • Fundraisers • Dinner Shows • Roasts
Office Parties • Dance Parties • Private Parties

Contact

800.364.1522
info@davidcooleyband.com
www.davidcooleyband.com

Price

Flexible, according to band size, venue & location

Clients & Venues

- MassMutual
- Rose Garden Arena
- Oregon Symphony Assn.
- Oregon Golf Club
- Honeywell
- Portland Art Museum
- Oregon Bankers Assn.
- Multnomah Athletic Club
- Pratt & Whitney
- OR Convention Center
- Microsoft
- WA State Conv. Center

RAVE REVIEWS

"David's a great professional to work with."
– Portland Hilton

"His music is absolutely perfect!"
– Evergreen Aviation Museum

"Without hesitation, I highly recommend the David Cooley Band for all who are in search of a fantastic band to work with and be entertained by."
– Miller Nash LLP

Bravo! Member Since 1994

www.bravoevent.com

Bands

6200 SW Virginia Suite 208
Portland, Oregon 97239
p. 503.335.0790
f. 1.866.720.9829
e. amy@patricklamb.com
www.patricklamb.com

About Patrick Lamb Productions

Patrick Lamb Productions currently represents Patrick Lamb - who tours internationally with Bobby Caldwell, Gino Vannelli & Diane Schuur, A Tribute to Ray Charles - an award winning show, and American Soul - which is Patrick's latest endeavor-a high energy horn driven dance band that's tailor made for corporate events. American Soul will take you on a journey from Motown to 70's funk and high energy soul dance music. We can also provide a more traditional sophisticated feel of Jazz perfect for that cocktail hour. Patrick Lamb Productions is known for bringing the best and you will be amazed at the energy, vitality and quality we will bring to your event. We specialize in providing high-quality music, talented musicians, and years of experience in the event/music industry.

Clients include:
- Intel
- Kaiser Permanente
- Nordstrom
- Chinook Winds Casino
- Pioneer Courthouse Square
- Bridgeport Village
- OHSU
- Reed College
- Portland Art Museum
- Portland Trail Blazers
- Oregon Symphony
- Wells Fargo
- And many more!

"I have never seen so many people dance at Reed College before."

— Jennifer Bates, Events Director, Reed College Portland, Oregon

Bravo! Member Since 1997

Contact
Amy Maxwell

Price
Starting at $800

Quick Facts
- Full production included
- Variety of music styles, jazz, R&B, soul, funk, disco & motown
- High-quality professional musicians
- Develop band selection tailored for your specific event needs
- Provide music for all occasions & events
- Provide specialty shows A Tribute To Ray Charles NW Gospel Project American Soul

CONTACT US
Call us today for a promotional packet, demo CD, and a personalized price quote!

www.bravoevent.com

p. 503.758.6587)
e. Seymour@seymourlovejoy.com
www.seymourband.info

About Seymour

We are Seymour – a variety / good-time rock 'n' roll quartet with drums, bass, keyboard, assorted guitars, and plenty of harmony vocals. Based in Portland, Oregon, we were founded in 1969, freeze-dried in '72, reconstituted in '91 and have been at it ever since.

Our roots were planted back when people cruised Yaw's and hung out at places like D Street, the Headless Horseman, the Torque Club, the Crystal Ballroom, the Pythian Hall and Springer's to catch live music around Stumptown.

We're Versatile

Besides occasional club dates, we play private and corporate events including block parties, company picnics, wedding receptions, award dinners and promotional events.

You'll Love Us

We're professional. We work with you to meet your particular needs. With our proven dependability, high-energy performances, musical and vocal excellence, and our repertoire of hundreds of songs, we've been creating happy (and repeat) customers for over 20 years.

References available upon request.

Contact
Seymour Lovejoy

Price
Varies by venue, cartage & type of event

Quick Facts
- The quintessential variety rock'n'roll band
- Covering the classics from the '60s forward
- Parties, events, festivals, concerts, dances
- Love Seed Records recording artists

WHAT'S NEW?
We keep our list fresh by rotating in new tunes all the time. Recent additions include tunes by The Mavericks, the Bodeans, Green Day and The Raconteurs.

Bravo! Member Since 2008

www.bravoevent.com

PO Box 2265
Lake Oswego, Oregon 97035
p. 503.781.8919
f. 1.914.470.7437
e. booking@stillpending.com
www.stillpending.com

About Still Pending

Still Pending, comprising three talented musicians ages 13 and 14, has been delighting Northwest audiences since they made their on-stage debut with Oregon Children's Theatre in the rock musical production, "Alexander, Who is Not, Not, Not, Not...Going to Move" at PCPA in the spring of 2006. Since then, the band has appeared at prestigious venues and events around Oregon such as McMenamin's Crystal Ballroom, The Eugene Festival and Baby Woodstock at the Portland Children's Museum. Still Pending wows crowds with their original, high-energy rock and pop/punk songs. Adults appreciate their impeccable covers of classic bands such as Led Zeppelin, The Who, The Red Hot Chili Peppers and Green Day. The band is highly professional and can work with your existing sound system and engineers, or provide full sound depending upon your needs. Still Pending will make your next event truly unforgettable. Be sure to check out the band's YouTube channel (www.youtube.com/stillpendingmusic) where their live performance videos have been viewed by fans around the world over two million times!

Contact
David Ellman

Price
Call for pricing

Our Clients Say
"Please share our enthusiasm with the band. I heard nothing but amazed comments from people in the audience reacting to their consummate set. I think they may have been just about the MOST PROFESSIONAL act of the whole event... In terms of preparation, delivery, stage presence &... they even thanked me from the stage!! Gotta love that!"

– Lisa Lepine
The Bite of Oregon

WHAT'S NEW

In 2009, Still Pending, along with 3 other local kid bands produced "KidsRock4Kids - A Benefit Concert for Mercy Corps." The event was hosted by the Crystal Ballroom where almost 800 fans showed up in support of impoverished kids around the world. KidsRock4Kids raised over $6200 for Mercy Corps' global childrens' programs.

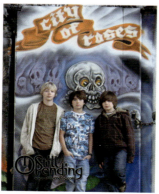

Bravo! Member Since 2007

Consultants

© Scott Duvall

Northwest Artist Management
Musicians, Concerts & Fine Events

Professional Musicians for all Occasions

p. 503.774.2511
f. 503.774.2511
e. nwartmgt@bigplanet.com
www.nwam.com

Contact
Nancy Tice

Price
Ensembles begin at $300

We Accept Visa and MasterCard

Testimonial
"The PDX Jazz Summit was a rich success due to your great commitment. Thanks for your fabulous work. We couldn't have done it without you."
— Maynard E. Orme, President & CEO Oregon Public Broadcasting

Also Featuring
- Jazz & cabaret theater, comedians, magicians, DJs, western entertainment including old time fiddlers, folk ensembles, country & rock bands.
- Dance Instructors: Country Line Dance, Salsa & Hula

About Northwest Artist Management
Since 1989, **Northwest Artist Management** has been proud to offer the finest in Classical, Jazz and International music for Concerts, Corporate Entertaining and Fine Occasions of all kinds. From Arias to Zydeco, soloists to elegant dance bands and hot jazz ensembles, we can accommodate just about any entertainment need or musical preference, including assistance with technical details.

Theme Parties Are Our Specialty
We are knowledgeable about all music, from the Grand Baroque period to the hottest Top 40. We coordinate the musical entertainment, food and decorations to create exciting and memorable events, and sizzling nights on the dance floor.

All of the artists on our roster are gifted, polished professionals with many years of experience helping our clients "custom-design" every detail of their musical needs. We are available to consult with you personally to help select the perfect ensemble and repertoire that will create and enhance the mood and ambiance of your event and accommodate the needs of your guests. Call for free promotional literature and/or demo CDs.

Dance Bands
You name it, we've got it: from Swing to Vintage Rock-n-Roll, Motown, Funk, R&B, Latin, Blues, Country, Caribbean, Folk, Top 40 and Variety.

International Roster
Go ahead, use your imagination! African and Cuban Rhythms, Caribbean, Reggae, Hawaiian, Latin Salsa, Italian, Irish, Mexican Mariachi and many more!

Member of Travel Portland, Jazz Society of Oregon & Association of Bridal Consultants

Bravo! Member Since 1992

Consultants

The Beatniks

PACIFIC TALENT INC.

PO Box 19145
Portland, Oregon 97280
p. 503.228.3620
f. 503.228.0480
e. andy@pacifictalent.com
www.pacifictalent.com

About Pacific Talent, Inc.

Pacific Talent Inc. is a full-service event and entertainment company providing the best available entertainment for events ranging from corporate events to festivals to wedding receptions. Our comprehensive resources and knowledge of the market enables us to provide the most diverse and quality talent available to our clients. We are dedicated to excellent customer service and quality event production.

Partial Artist Roster

Northwest Recording Artists: Pink Martini, Curtis Salgado, Linda Hornbuckle, Dirty Martini, Aaron Meyer, Quarterflash, Duffy Bishop, Katie Harman and Patrick Lamb; Jazz & World Music: Tom Grant, Michael Allen Harrison, Bobby Torres, Tall Jazz, Dan Balmer, Sam Bamboo, Mariachi Viva Mexico, Mary Kadderly, Barbara Lusch; Variety: Swingline Cubs, Design, Night Flight, The Antics, Cool-Ade, GruVbox; Misc: DJs, Comedians, Speakers, Magicians & more.

Contact
Andy Gilbert

Price Range
$500 and up

Quick Facts
- Total entertainment & event production services since 1975
- Representing entertainment of all varieties from top local & regional artists, to national headline attractions
- Serves corporate events, conventions, receptions, festivals, private parties & more
- Production & creative event services available

SPECIAL ATTRACTIONS
Johnny Martin, The Trail Band, Pepe & The Bottle Blondes, Hit Explosion, The Beatniks, The Retros, Super Diamond, Johnny Limbo and the Lugnuts, Riverboat Jazz Band, The Dickens Carolers, Joe Stoddard and The Coats

Barbara Lusch

Katie Harman

Bravo! Member Since 1994

www.bravoevent.com

All About Music Entertainment

TURN-KEY ENTERTAINMENT – READY FOR YOU!

You've done all the hard work - the planning, the preparation, now it's time to enjoy the fruits of your labor. Let us help you make your party something special.

We provide:

DJs – Our DJs are fully trained and prepared for every situation. We not only provide music, but also emcee services, audience participation activities, and host games.

Equipment – Whether you just need a PA system, Karaoke, or Music for a crowd of 1,000 people, we have the tools and the gear to get the party started!

Music – From the oldies but goodies to the newest songs on the radio, we have the music to accommodate every party and crowd. Please visit our website for a full music list.

Professionalism – Our DJs embody professionalism from attitude to attire, we work hard to provide the service you deserve.

Lights and effects – Change any venue to a club in minutes with our professional lighting package. Fog, foam, snow and bubbles are also available.

Environment – We are able to accommodate any theme or premise with music, attire, and décor to match.

Contract – We provide a written contract for our services so you know exactly what to expect including setup and breakdown times, start times, and space to include location-specific needs such as time limits and volume requirements.

Contact
Anthony Rice
PO Box 20444
p. 503.408.7857
e. info@allaboutmusicdj.com
www.allaboutmusicdj.com

Price
$595 - $2,000

Quick Facts
- MUSIC
- GAMES
- KARAOKE
- SPECIAL EFFECTS
- AUDIENCE INTERACTION

Bravo! Member Since 1996

AA
BUST-A-MOVE
Oregon's #1 DJ/ Entertainment Service

ANYONE CAN PLAY MUSIC, WE ENTERTAIN!

20391 S Meadow Avenue
Oregon City, Oregon 97045
p. 503.201.3710
f. 503.632.4233
www.bustamovedjservice.com

About AA Bust-A-Move DJ Service

Frank Bratcher, founder of Bust - A - Move DJ Services, has many years of experience in the Entertainment Industry. In the early 80's he was the front man and lead vocalist for a touring rock group that appeared with KISS, Fog Hat, the Scorpions, Quiet Riot, Head East, and too many others to list. Putting on a first rate performance is all he ever strives for, and expects out of his crew of DJ's.

"I don't care about being the biggest DJ company in Oregon, I just expect us to be the best. Whether it's a bride & groom, school function, or a business party, they all spend a lot of money to make their event special and fun, and we're gonna give them more than their money's worth."

– Frank Bratcher

"I cannot express how grateful we are to you. You made our wedding day the exact way we were hoping for. We had an incredible time. I will recommend you to every single person we know needing your services. You were fabulous! Thank you."

– Anthony & Nikki Kurtz

Contact
Frank Bratcher

Price
Affordable packages which can be custom-tailored for each event

Starting at $495

Quick Facts
- 27 Years of entertaining experience
- Fun, tuxedo dressed DJs
- State of the art lighting & sound
- Thousands of digitally recorded music selections
- Karaoke available
- Ceremonies starting at $125 if added into hours of chosen package
- Other services available

www.bravoevent.com

MOBILE MUSIC ENTERTAINMENT SERVICES

Professional DJ Services...

SINCE 1978

www.mobilemusicentertainment.com

Type of Music
Mobile Music has over 300 hours of music we bring to each event. Music selection ranges from big band, '50's, '60's, '70's, '80's, 90's, current hits, cocktail, lounge, country, Top 40, rock, hip hop and jazz. We always play the music you want.

Equipment
The sound systems Mobile Music uses are custom-built for mobile use. You won't find any home gear in our systems. The systems are compact and can be set up in 20 minutes. We do have larger setups for functions up to 3,000 people.

Experience
Mobile Music has been in business since 1978. We provide music and entertainment at more than 1,000 events each year. We base our business on providing friendly, professional service to our clients.

Corporate Events
For corporate events, Mobile Music has a wide variety of activities, including karaoke, casino games, contests and games – all hosted by a professional master of ceremonies. Please call for more information and rates on packages.

Music the Way You Want It!
We at Mobile Music pride ourselves on providing quality music the way you want it played. We use only professional disc jockeys with experience who will help make your event everything you want it to be. If you have any questions or special requirements, feel free to call.

Contact
Brian Smith
p. 503.638.0624
c. 503.209.0413
e. smittyosu1@hotmail.com

Price
The basic package starts at $500 for three hours & $100 for each additional hour; price subject to change

Services
- Also serving the Salem Area: 503.380.6319
- We have light shows & other special effects available for rent
- We also offer audio/visual equiment
- A 20% deposit & a signed contract hold your date for you

Award
Voted Best DJ of 2009 by the Oregon Bride Magazine

SPECIAL SERVICES
Mobile Music uses only professional mobile disc jockeys from around the Portland area. Whether you want a life-of-the-party DJ or just music, we have the disc jockey for your event.

Bravo! Member Since 1990

Guaranteed Customer Service

p. 503.331.9195
p. 866.530.1110
e. ct@prodjsoregon.com
www.prodjsoregon.com

About PRO DJs Oregon

PRO DJs Oregon has been serving Oregon and SW Washington with classy and fun DJ and Emcee services since 2001. We can bring musical excitement with lights for a disco party, surfing music including interactive games with hula hoops and limbo sticks for a beach party, emcee big band/swing era music in top hat tux and spats, or play low key smooth jazz background music. We can help craft the music and mood for the wedding of your dreams, as well as make your elementary school father/daughter dance or retirement party be a special memory for all. Consider PRO DJs Oregon for all your music intensive DJ, as well as emcee/interactive services: business functions, commitment ceremonies, weddings, community and school events, private parties, social events and more.

We care about the environment...as well as the environment of your event.

* Instead of purchasing new plastic CD's that pollute, we download all our music through iTunes.
* If you've got a sound system at your venue near the MAX line, we may be able to take MAX, cutting the carbon footprint of your event.
* We are a no-smoking/drinking/drugs company, so you know our attention will be only on you.
* We offer simplified packages for many of our non-wedding events, so you can choose the level of service that best fits your situation.
* We continue to seek innovative new ways to create a positive experience for your event.

Contact
Chris Taylor

Price
Non-wedding simplified parties starting at $425. See website for details.

Services
- Our interactive website provides you with an event planner to select your music and level of service, as well as communicate directly with Chris Taylor.
- Book early and often to make sure Chris Taylor is available for your events!

Client Approved
"I cannot say enough good things about working with Chris Taylor!! You made everything flow so smoothly. You were not only the DJ you were the coordinator of the whole day. It was wonderful. We would work with you again in a heart beat. Thanks so much."

– Calvin & Elisa Swain, Clackamas, Oregon

EXPERIENCE YOU CAN TRUST

Payment for services by check or PayPal

Bravo! Member Since 2003

ILLUSION MAGIC HUMOR MYSTERY ASTONISHMENT WONDER QUALITY

Alexander
Master of Marvels!

p. 503.331.8542
e. tim@parlorofwonders.com
www.parlorofwonders.com

About "Alexander, Master of Marvels!"

Your audience will laugh with amazement as I perform classics of magic and original tricks; things will appear, multiply, transform, and vanish at my fingertips, and in your guest's hands! With over ten years as a Willamette Valley professional, and two time Portland Area Society of American Magicians Annual Close-Up Contest Winner, I offer you the finest in magical entertainment. Your guests will be delighted as mystery, comedy, and sleight-of-hand create a uniquely entertaining and unforgettable magical experience!

Among Tim's Satisfied Clients

Boise-Cascade	Bristol Meyers Squibb
Nike	John L. Scott Reality
Bon Marche	State Farm Insurance
Intel	Jim Fisher Volvo
Hooters	Thompson Metal Fab
Xerox	Klarquist Sparkman, LLC
Adec	Microsystems Engineering
OMSI	Oregon State University
Hewlett-Packard	Wells Fargo Bank

Contact
Tim Alexander

Price
Call for pricing

Quick Facts
- Serving audiences of 1 to 1,000 throughout the Pacific Northwest
- Strolling Magic at receptions, cocktail parties, buffets, trade shows
- Parlor Show & Stand-Up Magic at meetings, banquets, parties, holiday gatherings
- Stage Show features music, sleight-of-hand, audience participation, levitation!

SAW YOUR CEO IN HALF!

Perfect for the holiday season- A hilariously magical illusion in which the boss, or anyone, is visibly sliced in half!

CALL FOR DETAILS!

Bravo! Member Since 2000

www.bravoevent.com

 Barbara Pikus Caricatures Since 1994

A caricature is a moment in time that you can keep forever

Let me capture the best of who you are as a caricature at your next event. My drawings are always meant to make people feel good, and are a unique addition to any occasion, corporate or private. I can draw anyone, age is no object, from new-born babies to 99 years. I've drawn them all.

Many guests will be fascinated just watching me do my 5 minute drawings. At your next event, as an ice-breaker and inter-active entertainment, please include Barbara Pikus Caricatures.

Praise for Barbara's Caricatures

"Thank you once again for bringing your superb talents to our Company picnic. Our employees truly appreciated you as indicated by the long lines."
– Spirit Boosters, Spirit Mountain Casino

"Thank you so much for being a part of our recognition event at the Portland Art Museum. We received many compliments on your work and it was such a pleasure to have you there!"
– Wells Fargo Recognition Committee

Bravo! Member Since 2002

Contact
Barbara Pikus
p. 503.238.4301
e. sketch@involved.com
www.barbarapikuscaricatures.com

Rates
Please call for pricing

Some Clients
- Art Institute of Portland
- Hewlett Packard
- Spirit Mountain Casino
- Sephora USA, Inc.
- Yoshida Group

Corporate & Private Events
- Parties
- Picnics
- Conventions
- Bar/Bat Mitzvahs
- Weddings

CARICATURES
Caricatures that capture the best of who you are.

See page 260 under Interactive Entertainment

www.bravoevent.com

brainwaves
IMPROVISATIONAL COMEDY

650 SW Meadow Drive
Unit #214
Beaverton, Oregon 97006
p. 503.520.8928
e. info@brainwavesimprov.com
www.brainwavesimprov.com

About Brainwaves Improvisational Comedy

Brainwaves is a unique comedy ensemble that can make your next event a hilarious success! Made up entirely of professional comedic actors, Brainwaves plays corporate functions, colleges and special events all over the United States. Formed in 1986, they are pioneers of the West Coast improv scene. The cast has years of experience working together, which gives them what *The Oregonian* called, "An almost psychic connection on stage." The cast is adept at incorporating anything about life about your company or event into their show.

Additional Information

A Brainwaves show consists of fast paced scenes based entirely on suggestions from the audience. These may include a live-action soap opera based on the life of a favorite employee, the wit, wisdom and humor of a two-headed psychic and a plethora of scenes that involve the 'Wavers quick wits and zany characters. *The Oregonian* calls a Brainwaves show "Smart Fun!"

Brainwaves has headlined at numerous National Improv Festivals including Chicago, Ill. and Austin, TX. The group has performed for hundreds of corporate and college clients, including Nike, Intel, Columbia Sportswear, Creighton University, University, METRO, St. Mary's Academy, and many more.

Contact
Daryl Olson
Tyler Hughs

Price
Average price for show in Portland Area: $1,500

Quick Facts
- Fast paced improvised comedy show ala "Whose Line Is It Anyway"
- Six very funny, professional comedic actors with credits in Film & TV
- Performances can be any length, held in almost any venue & incorporate themes from your office/group
- Portland's longest running improv group, celebrating more than 20 years of comedic life!

COME WATCH US
Brainwaves performs regularly for local audiences at The Shoebox Theater 2110 S.E. 10th Ave., Portland, Oregon.

See page 308 under Team Building

Bravo! Member Since 1995

Office: 3308 E Burnside Street
Portland, Oregon 97214

Theater: 1963 NW Kearney Street
Portland, Oregon 97209

p. 503.236.8888

e. portland@comedysportz.com

www.portlandcomedy.com

About ComedySportz

ComedySportz is improvisational theater played as a sport; it's a battle of wits between two teams of professional actors performing scenes, songs and games completely based on suggestions from your audience. It's topical – you tell us what it's about – and clean. We've never had a complaint about content in a ComedySportz Touring Company show (our referee keeps the offensive stuff out). We understand that laughter should bring people together without making anyone uncomfortable and we make it happen hundreds of times every year.

ComedySportz can travel to you, complete with a sound system, or you can create your own event at our theater. Our requirements are simple, and we pride ourselves on meeting your needs without extra work on your part. Planners from companies like Tektronix, Verizon, Intel, Mentor Graphics, AAA, Good Samaritan Ministries, Temple Beth Israel, Nike and Knowledge Learning Corporation have looked like geniuses by choosing CSz!

Go Even Further

ComedySportz Team-building workshops are a great way for your group to have fun, break down barriers and get more done!

We tailor each workshop to fit our clients' needs, using powerful and fun exercises from the world of improvisation. Workshops can stand alone, or combine with a ComedySportz Touring Company Show for twice the fun!

Contact
Patrick Short

Price
Call for pricing

Quick Facts
- Established in Portland in 1993, more than 3,300 shows
- Clean, fast-paced, tailored to your group & very funny
- Public shows every weekend—check us out before you buy
- We play for companies large & small, churches, schools, associations & any group gathering
- ComedySportz is available 24 hours a day anywhere in the USA

FULLY CUSTOMIZED

Our team of talented writers, actors, musicians and directors can also produce creative concepts – including branded theater and customized events. Clients include Burgerville, Metro, Old Navy and Oregon Food Bank.

See page 310 under Team Building

Bravo! Member Since 1994

www.bravoevent.com

2426 NE 88th Avenue
Portland, Oregon 97220
p. 503.880.1638
f. 815.927.0254
e. curt@curtisfrye.com
www.curtisfrye.com

Theatre of the Mind Show

A veteran of the defense and high technology industries, Curt has developed a wide range of mental skills that seemingly defy explanation. Whether he works out difficult math problems in a flash, solves a hard sudoku puzzle in under two minutes, or determines which word among tens of thousands a participant visualizes, he shapes demonstrations that entertain your audience and challenge them to make the most of their own capabilities.

Curt's shows are perfect for conferences, sales meetings, and award dinners. His presentations involve plenty of on-stage participation, so your audience gets to see their friends and co-workers in the spotlight! Most importantly, Curt treats his volunteers with respect. All of his humor comes from the moment — no one is ever made to look foolish.

Keynote Addresses

As a Microsoft Office Excel Most Valuable Professional, Curt is uniquely qualified to speak on using Excel as a business intelligence presentation and analysis tool. His other keynotes address how strategies found in classic games apply to modern business and how to cultivate effective individuals, teams, and enterprises.

Contact
Curtis Frye

Price
Call for pricing

Quick Facts
- Professional corporate entertainer since 1996
- Theatre of the Mind show demonstrates amazing mental abilities that inspire audiences to develop & share their own talents
- Shows feature audience participation that makes your attendees the stars
- Keynote addresses detail actionable business intelligence analysis techniques & strategy frameworks
- Microsoft has awarded Curt the Excel MVP distinction every year since 2006

CUSTOMIZED THEMES

Curt's shows and keynote addresses include elements he can customize to reinforce your event's theme. His rare combination of technical knowledge and performance skills enables him to communicate effectively with every audience.

Bravo! Member Since 2007

7527 SW 208th Place
Aloha, Oregon 97007
p. 971.227.8354
f. 503.591.1380
e. lisa@hulaaloha.org
www.hulaaloha.org

About Hula Halau 'Ohana Holo'oko'a

Our name means "school of hula where everyone is family" and in keeping with this spirit we are eager to share our love of hula with you at your next event! Our dancers are experienced and graceful performers who will help you create an authentic Hawaiian experience for your guests.

We can provide a single dancer for a backyard lu`au, private party or corporate event. For larger events, we have performance groups of 2 to 50 entertainers. We offer a wide repertoire of ancient and modern hula, with traditional music and authentic costuming with costume changes. With our variety and flexibility we are able to customize a package to fit your party and budget. No event is too big or too small!

Our past performances include appearances at the Portland Rose Festival, Uwajimaya Hawaiian Days, the Bravo! Wedding Affair, Columbia Gorge Interpretive Center, Encore Senior Village, and many other school and community events. Please contact us for pricing and scheduling details.

Contact
Lisa Chang

Price
Each show is custom-tailored for your event

Quick Facts
- Available for luaus, weddings, birthdays, business functions, school functions, picnics, retirement parties, retirement communities & community events
- A variety of show packages can be customized to fit your party & budget
- Audience participation with basic hula or Tahitian dance instruction
- We can provide lei greeters for your Hawaiian Event
- We can provide live musical accompaniment on request

Magic George

About Magic George

Magic George's style harkens back to the Magicians of the early 20th century—full of style, class and sophistication. No gimmicks; his magic is pure sleight-of-hand. His repertoire includes a variety of close-up magic that astonishes those who witness his work. You're just inches away from seeing the most amazing artful deception! His work leaves audiences in stunned silence, followed by great applause and whisperings of having seen the incredible.

TESTIMONIALS

• "Magic George definitely improves the whole mood of the party. His tricks and general demeanor break the ice so effectively that people were laughing, talking to each other and having fun from the start of the night. Far from being cheesy with the usual pat tricks, George makes an effort to be different, sharper and more engaging than the average 'magician.' And it really works well!!"

-Glotel, Inc.

• "George's magic helped me break the ice with a key customer at our first dinner meeting. Business talk came naturally after the customer was awed with one trick following the other while we dined. George created the precise relaxing environment that was conducive to effortless business conversation. I landed the account and my customer still comments about the artful show that George put together that evening. My company continues to hire George for company events."

-Freight Logistics, Inc.

Contact
Magic George

8423 SW Pointer Way Apt A
Portland, Oregon 97225
p. 503.946.8206
e. magicgeorge@gmail.com

Price
Hourly rates depend upon size of audience & nature of event

Quick Facts
- Over 20 years of professional experience
- Outstanding, mind-blowing sleight-of-hand, close-up magic
- Magic George is a hit at corporate events, trade shows, fundraisers & private parties
- Performed for TMobile, Glotel, Freight Logistics, Young Entrepreneurs Organization, Madonna, Cyndi Lauper, Tina Turner, and many more; featured performer at San Francisco's Café du Nord & Club Deluxe

Bravo! Member Since 2008

www.bravoevent.com

Musicians

One Performer, Endless Possibilities in Elegant Atmosphere & Event Entertainment
From the most Elegant Backdrops to Diverse and Exciting Entertainment, Scott Head, with his innovative solo performance is the answer to your next event's musical needs.

Professional Experience
Performing for Events for 10+ years, in some of the nation's finest venues, Scott's experience speaks for itself as soon as you begin working together. Highly recommended, Scott's Flexibility, Expertise, Professionalism and love of his craft shine through from day one making not just the entertainment incredible and one of a kind, but also working together a true pleasure!

Authenticity for your Event
Studying, performing, and most importantly living abroad in Brazil, Chile, Cuba, Mexico, Portugal, and Spain for over five years, Scott will leave your crowd with a true taste of the Elegant, Exotic, & Innovative in World & Classical Music!

Your Budget, Scott's gift!
Using live looping Scott showcases his accomplished performances in multiple instruments~ all tailored to just the musical atmosphere you're envisioning. The result is a live blending of instrumentation, vocals, and beautiful harmonies, allowing Musica Melodia to be a One Man Duet, Trio, Quartet or Jazz Combo piece.

All at a soloist' rates!

Contact
Scott Head
Musica Melodia
p. 503.867.2697
e. scotthead@musicamelodia.com
www.musicamelodia.com

Price
Call for incredible rates

Quick Facts
- Guitar, Trumpet, Flute, & Multi-lingual Vocals
- Classical, Mediterranean /Spanish style Guitar, American Jazz, Standards & Favorites, Sultry Latin Jazz, Brazilian
- All live - All one performer

Testimonials
"...He has crafted his art to perfection and when you hire this solo artist at 'solo' prices you feel that you have hired a whole band with multi-talented members!"

— Meri Kerekanich, The Kelly Group, Keller Williams & WOW Director

"As event planners we were thrilled with how easy Scott was to work with, both flexible and receptive to the exact atmosphere we were looking to create. We will definitely use him for future events!"

— eventBuilders.com

Bravo! Member Since 2008

www.bravoevent.com

Musicians

Duo con Brio

Duo con Brio is a professional ensemble founded by cellist Corey Averill. The duo may be augmented to a string trio or quartet; guitar, trombone, flute, voice, harp, and trumpet are also available. We have a large repertoire from Classical to Pop, Jazz, Jewish, Holiday, and more. We pride ourselves at arranging up to two special song requests at no additional fee.

Experience
Formed in 1989, the Duo has performed more than 2000 events. Over the years we have performed both locally and abroad in Europe and Asia. Our memorable events include performing at Timerline's Silcox Hut, Oaks Pioneer Church, University of Phoenix Graduation ceremonies, Sammy Awards, and many beautiful weddings. We are members of Better Business Bureau, and the American Federation of Musicians Local 99.

Bravo! Member Since 1991

Contact
Corey Averill
p. 503.526.3908
c. 503.407.6256
e. singandbow@comcast.net
www.duoconbrio.com

Price
Instant Quotes available on website

Solo cello $195 first hour ($95 each additional hour)

Duo $315 first hour ($165 each additional hour)

Trio $415 first hour ($210 each additional hour)

Quartet $515 first hour ($260 each additional hour)

We accept Visa/MasterCard/Discover

Notes of Celebration

Linda Smith, Piano Artistry

About Notes of Celebration

Not just a pianist, Linda is a piano artist, providing an uncommon level of musicianship and customer care to every event she performs at, going well beyond playing the notes on a page.

Whether playing music to make your spirit dance, classical stylings that relax and inspire, or music to create an elegant and romantic ambiance, the music Linda provides will frame your wedding or event with music that touches your heart!

"Linda, you were magnificent...your music added a significant element to the entire ambiance we were looking for...exactly what I wanted!"

— Debbie & Eric Rinell

Contact
Linda Smith

p. 503.645.2763
e. lindasmith@notesofcelebration.com
www.notesofcelebration.com

Quick Facts
- Over 20 years experience
- Customized piano programs
- Keyboard available
- Vocalist/strings can be added to the ensemble

Event Design, Production & Décor

Event Design
Floral
Floral & Balloon Décor
Lighting

Event Design

PARADYM EVENTS
EVENTS WITHOUT PRECEDENCE

Paradym Events

A full-service event production company specializing in creating unique and highly personalized events. We can handle all of your event needs, from themed décor, floral, specialty linens, A/V and lighting. From design and management, logistics to execution, we can handle all your companies' event needs.

Design: Linens and flowers, metals and paper, glass and wood: all mediums are utilized to create your unique event environment. Just as your company is one of a kind, so should your event.

Price Range: No matter the budget, we work to ensure that you remain on target while providing the largest impact possible. There are no surprises at the end of an event, just a clearly defined cost for every aspect of the production.

Location: We have traveled everywhere, from Hawaii to the Mediterranean and back. We will accommodate your every need while providing you the comfort that every detail of your event has been taken care by our knowledgeable staff. You no longer have to work with a company from out of town and hope they can execute the event to your standards. Paradym Events will take the guess work out of the equation while adding the peace of mind and flexibility of a local and dedicated staff.

Specializing: In the details, no matter how small, we have it covered so you don't have to. We create custom events to highlight you and your company. We can handle all your event needs from design and management, communications, to the execution and logistics.

Contact
Mary Bennett

4060 SW Macadam Avenue
Portland, Oregon 97239
p. 503.219.9290
f. 503.525.0675
e. info@paradymevents.com

www.paradymevents.com

Price
Call for quote

Capacity
10 people to 10,000, we help you plan and fulfill all your event needs.

Expectations
Meeting your expectations is not good enough; Paradym Events strives to exceed them in every detail.

Your Event
Give us a call and let us show you the possibilities of your next event.

EXPERIENCE
Putting 50 years of design production experience to work for you, any theme, any event, any time, any place you will know you have made the best choice.

Look for us on Facebook!

Bravo! Member Since 1998

Event Design

Peter Corvallis Productions
SINCE 1958

2204 N Clark Avenue
Portland, Oregon 97227
p. 503.222.1664
f. 503.222.1047
e. athena@petercorvallis.com
www.petercorvallis.com

About Peter Corvallis Productions
Distinguished for its exceptional service, Peter Corvallis Productions has provided quality tradition and experience in the event industry since 1958.

Event Coordination Service
Our event specialists will determine your event needs and apply our years of knowledge and expertise in planning, décor design and event layout. Lighting, sound and projection services are also available to complete your event.

Event Rental Inventory
As a full service event rental company our pledge is to grow our inventory according to our client needs. Visit our 100,000 sq. ft. warehouse to walk the aisles and view the thousands of theme décor items to enhance your next event.

Contact
Athena Paskill

Price
Varies on size of event; call for quote

Rentals and Services
- Tent & canopy rentals
- Party rentals
- Linens & chair covers
- Catering items
- Theme décor
- Audio visual services & rentals
- Tradeshow decorating
- Event planning services

PROVIDES MORE THAN JUST QUALITY PRODUCTS.

Here is a list of rental equipment and the many services we offer to make your function run smoothly so you can enjoy your event along with your guests. Having an event will never be easier.

See page 237 under Event Rentals

Bravo! Member Since 1994

www.bravoevent.com

ROYCE'S PROP SHOP

5406 N Albina Avenue
Portland, Oregon 97217
p. 503.283.8828
f. 503.283.3651
e. info@propshop.com
www.propshop.com

"The professionalism and integrity of the Prop Shop is unflinching."

Jeffrey A. Blosser
Executive Director
Oregon Convention Center

Event industry veteran Royce Mason and his dedicated team of professionals at the Prop Shop pride themselves on award-winning event design, décor, production and, most importantly, impeccable customer service.

Royce's Prop Shop is equipped with unparalleled national resources and can produce an extensive range of events, including corporate meetings, conventions, product launches, employee appreciations, educational seminars, team-building experiences, tradeshows, fundraisers, award ceremonies, galas, weddings, festivals, holiday celebrations and picnics.

Memberships include ABC, ACEP, ISES, MPI, and **Green Certified Member** of Travel Portland.

Contact
Royce Mason

Price
Customized to fit your budget

Quick Facts
- Award–winning event design
- Custom props, sets & lighting
- Backdrops, drape, linen & tabletop
- Complete production services
- Catering & entertainment assistance
- Permits, rentals & staffing

AWARDS

- 2007-2010 City of Portland Office of Sustainable Development RecycleWorks Award
- 2006-2007 MPI Supplier of the Year Award
- 2004 Event Solutions Spotlight Award for Designer of the Year
- 2003 Oregon Restaurant Association Award of Gratitude & Appreciation
- 2002 Bravo! Award for Best Theme Décor

See page 213 under Event Planners

Bravo! Member Since 1996

www.bravoevent.com

Event Design

About West Coast Event Productions

West Coast Event Productions is the premier event planning, design and rental company servicing the Pacific Northwest and the west coast – from Portland and Seattle to Los Angeles and Las Vegas.

We are an inspired team of event planners, designers and technicians committed to developing innovative solutions for special events. Our comprehensive product line, creative design services and broad range of technical expertise have gained us recognition as one of the top ten event production companies nationwide. Specializing in custom planning and fabrication, our inventive prop architects, visionary floral designers and innovative lighting and audio visual specialists are masters of creativity.

Whether planning a corporate gathering, personal celebration or wedding, you'll find an extensive and innovative range of services and products at your fingertips.

We invite you to come celebrate with us. Cheers!

Contact
Pat Smith
Elizabeth Hermann

1400 NW 15th Avenue
Portland, Oregon 97035

p. 503.294.0412
f. 503.294.0616
e. elizabeth@wcep.com
www.wcep.com

Price
Varies on service

Quick Facts
- Four locations & 30 years of experience: Portland, Bend, Las Vegas & Seattle
- Services include: Event & Wedding Consulting, Design & Rentals
- Creative Design Services: concept & theme development, rendering, fabrication, décor, floral & centerpiece design
- Technical Services: audio visual, lighting design & special effects, rigging & specialty trussing
- Over 120,000 square feet of rental inventory: linens, centerpieces & candles, china & glassware, tables & chairs, canopies & tents, staging & dance floors, props & life-size sets

See page 238 under Rentals

Bravo! Member Since 1990

www.bravoevent.com

CRYSTAL LILIES
exquisite flowers & events

134 SE Taylor Street
Portland, Oregon 97214
p. 503.221.7701
f. 503.200.1949
e. info@CrystalLilies.com
www.CrystalLilies.com

Exquisite Floral & Decor

Crystal Lilies is a specialty florist. Our expertise is in providing spectacular floral arrangements and décor for all events. We use fresh, unusual and interesting flowers and elements in every event.

Design, Coordination & Production

Crystal Lilies can help with the development of ideas for the design concept of your event, show or benefit. We work with your budget to coordinate the elements of your event from lighting, staging, rentals, audio, printing, entertainment, floral & décor and more. Whether your event is sophisticated or opulent, grand or intimate, simple and elegant, or fun and unusual we can coordinate all aspects. We provide production and setup for all events. We bring a team of professionals to each event to attend to all of the details.

With more than 20 years in business Crystal Lilies has the experience to make your event a success from the very beginning.

Contacts
Kimberley & Scott Lindsay

Pricing
No fee consultation; we will work within your budget

Events
- Corporate events
- Benefits
- Weekly lobby arrangements
- Trade show booths
- Holiday events & office decorations
- Grand openings & more

Custom Decor
- Displays for office, home, shows & events
- Holiday decorating; wreaths, garlands, Christmas trees
- Extensive unique rental items available

WE'RE HERE FOR YOU
To help you plan your event and/or floral needs, please call or email for a personal consultation.

Bravo! Member Since 1995

www.bravoevent.com

Extraordinary events

At Lavish we approach each event as a collaborative process with our clients. We start by getting to know what type of feel the client wants to communicate. Then we can begin to form an ambiance with a cohesive floral style that reflects the sensibilities of the host. This gives a wonderful personalization to each occasion.

When we plan our floral events we consider the experiential standpoint, thinking about what it feels like to be a guest. We love to include small surprises and twists that keep our designs innovative and leave a lasting impression on the guests.

Finally, we carefully orchestrate the entire process, ensuring that every element comes together with harmony and ease. The professionalism and execution of every detail are as important as the details themselves.

We look forward to working with you to create a memorable affair.

Open by appointment
4815 NE 17th Ave
Portland, OR 97211
p. 503.228.1558
e. info@lavishflora.com
www.lavishflora.com

Contact
Adria Lailer

Price
Your decor budget can take you as far as your imagination but we can make sure you stay on mark and get the absolute most out of your budget.

What we provide
From theme development and consulting to complete styling and installation of all your floral decor needs we can handle all of the details.

Bravo! Member Since 2006

Green – Organic options are available year round and we are happy to accommodate any event that wishes to go green!

www.bravoevent.com

Floral & Balloon Décor

Bouquets & Balloons

6650 NW Kaiser Road
Portland, Oregon 97229
p. 503.629.5827
f. 503.645.9404
e. bouquetsandballoons@juno.com
www.bouquetsandballoons.com

About Bouquets & Balloons

Bouquets & Balloons specializes in custom-designed floral and balloon sculptures and decor for every event from large corporate parties to company picnics, ground breaking and ribbon cuttings to grand openings and fundraisers. We also decorate for private celebrations including birthdays and weddings. We work with you to create unique and creative results for your special occasion.

Exceptional Designs

Balloons are the perfect decorating alternative for any occasion or event. Neon gumball, lighted balloons, blossoms and other shaped balloons add excitement to any arrangement. Create a focal point or give your room an air of festivity and elegance by using arches, columns, swags, balloon drops and sculptures. Balloons are perfect for your next Theme Party.

We pride ourselves in exceptional floral and balloon designs that are creatively different.

Contact
Cheryl Skoric, CBA

Price
Call for consultation

Quick Facts
- Floral, balloon & theme creations
- Impressive, personalized service
- Colorful floral or balloon centerpieces
- A reputation for quality
- Specialize in eye-catching backdrops, promoting your message
- Exciting, Exploding Wall and confetti-filled balloons
- All budgets welcome

CERTIFIED BALLOON ARTIST

Bouquets & Balloons offers Oregon's first Certified Balloon Artist to help with all of your decor needs

Bravo! Member Since 1994

www.bravoevent.com

We don't think you should have to choose between this....

....and this.

...stainable event lighting options
...m an award winning lighting company.

...sy choice.

...w.hollywoodlighting.biz
0-826-9881

5251 SE McLoughlin Boulevard
Portland, Oregon 97202
p. 503.232.9001
p. 800.826.9881
f. 503.232.8505
e. production@hollywoodlighting.biz
www.hollywoodlighting.biz

About Hollywood Lighting Services

Hollywood Lighting Services is ready to help you excite, motivate, and inspire your audience! We offer an award-winning design team, a complete line of state-of-the-art lighting equipment, and attentive service throughout your production. We understand what our competitors don't; that effective event lighting is not just about the gear...anyone can rent you a light fixture! What sets Hollywood Lighting apart is our passion for creativity and exceptional service. Unlike "rental" suppliers, we strive to find meaningful ways to add value and quality to your event's objectives. Do you want to imprint your brand in the minds of the attendees? Light your products for the best possible booth ROI? Motivate your team? Transform a plain-jane space into an elegant gala? By utilizing our talented staff of lighting design professionals and the Northwest's widest selection of equipment, we will strive to assist you in creating a memorable event experience.

What's New at Hollywood Lighting

It's been a GREAT year at HLS! We've rolled out our new "Skyline Branding" product, won 3 major awards including 2 national honors, added loads of new low-energy LED and HID fixtures to our rental inventory, hosted informative seminars and product showcases, and so much more! You can get in on the fun by visiting us on Facebook: Become a fan and get regular updates including special offers, event information, contests, education, and more. Just type "Hollywood Lighting" into the search box.

Contact
Sales Department

Trust Us For:
- Stage & scenic lighting
- Digital scenery & projections
- Low-energy lighting alternatives
- On-stage entertainment
- Galas, weddings, & fundraisers
- Corporate events
- Exhibits & product displays
- Grand openings & new product rollouts
- Sporting events
- Festivals
- Branding events

EXPERT EVENT LIGHTING

For over 60 years, Hollywood Lighting has been the Pacific Northwest's trusted leader in event lighting design, production, rentals, and sales. Whether your event is large, small, or in-between; bring your lighting challenges to us!

Bravo! Member Since 1999

www.bravoevent.com

© Maryhill Winery

Event & Meeting Sites

Boats
Casinos
Convention & Exhibition Facilities
Event & Meeting Sites

Willamette Star   Portland Spirit   Crystal Dolphin   Sternwheeler

The fleet and facilities of the Portland Spirit will provide a unique and memorable experience for your next event. Our knowledgeable sales staff and professional event planners will handle all the details, making your planning process easy and stress-free!

Portland Spirit
Capacity: up to 499 guests
Seating: up to 340 inside, plus outside seating

Willamette Star
Capacity: up to 144 guests
Seating: up to 100 inside, plus outside & lounge seating

Crystal Dolphin
Capacity: up to 120 guests
Seating: up to 50 inside, plus outside & lounge seating

Columbia Gorge Sternwheeler
Capacity: up to 499 guests
Seating: up to 225 inside, plus outside seating

Gorge Pavilion
Capacity: up to 300 guests
Seating: up to 225 inside, plus outside seating

Outrageous Jet Boat
Capacity: up to 35 guests

Bravo! Member Since 1996

Contact
Group & Charter Sales

110 SE Caruthers
Portland, Oregon 97214
p. 503.224.3900
p. 800.224.3901
e. sales@portlandspirit.com
www.portlandspirit.com

Price
Prices vary – please inquire

Vessel & Facility Amenities
- In-house catering provided
- Linen tablecloths & napkins provided
- House china, glassware & flatware provided
- Servers & bartender included with food & bar service
- Full service bar available
- Clean-up provided
- Commercial parking & street parking available
- ADA limited with assistance – please call for more information

See page 117 & 180 under Event & Meeting Sites

www.bravoevent.com

6823 Highway 8, PO Box 1240
Warm Springs, Oregon 97761
p. 800.554.4SUN (Reservations)
p. 888.220.9830 (Sales)
f. 503.768.9831
e. sales@kahneeta.com
www.kahneeta.com

About Kah-Nee-Ta High Desert Resort and Casino

Every great event begins with an extraordinary setting. Big Skies. Blue Waters. High Desert Vistas. Nestled in the heart of Central Oregon on the Warm Springs Indian Reservation, Kah-Nee-Ta High Desert Resort & Casino is the perfect destination for your next event. All 170 guestrooms feature balconies with panoramic views and captivating sunsets. The 15,000 square feet of meeting space is ideal for groups of all sizes and can accommodate business meetings, intimate gatherings, corporate events, and elaborate parties. Experience the taste of Native culture with a Salmon Bake complete with Native dancing or try our renowned Bird-in-Clay dinner.

We are the perfect playground for all ages with more recreation than any other resort in Oregon. Soak in the Village Hot Springs Pool, enjoy a round of golf, kayak down the Warm Springs River and see the high desert on horseback. Kah-Nee-Ta High Desert Resort & Casino – escape to where the fun shines!

Contact
Celia Lozano
Senior Sales Manager

Steve McDade
Sales Manager

Price
Varies by event. Please call for more information.

Capacity
Up to 620 people in a theatre-style setup and 360 in a formal dining atmosphere.

Quick Facts
- We offer 15,000 square feet of adaptable meeting space ideal for all size groups.
- 8 hole golf course, double Olympic-size hot springs swimming pool, horseback riding, kayaking & more.
- Full-service European Spa Wanapine.
- The 25,000 square foot casino offers more than 300 slots as well as blackjack & a dedicated poker room. In addition, we feature a major prize giveaway each month.

Bravo! Member Since 1997

See page 141 under Event & Meeting Sites

3201 Tremont Avenue
North Bend, Oregon 97459
p. 541.756.8800
p. 800.953.4800, Ext. 2288
f. 541.756.0431
e. ldinovo@themillcasino.com
www.themillcasino.com

Set in a picturesque location along the Coos Bay waterfront in North Bend, Oregon, The Mill Casino-Hotel & RV Park has become an entertainment destination on Oregon's South Coast. Owned by the Coquille Indian Tribe the historic mill facility shines as a gaming and hospitality center that has become a regular stop for coastal visitors and residents.

With over 14,000 square feet of meeting space and the right blend of rooms and services, The Mill is a prime location for meetings and conferences. The Salmon Room offers seating for up to 850 guests in addition to five new meeting rooms. Meeting facilities at The Mill include state-of-the-art audio and video systems and complimentary WiFi and broadband connectivity.

The Mill's professional catering services will create the right menu whether you are hosting a small group meeting or multi-day conference. You can count on The Mill's staff to make special events special indeed.

And don't forget to have fun. The Mill Casino offers 725 slots comfortably arranged on a gaming floor that includes our smoke-free slots room. Sharing the room is a full selection of table games and a classic Poker Room. After hours, guests can enjoy great live entertainment or catch the big game along with their favorite pub fare at Warehouse 101. Or, relax with our signature martini and special hors d'oeuvre menu in the smoke-free, bayside Whitecaps lounge.

Contact
Lucinda DiNovo

Capacity
Over 14,000 square feet of meeting space. We accommodate groups as small as 10 & as large as 500.

Amenities
- Slots, Blackjack, Craps, Roulette and Poker
- Bayside Hotel
- Waterfront RV Park
- Bayview Dining
- 5 Restaurants
- Indoor Pool and (2) Outdoor Hot Tubs
- Fitness Room
- Arcade
- Business Center
- Over 200 Hotel Rooms
- 8 Waterfront Suites
- 7 Meeting Rooms

Bravo! Member Since 2008

See page 160 under Event & Meeting Sites

www.bravoevent.com

Casinos

SPIRIT MOUNTAIN CASINO
The Northwest's Premier Entertainment Destination

27100 SW Salmon River Highway
Grand Ronde, Oregon 97347
p. 1.800.760.7977 ext. 3914
f. 503.879.6049
e. ashley.langley@spiritmtn.com
www.spiritmountain.com

About Spirit Mountain Casino

Our state-of-the-art Event Center was designed to make your next event perfect, with highly-trained staff to cater to your every whim. We offer all the conveniences necessary to host an intimate gathering of 10 up to a large group of 1,600. With more than **17,200** square feet of conference space for all occasions, we have the expertise and facilities to host your event.

And the entertainment possibilities are endless — we offer 2,000 Vegas-style slots, table games, Poker, Keno, Bingo, the exquisite Legends restaurant, Cedar Plank buffet, Raindrops nightclub, Mountain View sports bar and 254 comfortable lodge rooms.

Contact
Ashley Langley

Price
Price varies dependant upon services

Capacity
1,600

Amenities
- 17,200 sq. ft. of conference & meeting space
- Accommodations for groups of 10 to 1,600
- Gold medal chefs full service catering
- Largest buffet in Oregon
- Most diverse gaming options in the Northwest
- Top-name entertainment
- Raindrops Nightclub
- Mountain View Sports Bar
- Summit View Lounge
- Exquisite Legend's Restaurant
- 254 comfortable lodge rooms
- Secure Playworld facility
- Video Arcade
- Free Valet & RV parking
- 24-hour Mini-mart & gas station
- More than 3,600 parking spaces

Bravo! Member Since 1997

www.bravoevent.com

PORTLAND EXPO CENTER

expo

www.expocenter.org

A SERVICE OF METRO

2060 N Marine Drive
Portland, Oregon 97217
p. 503.736.5200
f. 503.736.5201
e. info@expocenter.org

www.expocenter.org

About The Portland Expo Center

The Portland Expo Center is one of the Northwest's Premier multi-purpose facilities, and home to some of the region's largest and most successful consumer-public shows, tradeshows and special events. The 60–acre campus includes five interconnected Exhibit halls comprising of 330,000 square feet of exhibit space, 11 meeting rooms, a full–service catering kitchen, and parking for more than 2,200 vehicles.

Hosting over 100 events annually that attract more than 500,000 attendees, the Expo Center is located in North Portland, just off the I-5 as well as via TriMet's Interstate Max Yellow Line. The Expo is easily accessible from the airport, S.W. Washington, and all of Oregon.

Owned by Metro regional government, and managed by the Metropolitan Exposition-Recreation Commission (MERC), the Expo continues to operate in a self sufficient manner, using zero tax dollars in supplying their clients and patrons with a world-class facility.

The Expo has a new on-line NEWSLETTER! Join the e-XPO Newsletter! www.expocenter.org/newsletter.htm

The Expo Center also has a Mobile program! For more details see here: www.expocenter.org/mobile.htm

Contact
Matthew P. Rotchford
Sales & Event Manager

Price
$100 – for Mtg Rm. D102, to $17,700 for Full Facility (Non-Ticketed).

Capacity
Up to 7,000 (concert style)
330,000 square feet of contiguous exhibit space

Amenities
- 5 exhibit halls (330,000 sq. ft.) & 11 Meeting Rooms
- On-site parking for over 2,200
- Ease of access for Exhibitors & on-line ordering
- Direct access via Interstate Max (Yellow Line - light rail)
- Experienced Staff
- High-speed internet, audio-visual & other services

Bravo! Member Since 2000

ENTER TO WIN!

Text EXPOSALES to 32075

For Discounts on Meeting Rooms and a chance for a Rent-Free Meeting! Call 503.736.5200 or visit www.expocenter.org for more info!

www.bravoevent.com

Home of the NW's Largest Consumer-Public Shows

Are you in the midst of planning a trade show? Has your fund-raising auction grown out of your traditional small ballroom? Do you need space for more than 1,500 10'x10' booths and a place for lunch? Has your load-in and load-out become a huge nightmare?

The flexibility of the Expo Center's five inter-connected exhibit halls – each with it's own unique characteristics - provide meeting planners with the solutions and limitless possibilities. From large public or private events to elegantly catered food and beverage functions, the Expo Center can handle the largest affair with exceptional service and style.

The Expo Center provides professional, friendly and knowledgeable staff to make your event an all-around success. With our flat floor (no stairs) load-in and loadout capability, the whole event immediately becomes less stressful. With eleven varied meeting rooms, the Expo provides up to 7,500 square feet of flexible space. Located just off the show floor within a spacious lobby, breakout rooms are easily accessible to patrons and offer a variety of configurations. Climate controls, audiovisual and lighting adjustments are available in each space.

The Expo Center has more 2,200 on-site parking spaces, so parking isn't just an afterthought. Now with the addition of TriMet Light Rail service, frequent train service runs direct to downtown every 15 minutes. We are conveniently located between Portland and Vancouver, just off the Interstate Five and within minutes to a number of hotels, restaurants and shopping. The Expo Center will be able to make your event – large or small, indoors or out – a seamless success!

www.bravoevent.com

About the Oregon Convention Center

The Oregon Convention Center features a one million square foot campus with 255,000 gross square feet of contiguous exhibit space, making it the largest such facility in the Pacific Northwest. Two beautiful grand ballrooms of 25,200 GSF and 34,300 GSF and 50 premier meeting rooms complement the exhibit space. Add in high speed wired and wireless (Wi-Fi) Internet connections throughout, on-site parking on two levels in our underground garage, extraordinary meals served up by ARAMARK/Giacometti Partners Ltd. and award-winning customer service, we are confident we can become your preferred meeting destination.

The OCC is located within Portland's city center, right around the corner from famous restaurants, popular cultural attractions and wide-ranging entertainment. The surrounding area's scenery, some of the most spectacular on the planet, is artfully complimented by the decor and atmosphere of the center's spacious interiors. Right from the start, you will realize that the OCC isn't only a great place to be, but a place where great things can happen.

Facility Specs

255,000 square feet of exhibit space

60,000 square feet of ballroom space - "Portland" & "Oregon" ballrooms

54,000 square feet of meeting space - 50 meeting rooms

19 loading docks

800 total parking spaces in underground garage

225 exhibitor parking spaces available on-site

777 NE MLK Jr. Boulevard
Portland, Oregon 97232
p. 503.235.7575
www.oregoncc.org

Contact
OCC Sales Department

Price
Determined by event size and menu.

Capacity
Individual Meeting Rooms:
From 10 to 700 people

Portland Ballroom:
From 250 to 3,500 people

Oregon Ballroom:
From 250 to 2,500 people

Skyview Terrace:
From 50 to 200 people for reception-style events

Amenities
- Tables & chairs provided
- Registration tables, coat racks, lecterns, podiums, staging & other essentials are available for rent
- Our in-house audio/visual team can provide the necessary equipment & technical support at a competitive price
- 800 parking spaces available in the underground parking garage; 225 exhibitor spaces in the adjacent parking lots

Bravo! Member Since 1994

www.bravoevent.com

Types of Events

The OCC can accommodate a wide variety of events - from an intimate meeting for 12 to a trade show for 60,000.

Exclusive Catering by ARAMARK/ Giacometti Partners Limited

Full-service catering provided exclusively by ARAMARK/Giacometti Partners Limited. In addition to the wide variety of menu suggestions, the ARAMARK catering department together with our executive chef can create a special menu to suit your needs. ARAMARK also offers sustainable menu selections, uses local, organically grown products whenever possible, and composts food waste.

Catering Amenities

Linens and napkins: Wide variety of colors to choose from.

White china and stemmed glassware provided complimentary.

Contract decorators available for exhibitors, booths, etc; ARAMARK/GPL can provide water fountains, multi-tiered buffet tables, mirrored bases, floral displays, "theme" breaks and food displays; ice sculptures, floral arrangements, silver service, and votive candles.

OCC and ARAMARK offer an upgraded level of sustainable services to help make your event as "green" as it can be.

Getting Around

Portland's MAX light-rail system makes getting around easy. It can pick you up or drop you off right at our front door - and it's free within most of the downtown area! Arriving from out of town? OCC is just eight short miles from the airport, and MAX can even bring you to us or take you home.

A Commitment to Sustainability

The OCC was the first U.S. convention center to receive LEED-EB certification for an existing building under the U.S. Green Building Council's Leadership in Energy and Environmental Design (LEED) program. The facility's many sustainable design features and the staff's commitment to continuous improvement of its practices have created one of the "greenest" venues in the country.

www.bravoevent.com

Salem Conference Center

200 Commercial Street SE
Salem, Oregon 97301
p. 503.589.1700
f. 503.589.1715
e. dearley@salemconferencecenter.org
www.salemconferencecenter.org

About The Salem Conference Center

Soon to be LEED certified, the Salem Conference Center is currently EarthWise Certified and is a member of the U.S. Green Building Council. SCC is committed to preserving the environment and we are constantly exploring new opportunities to better conserve and reuse our valuable resources.

Location

Located mid-way between Portland and Eugene, in the heart of historic downtown Salem, the Salem Conference Center is minutes from the State Capitol and surrounded by an array of unique shops, restaurants, art galleries, museums and theaters.

At the end of the day, conference attendees will enjoy refined hospitality at the adjoining 193 room Phoenix Grand Hotel. To unwind, visitors can choose fine dining in Bentley's Grill, a relaxing glass of premium wine in the lounge, a refreshing swim in the indoor pool and spa, or an exhilarating workout in the fitness center without leaving the facility.

Contact
Donna Earley

Price
Prices vary. Contact for direct quote.

Capacity
6 to 1,600; 30,000 square Feet of conference space

Amenities
- LEED Certified
- EarthWise Certified
- 30,000 square feet of event space
- 14 versatile meeting rooms
- Extensive pre-function & reception areas
- State of the art technology
- Complete on-site catering services with professional & experienced banquet staff
- Complimentary covered parking

Bravo! Member Since 2004

23800 NW Flying M Road
Yamhill, Oregon 97148
p. 503.662.5678
f. 503.662.5626
e. christy@5rockranch.com
www.5rockranch.com

About 5Rock Ranch

5Rock Ranch is a Christian non profit ministry. Our 108 acres are located in the beautiful mountains in Yamhill, Oregon... just 50 miles from Portland. Our mission at 5Rock is to help build and restore families with a focus on the fatherless child. Throughout the year, we offer free camps for fatherless children and their moms. We give them tools to re-build and restore their lives. We also hold dad drives to encourage dads, give them tools for effective fathering, and to train up mentors for the fatherless. In order to help offset costs for these free camps we offer our facility for events & retreats. Our beautiful 30,000 square foot log ranch house can be used for just about any event, big or small. We offer meals from family style to sit-down dinners. We also have a 17,000 square foot grass amphitheater right on the river that's perfect for outdoor events, services, or concerts.

Contact
Christy Bradley

Price
$1,000 - $12,000

Quick Facts
- Beautiful new amphitheater on the river
- Newly remodeled bunkhouse rooms & cabins
- Rustic log ranch house
- Indoor & outdoor site options

Bravo! Member Since 2008

WHAT'S NEW

Everything!!! 5Rock is the old Flying M Ranch. We've not only changed names, but we've changed the whole feel of the ranch. Our purpose is to share a place full of love in a way that restores the mind, body, and soul so each person who experiences the ranch grows in their personal relationships, and becomes part of God's family.

Abernethy Center
BALLROOM ♦ GARDENS

606 15th Street
Oregon City, Oregon 97045
p. 503.722.9400
f. 503.722.5877
e. corporate@abernethycenter.com
www.abernethycenter.com

About Abernethy Center

Abernethy Center, sitting a few blocks off I-205 in Oregon City, enjoys an enviable location easily accessible from the Portland airport, Vancouver, Portland, and Salem. Its proximity to the airport, hotels, downtown, and the highway makes it the perfect venue for local business and corporate America.

Conference & Meeting Space

We have the facility, staff, amenities and flexibility to handle board meetings, training sessions, seminars, political rallies, fundraisers, luncheons, banquets, auctions, holiday parties, and company picnics.

Catering & Event Coordination

Our on-site catering and event coordination take the stress out of planning your event and ensure a seamless execution of even the most detailed events. Custom menus and any dietary restrictions are easily accommodated.

Contact
Sales Department

Prices
Room rentals starting at $250

Capacity
4,500 square feet of event space

Amenities
- Flexible floor plans
- Retractable LCD projector & 9' x 12' screen
- High speed wireless internet
- Bose surround-sound stereo system, DVD, VCR & CD players
- Podium, staging, dance floor & microphones
- State of the art lighting capabilities
- Pre-event & day of event coordination

THE GARDENS

60' X 70' Reception tent and 3.5 acres of natural gardens, including one acre of flat grass. This space is perfect for your company picnic, team building events and even a lovely evening gala.

Bravo! Member Since 2001

www.bravoevent.com

10220 SE Causey Avenue
Happy Valley, Oregon 97086
p. 503.698.8020
f. 503.698.8060
e. info@elventures.com
www.TheAerieAtEagleLanding.com

About The Aerie at Eagle Landing

Perched atop Mt. Scott, our French chateau-style facility offers breathtaking views of the Willamette Valley and is conveniently located just 20 minutes from downtown Portland. The Aerie, meaning "eagle's nest," provides exquisite indoor and outdoor space for corporate events and private gatherings where you can experience a stylish mix of timeless elements and modern conveniences. The clubhouse is nestled within a 27 hole Executive Par 3 Golf Course with USGA-specified greens and fine white sand bunkers. Our grounds also offer a beautiful 36 hole Miniature Golf Course that winds around trees, waterfalls and natural rock formations.

Types of Events

The Aerie at Eagle Landing is your ideal location to host corporate meetings, banquets, award dinners, holiday parties, company picnics, golf tournaments, fundraisers, seminars, weddings, receptions and more.

Catering

Exclusive catering to create the most lavish or simple affair, just the way you want it!

Contact
Corporate Sales

Price
Varies according to event; please call for information

Capacity
Indoor seated: up to 160 guests, 2,543 sq. ft.
- Hors d'oeuvres/theater-style: up to 225 guests

Outdoors seated: up to 300 guests, 7,000 sq. ft.
- Hors d'oeuvres/theater-style: up to 450 guests

Outdoor Tent seated: up to 80 guests, 1,518 sq. ft.
- Hors d'oeuvres/theater-style: up to 150 guests

The Patio & Bellevue Gardens are the perfect setting for your outdoor event!

Amenities
- Indoor table & chair set up included in space rental
- Surround sound, DVD & CD Players, (3) 40" LCD TV's, 6' drop-down screen, podium, wireless internet & microphone
- Dance floor
- Ample FREE parking
- Linens, china, glassware & service items provided by catering service

Bravo! Member Since 2007

ALBERTINA'S
RESTAURANT AND SHOPS

424 NE 22nd Avenue
Portland, Oregon 97232
p. 503.231.3909
f. 503.408.5060
e. margarets@albertinakerr.org
www.kerrshops.org

About Albertina's Restaurant & Shops

Listed on the National Register of Historic Places and a Portland landmark, the stately 1921 Old Kerr Nursery is conveniently located a mile from downtown Portland. Refurbished in 2001, the Nursery is equally beautiful inside and out. The charming, homelike building and garden patios are the perfect setting for your special occasion.

With our four beautifully appointed rooms and two garden patios we can host a broad range of events from weddings, receptions and rehearsal dinners to business meetings, showers and parties.

Experience the history of the Nursery building and the gracious attention to detail provided by Albertina's dedicated volunteer staff. Albertina's Restaurant and Shops proceeds benefit Albertina Kerr Centers, providing stability and support to children, adults and families.

Contact
Margaret

Price
Varies with event & menu; please call for information

Capacity
Up to 200 for receptions;
Up to 90 for formal dinners

Quick Facts
- Champagne, wine & beer service, bartenders, servers & hostess/hosts provided
- China, glassware, silver service & linens supplied
- Dance floor available upon request; ample electrical hookups
- Clean-up included
- On-site & free street parking available
- ADA; accessible
- Beautiful fresh floral arrangements, including service tables, fireplace mantels & more

Bravo! Member Since 1996

ALDERBROOK
RESORT & SPA

10 East Alderbrook Drive
Union, Washington 98592
p. 360.898.2200
f. 360.898.5528
e. sales@alderbrookresort.com
www.alderbrookresort.com

Where Exceptional Gatherings Are a Natural

Nestled on the scenic shores of Hood Canal, Alderbrook Resort & Spa is two hours from Portland or Seattle. Yet it's a world away from the everyday. Established in 1913 and reinvented in 2004, Alderbrook is a breath of fresh air for meetings, retreats, social gatherings and special events. A place where groups from 8 to 200 come together to learn. Play. Share ideas. See things in a new light. Celebrate in one of the most scenic wilderness areas on earth.

Our incredible outdoor venues or our private yacht Lady Alderbrook are ideal for entertaining in the natural beauty of Hood Canal. The extraordinary views of mountains, trees, and gardens throughout the resort set the stage for a relaxing getaway. Numerous recreational opportunities for making your stay a complete event are offered, including golf, kayaking, swimming, and pampering services at The Spa.

Types of Events: We can accommodate all types of meetings, conferences, team building, conventions, and social events.

Capacity: Ten meeting rooms from 520 to 2,250 sq. ft.; we offer over 7,000 sq. ft. of flexible banquet and meeting space with additional outdoor venues for up to 200 and our Lady Alderbrook.

Contact
Marty McCormack

Price
Varies according to group size & date of event or meeting

Amenities
- Totally ADA-compliant
- Ample complimentary on-site parking
- All tables & chairs for up to 200 guests are provided
- Courteous & professional staff committed to making lasting memories
- Full-service, in-house catering provided
- Full-service bar for hosted or no-host functions
- Dance floor available upon request
- Linens & Napkins: Select from a range of options
- Silver, china, & glassware are provided
- Decorations: We are delighted to help with recommendations
- Cleanup provided by our staff

Amadeus Manor

"A unique, relaxing getaway & memorable meeting destination"

About Amadeus Manor

Amadeus Manor is the perfect setting for weddings, rehearsal dinners and annual, monthly or quarterly business meetings. You and your guests will enjoy fine continental dining in a wonderful old mansion overlooking the Willamette River on two wooded acres, filled with antiques, fireplaces, crystal chandeliers, candlelight and fresh flowers. We offer a full bar with a wide variety of Oregon and international wines. Outdoor dining and wedding ceremonies on our patio are also available. Piano music is included.

Availability and Terms

Reservations should be made as soon as possible to ensure availability. A deposit is required at the time of booking. Half the deposit is refundable if cancellations are made at least nine months prior to your event.

No cost for using the facility, bartending services, linens, flowers, candles, valet parking or classical piano.

Contact
Kristina Poppmeier

2122 SE Sparrow
(N. River Road. Exit / 22nd Street)
Milwaukie, Oregon 97222

p. 503.636.6154
p. 503.659.1735
e. kpoppmeier@aol.com
www.amadeusrestaurants.com

Price
Full course buffet-style dinners Saturday evening: $40 p.p.

Friday, Saturday & Sunday: $35 p.p.

Add $5 p.p. for served, sit-down, three-course dinners

Awards
"Voted Portland's most romantic restaurant."
- The Oregonian

Quick Facts
- Full-service in-house catering or off-location catering

TYPES OF EVENTS
Individual rooms for conferences, day-long seminars, private meetings and large group luncheons. Holiday parties and celebration dinners. From small intimate events up to 300. Weddings and rehearsal dinners.

Bravo! Member Since 1994

www.bravoevent.com

The AMBRIDGE
EVENT CENTER

1333 NE MLK Boulevard
Portland, Oregon 97232
p. 503.239.9921
f. 503.239.4246
e. dale@ambridgeevents.com
www.ambridgeevents.com

About The Ambridge

The Ambridge has crafted an unequalled reputation for personalized service, that uniquely complements events like yours. Grown in the tradition of hospitality, the Ambridge takes its name from a perfect, old fashioned rose designed specifically for the Portland area.

We are independent, privately owned and operated. For over 17 years, we have successfully hosted Corporate Events, Seminars, Workshops, Training Classes, Trade Shows, Company Retreats, Special Events, and much more. Remember, your event is as important to us as it is to you. Call and schedule a tour today!

Availability

Reserve early for desired dates. A deposit and signed contract will confirm your space. Our Account Executives will be happy to assist you with our current event policies.

Contact
Dale Allan

Price
Prices vary according to size of group & selection of service

Capacity
12 Private rooms – totaling 16,000 sq. ft of premium event space, including our Ambridge Ballroom. Conference style – to Standing Reception – up to 700 guests

Amenities
- Full in-house catering service
- Permanent hardwood dance floor
- In-house state-of the art audio visual equipment
- Wireless throughout building

GREAT LOCATION & ADA ACCESSIBLE

We have moved just down the street! To a new updated location! Parking available – MAX light rail two blocks away. All rooms comply to ADA standards.

Bravo! Member Since 1991

www.bravoevent.com

1314 NW Glisan
Portland, Oregon 97209
p. 503.228.9535
f. 503.228.0788
e. jennifer@andinarestaurant.com
www.andinarestaurant.com

About Andina

Andina is a proud ambassador of Peruvian cuisine. Our diverse menu features traditional dishes from the Andes as well as Novo-Peruvian creations, which combine a wonderful array of native ingredients with modern techniques and presentations.

Events are hosted in four private dining rooms. Tupai is our largest event space, able to accommodate 65 guests for a seated dinner or 100 guests for a standing reception or cocktail party. It features sophisticated Inca-inspired architecture, a dedicated kitchen and full service bar. Two versatile mid-size rooms, Tourmaline and George V, are decorated with warm earth tones and contemporary Peruvian artwork. For smaller groups, The Pearl Wine Shop seats up to 16 in an intimate wine cellar with a long rustic table, barrel-vaulted ceiling clad with stone and retractable screen.

Each room offers the opportunity for a unique private dining experience, whether for a special occasion, business meeting, or an evening amongst friends. We are delighted to customize a variety of prix fixe and tasting menus to ensure that every event is beyond memorable.

Contact
Jennifer Anderson

Price
Food & Beverage minimum per room, & price according to menu

Capacity
Tupai – 100 guests
George V – 50 guests
Tourmaline – 20 guests
Pearl Wine Shop – 16 guests

Highlights
- 100 Favorite Restaurants Worldwide – The Robb Report 2008
- 2005 Restaurant of the Year – The Oregonian
- Award of Excellence 2006, 2007, 2008, 2009 – Wine Spectator
- "Big Deal in Portland" – Gourmet Magazine 2004
- James Beard House Invitee – 2006, 2008
- Distinctive Peruvian Cuisine
- Extraordinary cocktails
- Extensive selection of artisan wines
- Friendly & knowledgeable staff
- Located in the heart of the Pearl District

Bravo! Member Since 2007

The Banker's Suite

1215 Duane Street
Astoria, Oregon 97103
p. 425.417.6512
e. bankerssuite@bluemars.com
www.thebankerssuite.com

About The Banker's Suite

Located in Astoria's downtown historic district, The Banker's Suite consumes the entire top floor of the historic Bank of Astoria building. The suite's 4,500 square feet of formal style was inspired by its original ornate plaster columns and capitals. Whether you are planning a romantic getaway for two or a social gathering for 50, the Banker's Suite is the perfect venue.

Opening on our main floor in January of 2010, will be The Banker's Ballroom and The Banker's Gift Shop. The Banker's Ballroom will mimic the formalness of The Banker's Suite in a 1920's grand style with hardwood floors, tall plaster columns and silk drapes.

The Banker's Gift Shop will carry unique gifts, custom cake toppers, and couture dresses and accessories by Boudoir Queen.

Contact
Trish Bright

Price
$650 - $750

Quick Facts
- The Banker's Suite occupancy 50
- The Banker's Ballroom occupancy 150
- Overnight Accommodations for 2
- List of approved caterers available upon request
- Air conditioned

WHAT'S NEW

The Banker's Ballroom and The Banker's Gift Shop opening January 2010.

www.bravoevent.com

"Big Al's: The Next Generation Of Entertainment!!!"

Big Al's, "The Next Generation of Entertainment" is 60,000 square feet of awe-inspiring FUN! Our full service venue offers premier accommodations, extraordinary atmosphere, and superior customer service. We have 42 state of the art bowling lanes, a 4,000 sq ft arcade, and the largest Sports Bar in the Pacific Northwest equipped with pool, shuffleboard, and an 8ft x 36ft big screen! If you're looking for an event to remember, mix business with pleasure and come see why so many companies keep coming back to Big Al's!

Event Offerings

- Team Building
- Fundraisers
- Holiday Parties
- Corporate Events
- Birthdays
- Summer Picnics

What's New

Big Al's has officially broken ground in Beaverton on its second location! Our new location is in the Progress Ridge town center and will be open in the summer of 2010.

Contact

Big Al's

16615 SE 18th Street
Vancouver, Washington 98683

p. 360.944.6118
f. 360.397.4128
e. events@ILoveBigAls.com
www.ILoveBigAls.com

Price

$15 to $50 per person

Quick Facts

- We can accommodate groups from 12 to 3,000
- Big Al's themed buffets come with decorations & a private party host
- FREE Wi-Fi
- Full audio/visual capabilities
- 2007 Brunswick Center of Excellence Award, 2008 & 2009 Best of Clark County awards for Best Family Fun Value, Best Bowling Alley, Best Place to shoot pool, Best place to watch the big game!

Bravo! Member Since 2007

20029 Highway 138 W
Elkton, Oregon 97436
p. 541.584.2295
f. 541.584.2395
e. bigkranch@cascadeaccess.com
www.big-k.com

Big K Guest Ranch

We are an all-inclusive guest ranch that offers a place for everyone to enjoy the outdoors. From scenic float trips down the Umpqua River to horseback rides on our 2500 acre property to local wine tours, there is always something to do. You will love the home style meals that wait for you when you come off the river after catching more fish than you ever thought possible. Our professional fishing guides and friendly staff will give your an unforgettable experience on the Umpqua.

We are the perfect venue for a variety of events from corporate retreats to weekend getaways. With 20 private cabins and a full service log lodge we can accommodate groups as large as 300. Our dining room and adjoining conference room create a relaxing and productive environment for any group.

Our packages are fully customizable and tailored for your group or event. We work with you every step of the way.

Contact
Kathie Larson

Price
Call for customized pricing

Amenities
- Event/Conference Room (250 capacity)
- Full Service Restaurant
- 20 uniquely appointed cabins
- Recreational Room
- Guided Fishing on the Umpqua River
- Horseback Rides

See page 286 under Resorts & Retreats

1252 East Cascade Drive
PO Box 356
N. Bonneville, Washington 98639
p. 509.427.7767
p. 509.427.9718
f. 509.427.9719
e. groupsales@bhsr.us
www.bonnevilleresort.com

Nestled in the heart of the Columbia River Gorge just 35 miles from Portland, Oregon, is Bonneville Hot Springs Resort and Spa. The resort features 78 spacious guest rooms and suites, all with a private balcony, many with fresh-air hot tubs filled with natural mineral hot springs water and no added chemicals. Fine dining is available in the Pacific Crest Dining Room offering a wide selection of local wines. Casual dining and exciting libations are found in the Cascade Lounge. Seasonal outdoor dining is available in the Courtyard.

Meeting and Special Event Space
Bonneville specializes in top of the line catering whether it is for business or pleasure. Our banquet menu accentuates traditional Northwest cuisine with fresh ingredients. Team building and recreational opportunities include; onsite miniature golf, near by hiking, biking, white water rafting, wine tasting, museum tours, golfing and kayaking.

Retreats and Incentives
Our full service spa is the perfect place for retreats and incentives. The spa includes a luxurious manicure/pedicure area with state-of-the art pedicure thrones, couple's rooms, complete with side-by-side massage tables, two person mineral water soaking tub, fireplace and shower. Specializing in over 40 body treatments. What better incentive or reward can you offer yourself, your employees or clients.

Contact
Camille Greenslade

Price
$139 to $424

Amenities
- 78 guestrooms all with fresh air balconies
- Specializing in small groups & corporate meetings & retreats
- Meeting & banquet space for 10 to 80 people
- 1,500 square feet of meeting space
- 25' pool, indoor & outdoor jetted pools, all filled with our Mineral Hot Springs water. Dry Sauna, miniature golf
- 14,500 square foot spa featuring mineral baths & wraps, massage, body treatments, manicures, pedicures, facials & waxing
- Friday and Saturday night wine tasting in the Great Room

WHAT'S NEW
Check out our meeting planner incentive program at www.bonnevilleresort.com

Bravo! Member Since 2003

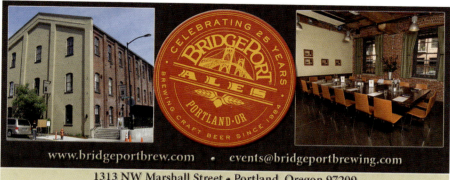

www.bridgeportbrew.com • events@bridgeportbrewing.com

1313 NW Marshall Street • Portland, Oregon 97209
p. 503.241.7179 ext. 310 • f. 503.241.0625

About bridgeport brewpub + bakery

Located in Portland's vibrant Pearl District since 1984, bridgeport brewpub + bakery resides in a hundred and twenty year old brick and timber building, fusing contemporary architecture, modern amenities and historic charm. The brewpub is a Portland landmark, tourist destination and beer lovers paradise. All foods are handcrafted using local, natural and organic ingredients whenever possible. Known internationally for award-winning ales, BridgePort is the oldest craft brewery in Oregon.

Heritage Room

The Heritage Room is a unique venue with rustic brick walls, large windows, wood floors, fir beams and a private full-service bar. We offer adaptable room layouts including options for break outs. The Heritage Room is fully wired with high quality audio visual equipment including a large cinematic screen, LCD Projector and integrated sound system.

Old Knucklehead Room

The Old Knucklehead Room provides privacy amidst the bustle of our busy pub. It is located next to our main bar for an authentic brewpub experience.

Bravo! Member Since 1995

Contact
Barbara Lee

Price
Call for price; minimums depend on day of the week

Capacity
Heritage Room: 30 to 110

Old Knucklehead Room: 5 to 25

Amenities
- Friendly & knowledgeable staff provided
- Private full-service bar in the Heritage Room
- Located on the street car line / close to freeways & downtown
- Audio visual system including Wi-Fi
- China, glass, silver, linens & candles provided
- Breakfast, Lunch & Dinner
- Private Entrance for the Heritage Room
- Sustainable business practices

REMODELED
bridgeport brewpub + bakery was remodeled in 2005. For a unique event we offer brewery tours & beer tasting.

4105 NW Camas Meadows Drive
Camas, Washington 98607
p. 360.833.2000
f. 360.834.7075
e. jduce@camasmeadows.com
e. sweishaar@camasmeadows.com
www.camasmeadows.com

About Camas Meadows Golf Club

Camas Meadows Golf Club's par 72, 18-hole Championship Course combines incredible scenery with a unique, challenging design that will satisfy both beginning and accomplished golfers. Camas Meadows offers excellent practice facilities that are covered and heated and on-site golf instruction. The Club House is spacious and accommodating and is ideal for golf tournaments, banquets (indoor or outdoor) and meetings. Visit the Oaks Bar & Grill after golf for a delicious meal and quenching beverage, or for happy hour from 3pm - 6pm daily. We are a public facility with numerous options to fit your group's special needs. Please contact us for pricing and availability. Reservations may be made on short notice based upon availability.

Contact
Jenny Duce
Stephanie Weishaar

Price
Call for Quotes

Capacity
Up to 250 People

Quick Facts
- 18-hole championship golf course
- Tournament packages for groups of any size
- Spacious indoor & outdoor banquet facilities
- Full service, in house catering
- Full service bar available

TYPES OF EVENTS
Wedding ceremonies & receptions, holiday parties, corporate business meetings & outings, reunions, private parties, anniversary parties, and customized tournaments.

See page 249 under Golf Courses & Tournaments

Bravo! Member Since 2007

www.bravoevent.com

Caples House Museum

Event & Meeting Sites

1925 First Street
Columbia City, Oregon 97018
p. 503.397.5390
e. caretaker@capleshouse.com
www.capleshouse.com

About Caples House Museum

The Dr. Charles Caples House Museum was the home of a pioneer doctor, who arrived in the 1844 wagon train, and his family. The grounds feature the 1870's home built upon the original site of his father's log cabin, a view of the Columbia River and Mt. St. Helens, magnificent trees and gardens, the 1870's Heritage Orchard of apple and pear trees, a collection of vintage toys and dolls, and a Country Store featuring fine American craft items and collectibles.

The Museum's Knapp Social Center is a cozy indoor meeting venue with views of the Columbia. Seated on its porch, you catch the soft breeze off the river and watch the ships pass by.

Whether you are looking for a large outdoor venue with a stunning river view or an intimate indoor venue, Caples Museum will transport you to another time and a peaceful, happy state of mind.

Contact
Christine Kramer
Caples House Museum Caretaker

Price
$1200 Full Day or call for Short Term rates

Capacity
Up to 300 Outdoors. 51 Seated indoors at tables or 110 seated in rows.

Amenities
- Ideal for weddings, receptions, corporate retreats, picnics, reunions & other events.
- Beautiful country setting with Columbia River and Mount St. Helens views.
- Expansive, level outdoor spaces under magnificent shade trees.
- Full kitchen facilities.
- Preferred caterers list upon request.

WHAT'S NEW
Catered teas available for 10 to 51 people at $20 each. 48 Hours notice required.

Bravo! Member Since 2008

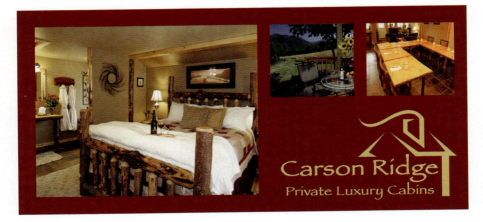

About Carson Ridge Luxury Cabins

Imagine a setting this beautiful and the privacy that goes with your very own venue. We offer a unique experience that will allow both corporate groups to clear their minds & focus and small groups to re-connect and enjoy each others company without strangers around.

We specialize in small groups providing a level of intimacy and attention you will not receive elsewhere, making sure your time together is just what you're looking for. Accommodating everything from corporate and spiritual retreats to reunions, small conferences, weddings and romantic or adventure getaways.

We are the ideal location for your intimate outdoor gatherings and weddings with landscaped grounds and breathtaking views of the Columbia River Gorge or enjoy our meeting space that offers an outstanding environment for retreats, corporate meetings & team building events.

Let our coordination team take the worry out of planning your special occasion and allow us to create those unforgettable memories for you.

Contact
Latisha & Pete Steadman
1261 Wind River Raod
Carson, Washington 98610
p. 877.816.7908
e. info@carsonridgecabins.com
www.carsonridgecabins.com

Capacity
50 indoor & 100 outdoor; lodging: 22

Amenities
- On site event planner, caterer & photographer
- Private luxury cabins with jetted tubs, fireplaces, log beds, luxury linens, private covered decks & log swings
- In cabin spa treatments
- Full breakfasts
- Endless activities: miles of hiking & biking trails, wine tours, waterfalls, world class fishing
- Or try something new: how about white water rafting, kite boarding or wind surfing?
- We specialize in small events & take the worry out of your planning

WHAT'S NEW
- 3 new custom built cabins
- Wellness center offering retreats, yoga, Thai massage & reiki

www.bravoevent.com

CATHEDRAL RIDGE WINERY

4200 Post Canyon Drive
Hood River, Oregon 97031
p. 541.386.2882
p. 800.516.8710
f. 541.386.5363
e. crw@cathedralridgewinery.com
www.cathedralridgewinery.com

About Cathedral Ridge Vineyard

Whether it's one person or a wedding party of 200 people, we love to have people visit our winery and vineyard. Beautiful in virtually every season, you will be amazed by the views of Mt. Adams as you rest on the bench overlooking the vineyards and by Mt. Hood as you tour your way south through the vines. Our charming winery and tasting room overlook manicured lawns and beautiful flower gardens, the perfect compliment to these stunning mountain views. Cathedral Ridge exists to provide a perfect event for you and will extend every effort to refer you to appropriate suppliers for whatever you may require. Our friendly and knowledgeable hospitality team is here to help make your wedding or event the most special day of your life!

Types of events: Company meetings, holiday parties, corporate picnics, private lunches, anniversary parties, special event celebrations, weddings & receptions, rehearsal dinners, etc.

Contact
Event Coordinator

Price
Varies depending upon the day of the week & type of event.

Capacity
Up to 200 Guests

Amenities
- Outstanding full-service caterers for all types of events. We offer a list of both Hood River & Portland Caterers with outstanding references.
- We provide seating for 100 & tables to match.
- We specialize in serving outstanding wines & also provide beer, water & soda as requested.
- Approximately 1200 square feet of dance floor.
- Linens, china & glassware: Usually included in catering price.
- Ample free parking.
- All facilities are ADA accessible.

See page 330 under Wineries & Custom Labeling

CITY OF HILLSBORO
Parks & Recreation

4400 NW 229th Avenue
Hillsboro, Oregon 97124
p. 503.681.6120
f. 503.681.6124
www.ci.hillsboro.or.us/ParksRec

Hillsboro Parks & Facilities Make For Unique Events

Whether you are planning a corporate picnic or team building event, a birthday party, wedding or family reunion, Hillsboro Parks & Recreation provides a variety of unique and versatile indoor and outdoor event spaces to fit the need.

From the sporty Gordon Faber Recreation Complex & Hillsboro Stadium, to the cozy River House at Rood Bridge Park, to the elegant and artistic Walters Cultural Arts Center, to the rustic and natural Jackson Bottom Wetlands Preserve Education Center, to the kid-friendly Tyson Recreation Center and Shute Park Aquatic and Recreation Center, to one of our many fun outdoor picnic shelters in various parks...we offer extraordinary event space for out-of-the-ordinary events. Our non-exclusive catering (bring your own caterer!) and experienced, customer-service oriented staff will also enhance your event.

Our Walters Cultural Arts Center in downtown Hillsboro is a beautiful and unique meeting venue offering auditorium space for up to 200. Call the Arts Center directly at 503-615-3485 for details.

Contact
Parks & Recreation Department

Price
Varies based on location and event

Capacity
From 10 to 7,000

Quick Facts
- 24 Outdoor Parks
- 7,000 seat Hillsboro Stadium with large plaza area, softball fields, parking for 1,600 cars
- Inspiring Walters Cultural Arts Center with event space, art gallery, classrooms, kitchen & outdoor terraces
- Two specialty rental facilities, including The River House with beautiful water & wetland views
- Indoor aquatic & recreation center with multipurpose event rooms
- Classroom space & 3,000 sq. ft. covered outdoor deck overlooking the beautiful Jackson Bottom Wetlands Preserve
- Non-exclusive catering

About The Keizer Civic Center

The brand new Iris Ballroom is the ideal location for your next meeting or special event. Located in the heart of Keizer, the Civic Center is just that—a place for the community to come together and celebrate with family and friends. With its warm and inviting space, the Keizer Civic Center is perfect for your special events, including fundraisers, dinners and weddings. You will also find all the modern technology to meet your corporate event needs already built into this facility. With three break-out rooms and A/V accommodations, the Iris Ballroom is a great location for your next meeting or conference.

Enjoy this beautiful Northwest facility for your next...
- Meeting
- Wedding
- Conference
- Holiday Party
- Fundraiser
- Auction
- Private Event
- Special Occasion

Contact
Class Act Events

930 Chemawa Road NE
Keizer, Oregon 97307
p. 503.371.8904
f. 503.589.9166
e. events@classactevents.net
www.keizer.org

Price
Rates vary. Please call for quote

Capacity
Up to 571

Amenities
- Three break-out rooms ideal for conferences
- Large lobby, pre-function area included in facility rental
- Exclusive caterers to meet your food service needs
- Ample free parking (up to 275 cars)
- Tables & chairs provided for up to 600
- A/V: LCD projector, 7'x12' screen, wireless internet, sound system, microphones, 6 channel mixer, & more available
- Stage & dance floor available
- ADA accessible

www.bravoevent.com

Clark County Event Center

The Clark County Event Center at the Fairgrounds is an established 170 acre campus with five multi-purpose facilities that host a wide variety of events each year. Our Exhibition Hall features 97,200 square feet of unobstructed, column-free show space. With two air-walls, this facility can become three halls, the smallest being just over 21,000 square feet.

Additional facilities on grounds include an Equestrian Arena, Outdoor Grandstands, a collection of Livestock Buildings and three additional large halls perfect for staging events.

Located at the perennially successful fairgrounds next to the Clark County Amphitheater, the Clark County Event Center gives unmatched flexibility for all types of shows. Highly successful events, such as Home and Garden Shows, Plant Sales, RV Shows, Conventions, Dinner Auctions, Sporting Events and Antique shows, have called the Clark County Event Center home.

The Clark County Event Center also features easy access for your patrons and exhibitors, nine miles north of the I-5 bridge just off of I-5. With four large roll-up doors your exhibitors can drive a semi right into the hall to unload, or use one of five loading docks right outside the hall, including one self-leveling bay.

The tremendous versatility of the Exhibition Hall gives show and event planners plenty of options. To see how we can meet your needs check out our charts and facility diagrams online and call to schedule an appointment today.

Contact
Justin Kobluk or Heidi Wilson

17402 NE Delfel Road
Ridgefield, Washington 98642
p. 360.397.6180
f. 360.397.6185
e. info@clarkcoeventcenter.com
www.ClarkCoEventCenter.com

Price
Please call for pricing

Amenities
- Layouts for theater, banquet & trade-show events, capacity figures available online
- Retain 100% of your ticket sales revenue
- Complimentary wireless access in Exhibition Hall
- Parking for 7,500 vehicles
- Easy access and high visibility from I-5, 15 minutes North of Portland
- Affordable venue offers exceptional value

CEDARVILLE PARK

3800 West Powell Loop
Gresham, Oregon 97030
p. 503.666.7636
e. amelia@cedarvillepark.net
www.clubpaesano.org
www.cedarvillepark.net

About Club Paesano-Cedarville Park

An unexpected retreat from the city, and only minutes away. Nestled upon 11.2 acres of lush wooded green space and surrounded by native cedar and fir trees. Cedarville Park the Home of Club Paesano is the true destination site showcasing the heart of the Pacific Northwest's regional natural scenic beauty.

Our facilities and park grounds will meet and accommodate to your business events/functions from professional corporate to simple casual:

- corporate meetings
- seminars
- conferences
- team-building workshops/retreats
- auctions/fundraisers
- brunches, luncheons, dinner banquets
- company picnics
- special occasions/weddings

Contact
Amelia Salvador
Marketing Representative

Price
Please contact us for venue & event package rates

Capacity
Indoors - Up to 300
Outdoors - Up to 2,500

Amenities
- Catering: Exclusive In-House full service catering Provided by: Special Occasions Catering & Events
- Bar-service available
- Ample & free onsite parking
- All Set-up & Clean-up included
- Pre-event Planning & Onsite Coordination
- Full sound system available
- Podium/Stage/Dance Floor/Microphone
- In-Focus Projector with full screen
- Rustic-log cabin lodge interior

www.bravoevent.com

Club Sport
OREGON
sports · fitness · adventure

18120 SW Lower Boones Ferry Road
Tigard, Oregon 97224
p. 503.968.4519
f. 503.624.5837
e. jessica.demonte@clubsports.com
www.clubsports.com/oregon

ClubSport fitness resort is a spacious, private sports facility offering all the amenities and features you need to motivate your meeting attendees. Our wellness meeting packages can inspire fresh ideas. If you're looking for something out of the ordinary to spice up your event, we'll create a theme party just for you.

In addition to meeting space you'll find a 150,000 square foot world class fitness resort offering a variety of spaces to accommodate small gatherings, team building events, company parties and even charity galas. ClubSport's spacious facilities can accommodate groups from 8 to 500+ with ample parking.

In addition to great meeting facilities ClubSport offers world class fitness amenities including the Northwest's largest indoor climbing gym, five full sized basketball courts, two mirrored dance studios, restaurant & bar, indoor and outdoor pools, massage services and on-site childcare.

Our expert event planners will see to every detail to help you plan an event that will inspire your attendees without breaking your budget. Catering is available from Courtside Bar & Grill our full service restaurant and bar. Audio visual is available as is complimentary wireless connectivity. ClubSport is ADA accessible.

Contact
Jessica DeMonte
Events Manager

Price
As low as $5.00 per person; call for rates & packages

Quick Facts
- Meeting & event spaces throughout this 150,000 sq. ft. facility
- Private conference room space for up to 65 classroom style seating
- Team building activities and expert planning for small & large groups
- Full service restaurant serving wine & beer
- Conveniently located off I-5, 15 minutes from downtown with ample parking & hotel rooms nearby
- Full event staff & free wireless internet connectivity

See page 278 under Recreation, Attractions & Sports & 309 under Team Building

Bravo! Member Since 2000

www.bravoevent.com

Event & Meeting Sites

"Easy to get to. Hard to leave."

3880 Westcliff Drive
PO Box 887
Hood River, Oregon 97031
p. 866.912.8366
p. 541.436.2660
e. info@columbiacliffvillas.com
www.columbiacliffvillas.com

Only One Hour East of Portland
On the sunny side of the Cascades the luxurious, Columbia Cliff Villas overlook the Columbia River Gorge with unforgettable views of the "The Hatchery" Windsurfing Beach, lush gardens and a 208' waterfall that has been the hallmark of historic Columbia Gorge Hotel.

Luxury Accommodations
29 different rooms and suites can be configured as 1-3 bedroom interconnected units to set the perfect stage for business meetings, retreats, wine excursions, outdoor adventures and weddings. All rooms feature gorgeous woodwork and exquisite appointments. Many offer gourmet kitchens and garages.

Extraordinary Services
Event and meeting coordination. Private chef dining and catering can provide any type of fare. Nanny services. Room service and spa services in all suites.

Area Attractions
World famous for breathtaking views, windsurfing and outdoor adventure. The Columbia River Gorge (a National Scenic Area) now offers 40 wineries, five golf courses, endless hiking and biking, fishing and water sports. Year-round skiing on Mt. Hood. Art galleries and award winning restaurants to suite any palate.

Contact
Steve Tessmer
Owner & General Manager

Price
$169 - $895

Capacity
Meetings up to 30

Amenities
- Kitchens
- Fireplaces
- Private Spa Services
- Nanny services
- Private chef dining
- Catering available
- Pet friendly

Testimonials

John & Michelle - Camas, WA:
"Wow, we were absolutely blown away with this place. The entire experience was the best in the Gorge."

Seth - Portland, OR:
"Serenity, immediate discovery, Columbia Cliff Villas creates an immediate connection with the lifestyle and unmatched splendor."

TYPES OF EVENTS
Business meetings, retreats, team building, achievement awards, wine dinners and weddings.

www.bravoevent.com

The Columbia Gorge Hotel

4000 Westcliff Drive
Hood River, Oregon 97031
p. 541.386.5566
e. kim.bosch@northp.com
www.columbiagorgehotel.com

Boring Meetings Banned!

An inspiring environment for your corporate retreat suddenly transforms the same old meetings into collaborative, creative-thinking sessions.

Just getting here inspires. One hour east of Portland International Airport (PDX), you'll travel along the Columbia River, with its wide swatches of greenery, across the foothills of the Cascade Mountain Range—no one is immune to this majestic beauty.

Our professional staff will assist you in creating an event—not just another meeting—with state-of-the-art audio/visual equipment, world-class dining and catering services, and an awe-inspiring setting unlike any other. Your next retreat will be miles away from ordinary.

Whether you need meeting space in a cozy elegant room for 10 or a training session for 100, we have over 5,000-sq. ft. of adjustable space to accommodate your event.

Built in 1921 by timber tycoon Simon Benson, the Columbia Gorge Hotel quickly became known as the "Waldorf of the West." A magnificent villa perched on a scenic cliff, the Hotel offered sweeping views of the majestic Columbia River as well as the very finest accommodations and dining in the northwest.

Contact
Kim Bosch, CMP

Price
Varies according to services, please call

Amenities
- 5,300 sq. ft. Banquet Seating accommodating up to 200 people
- 39 Guestrooms with historic charm, additional guestrooms within close proximity
- Onsite Restaurant & Lounge, full service catering provided by award winning culinary team
- World's Best Travel & Leisure Award Winner – 2007
- Complimentary High Speed Internet
- Stunning views of the Columbia Gorge
- Located in Hood River, Oregon just minutes from PDX

www.bravoevent.com

Sternwheeler

Gorge Pavilion

About Columbia River Adventure Cruises & Marine Park

With the beauty of the Gorge and an abundance of breathtaking views, the Columbia Gorge Sternwheeler and Marine Park continue to provide a unique venue for meetings, banquets, or any event. We can coordinate your event from start to finish, including transportation, catering and entertainment.

Columbia Gorge Sternwheeler

Enjoy an authentic riverboat experience on the scenic Columbia River. One-deck rentals, private charters of the entire vessel and public group reservations are available. Two levels are fully enclosed and heated, each with an independent sound system. The top Starlight Deck is an open air viewing deck.

Capacity: up to 499 guests
Seating: up to 225 inside, plus outside seating

Gorge Pavilion

The Gorge Pavilion in Marine Park is a year-round event center that offers a riverside facility suitable for any occasion. Complete with tongue and groove woodwork, ambient sconce lighting and a state of the art sound system, the Pavilion is the perfect location for your special occasion.

Capacity: up to 300 guests
Seating: up to 225 inside, plus outside seating

Outrageous Jet Boat

Enjoy a high speed Columbia River adventure aboard the Outrageous. Travel to one of three destinations – Historic Astoria, Portland Bridge Tour, or the Columbia River Gorge.

Capacity: up to 35 guests

Bravo! Member Since 1996

Contact
Group & Charter Sales

110 SE Caruthers
Portland, Oregon 97214
p. 503.224.3900
p. 800.224.3901
e. sales@portlandspirit.com
www.portlandspirit.com

Price
Prices vary – please inquire

Vessel Amenities
- In-house catering provided
- Linen tablecloths & napkins provided
- House china, glassware & flatware provided
- Servers & bartender included with food & bar service
- Full service bar available
- Clean-up provided
- Commercial parking & street parking available
- ADA limited with assistance – please call for more information

See page 84 under Boats and 180 under Event & Meeting Sites

www.bravoevent.com

10755 Cooper Spur Road
Mount Hood, Oregon 97041
p. 541.352.6692
p. 800.skihood
www.cooperspur.com

About Cooper Spur

Cooper Spur Mt. Resort is set on 875 acres surrounded by the Mt. Hood National Forest. The retreat center offers complete privacy in a tranquil setting. Our modern and comfortable facilities are an ideal setting for retreats, conferences and workshops.

Our variety of meeting spaces and friendly accommodations are designed to provide comfort within a variety of budget options. Our main meeting area can be set up for up to 70 people with several break-out spaces. Cooper Spur Mt. Resort is the perfect environment for board and staff retreats and conferences. It is also ideal for yoga retreats and teacher trainings, literary gatherings, artists' workshops and seminars, family reunions and meetings of all types.

Throughout the four seasons, visitors can enjoy the fresh mountain air and savor the natural beauty of the exquisite mountain and forest landscape. Take advantage of our tennis court, hiking trails and hot tubs. Wi-Fi is available in all of our rooms and as well as in the meeting areas. It is possible to have exclusive use of the center for a true retreat experience.

Cooper Spur Mt. Resort is conveniently located just 90 miles from downtown Portland, on the north side of Mt. Hood, offering numerous outdoor and cultural activities in the immediate area.

Contact

Jodi Gehrman
e. weddings@cooperspur.com

Price

Moderate to customized events, please inquire

Quick Facts

- Catering menus available
- Servers provided
- Full-service bar available
- Tent, dance floor & other fixtures available-inquire for pricing
- Ample complimentary parking available
- ADA

SPRING AND FALL WEDDING SPECIAL APRIL, MAY, OCT 15 - NOV 15

Host your entire wedding party at Cooper Spur Mountain Resort, including Wedding ceremony, lodging in our Honeymoon Cabin for Bride & Groom, reception dinner, wine, flowers, wedding cake. Price $3500 for up to 40 people (gratuity not included; limited number of dates available.) Call 541.352.6692 to book your date.

Bravo! Member Since 2008

PORTLAND CONVENTION CENTER

THE PLACE TO MEET.

1441 NE 2nd Avenue
Portland, Oregon 97232
p. 503.233.2401
f. 503.238.7016
e. sales@cpportland.com
www.cpportland.com

About Crowne Plaza Downtown/Convention Center

The Crowne Plaza-Downtown/Convention Center offers easy access from I-5 and I-84 and is just 20 minutes from Portland's International Airport. The hotel is just four blocks from the Oregon Convention Center and two blocks from the Rose Quarter and Memorial Coliseum. The Crowne Plaza is located in "Fareless Square" with access to the MAX Light Rail, where passengers can easily explore downtown Portland's incredible shopping, museums, galleries, and restaurants. The Lloyd Center Mall, Oregon's largest shopping mall, is located just seven blocks from the hotel and features an eight screen cinema and an indoor ice skating rink.

So Many Near-By Attractions

- Willamette River and the East Esplanade walking path – 4 blocks
- Oregon Museum of Science and Industry – 1 mile
- Chinese Gardens – 1 mile
- Saturday Market – 1 mile
- Oregon Zoo – 6 miles
- Japanese Gardens – 6 miles
- Multnomah Falls – 30 miles

Contact
Trisha Dirks
Executive Meetings & Events Manager

Price
Please inquire

Capacity
9,000+ square feet of meeting & banquet space; seating groups from 10 to 600

Quick Fact
- Recently completed a multi-million dollar renovation to become the new Crowne Plaza Portland.

WHAT'S NEW

241 newly remodeled, spacious guest rooms, featuring coffee makers, hairdryers, irons & ironing boards, deluxe-size work desks, microwaves and refrigerators and 42' flat screen TV's. All rooms include the Crowne Sleep Amenities.

See page 14 under Accommodations

Bravo! Member Since 1998

GLENN & VIOLA WALTERS CULTURAL ARTS CENTER

527 East Main Street
Hillsboro, Oregon 97123
p. 503.615.3485
f. 503.615.3484
e. seanm@ci.hillsboro.or.us
www.ci.hillsboro.or.us/wcac

Inspiring Meeting Space

Located in the heart of downtown Hillsboro, the Glenn & Viola Walters Cultural Arts Center houses an event space, five art studios, art gallery, kitchen & box office. Nestled in green space, the Center also has beautiful outdoor grounds and two terraces. The beautiful red stone walls and hardwood arches and accents make the Center an inspiring location for meetings, banquets and presentations.

The facility can be reserved and arranged to accommodate your individual event needs. The event space accommodates up to 200 seats in auditorium style and 136 in banquet style seating. Smaller groups are welcome in our art studios and gallery space for meetings and events. With gorgeous meeting, banquet, and reception spaces, the Center is a showplace for the arts as well as your event!

Find more information and photos on our website, www.ci.hillsboro.or.us/wcac.

Contact
Sean Morgan

Price
Prices vary according to spaces & amenities

Capacity
Up to 200 seats in auditorium style & 136 in banquet or meeting set up

Quick Facts
- Renters may work with the caterer of their choice
- Alcohol service & use of candles permitted with approval
- Facility opened in 2004 & has a state-of-the-art lighting & sound system
- The Center features year-round exhibitions of artwork for your guest's appreciation

WHAT'S NEW
Originally constructed as the Trinity Lutheran Church in the 1940s, the Glenn & Viola Walters Cultural Arts Center opened in 2004 to rave reviews as one of the west side's most beautiful exhibit & meeting spaces.

Tea is one of life's comforts that soothes the soul and warms the heart...

La Tea Da! If you are looking for a unique idea for a Bridal or Baby Shower, Afternoon Tea is a great choice. The Tea Room is a delightful place to spend time with family and friends to celebrate the milestones of your life. There is nothing more relaxing than a steaming pot of tea, accompanied by finger sandwiches, scones with jam and cream and an assortment of wonderful cookies and cakes.

Our Tea Room even has dress-up gowns and accessories that you can choose to use, if you wish. Take a group photo after spending some time "glamming" yourselves up!

The Doll House Tea Room is perfect for:

- Children's Parties
- Anniversaries
- Bridal Showers
- Graduation Parties
- Pampering Friends
- Birthdays
- Baby Showers
- Girls' Nights
- Celebrations
- Book Clubs

The Doll House Tea Room has been offering Fabulous Tea Parties for special celebrations since October 2000. Most often it is a birthday party but we have also done Fantasy Tea Parties for Brownies, Girl Scouts, granddaughters, etc. We look forward to seeing you!

The Doll House Tea Room

3223 SE Risley Avenue
Milwaukie, Oregon 97267
p. 503.653.6809
e. info@DollhouseTeaRoom.com
www.DollHouseTeaRoom.com

Quick Facts

- Minimum charge of $300 for up to 8 party participants plus $20 for each additional to a maximum of 25.

- Reservations should be made at least 2 weeks in advance, so call with your specific party need.

- A deposit of $100 is required to secure the date and time.

- In all fairness, the reservation will be given to the one who provides the earliest deposit.

- Parties last 2 hours.

www.bravoevent.com

DoubleTree® Hotel
Portland

1000 NE Multnomah
Portland, Oregon 97232
p. 503.331.4900
f. 503.249.3137
e. tdumas@portlanddoubletree.com
www.doubletreegreen.com

About The Doubletree Hotel Portland

The Doubletree Hotel is Portland's premier sustainable hotel, dedicated to making your event a success! Our professional staff will assist you in planning a flawless event. From menu planning to room décor and design, our experienced staff will take the stress and pressure out of planning. Our convenient location and ample parking make attending events easy. The hotel offers fresh, local, organic, sustainable, seasonal menus and impeccable attention to detail.

Training or planning meeting?

The Executive Meeting Center is specifically designed for training, offering ease of planning and comfort of attendees and trainers. Packages are generally inclusive of breaks, meals, AV and internet, and priced per person.

Contact
Tiona Dumas

Price
Please contact us for a customized proposal.

Quick Facts
- Full-service in-house catering provided exclusively by the hotel
- In-house audio visual services
- Parking for more than 650 vehicles
- ADA accessible
- Green Seal Certified Silver Level
- Energy Star Certified
- 2009 Best of the West Award Winner
- Oregon Business' Best 100 Green Companies to Work For
- 477 guestrooms
- More than 45,000 square feet of meeting space
- Visit our Executive Meeting Center, Portland's only true conference center

STYLE & COMFORT
Check out our newly renovated public areas, suites and guestrooms.

Bravo! Member Since 1997

Great Green Events

Ecotrust Event Spaces serves Portland with two unique green event venues: The Natural Capital Center and the Center for Architecture. We can accommodate meetings of many sizes, conferences, parties big and small, and weddings. Our beautifully restored historic buildings combine with state-of-the-art amenities to craft transformative events in a warm and creative atmosphere. We design our services to meet the specific needs of your event to make your planning process a pleasure and your event a success. Strategically situated in the heart of Portland's Pearl District, we are easily accessible from downtown by bike, foot, streetcar and car.

Availability and Terms

The Natural Capital Center's Billy Frank, Jr. Conference Center is available seven days a week. The Natural Capital Center's Outdoor Terrace is available Monday through Friday after 5 p.m., and all day Saturday and Sunday. The Center for Architecture is available for private rentals on the weekends.

Contact
Sales & Marketing Manager

721 NW Ninth Avenue
Portland, Oregon 97209
p. 503.467.0792
e. experience@ecotrust.org
www.ecotrust.org/events

Price
Please call for a quote.

Quick Facts
- Two historic, LEED-certified venues available: The Jean Vollum Natural Capital Center & The Center for Architecture. Both are located in the Pearl District.
- Exclusive list of sustainable caterers who offer local, organic & seasonal menus.
- Modern workshop-style furniture is included in the rental fee.
- State of the art audio-visual system is included in the rental fee.
- Electricity use is offset with Green Tag purchases.

Capacity
- The Center for Architecture: 100 standup reception
- The Billy Frank, Jr. Conference Center: 180 standup reception
- The Outdoor Terrace: 200 standup reception

Bravo! Member Since 2001

ELK COVE
VINEYARDS

27751 NW Olson Road
Gaston, Oregon 97119
p. 503.985.7760
p. 877.ELKCOVE
f. 503.985.3525
e info@elkcove.com
www.elkcove.com

About Elk Cove Vineyards

From atop a knoll with commanding views of premier vineyards and buttressing the scenic Oregon Coast Range, the Elk Cove facility is a superb site for that special event, yet only 45 minutes from downtown Portland.

The "Roosevelt Room", named after the herds of Roosevelt elk which roam the nearby mountains, will hold up to 150 people. With a full catering kitchen, Italian tiled floors, and a built-in dance floor, the Roosevelt Room's French doors open onto a full-length deck overlooking the vineyard and showcasing the marvelous spectacle that nature displays in one of Oregon's most picturesque locations.

Elk Cove is pleased to offer a wide range of wines, from our award-winning Pinot Gris (the 2005 was honored to be one of Wine Spectator magazine's top 100 wines of the year for 2007) to the much sought-after Pinot Noirs from our La Bohème vineyard, which have been served at two White House state dinners.

Contact
Hospitality Coordinator

Price
Please call for your customized quote

Quick Facts
- Available year round
- Capacity up to 150
- Roosevelt Room opens onto full length deck overlooking vineyards
- Plenty of on-site parking
- Utilize the vendors of your choice
- Tables & chairs in Roosevelt Room included

See page 331 under Wineries & Custom Labeling

www.bravoevent.com

An Outstanding Gathering Place

About Events at Copper Hill

Welcome to Events at Copper Hill, where the character of vaulted cedar ceilings, stone fireplaces, bronze chandeliers and detailed finishes merge with modern amenities in a newly renovated building.

This beautifully appointed facility, featuring over 10,000 square feet, has a variety of rooms ideal for gatherings of all sizes. Add to this a central location with ample free parking, state-of-the-art technology, and personalized service, you can expect nothing short of an outstanding event.

The Grand Hall, with soaring cedar ceilings and the "floor to ceiling" fireplace set the style for this immense room that will accommodate the larger events. Make your special event more memorable when held in this grand space.

You'll enjoy the atmosphere of our Lower Meeting Hall, with rough-hewn beams, large projection and flat screens, for presentations or slide shows. Versatility is the focus. Classroom, theater, conferences and receptions are just a sample of the possibilities for this special space.

Contact
Lacey Stark
Event Administrator

3170 Commericial St SE
Salem, Oregon 97302
p. 503.373.3170
f. 503.373.3171

www.eventsatcopperhill.com

Price
Price is determined by the event & services rendered

Capacity
Up to 250 people in Grand Hall; Up to 140 people in Lower Meeting Hall

Amenities
- Full-service, in-house catering
- Variety of room setups
- Exhibition kitchen, board room & lower gathering area also available for use
- Tables, chairs, white linens, china, flatware, and glasses provided at no additional cost
- On-site audio/visual systems available
- Wireless internet
- Room setup & clean-up provided
- Ample free parking & fully ADA accessible

Bravo! Member Since 2008

www.bravoevent.com

Awe-Inspiring Environment

The Evergreen Aviation & Space Museum's rental capacity is one of the largest in Oregon. Enjoy our unique atmosphere in the aviation museum: Surrounded by over 80 historic aircraft, including Howard Hughes' "Spruce Goose" and the SR-71 "Blackbird," every event in this 121,000 square-foot building is something special.

Availability and Terms

Reserve as early as possible for your desired date. Short notice events are available, space permitting. A 25% deposit is required to hold the space.

Special Services

An experienced event coordinator is available throughout the planning process and on site for every event. Volunteer docents are on-site for Gallery tours. We offer interior spaces for every kind of event, from intimate to over the top. For outdoor events, we offer the beautiful Oak Grove and several patio areas.

Included

Staffing; set-up and tear-down; tables and chairs; white, ivory or black table linens. Let us know what you need—we want to help you create the perfect event!

What's New

New this year is the Space Museum a perfect venue for memorable cocktail parties or other events. Call today to inquire about the available options.

Contact

Melissa Grace

500 NE Captain
Michael King Smith Way
McMinnville, Oregon 97128
p. 503.434.4023
f. 503.434.4188
e. events@sprucegoose.org
www.evergreenmuseum.org

Price

Varies according to rental space & size of group. Please call for specific information.

Capacity:

Aviation Museum: up to 3,000 reception style & 1,500 seated

Space Museum: up to 3,000 reception style & 1,500 seated

IMAX Theater: 232 seats

IMAX Lobby: 500 reception style

Outdoor Venues available

Amenities

- Preferred catering list available
- Wonderful contacts for music of all kinds
- Ample free parking; can accommodate motor coaches

www.bravoevent.com

Event & Meeting Sites

29111 SW Town Center Loop West
Wilsonville, Oregon 97070
p. 503.685.5000
f. 503.685.9694
e. groupsales@fun-center.com
www.fun-center.com

Family Fun Center & Bullwinkle's Restaurant

When it comes to FUN…
we don't "Moose" around!

This amazing 6-acre amusement park is easily accessible off I-5 in Wilsonville, just 18 miles from Downtown Portland. The Family Fun Center & Bullwinkle's Restaurant has something for everyone – and is open year round for ANY event! Let us do all the work – while you take all the credit for your successful Company Picnic, Off-site Meeting or Training, Employee Incentive/Teambuilding Event, Graduation All-Nighter, Church Group Outing, Team Party, Holiday Party, Birthday Party…any event, the possibilities are endless!

Contact the Group Sales office today for your VIP tour of the Fun Park & Event Center. Our experienced Event Planners will assist in making your event the easiest event you've ever planned – and the most fun!

Contact
Special Events Director

Price
Prices vary per package

Capacity
Up to 3,000 people

Amenities
- Six acres of fun for ALL ages!
- Indoor & Outdoor Attractions operate year-round, rain or shine!
- 4,000 sq. ft. of Event Space/Meeting Rooms
- Bullwinkle's Family Restaurant on-site
- Great location for Company Picnics
- Experienced Event Planners We put the pieces together for you!

ATTRACTIONS
- Go-Karts
- Lazer Tag
- Miniature Golf
- 28' Rock Wall
- Bumper Boats
- Batting Cages
- Sling Shot Bungee
- Max Flight Cyber Coaster
- Over 150 Arcade Games

See page 279 under Recreation, Sports & Attractions

Bravo! Member Since 1998

www.bravoevent.com

900 NW 11th Avenue
Portland, Oregon 97209
p. 503.525.2225
f. 503.525.2224
e. info@fenouilinthepearl.com
www.fenouilinthepearl.com

About Fenouil

Fenouil is an Urban Parisian Brasserie located in the heart of the Pearl District. The atmosphere is elegant, warm and inviting.

Our semi-private second floor mezzanine overlooks Jamison Square and is perfect for rehearsal dinners. We offer a variety of customized menus or you may meet with Chef Pascal Chureau to create a menu that is more personalized.

In addition, the entire restaurant is available for weddings and receptions as well as neighboring Jamison Square. It is a lovely setting for an outdoor event.

We also offer offsite, full-service catering for corporate events, rehearsal dinners, wedding receptions, cocktail receptions and many more occasions.

Contact

Janey Clark
e. JaneyC@fenouilinthepearl.com

Price

Please call for pricing

Capacity

- Full Restaurant
  120 people
  + patio 220 people
- Bar
  40 people - cocktail reception
- Mezzanine
  65 people - sit down dinner
  80 people - cocktail reception
- Full Restaurant & Jamison Square Park buyout available

Quick Facts

- Modern Brasserie
- Semi-private dining area available
- Serving lunch, dinner and Sunday brunch
- Seasonal outdoor dining
- Sommelier service
- Valet package available
- Streetcar line access
- Hotel accommodations nearby

Bravo! Member Since 2008

FIVE PINE
HEALTH • BALANCE • ADVENTURE

1021 Desperado Trail
Sisters, Oregon 97759
p. 541.549.5900
f. 541.549.5200
e. elena.mcmichaels@fivepinelodge.com
e. greg.willitts@fivepinelodge.com
www.fivepinelodge.com

Accommodations
32 craftsman cabins and lodge suites nestled in a pine forested meadow at the base of the Three Sisters mountains. All rooms are luxuriously appointed with a private deck or patio, fireplace, hand built furnishings, 42" plasma TV, waterfall soaking tub and Simmons very best super pillow top mattresses.

Conference Center
At FivePine, our wild flowered forest and blue sky set the ideal backdrop for your productive event. Cross the wood bridge to our Teresa Conference Center and you'll find meeting spaces in varying sizes and a staff dedicated to creating your perfect experience.

Wanderlust Tours
Wanderlust Tours is renowned for its professional, naturalist guides who provide vibrant natural and cultural history interpretation to bring your experience to life and create memories you'll never forget! Year round tours include kayaking, canoeing, caving, hiking and sightseeing, GPS tours, snowshoeing, moonlight and starlight canoe and snowshoe tours, Dinner Canoe Under the Stars, Brews and Views and Bonfire on the Snow 800-258-0757 or www.wanderlusttours.com

Contact
Elena McMichaels

Capacity
Seated 200, stadium 300

Amenities
- 4800 sq. ft. Teresa Conference Center
- 4600 sq. ft. outdoor creek side meeting space
- 19,000 sq. ft. athletic club
- Full service, in house catering
- State of the art audio visual
- Shibui spa
- Sisters movie house
- Three Creeks Brewing Company
- Chloe Fine Dining Restaurant
- Campus wide wireless Internet
- On site event coordinator

Guest Amenities
- Nightly wine reception at the lodge
- Natural Energy Breakfast
- Complimentary parking & WiFi throughout campus

Bravo! Member Since 2006

www.bravoevent.com

PO Box 100
Underwood, Washington 98651
p. 509.493.2026
f. 509.493.2027
e. info@gorgecrest.com
www.gorgecrest.com

The New Premier event location in the Gorge!

Gorge Crest Vineyards has created the first event site in the Gorge designed specifically for events to cater to your every need. We offer spectacular settings with expansive views of Mt. Hood, the Columbia River Gorge and the Hood River Valley. New traditional winery building with intimate inside settings and a custom rock fireplace. Spectacular views form the indoor and outdoor area, manicured lawns, cobblestone patios, covered porches, built in dance floor, tables & chairs, indoor/outdoor bars, dedicated catering facilities and elegant bathrooms makes Gorge Crest the perfect location for your special day!

"As a caterer, working at Gorge Crest Vineyards is just a dream. This is a venue that was created to host picture perfect weddings! As someone who works behind the scenes, this venue has really taken into account the needs of outside vendors. As for the rest of it, from the perfectly manicured grounds to the imported French light fixtures, no detail has been overlooked. With Mt. Hood as a backdrop, who could deny the magnificence of this place? In a word: exceptional."

– Talia, Cork & Bottle Catering

Contact
Ronda Crumpacker

Quick Facts
- Expansive views of the Columbia River Gorge, Hood River Valley & Mt. Hood
- Exquisite Indoor event room w/stone fireplace (in case of bad weather)
- Extensive manicured lawns w/concrete Dance Floor
- Dedicated catering facilities
- Elegant bathrooms
- Dressing room
- Covered porches
- Indoor/outdoor bars (including a wine serving area)
- Beautiful cobblestone patios
- Three dedicated band locations w/necessary electrical
- On-site parking facility & Valet Parking turn around
- Chairs & Tables
- Wonderful wine!
- On-site parking facility & Valet Parking turn around

Bravo! Member Since 2008

www.bravoevent.com

GRAND CENTRAL
Restaurant and Bowling Lounge

Grand Central Restaurant and Bowling Lounge: Providing Portland the ultimate dining and entertainment experience.

Grand Central can provide events with unparalleled versatility. Used alone or combined our meeting spaces create a spectacular atmosphere for events large and small. For parties from 10 – 1,000, Grand Central will ensure that each guest receives prompt, professional, friendly and attentive service.

Our private rooms are wired for sound, have high speed internet connections and Power Point presentation capabilities.

Our goal is to maintain a clean, safe and comfortable facility for our guests and staff. To provide an entertaining and dynamic bowling and billiards experience and produce high quality food and drinks with excellent value.

Grand Central is a restaurant and bar offering a fusion of contemporary American standard fare and Pacific Rim influenced cuisine featuring Northwest flavors. In addition to our full menu which is always available, choose from a list of our most popular selections for events.

Contact
Nichole Szymanowski

808 SE Morrison Street
Portland, Oregon 97214
p. 503.236.2695
f. 503.231.1928
e. grandcentralevents@cegportland.com
www.thegrandcentralbowl.com

Price
Varies with event type, menu selections and service options

Capacity
Up to 1,000

Amenities
- 12 Bowling lanes
- 2 Private Bowling Lanes
- 2 Anniversary Brunswick Billiards Tables
- Four 16' HD Projectors
- Twenty 50" Plasma HD TV's
- 3 Private Party Rooms – Wired for sound, high speed internet connections & Power Point Presentation capabilities

Bravo! Member Since 2008

Event & Meeting Sites

20500 SW Old Highway 99
Centralia, Washington 98531
p. 360.347.0027
f. 360.273.8406
e. jpoole@greatwolf.com
www.greatwolf.com/grandmound/waterpark

At Great Wolf, we understand it's more than just another meeting. It's your meeting and will be the event your attendees talk about and remember. Our Meeting Services team is ready and prepared. The logistics. The cuisine. The service. The technology. Perfect execution is our goal with each and every event. Our conference center features 12 separate rooms giving us the flexibility to accommodate events as small as 10 people and as grand as 1,050. There is a tastefully appointed pre-function area and a private registration counter to enhance your experience at Great Wolf Lodge, Grand Mound. From sales rallies and board meetings to team building events and product launches, Great Wolf adds a new dimension to your conference and meeting needs. When it is time to relax, our 60,000 square foot indoor waterpark, two full-service restaurants, Elements Spa Salon, Northern Lights Arcade and our proximity to beautiful golf courses and historic downtown Olympia makes it easy to see how Great Wolf Lodge creates excitement for all aspects of your event.

Contact
John Poole

Price
Please Inquire

Amenities
- State-of-the-art banquet rooms to accommodate groups of 10 to 1,050
- Wireless high-speed internet available in every guest room
- Full-service catering for all events
- Close proximity to beautiful golf courses
- Great Wolf's team of experienced meeting professionals

See page 311 under Team Building

www.bravoevent.com

Event & Meeting Sites

Sandy Boulevard
at NE 85th Avenue
Portland, Oregon 97220
p. 503.254.7371
f. 503.254.7948
e. meetings@thegrotto.org
www.thegrotto.org

About The Grotto

Retreat to The Grotto, a peaceful 62-acre oasis located minutes from downtown and the Portland airport. Set among towering firs, colorful rhododendrons and other native plants, The Grotto Conference Center has three well-appointed rooms that provide a unique setting for retreats, workshops, seminars, conferences, meetings, corporate team-building, Christmas parties and events. Complete meeting package options include catering and a full array of equipment.

The Grotto's experienced event planners can assist with all aspects of planning your event. Creative menus, attention to detail and excellent service will make your event memorable for all your guests. Admission to the upper level gardens or the Christmas Festival of Lights can be included in your meeting, event or holiday party package. Group tours, guided or informal, of the upper level gardens can be arranged in advance and included in your meeting package.

Come enjoy a peaceful break at The Grotto.

Contact
Conference Center Coordinator

Price
Please call for price schedule

Capacity
Up to 225 depending on room selection and set-up

Amenities
- Centrally located, minutes from both downtown & the airport
- Full-service in-house catering
- High-speed wireless internet access
- State-of-the-art audio/visual equipment
- Easy access to mass transit
- An oasis in the city
- Located on the grounds of an internationally renowned Catholic sanctuary

TYPES OF EVENTS
Corporate meetings, conferences, seminars, board meetings, retreats, corporate team-building, workshops, Christmas parties and fund-raising events.

Bravo! Member Since 1995

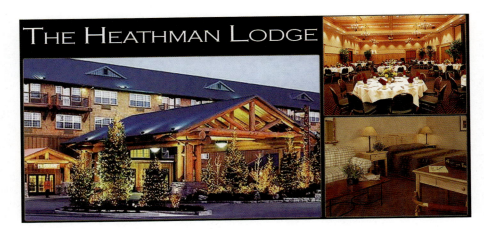

About The Heathman Lodge

The Heathman Lodge is Vancouver, Washington's full-service upscale hotel. An unexpected urban retreat, the Lodge offers travelers and locals from the Portland and Vancouver area a blend of heart-felt service, business amenities and rustic, mountain lodge comfort. Inspired by authentic Pacific Northwest decor and cuisine, the Lodge provides each guest a calm refuge and a memorable experience.

Guest Rooms

Discover what it means to experience a "Great Day" at The Heathman Lodge in one of our 162 guestrooms or 20 suites. With old-world craftsmanship and hickory peeled furnishings each guestroom captures the beauty of the Pacific NW.

Banquet / Meeting Facilities

The Lodge features nearly 10,000 square feet of meeting space which is located on the main floor of the hotel. Our two main ballrooms each feature their own private pre-function area and can be divided into three separate meeting rooms, we also offer 3 additional smaller meeting rooms and a mezzanine loft for fireplace receptions and more!

Contact

Maili Morrison

7801 NE Greenwood Drive
Vancouver, Washington 98662

p. 360.254.3100
f. 360.254.6100
e. maili.morrison@heathmanlodge.com
www.heathmanlodge.com

Price

Please inquire

Amenities

- 10,000 square feet of flexible meeting space to accommodate up to 400 people.
- 182 deluxe guestrooms & signature suites.
- In house catering provided by 4-star award winning Hudson's Bar & Grill.
- Complimentary parking, high speed wireless and airport shuttle service available.

WHAT'S NEW

The Heathman Lodge expansion is open for business! Featuring a brand new 4,200 square foot ballroom with private pre-function area and 40 new deluxe guestrooms!

Bravo! Member Since 2008

Hilton Garden Inn
Portland Airport

12048 NE Airport Way
Portland, Oregon 97220
p. 503.255.8600
f. 503.255.8998
e. Terrie.Ward@hilton.com
www.portlandairport.hgi.com

Four Star Service At A Three Star Price

Hilton Garden Inn Portland Airport offers spacious guest rooms full of thoughtful amenities complemented by friendly service and a relaxed atmosphere.

By focusing precisely on what guests have said they need and want, and less on what they don't use, we deliver the highest degree of service and cost savings to both business and leisure travelers, without sacrificing the quality associated with the Hilton name.

Stellar Location

We are located just three miles east of the Portland International Airport, by car or via our 24-hour complimentary shuttle. The Hilton Garden Inn is easily accessible off Interstate-205 and is only 12 miles from the Oregon Convention Center, the Rose Garden Arena and downtown Portland.

Special Services

We offer a special group rate with a booking of 10 or more guest rooms per night.

This hotel is a 100% smoke free facility.

Contact
Terrie Ward

Price
$91 to $131

Capacity
Four meeting rooms totaling 2,100 square feet, accommodating 10 to 80

Amenities
- Tables & chairs provided
- Servers included in price
- Full beverage service available; provided by hotel only
- Wide selection of linens & napkins provided
- China & glassware provided
- Wireless Internet access; full range AV equipment available at additional cost
- Cleanup provided by staff
- Complimentary parking
- ADA – yes

AWARD-WINNING INN
Awarded the JD Power Award, two years in-a-row

See page 16 under Accommodations

Bravo! Member Since 1999

Wilsonville, Oregon

25425 SW 95th Avenue
Wilsonville, Oregon 97070
p. 503.682.2211
f. 503.682.5596
e. dos@hiportlandsouth.com
www.hiportlandsouth.com

At the Holiday Inn Portland South/Wilsonville, we have built an unparalleled reputation for exceptional service. We are conveniently located off I-5, minutes from downtown Portland, 26 miles from the Portland International Airport, PDX. We are also just 30 miles north of Salem, Oregon's Capital City. There are plenty of extras to help you relax. We offer an indoor pool, whirlpool, and 24 hour fitness center. The hotel offers 170, indoor accessed, spacious, comfortable guest rooms with a full array of amenities including coffee makers, hair dryers, ironing boards, make-up mirrors, refrigerator, microwaves, oversized work desk and room service.

Meeting and convention space of over 11,000 square feet can accommodate from 8 to 800 people. We have a newly added executive conference boardroom. Our sales and catering team has over 75 years combined experience and are ready to help you plan your next event with us.

Contact
Sales & Catering Team

Price
Packages to fit most budgets – please call

Capacity
11,000 sq. ft. of flexible meeting space accommodating groups from 10 to 800

Amenities
- 170 guest rooms including 4 spacious suites
- Conveniently located just off I-5 between Portland & Salem
- On site restaurant & lounge serving breakfast, lunch & dinner daily
- Complimentary parking

New Ballroom

WHAT'S NEW
We have just completed a $3.5 million dollar renovation. Gorgeous guest rooms, public space and banquet facilities. Please come see us...

www.bravoevent.com

About Holocene

Holocene is a gorgeous, airy space with a comfortable and clean urban esthetic – located seconds across the Morrison bridge from downtown. Multiple rooms and modular furnishings let us adapt Holocene to suit your plans perfectly. We serve delicious, well-priced food, beautifully presented. Our bar makes amazing and unique cocktails. And our staff is famously sweet, attentive and charming.

Holocene operates year-round as a restaurant, lounge and performance venue, but can be reserved for private events any day of the week with good advance notice. It can be reserved with less notice for times we're normally shut – including many Mondays and Tuesdays, and most daytime hours. Please drop us an email or give us a ring with any inquiries.

Types of Events

Two large, airy rooms (4,000 square feet total) are available for cocktail parties, receptions, anniversary parties, holiday parties, fundraisers, corporate events, daytime meetings, theme parties, screenings, lectures and photo shoots.

Food and Drink

Full liquor bar, house specialty cocktails, domestic and imported beers and wines, plus espresso, coffee, tea and non-alcoholic drinks. We do wonderful in-house catering for any occasion; outside catering is welcome, too.

Availability and Terms

If possible, contact us two to six months in advance for best choice of dates.

Contact

Jarkko Cain

1001 SE Morrison Street
Portland, Oregon 97214

p. 503.239.7639
f. 206.457.6479
e. events@holocene.org

www.holocene.org/events

Price

Reasonable & flexible pricing, according to day, amenities & event size.

Capacity

Up to 300

Amenities

- Plenty of easy & free street parking
- Outside seating in the nice weather
- Excellent in-house full band/DJ sound systems & projection equipment
- Broadband & Wi-Fi
- Smoke-free

WHAT'S NEW

Ever-changing art installations and soundscapes keep the space current, while soaring white walls make a perfect canvas for your inspirations.

Bravo! Member Since 2008

Hotel Vintage Plaza

422 SW Broadway
Portland, Oregon 97205
p. 503.228.1212
www.pazzoristorante.com
www.vintageplaza.com

About Hotel Vintage Plaza

The Hotel Vintage Plaza has meeting space available to accommodate functions of many sizes. Our meeting rooms are located on the second floor and display the same European ambience seen throughout the hotel lobby, restaurant and guest rooms. Also available is the Pazzo Cellar, which has the capacity for seating up to 64 guests, 70 for a reception. The Pazzoria can accommodate up to 28 people for an evening event. We encourage you to reserve as soon as possible to secure your desired date. A deposit is required to confirm your space.

The Perfect European-Style Facility

Pazzo Ristorante offers exquisite food that embraces the warmth of Italian cuisine. You may have a spontaneous meeting in the living room of your Townhouse Suite and then relax with a glass of wine in our lovely lobby during our evening wine reception. You will quickly see why our guests return again and again to hold their events.

Contact
Sales & Catering

Price
Varies with menu selection

Capacity
Up to 150 (seated)

Amenities
- Full-service, in-house catering by Pazzo Ristorante
- Full-service bar available
- Custom linens & napkins available
- White china, sheer-rim wine glasses & flute champagne glasses available
- Recently renovated guest rooms & meeting space

TYPES OF EVENTS

Board meetings, conferences, trainings, breakfasts, lunches, dinners and cocktail receptions.

117 guest rooms and suites available for overnight guests.

Bravo! Member Since 1990

www.bravoevent.com

Inn At Spanish Head
RESORT HOTEL

4009 SW Hwy 101
Lincoln City, Oregon 97367
p. 800.452.8127
f. 541.996.4089
e. tonya@spanishhead.com
www.spanishhead.com

The Most Inspiring Meeting Facilities on the Oregon Coast

The Inn at Spanish Head Resort Hotel in Lincoln City is Oregon's only resort hotel built right on the beach. The Inn offers breathtaking views of the Pacific Ocean & easy access to the wonders of nature. As a smoke-free condominium hotel, each of the Inn's 120 guest rooms & all meeting rooms are oceanfront with floor-to-ceiling windows. A wide variety of suites, studios & bedrooms are available. Most have balconies & are equipped with a kitchen, kitchenette, or wet bar.

We can graciously accommodate groups from 10 to 150 people, complete with on-site catering & an experienced staff who take meticulous care of each detail. Elevators take you directly to the beach for mid-day breaks, barbecues or a nice walk to unwind at the end of the day.

Nearby there is exceptional hiking, golfing, fishing, tide pools, galleries & unique shops, a major casino and outlet shopping center.

Come & enjoy the Inn's excellent service & spectacular setting. It's the perfect combination to inspire your meeting, reward achievement or celebrate any occasion.

Contact
Tonya Weaver
Group Sales

Price
Guest room rates vary by season & days of the week

Capacity
Up to 150

Amenities
- Five oceanfront meeting rooms featuring floor-to-ceiling windows & more than 3,500 square feet of space; wireless access in meeting & guest rooms
- Two meeting rooms open directly to poolside & the beach offering opportunities for poolside receptions & bonfires
- Heated outdoor pool, ocean view spa, saunas, recreation/exercise room, easy beach access

AWARD WINNING OCEANVIEW RESTAURANT

Fathams Restaurant & Bar was awarded Best Overall Restaurant, Best Sunday Brunch & Best Restaurant to Take Guests To.

See page 289 under Resorts & Retreats

Bravo! Member Since 1996

Jake's CATERING
AT THE GOVERNOR HOTEL

614 SW 11th Avenue
Portland, Oregon 97205
p. 503.241.2125
f. 503.220.1849
www.jakescatering.com

A Historic Gem

Listed on the National Register of Historic Places, The Governor Hotel is an architectural beauty. Built in 1909, the hotel has been completely restored to its original grandeur. The recently completed renovation of the Heritage Ballroom unveils Portland's best-kept secret, resurrecting this one-of-a-kind grand space for events after a hiatus of more than 60 years. The classic design and ornate craftsmanship were preserved in the original Italian Renaissance styling. The room's high vaulted ceilings, marble floors and black-walnut woodwork and walls are truly unique.

Jake's Catering...A Tradition

Jake's Catering is part of the McCormick & Schmick's family of restaurants, including Jake's Famous Crawfish. Jake's is one of the oldest and most respected dining institutions in the Portland area, and Jake's Catering upholds this prestigious reputation.

Known for offering an extensive range of Pacific Northwest menu selections, including fresh seafood, pasta, poultry and prime cut steaks, Jake's Catering has the variety, flexibility and talent to cater to your needs.

Availability and Terms

Our Italian Renaissance-style rooms offer variety and flexibility for groups of 25 to 700. The newly renovated Heritage Ballroom, Renaissance Room, Fireside Room, Library and eight additional rooms gracefully complement the charm of The Governor Hotel. We require a 50% deposit to confirm your event and payment in full 72 hours prior to event for estimated charges.

Bravo! Member Since 1994

Contact
Catering Director

Price
$25 to $55

Capacity
700 reception; 500 sit-down

Amenities
- Tables & chairs for up to 500
- Professional, uniformed servers
- Full-service bar & bartender
- Cloth napkins & linens in variety of colors
- Fine china & glassware provided
- A/V available upon request
- Ample parking

TYPES OF EVENTS
From stand-up cocktail and appetizer receptions to fabulous buffet presentations to complete sit-down dinners for groups and gatherings of all sizes.

See page 44 under Full-Service Catering

HIGH DESERT RESORT & CASINO

6823 Highway 8, PO Box 1240
Warm Springs, Oregon 97761
p. 800.554.4SUN (Reservations)
p. 888.220.9830 (Sales)
f. 503.768.9831
e. sales@kahneeta.com
www.kahneeta.com

About Kah-Nee-Ta High Desert Resort and Casino

Every great event begins with an extraordinary setting. Big Skies. Blue Waters. High Desert Vistas. Nestled in the heart of Central Oregon on the Warm Springs Indian Reservation, Kah-Nee-Ta High Desert Resort & Casino is the perfect destination for your next event. All 170 guestrooms feature balconies with panoramic views and captivating sunsets. The 15,000 square feet of meeting space is ideal for groups of all sizes and can accommodate business meetings, intimate gatherings, corporate events, and elaborate parties. Experience the taste of Native culture with a Salmon Bake complete with Native dancing or try our renowned Bird-in-Clay dinner.

We are the perfect playground for all ages with more recreation than any other resort in Oregon. Soak in the Village Hot Springs Pool, enjoy a round of golf, kayak down the Warm Springs River and see the high desert on horseback. Kah-Nee-Ta High Desert Resort & Casino – escape to where the fun shines!

Contact
Celia Lozano
Senior Sales Manager

Steve McDade
Sales Manager

Price
Varies by event. Please call for more information.

Capacity
Up to 620 people in a theatre-style setup and 360 in a formal dining atmosphere.

Quick Facts
- We offer 15,000 square feet of adaptable meeting space ideal for all size groups
- 8 hole golf course, double Olympic-size hot springs swimming pool, horseback riding, kayaking & more
- Full-service European Spa Wanapine
- The 25,000 square foot casino offers more than 300 slots as well as blackjack & a dedicated poker room. In addition, we feature a major prize giveaway each month.

See page 85 under Casinos

Bravo! Member Since 1997

www.bravoevent.com

PORTLAND'S IRISH RESTAURANT & PUB

112 SW Second Avenue
Portland, Oregon 97204
p. 503.227.4057
f. 503.227.5831
e. tracey@kellsirish.com
e. brad@kellsirish.com
www.kellsirish.com

About Kells Irish Restaurant and Pub

Located on the second floor of the 1889 Historic Glisan building, Kells provides an Irish ambiance with excellent service and outstanding food. Our elegant facility invites your guests to celebrate in the stately Ceili Ballroom and mingle in the Irish Writers, Ulster Bar and Hibernian Rooms.

We provide buffet and formal sit-down service for receptions, rehearsal dinners and more.

Meeting and Banquet Facilities

With more than 2,500 square feet of accommodations, Kells banquet facilities can be modified into separate, more intimate rooms for a rehearsal dinner or one large space for your grand reception.

Both rooms include the latest technology in high-definition, overhead projector televisions, wireless microphones and Internet connectivity.

Kells truly offers all the bells and whistles, along with classic style.

Contact
Tracey Murphy
Brad Yoast

Price
We credit back room fees when minimums are met; call for more information

Capacity
Seated 15 to 120;
Reception 250;
Private banquet facilities on 2nd floor

Amenities
- Full-service, in-house, award-winning catering
- Upgraded air conditioning & heating
- Unique grand ballroom, circa 1889
- Two separate full-bar facilities
- Linens & candles included in service
- China & glassware included in service

GREAT DOWNTOWN LOCATION
Kells is located in the classic Old Town Area, close to the waterfront, Max Light Rail, Convention Center and many upscale hotels.

Bravo! Member Since 1990

www.bravoevent.com

LAKESIDE GARDENS

16211 SE Foster Rd.
Portland, Oregon 97236
p. 503.760.6044
f. 503.760.9311
e. lgardens@easystreet.net
www.lakesidegardensevents.com

About Lakeside Gardens

Lakeside Gardens offers you the ultimate Oregon setting, a grande estate and royal service. We are a Private Event Facility situated on approximately seven acres. You can proudly invite guests from all over the world to the natural miracle of Oregon. Lakeside Gardens blends tall cedars, weeping willows and lakes surrounded by a garden paradise.

Right in your own backyard we have the ideal Oregon meeting place. Lakeside Gardens is a beautiful and productive setting for such activites as conferences, seminars, workshops. business association meetings, annual company dinners, commemorative events and Celebrations of Life.

Besides plenty of meeting space, lakeside Gardens offers superb catering. Our "culinary cuisine" trained chef creates the menu to fill you every need and appetite. We are able to provide ice sculptures by our chef and other decorations to create the setting of your choice.

Contact
Office

Price
Price is determined by the event & menu selected

Capacity
Up to 300 people for a hors d'oeuvre buffet

Up to 200 people for a sit-down buffet dinner

Amenities
- Full-service, in-house catering
- Tables & chairs are provided; terrace & garden seating available
- We offer beer, wine & champagne; we provide all beverages & bartenders
- China & glassware provided, linen tablecloths provided, linen & paper napkins available

WHAT'S NEW

Lakeside Gardens brings the place, the plan, and the people together. Our professional and friendly staff look forward to contributing to the success of your event.

Bravo! Member Since 1990

24377 NE Airport Road
Aurora, Oregon 97002
p. 503.678.GOLF (4653)
www.langdonfarms.com

About Langdon Farms Golf Club

Langdon Farms Golf Course is conveniently located 20 minutes south of Portland off I-5. The course is situated on several acres of pristine greens designed from the former farmland of the Langdon Family. This tranquil setting is a versatile venue ideal for events ranging from a casual golf outing and luncheon to an elegant reception. The staff at Langdon Farms is dedicated to providing exceptional service and will go the extra mile to make your event a success. Whether your event is outdoors or in, your guests will delight in the serenity and splendor of the surroundings.

Availability and Terms

Reservations can be made anytime, but it is recommended that they be made at least six months in advance. A deposit is required to hold a reservation date.

Types of Events

Corporate golf tournaments, fundraisers, auctions, company picnics, breakfast, lunch and dinner meetings, cocktails and hors d'oeuvres, corporate parties, sit-down and buffet dinners, wine tastings, private parties, barbeques, and retreats.

Contact
Golf Outings
p. 503.678.4775
Non-Golf Events
p. 503.678.4723

Price
Price varies according to menu selection

Capacity
Up to 500 people depending on type of event

Amenities
- Full-service, in-house catering
- Fully trained & licensed professional servers
- Full-service bar & licensed bartender(s) provided; full selections of liquor, beer, wine & champagne
- Ample FREE parking
- ADA: Fully accessible

PUBLIC WELCOME
Langdon Farms Golf Club is open to the public. Call the Golf Shop for seasonal rates and to request a tee time.

See page 250 under Golf Courses & Tournaments

Bravo! Member Since 2001

www.bravoevent.com

LAWRENCE GALLERY

903 NW Davis
Portland, Oregon 97209
p. 503.224.1591
f. 503.224.5953
e. info@fireworkseventproductions.com
www.lawrencegallery.net

Portland's trendy Pearl District is home to the prestigious Lawrence Gallery with it's multi-million dollar art collection. Classic European sculpture and paintings of masters such as Chagall, Dali, Miro and Picasso rub elbows with a vast collection of works by extraordinary Northwest artists.

Your experience in this 14,000 square-foot environment will be unique and truly unforgettable.

Our spatial flexibility allows us to create visually exciting combinations of areas to suit your special event. Among the areas to consider are the Main and Middle Galleries, the exquisitely focused Side Galleries, Vermillion Wine Bar, the intimate Vermillion Wine Cellar, the Floral Wine Patio, as well as the art-filled oasis of the Sculpture Garden. These elements are each designed to impart a sophisticated ambience to each event that truly delights.

Professional event management which includes the detailed and creative focus provided exclusively by FireWorks! will bring all of the necessary elements together to help you achieve a flawless event.

Contact
Teresa Beck

Capacity
Up to 200 seated in one area; additional seating available in combined areas
Up to 300 reception-style

Quick Facts
- Find us by taking the Portland Streetcar to our fabulous sculpture garden entrance on N.W. 10th & Everett, conveniently located in Portland's renowned Pearl District

WHAT'S NEW
We're always new! Lawrence Gallery continuously displays new works of art so our patrons will experience a fresh venue each time they visit us!

Bravo! Member Since 2007

Event & Meeting Sites

13300 Highway 20
Sisters, Oregon 97759

p. 541.595.2628 Ext. 209 or 283
f. 541.595.2267
e. eventdirector@
   thelodgeatsuttlelake.com

www.thelodgeatsuttlelake.com

Your Event at The Lodge at Suttle Lake

The intimate setting of The Lodge at Suttle Lake will transport you….

….family reunions will be as personal as your signature

…events are like fingerprints…there are no two alike…

From board meetings to conferences, seminars to office retreats, we like you, are unique.

Nestled in the heart of the Deschutes National Forest amid soaring pines, Suttle Lake Resort provides an enchanted escape. Our focus will always lie in the details of your comfort and the quality of your experience.

Dining at the Boathouse Restaurant or having Chef Michael Valoppi cater your affair will make your guest know how special they are. Approachable NW Cuisine accompanied by our dynamic wine list and full bar.

The Lodge at Suttle Lake invites you to…
Come find your way…

Contact
Cynthia Willams or
Kasandra Scevers

Price
Please call for details

Capacity
12 to 80 indoor;
up to 200 outdoor

Quick Facts
- 11 lodge rooms, 13 cabins & private boardroom
- Several onsite event locations to choose from; including private outdoor settings and rustic elegant in-door facilities
- Team building activities upon request that capture the local surroundings of Beautiful Central Oregon
- Personal memorabilia for your event upon request
- Extra rooms for breakout sessions

Amenities
- Onsite Catering
- Spa
- Full Service Bar
- A/V available
- Wireless connectivity

www.bravoevent.com

An Historic Oregon Ranch

7115 Holmes Road
Sisters, Oregon 97759
p. 541.923.1901
e. howdy@lhranch.com
www.lhranch.com

About Long Hollow Ranch

Long Hollow Ranch, Oregon's only working dude ranch, is nestled in between two rocky plateaus, with views of world famous Smith Rock to the East and the Cascade Mountains to the West. Long Hollow is the ideal setting for your unique western wedding or corporate retreat.

Our farm house, built in 1905, is the original headquarters for the Black Butte Land and Cattle Company. It features 5 bedrooms with private baths and a guest cottage perfect for the Bride and Groom.

At Long Hollow, we will assist you with all of your needs or simply step back and let you create the wedding of your dreams. You can plan a garden wedding, be adjacent to the farm house on the beautiful lawn, or be down at the barn, with high desert sunsets being our specialty.

If it is peace and tranquility you desire, then Long Hollow Ranch is your perfect combination, mixing the past and the present.

Contact
Dick & Shirley Bloomfeldt

Price
$200 - $10,000

Quick Facts
- 562 acre working dude ranch / Bed & Breakfast
- Catering on site with our chef or caterer of your choosing
- Weddings or corporate events up to 200
- Historic barn, original farm house
- 3 ponds for fishing and access to the Deschutes River; trail rides; cattle drives
- Easy access to municipal airport and major airline carriers

WHAT'S NEW
There is always something new at the ranch. In the fall of 2009 the corral remodel started and the barn got old siding replaced with sustainable boards.

See page 312 under Team Building

Event & Meeting Sites

147

MAJESTIC INN & SPA

419 Commercial Avenue
Anacortes, Washington 98221
p. 360.299.1400 ext. 110
f. 360.299.8835
e. kristine@majesticinnandspa.com
www.majesticinnandspa.com

The Majestic Inn and Spa has been beautifully restored to its original grandeur. The historic Majestic Inn and Spa, located in the heart of downtown Anacortes WA, is your perfect getaway. Nestled in the natural beauty of the Pacific Northwest, surrounded by marinas, evergreen trees and the Puget Sound, Anacortes is the ideal location for shopping, hiking, boating or simply relaxing.

Our facilities are ideal for special events. From formal dinners to cocktail receptions, from memorable weddings to extraordinary family reunions and birthdays, our professional event planning staff will guide you every step of the way to ensure an unforgettable experience.

The Chrysalis Day spa invites you to come relax in our eucalyptus steam rooms or schedule an appointment for one of the many euphoric treatments and massages. The Ryan Chanel hair salon offers several services which include a trim, color, cut, style or a full group service with your choice of catering. Let our on-site spa and salon staff pamper you and your guests during your stay.

Plan your next meeting, corporate retreat or private event in the comfort and grace of the Majestic. Your group will appreciate the beautiful building, caring staff, elegance and warm ambiance of our Inn and Spa.

Contact
Kristine Ells

Price
Varies by event. Please call for information.

Quick Facts
- Picturesque setting with indoor & outdoor meeting & banquet facilities
- Accommodates up to 75 indoors; expands to 200 using the outside courtyard
- On site catering & event coordinating
- 21 luxurious guest rooms
- Complimentary Wi-Fi, cable TV, DVD player, Mini Refrigerators
- Complimentary Athletic club access
- Majestic restaurant & pub offers elegantly casual dining
- 4 meeting rooms of various sizes

WHAT'S NEW
The Majestic Boardroom, perfect for small corporate meetings accommodating up to 12 guests. Well equipped with a 42" flat screen TV for LCD projection, conference phone, and personal Fax/copy machine.

www.bravoevent.com

About Courtyard by Marriott - Portland North Harbour

The Courtyard by Marriott – Portland North Harbour is the perfect location for an outdoor celebration. Our 7,500 square foot, secsonally landscaped courtyard patio overlooks the Columbia River channel and has magnificent views of Mount St. Helens and Mount Adams. Complete with gazebo & fountain, the Courtyard by Marriott Portland North Harbour is an ideal setting for ceremonies, receptions, rehearsal dinners, cocktail & holiday parties!

About Residence Inn by Marriott - Portland North Harbour

North Harbour Residence Inn by Marriott provides the comforts of home and functionality for business. With over 2,500 square feet of flexible meeting space we can accommodate up to 150 people. Complimentary wireless internet access is available throughout the entire hotel.

Contact
Kristina Shipley

Courtyard Marriott:
1231 N Anchor Way
Portland, Oregon 97217

p. 503.735.1818
f. 503.735.0888
e. kristina.shipley@marriott.com
www.marriott.com/pdxnh

Residence Inn by Marriott:
250 N. Anchor Way
Portland, Oregon 97217

p. 503.285.9888
f. 503.285.5888
e. kristina.shipley@marriott.com
www.marriott.com/pdxph

Quick Facts
- Complimentary parking
- ADA compliant & complimentary airport transportation
- MAX Lightrail is within walking distance

Bravo! Member Since 2007

www.bravoevent.com

9774 Highway 14 W
Goldendale, Washington 98620
p. 877.MARYHILL
f. 509.773.0586
www.maryhillwinery.com

About Maryhill Winery

Established in 1999 by Craig and Vicki Leuthold, Maryhill Winery is one of Washington state's largest family-owned wineries producing 80,000 cases annually. Located in the picturesque Columbia Gorge scenic area in Goldendale, Washington, the winery is perched on a bluff overlooking the Columbia River against the stunning backdrop of Mt. Hood. Nestled among rows of vines, Maryhill is a popular destination for picnics and special events, with an adjacent 4,000-seat outdoor amphitheatre that hosts a world-class summer concert series.

Maryhill's 3,000 sq. ft. tasting room draws more than 75,000 wine enthusiasts from around the globe each year, ranking among the top five most visited wineries in the state. Maryhill sources grapes from some of the most highly-regarded vineyards in the state to produce 23 varietals and 28 award-winning wines. Offering something for every palate, Maryhill's wines offer tremendous value with exceptional quality at accessible price points. For more information or to order wines online, visit *www.maryhillwinery.com*.

Contact
Joe Garoutte

p. 877.MARYHILL ext. 342
e. joeg@maryhillwinery.com

Maryhill provides a selection of 4 sites including:

- Ceremony site on the bluff of the Columbia River
- Amphitheatre & Stage
- Recreation area
- Arbor after hours

Price
Fee is $6,500 & includes the following:

- Selection of sites
- Event Planner Assistance
- Day of event coordination
- 20 tables, 360 chairs

Quick Facts
- "2009 Washington Winery of the Year" ~ Winepress NW
- "Best Destination Winery" ~ Seattle Magazine
- Excellent caterers available for hire
- Personalized Wine labels available for additional charge
- Handicap accessible

www.bravoevent.com

McMENAMINS EDGEFIELD

2126 SW Halsey Street
Troutdale, OR 97060
p. 503.492.2777
p. 877.492.2777
e. salesed@mcmenamins.com
www.mcmenamins.com

About the Edgefield
Built as the county poor farm in 1911 at the mouth of the Columbia River Gorge and later used as an old folks' home, Edgefield was marked for demolition until the McMenamin brothers renovated the property in the mid-1990s. Today, this destination resort and national historic landmark offers over 100 guestrooms, along with indoor and outdoor meeting and event spaces that can accommodate up to 225 and include WiFi, original artwork and onsite catering. Or perhaps organize a golf tournament on one of our two par-3 courses. After your event, visit the fine-dining Black Rabbit Restaurant, the Power Station Pub, our many small bars, gardens, distillery, winery and tasting room, Ruby's Spa and soaking pool, movie theater and more! Photos, menus and room layouts available at *mcmenamins.com*.

Contact
Group Sales Office

Price
Food & beverage minimum; varies based on size of room & time of day

Capacity
Up to 200 guests seated
250 guests reception-style
300 guests reception-style available in summer

Amenities
- 114 guestrooms
- Restaurants & small bars
- Ruby's Spa & soaking pool
- Two par-3 golf courses
- Pool tables & shuffle board
- Movie Theater
- Brewery
- Winery
- Distillery
- Wifi

See page 290 under Resorts & Retreats

Bravo! Member Since 1991

3505 Pacific Avenue
Forest Grove, Oregon 97116
p. 503.992.9530
p. 877.992.9530
e. salesgl@mcmenamins.com
www.mcmenamins.com

About the Grand Lodge

Located in Forest Grove, halfway between Portland and the Oregon coast, this stately 1922 Masonic lodge turned hotel in Oregon's wine country welcomes you! Relax in comfortable guestrooms, order a Northwest-inspired meal in the Ironwork Grill or Yardhouse Pub and enjoy handcrafted McMenamins ales, wines and spirits in the Doctor's Office or Bob's Bar. You and your guests can schedule massage, facials and more at Ruby's Spa. During your visit, take in the estate's original artwork and architecture, its ornate theater featuring recent-run films, a rambling 10-hole disc golf course, heated saltwater soaking pool, lush year-round gardens — that's just the beginning! Photos, menus & room layouts available at mcmenamins.com.

Contact
Group Sales Office

Price
Food & beverage minimum; varies based on size of room & time of day

Capacity
Indoors, seated 200, reception-style 200
Outdoors, seated 500, reception-style 500

Amenities
- 77 guestrooms
- Restaurants & small bars
- Ruby's Spa
- Outdoor year-round soaking pool
- Movie theater
- Disc golf course
- Gardens
- Artwork

Bravo! Member Since 1991

310 NE Evans Street
McMinnville, Oregon 97128
p. 503.472.8427
p. 888.472.8427
e. saleshoto@mcmenamins.com
www.mcmenamins.com

About the Hotel Oregon

Set in McMinnville's charming downtown district in the center of wine country, Hotel Oregon (built in 1905) is an ideal spot for an event or meeting. Along with comfortable spaces equipped with WiFi that hold up to 120 guests, your participants will enjoy the original artwork, extensive wine list, cozy guestrooms and more. Hold breakfast, lunch or dinner meetings in the inviting McMenamins Pub. Gather for a friendly round of pool in the Paragon Room. Relax in the Cellar Bar with your colleagues or guests. Take the elevator up to the legendary Rooftop Bar for happy hour to sample McMenamins ales and wines while drinking in the spectacular sight of Oregon's Coastal Range, vineyards and orchards stretching for miles in every direction. Photos, menus and room layouts available at mcmenamins.com.

Contact
Group Sales Office

Price
Food & beverage minimum; varies based on size of room & time of day

Capacity
Up to 80 guests seated
Up to 120 guests reception-style

Amenities
- 42 guestrooms
- Restaurants & small bars
- Pool tables
- Wifi

Bravo! Member Since 1991

www.bravoevent.com

5736 NE 33rd Avenue
Portland, Oregon 97211
p. 503.288.3286
p. 888.249.3983
e. salesken@mcmenamins.com
www.mcmenamins.com

About Kennedy School

Rescued from demolition and renovated for a 1997 opening, McMenamins Kennedy School is a Portland institution, featuring the city's most whimsical lodging and event space. This former 1915 elementary school offers 35 classroom-turned-guestrooms (with original chalkboards and cloakrooms), comfortable meeting rooms for groups both large and small and including WiFi, an array of colorful artwork, an outdoor soaking pool, the Courtyard Restaurant serving breakfast, lunch and dinner and a brewery where handcrafted ales are made with care. After your event, sip a fresh-juice cocktail in the Honors Bar with the good kids or savor a whiskey and a cigar with the wild ones in the Detention Bar. The Cypress Room and Boiler Room Bar also feature full bars and menu options. Photos, menus and room layouts available at *mcmenamins.com*.

Contact
Group Sales Office

Price
Food & beverage minimum; varies based on size of room & time of day

Capacity:
Up to 200 seated theater style
Up to 112 seated meal
Up to 120 reception-style

Amenities
- 35 guest rooms
- Restaurant & small bars
- Heated soaking pool
- Movie Theater
- Pool tables & shuffle board
- Wifi

Bravo! Member Since 1991

www.bravoevent.com

700 NW Bond Street
Bend, Oregon 97701
p. 541.330.8567
e. salesbend@mcmenamins.com
www.mcmenamins.com

About Old St. Francis School

Hold your meeting, reunion, retreat or other big event in this former Catholic elementary school – no worries about goofing off in class here! We encourage all forms of fun and merriment. You and your guests will revel in the many indoor and outdoor spots to enjoy a handcrafted ale, wine or spirit and Northwest-inspired pub fare. Have a scotch and some spirited conversation at an outdoor table in O'Kanes Square. Enjoy a cool pint in the cozy Fireside Bar. Take in a recent-run film in the movie theater (with refreshments including beer and pizza delivered to your seat), or rest your aching bones in our beautiful open-air soaking pool.

For more than 20 years, Mcmenamins' historic hotels, pubs and breweries throughout Oregon and Washington have been well known as being friendly, familiar places to enjoy handcrafted ales, wine, spirits and Northwest-inspired pub fare with family and friends. Photos, menus & room layouts available at mcmenamins.com.

Contact
Group Sales Office

Price
Food & beverage minimum; varies based on size of room & time of day

Capacity
Indoors, seated 100, 120 reception-style

Outdoors, 100 seated, 150 reception-style

Catering
In-house catering only

Amenities
- 19 guestrooms & four cottages
- Restaurant & small bars
- Soaking pool
- Movie theater
- Onsite brewery
- Outdoor seating in summer

Bravo! Member Since 1991

About the Sand Trap

Make your next event – employee retreat, family reunion, birthday party or what-have-you – a fun getaway for everyone by holding it on the Oregon coast! McMenamins Sand Trap Pub, just 5 miles north of Seaside, overlooks the historic 1892 Gearhart Golf Links and is just a short stroll across the street to the mighty Pacific Ocean. Enjoy a full menu featuring McMenamins' signature burgers and sandwiches, along with seasonal salads and fresh seafood specials. We offer a large event space called Livingstone's to accommodate all size of groups. Your guests will undoubtedly enjoy our selection of McMenamins handcrafted ales, wines and spirits along with other fine products. Photos, menus & room layouts available at mcmenamins.com.

1157 North Marion Avenue
Gearhart, Oregon 97138
p. 503.717.8502
e. salessandt@mcmenamins.com
www.mcmenamins.com

Contact
Group Sales Office

Price
Food & beverage minimum; varies based on size of room & time of day

Capacity
Up to 180 indoors plus an additional 100 outside

Amenities
- Restaurant & small bar
- Outside deck overlooking Gearhart Golf Links
- Indoor & Outdoor event space

Bravo! Member Since 1991

About The McMinnville Grand Ballroom

The McMinnville Grand Ballroom epitomizes simple, natural elegance. Light floods the room from the north and south facing windows. Beautiful Douglas fir floors stretch from wall to wall throughout the 5600 square foot ballroom. Turned pillars support high ceilings. The building was designed in 1892 in the Arts and Craft Style for the McMinnville Ballroom Association. This elegant space is located in the heart of downtown McMinnville overlooking historic Third Street.

Location

Central downtown wine-country location. Easy walking distance from hotels and churches. Less than an hour from Portland, Beaverton, Tigard, Wilsonville and Salem.

Rentals

Linens, placesettings, glassware, napkins, center pieces, dual projection system with large retractable screens, sound system with full set-up and microphones, podium.

Contact

Steven Battaglia

325 NE Third Street
McMinnville, Oregon 97128
p. 503.474.0264
e. info@mgballroom.com
www.mgballroom.com

Price

Starting from $500 up to $2,500

Capacity

From 50 to 350

Catering

Preferred caterer, outside caterer or self-catering & bartending

Amenities

- Tables & chairs
- Changing room
- Set-up & clean-up
- Adjustable chandelier lighting
- Two extra large bars
- Sinks, refrigerator & dishwasher

Bravo! Member Since 1995

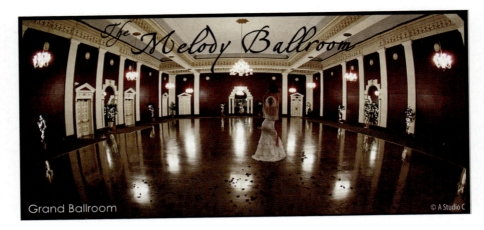
Grand Ballroom

About The Melody Ballroom

The Melody Ballroom is a unique, historic facility, built in 1925, featuring two beautiful ballrooms. We specialize in producing events that are customized to suit your desires. Our catering staff can produce a diversity of menus, from ethnic, themed, or locally sustainable, to your grandmother's own recipes prepared for you in our kitchen. Our caring staff will provide expert service that will make you and your guests feel well cared for and welcome.

Special Services

The Melody Ballroom rents on a per day basis, giving you the flexibility for decorating and music setup at your convenience. Our on-site event coordinators are always happy to help you plan and execute your event to perfection.

Extraordinary Food and Friendly Service

We offer sit-down, buffet, theme dining, as well as cocktail and hors d'oeuvres styles of celebration.

Our extraordinary food and friendly service will make your event a success!

Contact

Kathleen Kaad

615 SE Alder
Portland, Oregon 97214
p. 503.232.2759
f. 503.232.0702
e. kathleen@themelodyballroom.org
www.themelodyballroom.org

Price

Varies, please call

Capacity

Two rooms totaling 1,100 people. Individually, up to 300 or 800 people.

Services

- In-house catering & beverage services only
- Outside catering with some restrictions
- Staff included in catering costs; gratuity on food & beverage
- Full-service bar provided; host or no-host; liquor, beer, & wine
- Fresh flowers, linens & some decorating accessories provided
- 30'x30'; 300 capacity dance floor, plus stage
- Free street parking

Lower Ballroom

Bravo! Member Since 1994

www.bravoevent.com

Meriwether's Restaurant

Event & Meeting Sites

2601 NW Vaughn Street
Portland, Oregon 97210
p. 503.228.1250
e. info@meriwethersnw.com
www.meriwethersnw.com

About Meriwether's Restaurant

Meriwether's is located in the historic 2601 NW Vaughn building in the NW Industrial area of Portland. We have several shared or private spaces that can accommodate parties between 15 and 300 guests for a variety of events from cocktail & hors d'oeuvres, corporate dinners and gatherings to showers, rehearsal dinners, weddings & receptions.

Our unique outdoor covered, heated (and enclosed if needed) patio, gardens and gazebo with fire pit are year-round event venues. Our outdoor spaces are surrounded by "four-season" gardens, which means something is in bloom year round. Inside, rustic stone fireplaces, hardwood floors, stained glass and copper accents are the décor.

About our food…events menus are created from our own 4-acre Meriwether's Skyline Farm, located 20 minutes from the restaurant. We are growing a full array of traditional garden vegetables, flowers and herbs with an emphasis on heirloom and Italian varietals. Whenever possible, our seasonal events menus are created using Meriwether Skyline Farm ingredients.

Contact
Events Coordinator

Capacity
From 10 to 240 for a seated event & 300 for cocktails & hors d'oeuvres

Types Of Events
Corporate dinners, lunches & brunches, cocktail & hors d'oeuvre parties

Wedding ceremonies, receptions, rehearsal dinners, showers, cocktail & hors d'oeuvres, wedding party events

Special events, holiday parties, winemaker dinners, birthdays, anniversaries, Bar/Bat Mitzvah's

Highlights
- Five minutes from downtown Portland
- Private rooms available
- On-site parking
- "Year-round" outdoor covered & enclosed patio, gardens & gazebo
- Historic indoor rooms with stone fireplaces
- Menus created from our own working farm

Bravo! Member Since 2007

www.bravoevent.com

Event & Meeting Sites

3201 Tremont Avenue
North Bend, Oregon 97459
p. 541.756.8800 or
   800.953.4800, Ext. 2288
f. 541.756.0631
e. ldinovo@themillcasino.com
www.themillcasino.com

Set in a picturesque location along the Coos Bay waterfront in North Bend, Oregon, The Mill Casino-Hotel & RV Park has become an entertainment destination on Oregon's South Coast. Owned by the Coquille Indian Tribe the historic mill facility shines as a gaming and hospitality center that has become a regular stop for coastal visitors and residents.

With over 14,000 square feet of meeting space and the right blend of rooms and services, The Mill is a prime location for meetings and conferences. The Salmon Room offers seating for up to 850 guests in addition to five new meeting rooms. Meeting facilities at The Mill include state-of-the-art audio and video systems and complimentary WiFi and broadband connectivity.

The Mill's professional catering services will create the right menu whether you are hosting a small group meeting or multi-day conference. You can count on The Mill's staff to make special events special indeed.

And don't forget to have fun. The Mill Casino offers 725 slots comfortably arranged on a gaming floor that includes our smoke-free slots room. Sharing the room is a full selection of table games and a classic Poker Room. After hours, guests can enjoy great live entertainment or catch the big game along with their favorite pub fare at Warehouse 101. Or, relax with our signature martini and special hors d'oeuvre menu in the smoke-free, bayside Whitecaps lounge.

Contact
Lucinda DiNovo

Capacity
Over 14,000 square feet of meeting space. We accommodate groups as small as 10 & as large as 500.

Amenities
- Slots, Blackjack, Craps, Roulette and Poker
- Bayside Hotel
- Waterfront RV Park
- Bayview Dining
- 5 Restaurants
- Indoor Pool and (2) Outdoor Hot Tubs
- Fitness Room
- Arcade
- Business Center
- Over 200 Hotel Rooms
- 8 Waterfront Suites
- 7 Meeting Rooms

Bravo! Member Since 2008

See page 86 under Casinos

www.bravoevent.com

MJCC
MITTLEMAN JEWISH COMMUNITY CENTER

About Mittleman Jewish Community Center

Exceeding your Expectations

Whether you're planning a luncheon for eight, a sit-down dinner for 375, or a team-building event with rock climbing followed by a pool party, the MJCC has everything you need to make your next event or meeting memorable. With our elegantly-renovated ballroom, lobby and café, we've spared no expense to make our event space both gracious and welcoming.

Our in-house caterer will work with you to devise a mouth-watering menu and our friendly and efficient staff will attend to every detail. Our facility also features top-notch sports and fitness facilities (including rock wall, fitness room, swimming pools, gymnasium, indoor soccer, gymnastics, batting cages and much more), classrooms and conference rooms. Come see the best kept secret in Portland!

FIND YOURSELF AT THE J

Bravo! Member Since 2007

Contact
Jordana Levenick

6651 SW Capitol Highway
Portland, Oregon 97219
p. 503.535.3555
f. 503.245.4233
e. Jlevenick@oregonjcc.org

www.oregonjcc.org

Price
Please call for more information

Capacity
Ballroom banquet seating for 375. Capacity varies depending on style. Call for details.

Quick Facts
- Free on-site parking
- State-of-the-art A/V system
- Moveable stage & walls
- Dance floor
- On-site kosher catering
- Podium & Microphones

Photos taken by: LeeAnn Gauthier & Katharine Kimball

PORTLAND'S BEST KEPT SECRET
Open to Everyone. Call today for a tour.

THE STEAKHOUSE

213 SW Clay Street
Portland, Oregon 97201
p. 503.248.2100
f. 503.248.2005
e. cm.mpo@mortons.com
www.mortons.com

Renowned for its signature menu and legendary hospitality, Morton's sets the standard for fine steakhouse dining. Morton's serves only the finest quality foods, featuring USDA prime aged beef, fresh seafood and an award-winning wine list.

The perfect setting for any social or corporate occasion including seminars, launch parties, rehearsal dinners, intimate weddings and anniversary parties with a dedicated Sales Manager to attend to your every need.

Morton's is also the perfect solution for all your morning and day time meeting needs, serving signature breakfast and lunch selections in a refined and elegant private dining space. Our variety of menu options offer items for every palate and any occasion.

Assemble audiences anywhere...all at once! Velocity provides digital access at 72 Morton's locations in 44 markets. Custom broadcasts include high-level production, talk-show style formatting, compelling video arrangement, and expert guests offering insightful, interactive content. Contact our Sales and Marketing Manager for more details.

Contact
Jenna Zak

Price
Varies according to menu selection and size of event

Quick Facts
- Private dining available for groups of 10 to 120 guests
- A personalized menu available for every occasion including breakfast, luncheon, cocktail reception & dinner
- State-of-the-art media suites with audiovisual capabilities & Wi-Fi technology
- All the extras...including floral arrangements, wine tastings & valet service
- Located in the heart of downtown within walking distance of Portland's finest theaters, the riverfront and a short drive from the Arena & Convention Center.
- No room rental fees

WHAT'S NEW
Morton's is pleased to introduce Power Hour! Enjoy 'Bar Bites' for $5 paired with specially priced cocktails starting at just $4, daily from 5pm – 6:30pm and 9pm - close.

www.bravoevent.com

Mt. Hood
bed & breakfast, LLC

8885 Cooper Spur Road
Parkdale, Oregon 97041
p. 541.352.6858
e. mthoodbnb@gorge.net
www.mthoodbnb.com

Enchanting Country Setting With Spectacular Mountain Views

Mt. Hood Bed & Breakfast, LLC has everything you need for your wedding and reception. Situated on the north shoulder of Mt. Hood, the facility offers spectacular panoramic views.

Let your mind rest easy. Our professional staff can take care of your every need. We can move indoors if the weather is inclement.

Our grounds are completely private. This means only your guests and people working on your wedding are allowed on site during your event.

We care about you. Yes, we have done hundreds of weddings but our goal is for you to be our "only client" when we work with you for your wedding and reception.

So please call us and tell us your wants and desires. Let us make your wedding day the way you have always dreamed it should be.

Contact
Rebekah Rice

Price
Available upon request

Capacity
Up to 350

Amenities
- Event site from 2:00 p.m. until 10:00 p.m.
- Four complimentary guest rooms
- Overnight accommodations for 8 persons
- Ceremony & reception site
- Cocktail/appetizer garden
- Twinkle lights in reception area
- Outdoor dance floor
- Bar stations
- Stage for band/DJ
- Restrooms - two indoor/two outdoor
- Parking attendants
- White folding chairs
- Green working B&B farm

WHATS NEW

Voted one of the top 10 most romantic places to get away to.
- Sunset Magazine, Feb. 08

Bravo! Member Since 1997

14040 Highway 35
35 miles South of Hood River
Mt. Hood, Oregon 97041
p. 503.659.1256
p. 800.ski.hood
e. george.evans@skihood.com
www.skihood.com

About Mt. Hood Meadows

Mt. Hood Meadows is located just 65 miles east of Portland on beautiful Mt. Hood. Mt. Hood Meadows has the most diverse skiing and snowboarding in Oregon. Our location and views are breathtaking! When you combine the views with our meeting and event facilities you have the best event site in Oregon. If you want to mix business with pleasure, we also have the finest winter recreation on Mt. Hood.

The Lodge

Our lodge facility is built for groups that enjoy the beauty of the mountains. We are equipped to accommodate groups of all sizes. Our lodge facilities can service groups as small as 25 or as large as 600, our on-hill capacity is much higher. Our professional banquet and catering staff offers an array of delicious menu items and our views offer the perfect atmosphere for a first class event. We also offer group rates on lift tickets, rental equipment, lessons and custom clinics.

Contact
George Evans

Price
$350 – $3,500/room rental; discounts available

Capacity
25 to 600, on hill much more

Amenities
- Tables & chairs provided
- Bar facilities available
- Audio visual equipment available
- Parking ample – sno-park permit required during the winter months
- Activities: downhill & cross-country skiing, snowboarding, hiking & on-snow activities

WHAT'S NEW

The "Uplift Special" provides a lift ticket and catered lunch for groups of 15 or more adults for just $59/each (midweek, non-holiday) when arranged in advance. Those new to the sport in your group receive a beginner's special (beginner lift, lesson and equipment rentals) and lunch!

See page 281 under Recreation, Attractions & Sports

Bravo! Member Since 1990

www.bravoevent.com

PO Box 280
Government Camp, Oregon 97028
p. 503.658.4385
f. 503.272.3554
e. knorton@skibowl.com
www.skibowl.com

Discover Mt. Hood SKIBOWL

With Mt. Hood as the backdrop, encompassed in over 1,000 acres and less than an hours drive from Portland, SKIBOWL provides the perfect setting for any group outing. Whether you have a group of 15 or 5,000 looking to do team building, a corporate retreat, or company picnic, our expert staff will customize an unforgettable yet affordable event. If your looking for a unique and memorable experience for your group — look no further.

Winter Activities

America's Largest Night Ski Area; 65 day runs, 34 night runs, 300 acres of outback terrain, snow tube tow and rentals, adventure park, terrain park, horse drawn sleigh rides, and snowmobile rentals.

Summer Activities

Over 20 mountain adventures offering fun for all ages where you are in control; including bungee trampoline, half-mile dual alpine slide, two scenic sky chairs, interpretive hiking trails, lift-assisted mountain bike park with 40 miles of trails, plus rentals and tours. We offer indy karts, disc and miniature golf, automated batting cages, zipline, free-fall bungee, kiddy jeeps and kiddy canoe rides, an indoor two story 2,400 sq ft play zone and more.

We can customize any package – from no-cost Company Day to closing the facility down exclusively for your company. Our professional and friendly staff knows just what it takes to make your event an unforgettable one.

Contact
Karen Norton

Price
Customized packages to fit any budget

Capacity
Up to 6,000 people (more with off-mountain shuttle)

Facility & Services
- Ample parking and free (east to west) shuttle on weekends
- Two yurts, three day lodges & a historic mid-mountain Warming Hut
- Tented picnic areas offer dining capabilities
- Three full-service host/ no-host bars available
- We customize any package to meet your needs & budget

TYPES OF EVENTS
Company picnics, corporate events, meetings, team building, weddings, private parties, concerts, reunions and graduation parties.

See page 282 under Recreation, Attractions & Sports

Mt. Hood Winery

2882 Van Horn Drive
Hood River, Oregon 97031
p. 541.386.8333
f. 541.387.2578
e. linda@mthoodwinery.com
www.mthoodwinery.com

About Mt. Hood Winery

Mt. Hood Winery is located just 4 miles south of downtown Hood River, off hwy 35. The newly completed facility opened in July of 2009. Situated on 16 acres of vineyard our 2,500 sq. ft. Northwest Lodge style Tasting Room welcomes guests with a 30 ft. oak and walnut marble top bar. The amazing views of Mt. Hood and Mt. Adams create an inviting and relaxed atmosphere.

Mt. Hood Winery is a perfect destination for weddings, rehearsal dinners, receptions and corporate business meetings. If your event needs to be catered, we would be happy to arrange professional food service for you. The staff at Mt. Hood Winery is dedicated to providing exceptional service in making your event a success.

Contact
Linda Barber

Price
$250 to $5,000

Capacity
250

Amenities
- Estate grown and produced award winning wines
- Family Owned Century Farm
- Winery founded in 2002
- Stunning mountain and vineyard views
- Brand new 2,500 sq. foot Tasting Room
- Conference room with surround sound and projection screen for presentations
- Ample parking

See page 334 under Wineries & Custom Labeling

About Old McDonald's Farm, Inc.

Enjoy a fantastic family reunion, birthday party or company picnic at Old McDonald's Farm, Inc. Nestled among 68 acres are our 30+ farm animals, forest, raspberry fields and a trickling stream in the Columbia River Gorge area. Our picturesque Farm is ideal for your special day.

The Farm's amenities include a cozy family sleepover room in the barn, rustic schoolhouse, outdoor fire pit, lovely and historic home, restroom facilities, a garden, a farm store and lots of green space. We are conveniently located just 25 minutes to downtown Portland.

When choosing Old McDonald's Farm, Inc. for your special day, you will also be supporting a local non-profit organization dedicated to providing children in the Portland metropolitan area healthy life experiences utilizing animals, agriculture gardens and natural resources as educational tools.

Contact
Stephanie Rickert

PO Box 326
Corbett, Oregon 97019
p. 503.695.3316
e. omf@oldmcdonaldsfarm.org

Price Range for Service
Varies depending on your needs

Quick Facts
- Beautiful 68-acre, raspberry farm.
- Picturesque location with a creek, fields, forest & off-the road privacy.
- We are located just off the East Historic Columbia River Highway minutes from the Vista House.
- We can accommodate small or large groups.
- See the 30+ farm animals, rope a cow, climb on a tractor, play horseshoes, enjoy the fire pit, shop in the farm store & more.
- Your funds helps us help children as we are a private, non-profit, children's program.

WHAT'S NEW
Horse rides, hayrides, a bar-be-que in our fire pit, u-pick berries and more.

www.bravoevent.com

1945 SE Water Avenue
Portland, Oregon 97214
p. 503.797.4671
e. eventsales@omsi.edu

www.omsi.edu

About OMSI

Featuring breathtaking riverfront views and exciting interactive entertainment, OMSI offers both an elegant dining experience and brain-powered fun. Located on the east bank of the Willamette River near the Oregon Convention Center, the museum features hundreds of exhibits and displays, an OMNIMAX dome theater, a world-class planetarium and a real submarine. Free parking, room to entertain 25-2500 guests, and sustainable food service from our exclusive caterer Bon Appétit makes OMSI your unique event destination.

Availability and Terms

Reservations should be made as soon as possible to ensure availability. A 50% non–refundable deposit of rental charges is due upon signing an agreement. The balance is due five days before your event. Events held among exhibits typically begin after regular museum hours.

Event Enhancements

Add to your party with a private show in the OMNIMAX Theater or Harry C. Kendall Planetarium Try a wild ride on our motion simulator or hop aboard the USS Blueback Submarine for a personalized tour. We encourage live musical entertainment during after-hours events and would be happy to assist you with arrangements.

Catering

Catering provided exclusively by Bon Appétit. Creative menus are based on budget requirements and/or type of food and beverages requested.

Contact
Event Sales

Price
Please call or email for an estimate

Capacity
Up to 2,500 reception-style; 250 to 750 for a banquet; 300 for meetings

Amenities
- Bar Services & skilled servers provided by Bon Appetit
- A variety of linens, china, & tableware to suit any event
- OMSI's Dining Room is ideal for dancing & live entertainment
- 800 parking spaces available free of charge
- Meets all ADA requirements

SPECIAL SERVICES
Our experienced event coordinators will assist you with planning virtually every aspect of your event. Creative menus, outstanding service and close attention to detail will provide you with a magnificent event your guests will remember!

Bravo! Member Since 1995

PO Box 155
879 W Main Street
Silverton, Oregon 97381
p. 503.874.6005
f. 503.874.8200
e. events@oregongarden.org
www.oregongarden.org

About The Oregon Garden

The Oregon Garden is a year-round, 80-acre botanical display garden showcasing water features, garden art, and thousands of plants in more than 20 specialty gardens. These elements provide a beautiful and peaceful setting for any event, from retreats to trade shows.

The Oregon Garden Resort is the newest addition to the property, featuring 102 guest rooms, a restaurant, cocktail lounge, day spa and private event space. The two properties together provide over 18,000 square feet of indoor meeting space with rooms ranging in capacity from 20 to 600 people. We have a variety of outdoor venues as well, which are perfect for meal functions or social gatherings.

One venue of note on the property is the Grand Hall in the J. Frank Schmidt Jr. Pavilion. The Hall features a state of the art sound system, stage lighting and power screen. Situated within the Garden itself, the large windows provide beautiful views of the scenery, and the 9,000 square feet of space give us flexibility for very large scale events, from trade shows to car shows.

Contact
Christine Bradbury
Catering & Conference Services Manager

Price
From $20 to $3,000

Capacity
Up to 600, theater seating for up to 1,000 indoors, with adjacent breakout rooms

Amenities
- 18,000 feet of combined meeting space
- Newly constructed Resort provides guest rooms & amenities for overnight retreats & conferences
- 10 different indoor venues provide flexibility for any size or type of group
- Full-service catering on-site through the Oregon Garden Resort

VISIT US ONLINE
Watch for Resort updates and upcoming events on our website:
www.oregongarden.org

Bravo! Member Since 1995

THE OREGON HISTORICAL SOCIETY
FOUNDED 1898

1200 SW Park Avenue
Portland, Oregon 97205
p. 503.306.5281
f. 503.896.5237
e. events@ohs.org
www.ohs.org

Give your event a place in history!

Located in the South Park blocks of downtown Portland, the Oregon Historical Society is surrounded by culture, history and beauty. The Society offers two indoor and two outdoor venues capable of accommodating a variety of events.

The James F. Miller Pavilion is an ideal location for staging an elegant downtown event with a unique Oregon flare. The adjacent outdoor Plaza can be combined with the Pavilion to create a unique indoor outdoor event.

The Broadway Terrace is the perfect setting for smaller gatherings or as added space for larger events. Surrounded by boxwoods and encompassing a southern view of the Haas Mural, the Terrace truly emotes urban living.

The Madison Room is designed for meetings or lectures of 60 people or less and is the perfect venue for a board meeting, power breakfast or off-site staff retreat. On sunny days, take a break on a private balcony directly off the room.

Contact
Rachael Snow

Price
Based on size of event, please call for pricing

Quick Facts
- Miller Pavilion – 150 banquet style, 250 reception, 160 theater
- Plaza – 150 banquet style, 200 reception, 200 theater, able to be tented
- Broadway Terrace – 60 banquet, 125 reception, 80 theater, able to be tented
- Madison Room – 40 banquet, 100 reception, 60 theater

Bravo! Member Since 2004

WHAT'S NEW
Include exhibit space during your event to create an especially memorable night for your guests.

www.bravoevent.com

40 N State Street
Lake Oswego, Oregon 97034
p. 503.636.4561
f. 503.636.4871
e. kathy@oswegolakehouse.com
www.oswegolakehouse.com

About the Oswego Lake House

Elegant lakeside dining is what you will find at the Oswego Lake House. This historic restaurant is located on State Street in Lake Oswego next to the theater. Our staff of seasoned professionals will provide an effortless event for you, and a memorable experience for your guests. From your first phone call throughout the day of your event you can expect personalized service. Our restaurant is ideal for corporate events, holiday parties and wedding receptions.

The view from our 3,000 sq ft deck is spectacular with the lake as a back drop to a wonderful dining experience. We accommodate quite comfortably 250 guests on the deck for any occasion. The comfortable yet elegant main dining room and adjoining private room with its own bar, also have wonderful views of the lake. Patio includes gas fire pits and heaters, while a fireplace adorns the main dining room.

We understand the success of any event lies greatly in the hands of the staff and simply put, our staff is a cut above. Our entire staff truly looks forward to ensuring the greatness of your event.

Contact
Kathy Krech

Price
Customized by the event, menu choices & services

Capacity
20 to 300

Amentities
- Fireplace
- Cozy lounge
- Private wine lockers
- Three separate bars, including large outdoor bar
- Five decks and patios
- Two firepits
- Stunning views

OFF-SITE CATERING

Consider us for your next event at the location of your choice. Boxed lunches or buffet lunches to go. Light or heavy appetizer platters. Dinner buffets. On-site live cooking (your location). Brunch or breakfast service.

10500 NE Parrett Mountain Road
Newberg, Oregon 97132
p. 503.625.6821
e. contact@parrettmountainfarm.com
www.parrettmountainfarm.com

Where History Happens Everyday

Your special day marks an historic moment in your life. The Parrett Mountain Farm is a Living History Farm located on beautiful Parrett Mountain just twenty five miles southwest of Portland.

Featuring a spectacular panoramic view of Mount Hood, the Farmhouse offers a beautiful setting for both ceremony and reception. For your ceremony, a lovely pergola is set among landscaped gardens and a soothing water pond. A large veranda and manicured lawns provide the perfect space for your reception.

At the Parrett Mountain Farm more than 150 years of history and tradition create a charming backdrop for your special day. Experience traditional crafts and demonstrations all designed to make your day that much more memorable for both the bride and groom and your guests.

On your special day, make history, at the Parrett Mountain Living History Farm.

Contact
Elizabeth Rhode

Price
$2,500 and up
Packages available

Capacity
Up to 200 guests

Amenities
- Historic crafts & demonstrations
- Catering kitchen
- Tables, chairs, linens, & china on site
- Beautiful photo settings
- Bride's and groom's dressing rooms
- ADA accessible
- Clean-up provided
- Full-service catering

Bravo! Member Since 2008

AN HISTORIC SETTING
Surround yourself with the peace and tranquility of this special place. Featuring country charm and urban elegance.

www.bravoevent.com

Portland Community College

12000 SW 49th Avenue
Portland, Oregon 97219
p. 503.977.4316
f. 503.977.4233
e. jsanchez@pcc.edu
www.pcc.edu/events

About Portland Community College Sylvania Campus

The PCC Sylvania Campus is located in Southwest Portland between Lake Oswego and Tigard. The campus rests on a gently sloping hillside, bordered by a forest of Douglas firs, oaks, maples and alders, with breathtaking views of the Tualatin Valley, Bull Mountain and the Oregon Coast Range. Plan your next event in these beautiful collegiate surroundings.

Facilities and Services

Types of events: corporate conferences and business meetings, seminars, banquets, dinners, receptions, holiday parties and any social gatherings. Meeting and banquet facilities (8,800 square feet) can seat up to 350. Conference meeting rooms can seat 10 to 100. Please discuss decorations with coordinator; some restrictions apply.

Contact
Jana Sanchez

Price
Meeting room prices vary depending on the menu selection & size of event

Capacity
Seating up to 350 banquets or events

Amenities
- Full-service, in-house catering
- Beer & wine service available
- China, glassware, linen & napkins included with food & beverage
- Audiovisual at additional cost
- Ample parking, fully accessible facilities

AVAILABILITY

The best opportunity is June 19 - September 14 and December 13 - January 5. Throughout the year space is available Friday, Saturday and Sunday. Depending on the time of year, more meeting spaces may be available, please call.

Bravo! Member Since 2006

33180 Cape Kiwanda Drive
Pacific City, Oregon 97135
p. 503.965.3674
p. 866.571.0581
f. 503.965.0061
e. Events@pelicanbrewery.com
www.pelicanbrewery.com

Located on the oceanfront at the stunning Cape Kiwanda Natural Scenic Area, and only two hours from Portland, the Pelican Pub & Brewery is the perfect place for your special event, meeting, or retreat.

Our banquet room offers privacy for your group without sacrificing the unique personality of the restaurant and its location. The room opens to the sand for beach events or expanded dining and reception areas.

The award-winning kitchen can prepare meals from simple to extravagant, with the ability to customize menus to your taste and whimsy.

Our in-house brewery has won awards all over the world, and can provide these fresh craft beers directly to your event. In addition, great wines and full bar are available.

Our lodging properties, The Inn at Cape Kiwanda, Shorepine Vacation Rentals, and The Cottages at Cape Kiwanda provide first-class accommodations for your group. From luxury boutique hotel rooms to fully furnished vacation homes and oceanfront suites, we have the flexibility to house any group in style and comfort.

Call and let us know how we can make your event as special as it can be!

Contact
Event Coordinator

Price
Varies based on season & menu

Quick Facts
- Award-winning craft brewery on site
- First class kitchen prepares meals from simple to extravagant
- Oceanfront
- Private beach for outdoor events
- Full bar and attentive service
- Flexible overnight accommodations, from hotel rooms to vacation rentals.
- Dedicated event planner

Bravo! Member Since 2008

Country Club

500 SE Butler Road
Gresham, Oregon 97080
p. 503.674.3259
f. 503.667.3885
e. membership@persimmoncc.com
www.persimmoncc.com

Event & Meeting Sites

About Persimmon Country Club

At Persimmon you will discover the atmosphere of a fine country club, one that ensures your event will be a memorable affair. Your guests will enjoy spectacular views of Mt. Hood, and our own impressive 18-hole championship golf course.

For a location as special as your events, let Persimmon Country Club be your host. From the menu, room arrangements, decoration and ambiance, no detail will be overlooked. Whatever your particular needs may be, we are certain you will find Persimmon the perfect choice.

Contact
Tournament & Membership Sales

Price
Seasonal, call for pricing

Capacity
300 for banquets

Quick Facts
- Gresham Chamber of Commerce & POVA member
- 4900 square feet of banquet space
- Spectacular views of Mount Hood
- Complimentary self parking
- Outdoor dining with scenic views
- 30 minutes from downtown Portland

Bravo! Member Since 1995

See page 251 under
Golf Courses & Tournaments

www.bravoevent.com

Event & Meeting Sites

1844 SW Morrison Street
Portland, Oregon 97205
p. 503.553.5523
f. 503.553.5510
e. atolonen@pgepark.com
www.pgepark.com.com

About PGE Park
PGE Park is a multi-use facility on the MAX line located in the heart of downtown Portland

We are available for
- Company parties
- Concerts
- Music festivals
- Sports tournaments
- Cultural events
- Swap meets
- BBQ's
- Graduations
- Anything you can think of!

Contact
Andrea Tolonen

Price
Call for rates

Quick Facts
- Portland's largest outdoor amphitheater
- Portland's largest event venue (100,000-square foot field area)
- Located in the heart of downtown
- Ticket services, concessions & catering available
- Back of the house facilities include dressing/locker rooms, green room, commissaries
- Small Indoor meeting space available (Pavilion Suites)
- In-house sound system, video wall, ample power, field lighting
- Kids games/ activities available (inflatables, volleyball, baseball, football, badminton, tug-o-war, gunny sack races)
- Activity Leaders
- Easy access to the MAX line

Bravo! Member Since 2000

www.bravoevent.com

Pomeroy Farm

Event & Meeting Sites

20902 Lucia Falls Road
Yacolt, Washington 98675
p. 360.686.3537
f. 360.686.8111
e. danielbrink@pomeroyfarm.org
www.pomeroyfarm.org

About Pomeroy Farm

Let the serene and beautiful 677 acre Pomeroy Farm, nestled among towering fir trees and situated on the East Fork of the Lewis River, be the setting for your coming event. Located just 45 minutes North of Portland, this picturesque historic farm offers a memorable venue for your event. Amenities include the newly renovated "Gathering Place", cavernous 1940's bar, 1920's log home, and expansive fields.

The Farm offers colorful seasonal vistas of the remote and beautiful Lucia Valley and the charming herb and flower garden offers an idyllic backdrop for photographs.

Contact
Daniel Brink

Price
$150 - $1,500

Quick Facts
- Can accommodate over 500
- Various indoor & outdoor settings
- Onsite commercial kitchen

www.bravoevent.com

PORTLAND ART MUSEUM

1219 SW Park Avenue
Portland, Oregon 97205
p. 503.276.4291
f. 503.276.4377
e. doug.froman@pam.org
www.portlandartmuseum.org

About the Portland Art Museum

Portland's premier event venue for:

- Weddings
- Meetings
- Fundraisers
- Holiday parties
- Elegant receptions

Mingle with the art in newly-available gallery reception spaces.

Dance under the stars in the city's most sophisticated outdoor courtyard.

Entertain in style in Portland's most glamorous ballrooms.

Location
Our landmark campus is located in the heart of the beautiful downtown Park Blocks, in the midst of the city's cultural district.

Options
Combine an exhibition viewing or gallery tour in conjunction with your event. Choose from a variety of floor plans.

Contact
Portland Art Museum

Price
Prices vary; please call for details

Capacity
The 9,000 square-foot Kridel Grand Ballroom accommodates 560 for a seated dinner & 1,200 for a reception; the 6,100 square-foot Fields Ballroom accommodates 220 for a seated dinner & 400 for a reception.

Amenities
- Rooms fully supported by in-house A/V.
- Exclusive caterer offers full-range catering options including bar, décor, floral, and staffing.

Bravo! Member Since 1992

www.bravoevent.com

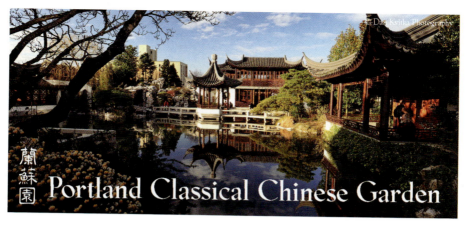

Portland Classical Chinese Garden

Portland's Most Unique Venue

Winding walkways, a bridged lake and open pavilions frame an exquisitely arranged landscape of plants, water, stone, architecture, and poetry. The Garden is the perfect backdrop for any occasion you wish to celebrate.

A heated, two-story Chinese Teahouse is available year round and can accommodate up to 50 guests. Furnished with authentic, artisan Chinese furniture and hanging lanterns it has unsurpassed views of Lake Zither and the Garden. This not-to-be-found-anywhere-else venue offers you and your guests a spectacular event experience.

The Garden and Teahouse can be rented before or after regular public hours. Within walking distance from all downtown hotels and a five minute MAX train ride from the Oregon Convention Center, the Garden is the easy venue for your next private event.

Experienced Garden event staff are available, at no additional cost, to guide, advise and assist as you plan and stage your event. Garden docents are available to mingle with your guests to share history and information about this rare space.

Contact
Gary Wilson & Michele Starry

239 NW Everett
Portland, Oregon 97209

p. 503.228.8131
f. 503.228.7844
e. rental@portlandchinesegarden.org
www.portlandchinesegarden.org

Price
$1,200 - $3,200

Capacity
Up to 300

Amenities
- Exclusive after hour use of the facility
- On-site event management
- Complimentary site visits
- Approved list of caterers to meet your needs
- Chairs (up to 100) available for rent on-site
- Greeter/Security posted at entrance
- Easily accessible via MAX light rail
- ADA accessible

Special rates available for morning events.

www.bravoevent.com

Willamette Star

Portland Spirit

Crystal Dolphin

Portland SPIRIT

The fleet and facilities of the Portland Spirit will provide a unique, memorable experience for your next event. Our knowledgeable sales staff and professional event planners will handle all the details, making your planning process easy and stress-free!

Portland Spirit

Our flagship yacht combines a classic nautical experience with a fine dining atmosphere. One-deck rentals, private charters of the entire vessel and public group reservations are available. Two levels are fully enclosed and climate controlled, each with an independent sound system and baby grand piano. A built-in marble dance floor is available on the Columbia Deck (2nd level). The top Starlight Deck is an open air viewing deck.

Capacity: up to 499 guests
Seating: up to 340 inside, plus outside seating

Willamette Star

Elegance and style has been custom built into the Willamette Star, from its solid cherry wood interior to brass accents and plush carpeting. The Willamette Star has two enclosed, temperature-controlled levels, two outdoor viewing decks, piano and sound system.

Capacity: up to 144 guests
Seating: up to 100 inside, plus outside & lounge seating

Crystal Dolphin

This sleek and luxurious vessel provides a bright, contemporary setting for any event. The Crystal Dolphin features three fully enclosed and climate controlled levels, a grand piano, outdoor viewing decks and sound system.

Capacity: up to 120 guests
Seating: up to 50 inside, plus outside & lounge seating

Bravo! Member Since 1996

Contact
Group & Charter Sales

110 SE Caruthers
Portland, Oregon 97214
p. 503.224.3900
p. 800.224.3901
e. sales@portlandspirit.com
www.portlandspirit.com

Price
Prices vary – please inquire

Vessel Amenities
- In-house catering provided
- Linen tablecloths & napkins provided
- House china, glassware & flatware provided
- Servers & bartender included with food & bar service
- Full service bar available
- Clean-up provided
- Commercial parking & street parking available
- ADA limited with assistance – please call for more information

See page 84 under Boats and 117 under Event & Meeting Sites

www.bravoevent.com

Pumpkin Ridge
GOLF CLUB

12930 Old Pumpkin Ridge Road
North Plains, Oregon 97133
p. 503.647.4747
f. 503.647.2002
e. eventsales@pumpkinridge.com
e. catering@pumpkinridge.com
www.pumpkinridge.com

Events With Elegance & Class

At Pumpkin Ridge Golf Club we pride ourselves on creating memorable, lasting events. Set on the edge of the beautiful Willamette Valley, yet convenient to downtown Portland, our Ghost Creek facility offers a gracious 18,000-sq. ft. clubhouse featuring dramatic architecture and an old Portland flavor. Your guests will delight in views of our two championship courses where golfing legends have made history on numerous occasions. Our Sunset Room is a spacious banquet facility with open beam ceilings, skylights, a generous deck and sweeping golf course views. Our expert event staff promise to deliver culinary expertise and an event that far exceeds your expectations. Whether you're planning an intimate gala or a corporate outing, you can relax knowing you and your guests will enjoy nothing less than perfection.

We suggest early reservations, but can accommodate events on short notice if space is available. A deposit is required; payment in full is due seven days prior to your event.

Contact
Event Sales Department
503.647.2527 or
503.647.2507

Price
Varies according to menu selection

Capacity
Up to 300, plus outside seating

Amenities
- Full-service, in-house catering provided
- Tables & chairs provided up to 300 guests
- Full-service bar provided
- Parquet dance floor available in a variety of sizes
- China, glassware, linens & napkins provided

TYPES OF EVENTS
Weddings, receptions, rehearsal dinners, showers, formal sit-down, buffet, cocktail & hors d'oeuvres, reunions, anniversary parties, corporate business meetings, holiday parties & groomsmen golf outings.

See page 252 under Golf Courses & Tournaments

Bravo! Member Since 1998

Event & Meeting Sites

1441 North McClellan
Portland, Oregon 97217
p. 503.283.3224
f. 503.283.5645
e. queenannevictorianmansion@yahoo.com
www.queenannevictorianmansion.com

A Magical Storybook Place

The Queen Anne staff is very detail oriented and will make sure you and your guests are at ease knowing everything is taken care of start to finish. Easily accessible and very private setting on over two acres, the mansion is a beautiful and perfect location for your event. Built in 1885 by David Cole as a wedding gift for his wife, the mansion is truly a work of art. It features incredible original woodwork, chandeliers and one of the largest private collections of Povey stained glass windows in the world. Call to set up your appointment and allow our staff to dazzle you with a tour of the grounds and mansion. Appointments are made through the week.

Availability and Terms

The mansion is a 6,300-square-foot beautiful Victorian with a 42' round enclosed gazebo. Reserve as early as possible. Reservations have a 90-minute and six-hour time limit per function.

Contact
Event Manager

Price
Rates vary. Please call for specific pricing.

Capacity
Up to 400 seated; 300 reception

Amenities
- Irresistible house catering
- Tables & chairs for up to 400 provided
- Gazebo is a perfect location for dancing
- Completely decorated in Victorian-era antiques, colorful floral garlands & arrangements throughout the home; meticulously landscaped gardens
- Full bar service available
- Plenty of free parking
- All inclusive in house catering

TYPES OF EVENTS
Cocktail parties, corporate meetings, fund-raisers, weddings, receptions, rehearsal dinners, buffets, class reunions, picnics, birthdays, anniversaries, photoshoots and movies.

Bravo! Member Since 1994

RED LION HOTEL ON THE RIVER
JANTZEN BEACH • PORTLAND

909 N Hayden Island Drive
Portland, Oregon 97217
p. 503.283.4466
f. 503.735.4847
e. info@redliniontheriver.com
www.redlion.com/jantzenbeach

Event & Meeting Sites

About Red Lion On The River

Located on the banks of the Columbia River, yet right here in Portland, the Red Lion Hotel on the River offers a truly unique venue providing the ambience of a resort with the convenience of the city. We offer easy access to I-5, just 10 minutes north of downtown and the airport.

Create your perfect event starting with the largest 18,000-square-foot pillar-free ballroom in Portland with floor to ceiling windows showcasing breathtaking views of the river. Our 18 flexible breakout rooms—most with views—offer easy flow and great traffic for tradeshows.

Our reputation for extraordinary cuisine and exceptional service makes us the ideal location for your next event! Your guests will enjoy casual breakfast dining in Shenanigans' Café, and river view lunch or dinner in Shenanigans' Restaurant. After hours, your group can relax in Tuxedo Charley's Lounge.

Docking is available for all Portland area riverboats as well as spacious patios for riverside events. In addition, tours from our float plane dock to see Mt. St. Helens or the Columbia Gorge are available for your guests.

Contact
Catering Department

Price
Call for pricing

Amenities
- 320 guest rooms with private balconies & 24 suites; now 100% non-smoking
- Outdoor pool, spa, fitness room & tennis courts
- 18 flexible meeting rooms
- Over 34,000 square feet of meeting space
- Award-winning convention services & catering staff
- Free wireless high speed Internet access throughout the hotel
- Free parking
- Free airport shuttle
- Restaurants & shopping within walking distance

WHAT'S NEW
Updated public space and guest rooms with private balconies, pillowtop mattresses, refrigerators and microwaves.

Bravo! Member Since 1997

Event & Meeting Sites

RED LION HOTEL
PORTLAND · CONVENTION CENTER

1021 NE Grand Avenue
Portland, Oregon 97232
p. 503.820.4156
f. 503.235.0396
e. janet.kearney@gaha.biz
www.redlion.com/conventioncenter

About Red Lion Hotel Portland Convention Center

Beautiful 173 room hotel, including three suites, centrally located across from the Oregon Convention Center, on the MAX light rail line in fareless square. Over 8,000 square feet of meeting/event space on the 6th floor with beautiful views of OCC, downtown and the west hills. Comfortable café for breakfast, lunch and dinner; room service; lounge with view; marketplace for sundries and snacks; guest laundry; fitness center.

Complete renovation of hotel rooms including bathrooms, meeting space, lobby, café and lounge. Finished in 2009.

Guest rooms include coffee maker, iron and ironing board, refrigerator, hairdryer, dataports, cable television with premium channels and Nintendo. All rooms have one king or two queen beds.

We are the pet-friendliest hotel around! Only $20.00 charge per stay, however, join the Red Lion R&R frequent guest program and your pet stays free!

Contact
Janet Kearney, CMP

Price
Varies according to event

Amenities
- Located adjacent to the Oregon Convention Center, near the Rose Garden. 5 minutes to downtown Portland!

- Recent renovation includes a new bright, contemporary atmosphere in all meeting/event space; guest rooms; lobby & other public spaces.

- Beautiful Windows Skyroom event space with outdoor terrace overlooking the city for up to 250 people. Gorgeous!

- 4,000 square foot Grand Ballroom, completely renovated this year!

- Premier conference suite with executive style seating overlooking the city!

- Pet friendly! Red Lion is the pet-friendliest hotel chain around!

WHAT'S NEW
Renovation....the Red Lion is "brand new again"!

Bravo! Member Since 1997

www.bravoevent.com

3301 Market Street NE
Salem, Oregon 97301
p. 503.370.7888
f. 503.370.9985
e. sales@redlionsalem.com
www.Redlion.com/salem

About The Red Lion - Salem

Expect the unexpected in the "Heart" of the Willamette Valley at the newly renovated Red Lion Hotel Salem. The Hotel is located just off interstate 5 and minutes from downtown Salem, the Oregon State Capitol, Oregon State Fairgrounds and the Woodburn Shopping Outlets. The Red Lion Salem features 148 spacious guest rooms and six executive suites. Groups and guests will also enjoy ample complimentary parking, free high speed wireless internet access, indoor pool, fitness room, dry sauna, 24 hour business center and the Travel Salem Visitor Center onsite in the hotel lobby. While visiting the hotel be sure to leave room to indulge in the flavors of the great Northwest at "Willamette Valley Grill" Restaurant and Lounge, open daily for breakfast, lunch and dinner and providing catering services to the hotel's 10,000 square feet of meeting space which can accommodate up to 600 guests for your next conference or social occasion.

Contact
Sales Manager

Price
$110 - $279

Capacity
148 guest rooms, 10,000 square feet of flexible meeting space

Amenities
New Sealy Pillow top beds, refrigerator & microwave, brand new showerheads, curved shower rods and marble vanities in all guest rooms. Complimentary parking for hotel guests. 100% non-smoking hotel, restaurant and lounge.

Bravo! Member Since 2000

www.bravoevent.com

Event & Meeting Sites

4805 SW 229th Avenue
Aloha, Oregon 97007
p. 503.259.2018
f. 503.848.3425
e. rebecca.bliss@reservegolf.com
www.reservegolf.com

About The Reserve Vineyards and Golf Club

Nestled amongst the grapevines of Oregon's fabulous wine country is a magnificent celebration of golf and pleasure. The Reserve's merger of championship golf and resort-style amenities makes it the region's premier host for group events and meetings from company parties and corporate retreats, to family reunions and wedding receptions. On-site event and catering coordinator make plans and preparations pleasurable and uncomplicated. You choose all the elements that comprise the special character of your meeting or event, and we make it happen.

Catering

The Reserve's in-house catering staff provides a variety of menu options; all dishes are prepared fresh on-site and served with impeccable care. From formal sit-down dinners to casual receptions, the choices encompass BBQs, continental breakfasts, themed buffets and more.

Contact
Rebecca Bliss

Price
Please call for information

Capacity
Harvest Room: 150
Private Dining Room: 20
Board Room: 12
Vintner's Pavilion: 300

Amenities
- Servers, china & glassware, tables & chairs provided as needed
- In-house catering only
- All ADA–accessible
- Ability to host golf tournaments, corporate meetings, wedding-receptions & other social events

EVENT SPACE
The Reserve offers a variety of rooms and spaces to suit your needs. Our most popular, all weather outdoor site is the Vintner's Pavilion, available May through mid-October.

See page 253 under Golf Courses & Tournaments

Bravo! Member Since 1997

www.bravoevent.com

Event & Meeting Sites

5100 NW Neakahnie Avenue
Portland, Oregon 97229
p. 503.645.1115
f. 503.645.1755
e. theclubhouse2@rockcreekcc.com
www.rockcreekcountryclub.com

About Rock Creek Country Club

RCCC offers the finest in professional services, culinary delights, event planning and catering.

Enjoy a classic setting at our clubhouse and impressive 18-hole golf course. Relax and let Rock Creek Country Club insure your event is a memorable affair.

Special Services

Rock Creek Country Club's experienced event planners can assist with all aspects of planning your event, whether at the club or off-premise at your business or facility. Our beautiful park-like setting makes us the perfect choice for your next special event.

RCCC offers extensive full service catering in our clubhouse as well as off-premise catering at your facility or business. Customized menus may be designed to make your event truly memorable.

Contact
Catering Department

Price
Price/fees vary according to menu selection & event size

Capacity
Up to 225 guests in our Banquet Room, Second Floor Banquet Room up to 100, Lower Floor up to 275, Seasonal Pavilion Tent up to 300; Clubhouse Bar & Grill up to 65.

Amenities
- Professional and courteous staff provided to ensure outstanding service
- Full service, licensed bar available
- 10' x 30' dance floor
- 40' X 80' seasonal pavilion tent
- Ample parking available

TYPES OF EVENTS
Golf tournaments, manager retreats, holiday parties, conferences, seminars, auctions, receptions, outdoor and indoor ceremonies and rehearsal dinners.

See page 254 under Golf Courses & Tournaments

Bravo! Member Since 2002

www.bravoevent.com

ROSE QUARTER
Rose Garden * Memorial Coliseum * Rose Quarter Commons

One Center Court, Suite 150
Portland, Oregon 97227
p. 503.797.9705
f. 503.736.2184
e. cathy.walsh@rosequarter.com
www.rosequarter.com

About Rose Quarter
The Rose Quarter Campus features three fabulous facilities: the Rose Garden, Memorial Coliseum and the Rose Quarter Commons.

ROSE GARDEN
The Rose Garden is a 20,000-plus seat arena. Check out the Rose Room for your next meeting. Covered parking brings you just steps away from your meeting.

The Rose Garden's unique acoustic clouds provide the ability to adjust the acoustics to meet your needs. The "Theater of the Clouds" set, with spectacular theater curtains, provides a more intimate setting and can accommodate groups from 1,000 to 6,500.

MEMORIAL COLISEUM
The Memorial Coliseum has an 11,000-plus-seat arena, a 40,000 square foot Exhibit Hall and seven meeting rooms. The "Half House" configuration accommodates groups as small as 1,000.

ROSE QUARTER COMMONS
The Rose Quarter Commons, Portland's largest outdoor plaza, connects the Rose Garden and the Memorial Coliseum and can accommodate everything from open-air concerts with seating for 3,000 to outdoor festival and fairs up to 5,000 people.

Contact
Cathy Walsh

Price
Call or visit our website

Capacity
Up to 20,000

Meeting & Banquet Rooms
Rose Garden:
- Rose Room – 250
- Courtside Club – 140
- Private Dining Room – 40

Memorial Coliseum:
- Georgia Pacific – 350
- Fountain – 80
- US Plywood – 120

DID YOU KNOW?
Need a change of scenery? The Rose Room is a great place for your next meeting.

Bravo! Member Since 1994

www.bravoevent.com

3839 NE Marine Drive
Portland, Oregon 97211
p. 503.288.4444 ext 4108
f. 503.281.6353
www.saltys.com/portland

About Salty's

Salty's exceptional Northwest cuisine, warm hospitality, and spectacular views of the mighty Columbia and majestic Mount Hood will make your event a very special occasion! Only 15 minutes from downtown Portland, Salty's has the perfect recipe for all-day meetings, board meetings, seminars, employee recognition, business breakfasts, dinners, luncheons, buffets, cocktails and hors d'oeuvres for up to 200 guests.

Availability and Terms

We recommend reserving your space three to six months in advance. But if you need assistance with last minute planning – we can help! A deposit is required to reserve your date. Room fees are waived with a minimum purchase of food and beverage.

Description of Facility and Services

We have a variety of table sizes and seating options with house color linens, restaurant silver, china and glassware available at no additional charge. After gratuity, servers are provided at no charge. A/V equipment available to rent. Salty's staff handles clean-up.

Contact
Dorothy Lane

Price
Call for current pricing

Capacity
Up to 200 guests

Amenities
- Full-service catering; in-house
- First floor ADA accessible; Wine Room and North Shore View Room are on second floor
- Plenty of free parking; complimentary valet service
- Full-service bar provided courtesy of Salty's; host/no-host; liquor, beer and wine

SPECIAL SERVICES

Our catering director works closely with you to ensure your event's success. We print a personalized menu for you and your guests. We are happy to refer you to florists, DJs and musicians. At Salty's, we pride ourselves on catering to your every whim.

Bravo! Member Since 1991

www.aplaceforweddingspartiestheatre.com

Scottish Rite Center

709 SW 15th Avenue
Portland, Oregon 97205
p. 503.226.7827
f. 503.223.3562
e. admin@oregonscottishrite.org

About The Scottish Rite Center
Featuring a large ballroom and 587 seat auditorium, the Scottish Rite Center is a unique Northwest landmark. Completed in 1902, this immaculately maintained and updated building has been a part of Portland's social and business fabric for decades.

Location
Situated in downtown Portland, the Scottish Rite Center will make your special occasion a cherished memory for years to come. Conveniently located next to Hotel deLuxe makes it perfect for out of town guests.

Let the beauty of this elegant building add to the grandeur of your event.

Terms
A $100 deposit is required to reserve your date. Payment in full is required two weeks prior to event.

Types of Events
Specializing in weddings, receptions, anniversaries, banquets, dances, proms, corporate and private meetings, graduations, award ceremonies, wine tastings, concerts, reunions and theatre productions.

Contact
Connie Shipley

Price
Varies according to event

Capacity
Up to 300 for seated dinners;
500 for a dance;
587 seat theatre;
Smaller rooms also available

Amenities
- Tables, chairs, set-up & clean-up included in rental
- Convenient street parking & commercial lot parking
- ADA accessible
- Piano, pipe & electric organs, podium, whiteboard & easels available
- TV/VCR, In Focus projector, large screens
- Wi-Fi access
- Air conditioned

KATERING BY KURT
Katering by Kurt, a preferred caterer of the Scottish Rite Center, can provide servers, catering and bar service as well as linens, china, glassware and flatware.

www.bravoevent.com

SEVENTH MOUNTAIN RESORT

18575 SW Century Drive
Bend, Oregon 97702
p. 800.452.6810 (reservations)
p. 541.382.8711
f. 541.382.3475
e. info@seventhmountain.com
www.seventhmountain.com

About Seventh Mountain Resort

Seventh Mountain Resort is in the heart of Central Oregon, on the Deschutes River, one of Oregon's premier whitewater rivers. The Seventh Mountain Resort is the closest lodging to Mt. Bachelor, Oregon's most celebrated ski and snowboard area.

The resort offers 240 condominium units with full kitchens, living areas, fireplaces and private decks.

With 11,000 square feet of meeting space indoors and outdoors, Seventh Mountain Resort can accommodate groups of 10 to 350 for meetings, conferences and retreats. We provide a comfortable natural setting in a relaxing atmosphere with the ability to escape into the Deschutes National Forest.

Seventh Mountain Resort is also a premier location for recreational activities from hiking and biking to horseback riding, we even offer on-site whitewater rafting. And for the golfers in the group, we are located right next door to one of central Oregon's finest golf courses, Widgi Creek.

Contact
Vanessa Berning

Price
Varies; please call

Capacity
Conference center – up to 250; individual breakout room; Mt. Bachelor Events Center – up to 400; outdoors – up to 1000

Amenities
- Closest resort to Mt. Bachelor, on the Deschutes River
- Seasons, serving Pacific Northwest Cuisine, is open seven nights a week
- In-house catering by Season's Restaurant

NEWLY RENOVATED

We just finished a property wide renovation including 100 condos fully renovated, two new restaurants, 11,000 square feet of brand new meeting space, new guest arrivals building, fitness center, two year-round outdoor heated swimming pools and a new children's pool.

See page 291 under Resorts & Retreats

Skamania Lodge
Scenic Columbia River Gorge

1131 SW Skamania Lodge Way
Stevenson, Washington 98648
p. 800.376.9116
p. 800.221.7117
e. slmeetings@destinationhotels.com
www.skamania.com

Contact
Sales Office

Price
Varies on event size & menu selction; call for quote

Capacity
Up to 500 guests

Quick Facts
- 254 newly renovated guest rooms with views; suites & fireplace rooms available
- 23 meeting rooms with 22,000 square feet of IACC approved space
- More than 40,000 square feet of seasonal outdoor venue space
- On-site recreational facilities including an 18-hole golf course
- Waterleaf Spa & Fitness Center, indoor pool, Jacuzzis & dry saunas, outdoor whirlpool & sundeck, hiking trails, tennis & basketball courts & volleyball.

SKAMANIA LODGE
Skamania Lodge is a distinctive experience provided by Destination Hotels & Resorts.

Accommodations

Skamania Lodge, designed to be reminiscent of the great lodges of the early 1900s, has charm and appeal, yet contains all the guest conveniences of a modern resort. The lodge features 254-guest rooms boasting either a peaceful forest or scenic river view. Guestrooms feature original artwork, terrycloth robes, coffee makers, hairdryers, data points hi-speed internet access, Wi-Fi, color televisions with remote control, in-house movies and video games.

Conference Center

Skamania Lodge, a member of the International Association of Conference Centers, offers 23 meeting rooms and more than 22,000 square-feet of dedicated flexible conference and event space, including two ballrooms, accommodating up to 500 people. The Lodge also offers more than 40,000 square feet of outdoor seasonal venue space. Our professional conference planners and full-service business center are on staff to assist you with all of your meeting needs.

Dining

The Cascade Room, a full-service restaurant, reflects a stately, warm atmosphere and features delectable Native Northwest cuisine. On Friday evenings, experience the Gorge Harvest Buffet featuring seafood, a carving station and delicious selection of desserts. And don't forget our fabulous Sunday Champagne Brunch. Dining in the casual ambiance of the River Rock offers a lighter fare menu and lounge. In addition, Skamania Lodge offers a full array of catering opportunities.

Bravo! Member Since 1995

901 SW Salmon Street
Portland, Oregon 97205
p. 503.326.1300
f. 503.326.1301
e. karin.devencenzi@northp.com
www.southparkseafood.com

About Southpark Seafood Grill & Wine Bar

Located downtown in the heart of Portland's cultural district, Southpark Seafood Grill and Wine Bar draws upon the freshest Northwest seafood and produce available to create dishes inspired by the culinary traditions of the Mediterranean. Utilizing fresh local ingredients and the finest imported specialty foods, Southpark serves authentic Mediterranean inspired cuisine in a lively urban setting.

Appreciating the culinary landscape of the Mediterranean regions would be incomplete without pairing the cuisine with the regions' wines. To complement Southpark's menu, the list includes wines from Portugal, Spain, France, Italy and Greece as well as many local wineries from around Oregon and the Pacific Northwest.

Southpark has been recognized by Bon Appetit, Restaurant Hospitality, Santé and Sunset magazines as well as the Oregonian, The New York Times and The Seattle Times for excellence in food and wine and received an award for "America's Best Wine List".

Contact
Karin Devencenzi

Price
Lunch menus starting at $14 and three course dinner menus starting at $35

Quick Facts
- Southpark can accommodate up to 75 people in a restaurant setting
- We have no room rental, set up fees or minimums
- We are happy to put together a custom menu based on your preferences and budget
- Our wine director can select wonderful wines for your menu that will meet your budget needs
- We validate parking after 5:00 p.m. at the Southpark Garage located right next door

Our commitment to sustainable and environmentally friendly practices extends from our farmers and growers to how we reduce, reuse and recycle. In 2008, Southpark earned the Recycle Works award from Oregon's Office of Sustainable Development.

27100 SW Salmon River Highway
Grand Ronde, Oregon 97347
p. 1.800.760.7977 ext. 3914
f. 503.879.6049
e. ashley.langley@spiritmtn.com
www.spiritmountain.com

About Spirit Mountain Casino

Our state-of-the-art Event Center was designed to make your next event perfect, with highly-trained staff to cater to your every whim. We offer all the conveniences necessary to host an intimate gathering of 10 up to a large group of 1,600. With more than **17,200** square feet of conference space for all occasions, we have the expertise and facilities to host your event.

And the entertainment possibilities are endless – we offer 2000 Vegas-style slots, table games, Poker, Keno, Bingo, the exquisite Legends restaurant, Cedar Plank buffet, Raindrops nightclub, Mountain View sports bar and 254 comfortable lodge rooms.

Contact
Ashley Langley

Price
Price varies dependant upon services

Capacity
1,600

Amenities
- 17,200 sq. ft. of conference & meeting space
- Accommodations for groups of 10 to 1,600
- Gold medal chefs full service catering
- Largest buffet in Oregon
- Most diverse gaming options in the Northwest
- Top-name entertainment
- Raindrops Nightclub
- Mountain View Sports Bar
- Summit View Lounge
- Exquisite Legend's Restaurant
- 254 comfortable lodge rooms
- Secure Playworld facility
- Video Arcade
- Free Valet & RV parking
- 24-hour Mini-mart & gas station
- More than 3,600 parking spaces

Bravo! Member Since 1997

www.bravoevent.com

SUNRIVER RESORT

Event & Meeting Sites

57081 Meadow Road
Sunriver, Oregon 97707
p. 541.593.4605
f. 541.593.2742
e. weddings@sunriver-resort.com
www.sunriver-resort.com

About Sunriver Resort

Located near the breathtaking Cascade Mountain range, just 15 miles south of Bend, Oregon, Sunriver Resort offers a unique experience for all ages. A unique Northwest resort destination for all seasons that creates togetherness and memories among families and groups, Sunriver Resort provides unmatched activities and experiences in a serene, natural setting.

With more than 44,000 square feet of flexible meeting and banquet space, guests can choose from a wide variety of flexible indoor space featuring Northwest-style ambiance, or naturally gorgeous outdoor space, including the scenic Bachelor Lawn or the Great Hall Courtyard.

Whether planning a vacation, corporate meeting or a dream wedding, our state-of-the-art meeting facilities combined with the world-class recreation of Sunriver Resort will help execute your distinct vision with unrestricted flexibility and creativity that exceed your expectations.

Contact
Sunriver Catering Office

Price
Varies

Quick Facts
- Experienced professional staff to attend to every need
- Custom weddings
- Wedding packages are available for ease of planning
- Multiple locations, both indoors and out, that can accommodate weddings and groups of all sizes

See page 293 under Resorts & Retreats

www.bravoevent.com

SURFSAND resort
Cannon Beach, Oregon

148 West Gower
Cannon Beach, Oregon 97110
p. 503.436.2274
p. 1.800.797.4666
f. 503.436.2885
e. groups@surfsand.com
www.surfsand.com

Located on the Pacific Ocean shores of Cannon Beach, Oregon, the Surfsand Resort is a premier northwest destination resort featuring spectacular views, unparalleled luxury and world-class amenities.

Rooms and suites, which feature breathtaking views of world famous Haystack Rock and Tillamook Lighthouse, offer the ultimate in comfort. Decorated in subtle earth tones inspired by the grandeur of the Pacific Ocean and nearby coastal forests, each room is carefully designed to enhance each guest's beach experience.

Indulge in the luxury of natural finishes and fine furnishings, including gas fireplaces, flat screen televisions with DVD players, iHome audio systems and wet bars in every room. Special touches include Tempur-Pedic mattresses, custom lighting, tile and wood work. Some rooms feature elegant ocean view jetted tubs, separated from the main room by a sliding shoji screen.

The resort provides stunning views of the rugged coastline for storm watching or enjoying the sunset. Our goal is to make the Surfsand Resort your beachfront home-away-from-home.

Contact
Group Events

Price
Call for pricing

Capacity
Seating for 200 guests

Amenities
- Full-service catering provided by The Wayfarer Restaurant & Lounge
- 32 inch flat-screen LCD televisions in all suites & 15 inch LCD televisions in all bathrooms
- Complimentary high-speed wireless internet
- Seasonal Beachfront Cabana Service
- Pet-free and pet friendly accommodations available

ON SITE FACILITIES
- Heated indoor pool and hot tub
- Comprehensive fitness center that features state-of-the-art workout equipment and cedar-lined saunas
- On-site massage rooms and services

See page 294 under Resorts & Retreats

Bravo! Member Since 1998

1410 S.W. Morrison
Portland, Oregon 97205
p. 503.222.0703
f. 503.243.7147
e. info@tiffanycenter.net
www.tiffanycenter.net
www.rafatiscatering.com

Portland's Premier Event Center

Stunning entrance features local artist's reproduction of Michelangelo's Sistine Chapel, which underscores the historic 1920's elegance of Portland's premier event facility! The Tiffany Center is centrally located in downtown Portland, features expansive ballrooms and cozy foyers together with gilded mirrors, gleaming refinished hardwood floors and emerald green accents which will provide you with an elegant setting for business meetings, fundraisers, auctions, corporate dinners or lavish holiday events! Our experienced, professional staff will provide you with everything you need to ensure that your event is a treasured memory.

Catering is available exclusively by Rafati's Elegance in Catering, prepared onsite in their commercially licensed kitchen. Rafati's full service catering can assist you with your selection of the perfect menu for your event, ranging from brunch to casual or formal reception dinner services, all events are customized to reflect each client's individual taste and style. Personalized menu planning in all price ranges.

Contact
Leslie Best

Price
Call for rental rates

Capacity
From 30 to 1,100; call for specifics

Amenities
- Table & chair set up included in the room rental
- Average six-hour event contract, plus early set up access
- Linens, china, glassware, service staff & bartenders included in catering charges
- Convenient street & commercial lot parking, located on MAX line
- Central air conditioning in the second floor ballroom, spot cooling available on the fourth floor for rental

APPOINTMENTS
Appointments are available Monday – Friday, 10:00 a.m. to 5:00 p.m. After hour and Saturday appointments can be arranged as needed. Please call for appointment.

Bravo! Member Since 1994

www.bravoevent.com

About Timberline Lodge

Timberline Lodge is a year 'round historic lodge on Mt. Hood and considered by many as one of the most unique meeting venues in Oregon. As the "crown jewel" of the Cascades, The Lodge's inspirational art, craftsmanship, warmth and majesty make for memories that you and your attendees will always remember. Great outdoor opportunities available for groups interested in team-building activities.

With 60 rooms on-site as well as luxury condominiums available at The Lodge at Government Camp, you and your attendees can enjoy the convenience of your meetings, meals, reception and overnight accommodations together.

Banquet rooms have massive vaulted ceilings, timber beams, lofts, hand wrought iron, carved wood accents and soaring windows with spectacular views of Mt. Hood, and Mt. Jefferson.

Timberline Lodge is a masterpiece of mountain lodges located at the 6,000 feet level on the south side of Mt. Hood just an hour drive from Portland International Airport. The Lodge has all the amenities and services you would expect from a quality resort with a unique rustic elegance, yet a comfortable feel. In addition to meetings and conferences, Timberline is the perfect place for any special occasion.

Contact
Sales & Catering

Timberline, Oregon 97028
p. 503.272.3251
f. 503.272.3187
e. sales@timberlinelodge.com
www.timberlinelodge.com

Price
Starting at $20 per person

Capacity
Meetings for 10 to 300

Amenities
- One of the Greatest Historic Lodges in America
- Just an hour from Portland & International Airport
- Ullman Hall (2,400 square feet) divisible with patio & mountain views
- Barlow Room (1,500 square feet) with original hewn wood interior
- Raven's Nest (1,100 square feet) with soaring ceilings, view & bar
- Nationally recognized, on-premise food & beverage services. Award winning dining room & NW Wine Vault
- Free WiFi available in all lobbies & private meeting rooms

Bravo! Member Since 1993

Event & Meeting Sites

THE TREASURY

326 SW Broadway Street
Portland, Oregon 97204
p. 503.226.1240
e. events@treasuryballroom.com
www.treasuryballroom.com

About The Treasury Ballroom

The elegant, historic Treasury Ballroom is located conveniently downtown near some of Portland's finest hotels. A grand staircase descends into the Ballroom, which features neo-classical architecture, arches, and floors and columns of Italian marble. The turn-of-the-century bar, restoration light fixtures, stained glass, steel vault door and rich velvet curtains complete the extraordinary and unique atmosphere.

With a seating capacity of 225, The Treasury is ideal for weddings or rehearsal dinners. The Lounge is perfect for bridal preparations, and the Rooftop Terrace is a nice addition to your rental of the Ballroom for a breath of fresh air, an outdoor reception or a view of downtown Portland.

The Board Room

The magnificent Board Room, designed by Pietro Belluschi, features elegant woodwork and backlit stained glass windows. Gold cherubs on the chandelier fly above the large hardwood table and accent the grand marble fireplace.

Contact
Kurt Beadell

Price
Options include all-inclusive packages. Please contact us for a free consultation.

Capacity
Ballroom up to 225;
Board Room up to 25

Amenities
- We offer full event planning services including: customized menu, décor, floral, entertainment & day-of event management.

- Exceptional catering by Vibrant Table Catering & Events allows you to choose from a variety of menus or have one custom created just for your special event.

- Tables, mahogany chiavari chairs, china, linens & glassware are just some of the elements included in your package when you book The Treasury.

TOUR THE TREASURY

Take a virtual tour of The Treasury on the Bravo! website www.bravoevent.com/virtualtours

Bravo! Member Since 2006

www.bravoevent.com

220 A Avenue
Lake Oswego, Oregon 97034
p. 503.697.3383
f. 503.697.3387
e. tucciposta@tucci.biz
www.tucci.biz

About Tucci

Tucci is a family owned Italian restaurant in downtown Lake Oswego. We are celebrated our 5th anniversary, November 2007. We are a local favorite open Monday through Friday for lunch and dinner, Saturday and Sunday for dinner only. We feature live music in our bar on Saturday nights. We recently added the new Bacchus Room that will accommodate up to 24 people for private dining. If additional space is needed, the bar area, which adjoins the Bacchus Room can also be used for private events. The two spaces together can accommodate up to 50 people comfortably, and includes a fireplace.

Contact
Suzie Regan

Price
Dependent on night of the week, if it is buffet style, sit down, etc.

Capacity
Bacchus Room holds up up to 24 people; bar & Bacchus can accomodate up to 50 people

Bravo! Member Since 2007

URBANSTUDIO

Event & Meeting Sites

206 NW 10th Avenue
Portland, Oregon 97209
p. 503.860.0526
e. via@urban-restaurants.com
www.urbanstudiopdx.com

About Urban Studio
Urban Studio is an event facility located in the heart of the trendy Pearl District. Ideal for weddings, corporate events and private parties, Urban Studio is the quintessential contemporary event location. Light and airy, Urban Studio features a sunken banquet room accented in soaring radiant walls of pewter, chocolate brown and pearly white. Guests are first greeted with a slightly raised reception area trimmed in chandeliers, natural stone and large windows that usher in natural light. The 5,000 square-foot space offers a flexible floor plan which can accommodate your guests in a variety of ways such as a stand-up reception, lounge-style cocktail party, or banquet dinner. Our experienced event staff will meet your needs in planning and coordinating the perfect event.

Catering
Pearl Catering, our exclusive in-house full-service caterer, delivers a menu of crowd pleasing favorites richly influenced by Northwest ingredients, beautifully presented and full of flavor!

Types of Events
Weddings, receptions, conferences, reunions, birthdays, holiday parties, fashion shows, dances, fundraisers, art shows, and so much more!

Contact
Via Hersholt

Price
Please call for pricing

Capacity
275 banquet style,
375 cocktail style

Quick Facts
- 5,000 square-feet; flexible floor plan
- Complete audio/visual system; iPod hookup
- Ample parking, with valet service available
- Full service, in-house caterer; built in bar with full bar service
- On the Portland Streetcar line!
- ADA compliant
- Perfect for your holiday party!

WHAT'S NEW?
Space rental is waived with a minimum food and beverage purchase with Pearl Catering. Call for more information 503.860.0203.

See page 46 under Full-Service Catering

VILLAGE LAKE CONFERENCE
| IN FIRST ADDITION |

630 B Avenue
Lake Oswego, Oregon 97034
p. 503.675.1380
f. 503.675.1204
e. denise@bravoportland.com

About Village Lake Conference in First Addition

Located in the First Addition neighborhood of beautiful downtown Lake Oswego, this state-of-the-art conference room is perfect for off-site conferences needing a bright, private and creative space to work. Village Lake Conference is conveniently located to boutiques and is walking distance from Tucci's, Manzana, Five Spice and Zeppos among other fine dining restaurants.

Conference Room

- Flat screen television with DVD and VCR for presentations
- PC monitor plug-in for computer presentations
- Conference table can break apart for small group team building
- Break out areas for team building
- Cable Internet connection for web access
- Phone provided for conference calls
- Easy access to downtown and surrounding areas

Contact
Denise Hall

Price
$75/hour with a two hour minimum

Capacity
Up to 30; conference table seats 20

Types of Events
- Seminars
- Conferences
- Social meetings
- Small receptions
- Business meetings

Amenities & Services
- On-site parking available
- Outside catering welcome
- Available for day, evening or weekend events

LOCATION!
Village Lake Conference Center is located in First Addition - the heart of downtown Lake Oswego.

www.bravoevent.com

13315 NE Airport Way
Portland, Oregon 97230
p. 503.224.0134
www.wildbills.com

About Wild Bill's

Host your next party in our new 2,000 sq ft event space!

Its a great space for:

- Company Parties and Meetings
- Birthday and Anniversary Parties
- Wedding Receptions
- Bar/Bat Mitzvahs
- Graduation Parties
- Charity Fundraising

Our Specialties:

- Casino Nights
- Murder Mystery Dinners
- The Great American Game Show
- A Vegas Wedding in Portland
- And Much More!

Contact

Shannon Walker

The Room Includes:

- 14ft Bar
- Built in Sound System
- Catering Room
- Bartender
- Private Lounge
- Tables & chairs
- Custom lighting
- LED Projector & Screen
- On-Site Free Parking
- Your Caterer or Choose from our Preferred List

See page 28 under Casino & Theme Parties & 265 under Interactive Entertainment

www.bravoevent.com

800 NW 6th Avenue
Portland, Oregon 97209
p. 503.223.0070
f. 503.223.1386
e. candace@wilfsrestaurant.com
www.wilfsrestaurant.com

About Wilfs Restaurant & Bar

Wilfs Restaurant & Bar at Union Station, minutes from downtown, offers a unique, convenient location for all your events: lunch, dinner, meetings, wine tasting, family celebrations, to the perfect wedding! Our catering includes box lunches to a formal sit-down affair.

Easy as 1-2-3

Wilfs offers coordinating services to help unravel the complexities of event planning. Expert staff offers personal service and attention to the details, and Candace, our event coordinator, will create a seamless event. Our experience in asking the "right" questions from the start, assures you, your event for 10 to 1,000, will be effortless.

The Perfect Plan

Our packages are created for your moment. We offer reception-style, sit-down, or a cocktail party atmosphere; either at the restaurant or an event site. We source our ingredients from our NW backyard, creating contemporary cuisine with a classic touch for every palate.

Contact
Candace McDonald

Price
Starting at $15 per person

Quick Facts
- Capacity from 2 to 1,000
- Settings include Union Station Depot Lobby, Rose Garden, entire restaurant.
- Outdoor urban roof top venue over looking the city
- Off-site catering services
- Event coordinator
- Easy parking
- A sustainable company
- Open warehouse setting up to 800

WILF'S RESTAURANT & BAR
- Unique location
- Outdoor urban roof top venue
- Locally grown products from the NW
- Open warehouse setting up to 800

See page 50 under Full-Service Catering

Bravo! Member Since 1992

www.bravoevent.com

Windrose, llc
conference & meeting center

809 West First Street
Newberg, Oregon 97132
p. 503.701.7273
e. lynn@windrosecenter.com
www.windrosecenter.com

About Windrose Conference & Meeting Center

Located just 25 miles from Portland or Salem in the heart of Oregon wine country, Windrose has gorgeous meeting facilities for your corporate retreat, meeting, seminar, training, company or family event, wine tasting, holiday party, dinner, wine and hors d'oeuvre reception, anniversary, or wedding.

Outside boasts a large brick courtyard surrounded by flowers that can seat 70 people and is perfect for outside meetings, weddings, receptions, wine and hors d'oeuvre functions, or to just take a break or have lunch. The smaller courtyard is perfect for smaller groups and has a 3-tiered water fountain and a bar. The back lawn area overlooks the canyon and creek and has an arbor for wedding ceremonies and a small brick patio that is WiFi accessible. **Inside** has the feel of an old English library, with 2 fireplaces, kitchenette, reception area, and meeting space for up to 50 people. We have an *exclusive use policy*, which means we cater to only one group at a time and you have use of the entire facility and grounds, including the loop trail to the creek.

Windrose is available for reservations any day or evening of the week and bookings are confirmed with a deposit and signed agreement. Ample free parking is available in the lot adjacent to Windrose.

Contact
Lynn Weygandt
Owner & Manager

Price
$100 - $1,500, depending on event & size of group

Capacity
50 indoors/70 outdoors

Amenities:
- All A-V equipment is provided at no extra charge: InFocus projector, overhead projector, screen, TV/VCR, flip charts & paper, hi-speed wireless internet, conference call phone, built in music system, & the coffee!

- Price includes all tables & chairs for your function

- 2 outside courtyards full of flowers, one with a 3 tiered water fountain

- Terraced back yard overlooking the canyon & creek that can be used for a wedding ceremony or to just sit & use the free WiFi

- Close to the new Chehalem Glenn Golf Course, Vista Hot Air Balloon rides, Spruce Goose & Evergreen Aviation Museum, & over 100 wineries (20 within a 5 mile radius of Windrose!)

Bravo! Member Since 2005

WORLD FORESTRY CENTER

4033 S.W. Canyon Road
Portland, Oregon 97221
p. 503.488.2101
f. 503.228.4608
e. amorrison@worldforestry.org
www.worldforestry.org

About The World Forestry Center

The World Forestry Center in Washington Park offers one of the most unique and beautiful settings in Portland for your social or business event. The natural warmth of wood tones in Miller and Cheatham Halls create inviting spaces with large, open ceilings. The Mt. Hood Room, our newest meeting space, is located on the second floor of the Discovery Museum with a balcony overlooking Washington Park and Mt. Hood.

Our 10,000 square foot plaza can be enjoyed on a star-studded evening or tented to create an elegant and protected outdoor event. Combined with the Discovery Museum, your event can be the best party of the year giving your guests a fun and memorable experience.

We offer a natural setting with all the modern amenities creating an inviting and relaxed atmosphere. Our extensive preferred caterers' list gives you the opportunity to choose from some of the finest establishments in town for your banquet needs.

Contact
Amber Morrison

Price
Call for pricing

Capacity
250 banquet, 300 reception

Amenities
- Conveniently located in Portland's beautiful Washington Park
- Extensive preferred caterers' list
- Wi-Fi available
- Wide variety of facilities available to rent from small classrooms to large banquet halls

CONVENIENTLY LOCATED

Located only 10 minutes from downtown or right off the Washington Park MAX tunnel stop, the World Forestry Center is conveniently located for both in town and out-of-town guests.

Bravo! Member Since 1999

www.bravoevent.com

Event & Meeting Sites

WORLD TRADE CENTER PORTLAND

Two World Trade Center Portland
25 SW Salmon Street
Portland, Oregon 97204
p. 503.464.8688
f. 503.464.2300
www.wtcpd.com

Make Your Next Event One to Remember
Whether your event is large or small, the World Trade Center Conference Center is the ideal setting. You'll be in the heart of vibrant downtown Portland in one of the city's most elegant and spacious buildings.

Distinctive Urban Elegance
Our beautiful building overlooks the Willamette River and Tom McCall Waterfront Park. Let our award winning architecture and unique meeting space play host to your next event.

In addition to our prestigious location, you'll have a professional and attentive staff eager to fulfill your every need. Special requests and last minute changes are handled efficiently and promptly. Our expert sales managers and banquet staff will anticipate your needs and offer a level of service that will delight you and your guests.

Price
Price varies – please call

Capacity
Varies depending on number of guests, day of the week & season of the year, please call

Amenities
- On-site executive chef with full-service catering
- 11,000 square foot Outdoor Plaza
- Our Mezzanine Level & Sky Bridge Terrace offer views of the city
- 15 conference & meeting rooms
- Hourly rate weekday parking & flat rate evening & weekend parking available in building
- DSL & audioviusal support

Bravo! Member Since 1994

BUSINESS READY
Our facility has DSL plus full audiovisual and electrical support.

www.bravoevent.com

Notes

Event Planners

P.O. Box 28036
Portland, Oregon 97228
p. 503.620.9656
e. info@bellanotte-events.com
www.bellanotte-events.com

No matter what the occasion, your event should be alive with magic and flawlessly executed. Even if you have no idea where to start, we can create an environment that takes your party to another level. Our motto is, 'Let us handle the details so you can entertain'.

Give us the concept, we'll give you an affair to remember.

Choose any or all of the event planning services we have to offer, including:

- Budgeting, contract negotiations rental arrangements, security requirements
- Site selection, meeting space preparation, on-site management
- Travel and lodging arrangements, equipment and product transportation
- Marketing and theming — from menu planning through entertainment
- Guest speakers, entertainment
- Photography or video taping

Contact
Cindy Danbom

Price
Call for quote

Quick Facts
- Recommended and published in Daily Candy, Splendora, Grace Ormond
- Available for Travel, locally and International
- We have been in business for 8 years
- Believe you should enjoy planning your event

WHAT'S NEW
New office in Portland! Yes we are here full time, but also still planning in San Francisco and beyond!

www.bravoevent.com

Event Planners

![Class Act Event Coordinators, Inc. logo]

Portland: 503.295.7890
Salem: 503.371.8904
Lake Oswego: 503.636.1083
Bend: 541.382.1816
f. 503.589.9166
e. events@classactevents.net
www.classactevents.net

About Class Act Event Coordinators, Inc.

Since 1987, Class Act has been designing and coordinating some of the most creative and memorable corporate events in the area. From budgeting to floor plans to entertainment, event management is a demanding job that calls for impeccable taste, exacting attention to detail and a thorough knowledge of available resources.

Class Act eliminates the uncertainty and anxiety related to planning meetings and special events— leaving you free to enjoy the planning process, as well as the event!

"If you are looking for an experienced, creative, professional coordinator who is able to transform an empty space into a true experience, look no further."

– Cynthia J. Sparacio, SPHR, EVP HR and Administration, West Coast Bank

"All of our guests were awed and amazed by our evening – that was in large part due to Class Act's creativity and diligence."

– Shelley Hanson, Director, Spirit Mountain Community Fund

Contact
Class Act Event Coordinators
Price
Custom quote per event
Quick Facts
- Specializing in corporate events, conferences, festivals, tradeshows, auction & non-profit fundraisers, golf tournaments, conventions & more.
- Years of expertise assisting non-profits creating new events and raising the level of existing events.
- We offer a complimentary consultation & would love to talk with you today about your special event!

Professional Membership
- Member ISES (International Special Events Society).
- Member of Oregon Festivals & Events Association.

WE CONTINUE TO GROW!
Now serving Central Oregon Ring: 541.382.1816
Now offering full-service festival event planning

Bravo! Member Since 1998

www.bravoevent.com

We meet all of the benchmarks.

- Creative, affordable, detail oriented
- Professional, experienced coordination
- Full-service event production
- Exceed all client expectations
- Network of savvy local sources

Looking for more?

- Inspired concept development
- Define-the-edge design
- Collaborative planning
- Integrated event management
- Focused logistics management
- National vendor relationships
- Flawless execution

Much More!

Passionate drive to develop exquisite events is the elemental nature of the very fire that defines our work.

Environmental Commitment.

Special attention is given to the "greener" aspects of event stewardship, with an eye towards local and sustainable products.

Contact

Teresa Beck
903 NW Davis Street
Portland, Oregon 97209
p. 503.224.1591
f. 503.224.5953
e. teresa@fireworkseventproductions.com
www.fireworkseventproductions.com

Price
Call For Information

Quick Facts

- All corporate/social events
- Regulatory compliance
- Media & publicity services
- Venue selection
- Menu planning
- Vendor coordination
- Décor design
- Equipment rentals assistance
- Production services
- Theme, concept & branding development
- Entertainment
- Gift services
- Destination management

ROYCE'S PROP SHOP

Event Planners

5406 N. Albina Avenue
Portland, Oregon 97217
p. 503.283.8828
f. 503.283.3651
e. info@propshop.com
www.propshop.com

"The professionalism and integrity of the Prop Shop is unflinching."

Jeffrey A. Blosser
Executive Director,
Oregon Convention Center

Event industry veteran Royce Mason and his dedicated team of professionals at the Prop Shop pride themselves on award-winning event design, décor, production and, most importantly, impeccable customer service.

Royce's Prop Shop is equipped with unparalleled national resources and can produce an extensive range of events, including corporate meetings, conventions, product launches, employee appreciations, educational seminars, team-building experiences, tradeshows, fundraisers, award ceremonies, galas, weddings, festivals, holiday celebrations and picnics.

Memberships include ABC, ACEP, ISES, MPI, and **Green Certified Member** of Travel Portland.

Contact
Royce Mason

Price
Customized to fit your budget

Quick Facts
- Award–winning event design
- Custom props, sets & lighting
- Backdrops, drape, linen & tabletop
- Complete production services
- Catering & entertainment assistance
- Permits, rentals & staffing

AWARDS
- 2007 – 2010 City of Portland Office of Sustainable Development RecycleWorks Award
- 2006 – 2007 MPI Supplier of the Year Award
- 2004 Event Solutions Spotlight Award for Designer of the Year
- 2003 Oregon Restaurant Association Award of Gratitude & Appreciation
- 2002 Bravo! Award for Best Theme Décor

See page 76 under Event Design

Bravo! Member Since 1996

About Successful Creations

Successful Creations has been planning events throughout the U.S. for the past 17 years. Extreme care and meticulous attention to detail are our forte'. We take big picture ideas, combine them with the overall goal of the event and then break the planning process down to smaller steps that are easily achieved. It is our belief that each of these individual elements link together to form an outstanding experience for you and your guests.

Successful Creations is dedicated to assisting organizations and individuals whose work benefits our world. One of the ways we do this is by offering reasonable prices. Another way that we do this is by specializing in Volunteer Management. We regularly work with organizations that rely on volunteer support. Together, our team along with your staff and volunteers create events that are a huge success!

Accolades

"Thank you for making our annual convention such a tremendous success. Each year, you take control of the myriad of details that usually frustrate and overwhelm many unaccustomed to working with the Guild. Your professionalism, meticulous organization, and good humor are tremendously appreciated. What a joy it is to work with you!"

– H. Boghosian, National Lawyers Guild

Successful Creations
p. 503.704.5856
e. HiediSimon@comcast.net
www.SuccessfulCreations.com

Contact
Hiedi Simon

Price
Please call for a complimentary consultation

Comprehensive Event Planning
Including these a la carte services:

- Food & beverage arrangements
- Housing accommodations
- Merchandise & product sales
- On-site coordination
- Registration
- Site Selection & Contract Negotiation
- Speaker and/or musician arrangements
- Virtual communication
- Volunteer management

TYPES OF EVENTS
National, Regional & Local conventions, conferences, retreats, fundraising events, concerts, private and social functions.
You Name It – We Plan It!

Event Professional Organizations

ASSOCIATION OF CATERING & EVENT PROFESSIONALS

About Association of Catering & Event Professionals (A.C.E.P.)

For those of you working in the catering and special events industry, this is the association for you. And if you're planning an event, we can help with that too!

Our Mission Statement

- To identify and give status to the catering and event planning industry as a whole and to represent its desires and best interests to the community at large.
- To promote the exchange of common ideas and solutions.
- To develop a cordial relationship among its members.
- To present the members programs of educational value relating to the catering, event industry and allied businesses.

Member Benefits

Monthly Industry Event with Networking and Educational Opportunities and of course Referrals. There are ten meetings per year with no meeting in August or December. Each meeting is at a different location; either the in-house or a selected caterer provides catering. Each meeting offers educational opportunities consisting of speakers or panel discussions with themes ranging from weddings to sales techniques. Member companies are listed in the annually published Membership Directory an in the www.acep.com website which are widely distributed and a useful resources.

Targeted Event Professional Advertising

Each member may advertise in the monthly newsletter for a low fee per ad per month, or may choose to prepay for the entire year of advertising at a discounted rate.

Bravo! Member Since 2000

Contact
Don Richardson
2010 President

P.O. Box 14233
Portland, Oregon 97292

www.acep.com

Quick Facts
- Great Networking
- Educational Opportunities
- Informational Speakers
- Membership Directory
- Monthly Newsletter
- Includes Web Page
- Community Involvement

www.bravoevent.com

P.O. Box 176
Astoria, Oregon 97103
p. 503.325.6311
p. 800.875.6807
f. 503.325.9767
e. reginawillkie@charter.net

www.oldoregon.com

"Astoria has an edge of the world beauty that wins your heart. A quirky, supernatural aura hovers over it." National Geographic Traveler Magazine, Sept. 2006

The area of Astoria and Warrenton is a nationally significant historic region where the Columbia River meets the mighty Pacific Ocean. Picturesque Astoria is the oldest American settlement west of the Rockies. Visitors have an opportunity to escape into an appealing, intriguing past in a place that takes you back to simpler times. Its architecture is dominated by hundreds of Victorian homes clinging to steep wooded hillsides with a revitalized 1920's era downtown and working waterfront, all set against a backdrop of tremendous natural beauty in the temperate rain forest at the mouth of the Columbia. The area offers several first-class attractions including the Lewis and Clark National Historical Park, Columbia River Maritime Museum, Heritage Museum, Flavel House, Astoria Riverfront Trolley, Astoria Column, Fort Stevens State Park, and beaches for exploring in Warrenton.

Experience the magic.

Contact
Regina Willkie

Price
Varies based on location & event

Capacity
From 10 to 600

Quick Facts
- Meeting spaces vary from a 1920's vaudeville theater to riverfront banquet rooms.

- Unique group activities include a ride on our 1913 trolley, seafood cooking demonstrations, museum tours and more.

- Find handcrafted items made locally, works from local artists, antiques, collectibles, jewelry and vintage apparel.

- The region's booming restaurant scene continues to grow, boasting some of the best cuisine along the Oregon Coast.

- The Chamber of Commerce partners with dedicated professionals to help you plan your memorable event.

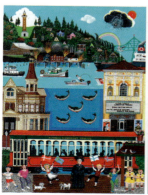

Bravo! Member Since 2001

Event Professional Organizations

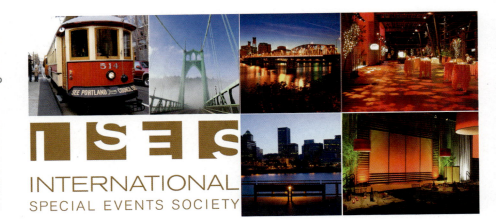

About ISES
The International Special Events Society (ISES) was founded in 1987 to foster enlightened performance through education while promoting ethical conduct.

WHY ISES
The solid peer network ISES provides helps special events professionals produce outstanding results for clients while establishing positive working relationships with other event colleagues.

OUR MISSION
The mission of ISES is to educate, advance, and promote the special events industry and its network of professionals along with related industries.

To that end, ISES members strive to...
Uphold the integrity of the special events profession to the general public through ISES' "Principles of Professional Conduct and Ethics".

Acquire and disseminate useful business information.

Foster a spirit of cooperation among its members and other special events professionals, and...

Cultivate high standards of business practice

Contact
ISES Portland Chapter

e. info@isesportland.com

ISES Membership Benefits
- Distinguish yourself from the competition
- Belong to an international community dedicated to professionalism in special events.
- Network with fellow special event professionals & service providers.
- Benefit from local monthly educational programs.
- Enjoy chapter meetings held in new event venues.
- Monthly event menu courtesy of rotating catering companies.
- ISES International education & recognition programs.
- Certified Special Events Professional program.
- Special Events magazine.
- Esprit! Awards.
- The Special Event & EventWorld annual conferences.

Bravo! Member Since 2001

OREGON CHAPTER MPI

MEETING PROFESSIONALS INTERNATIONAL

Contact: Stephanie Kennedy
p. 503.626.8197
e. info@mpioc.org
www.mpioc.org

The purpose of Meeting Professionals International Oregon Chapter is to provide its membership with quality education, to promote professionalism within the meetings industry and to provide marketplace opportunities to enhance business relationships. Membership is open to all professionals in the meetings industry.

Chapter Meetings: Monthly meetings take place from September to June, with special/social events throughout the year. Meetings are usually held in the Portland metropolitan area. Visit our Calendar of Events for information on our next meeting and educational topic.

- **September 15** – The Nines, Portland, OR, 11:30am
- **October 14** – Oregon Convention Center, Portland OR, 9:00am
- **Nov. 17** – Embassy Suites Portland Airport, Portland OR, 3:00pm
- **Dec. 15** – Hilton Vancouver, Vancouver WA, 11:30am
- **Jan. 19** – Embassy Suites Downtown, Portland OR, 11:30am
- **March 16** – The Allison Inn & Spa, Newberg OR, 3:00pm
- **April 20** – Red Lion on the River, Portland OR, 11:30am
- **May 18** – Location TBA, 9:00am

Annual Regional Cascadia Conference will be held March 7-9, 2010 at the Tualip Resort and Spa in Tualip, Washington. For more information, go to www.mpicascadia.com.

85 meetings per year on average are planned by each MPI Oregon planner. More than 1,200 room nights per year are booked by each MPI Oregon planner. The meetings industry contributes $102.3 billion annually nationwide.

Partnership Opportunities

Does your company want to be in front of more meeting planners and suppliers? Are you interested in sponsoring a monthly meeting? Do you want to have a display at the Speaker Showcase? Would you like to be an elite supplier at a Planner Roundtable? Do you want to advertise on the MPI-OC website? Check out the MPI-OC website – www.mpioc.org – to learn about this year's opportunities and many more with the MPI-OC Partnership Guide. Join Today and Become Part of the Organization that Benefits You…

Quick Facts

- We are approximately 237 members in our chapter.
- We strive to keep the meeting planner/supplier ratio at 50:50.
- The Oregon Chapter is part of the world's largest association of meeting professionals with more than 24,000+ members in 80 countries & 69 chapters globally.
- Membership is open to all professionals in the meeting industry.

Bravo! Member Since 1996

P.O. Box 862
Salem, Oregon 97308
p. 503.378.2497
f. 503.373.1626
e. nancy.a.ahlbin@state.or.us
www.gosgmp.com

About GOSGMP

GOSGMP – is Oregon's local chapter of the Society of Government Meeting Professionals – a nonprofit professional organization specializing in government meeting and conference planning. We are dedicated to improving the knowledge and expertise of individuals in the planning and management of government meetings through education, training, and industry relationships.

Benefits of Membership

GOSGMP encourages and improves communication, understanding and cooperation between meeting planners and suppliers.

GOSGMP expands knowledge and abilities of planners and suppliers through formal educational conferences, workshops, and monthly meetings.

GOSGMP aids planners in locating and evaluating commercial meeting facilities and support services.

GOSGMP provides up-to-date information regarding per diem rates, regulatory policies, and legislative issues which effect state and federal government meetings.

Contact

Nancy Ahlbin

President

Services

- Encourages & improves communication.
- Expands knowledge & abilities of planners & suppliers.
- Aids planners in locating & evaluating commercial meeting facilities.
- Provides up-to-date information regarding per diem rates, regulatory policies & legislative issues.

travel PORTLAND

1000 SW Broadway
Suite 2300
Portland, Oregon 97205

p. 503.275.9750
f. 503.275.9774
e. partnerservices@travelportland.com
www.travelportland.com

About Travel Portland

Travel Portland is Portland's official convention and visitors bureau, reaching millions of visitors each year. Travel Portland's mission is to strengthen the region's economy by marketing the metropolitan Portland region as a preferred destination for meetings, conventions and leisure travel.

In 2008, Portland metro area visitors spent more than $3.8 billion, supporting 30,500 jobs and generating $151 million in state and local tax receipts.

Travel Advice

Travel Portland operates a busy downtown information center at Pioneer Courthouse Square, assisting more than 600,000 visitors annually with recommendations for restaurants, tours, attractions, shopping and more.

Travel Portland partners have the opportunity to display brochures at the Travel Portland Information Center. Additionally, partners can promote their businesses on Travel Portland's website, www.travelportland.com, which receives 510,000 page views a month.

Contact
Marsha Stout, Director of Partner Services

Price
$300 – $2,000

Services
- Travel Portland provides marketing opportunities to help Pacific Northwest businesses reach visitors.
- Travel Portland partners can market their businesses to clients planning conventions or meetings; tour operators; and business and leisure travelers.
- Travel Portland partners with more than 1,000 businesses throughout the metropolitan area, the state of Oregon and the Pacific Northwest.

WHAT'S NEW
For more information on partnering with Travel Portland, call the Partner Services team at 503.275.9750.

Bravo! Member Since 1994

181 High St. SE
Salem, Oregon 97301
p. 503.581.4325
p. 800.874.7012
f. 503.581.4540
e. dmccune@travelsalem.com
www.travelsalem.com

Absolutely Hospitality

Unique venues that meet your exact needs and affordable accommodations. These are just a few reasons Salem should be on your meeting, event, conference, wedding, retreat, reunion 'short list.' We invite you contact us for more information and free planning assistance.

Meeting Facilities

Salem offers an incredible variety of meeting venues, from modern facilities to restored historic sites. The city offers 450,000 square feet of meeting and exhibit space, for groups from 10 to 7,000.

Transportation

Portland International Airport is 50 minutes north of Salem and is serviced by all major airlines. Ground transportation is available and easily coordinated by your travel professional.

Where to Stay

Salem offers more than 1,900 quality guestrooms, from small independent hotels to premier business-class accommodations. Most hotels have meeting facilities, and many offer 'turn-key' service for groups from 10 to 300.

What to Do

Our wineries, rivers, gardens and historic sites offer discoveries at every turn. Golfers will enjoy courses from breathtaking alpine to classic parkland layouts along the Willamette River. Groups can visit our award-winning wineries. And for strolling and shopping, Salem's historic downtown offers a charming mix of stores, galleries, restaurants and parks.

Bravo! Member Since 1999

Contact
Debbie McCune

Price
Complimentary

Quick Facts
- Full Service Destination Marketing Organization.
- Coordination of bid proposals for accommodations, conference and meeting venues.
- Arrange site tours.
- Assist with pre and post tours.
- Provide group services, welcome packets, visitor information tables.

LET US HELP

We'll work as an extension of your team to fashion a meeting that will be absolutely inspired. Travel Salem can help in all aspects of planning including service-related bids, day tours and break-out activities, dining and hotel accommodations, transportation and information packets.

P.O. Box 774
McMinnville, Oregon 97128
p. 503.883.7770
e. info@yamhillvalley.org
www.yamhillvalley.org

About Yamhill Valley Visitors Association

Located in the heart of Oregon's wine country, the Yamhill Valley Visitors Association represents the finest attractions, lodging, dining, wineries, shopping, event facilities and events throughout Yamhill Valley.

Our staff specializes in assisting area guests with itineraries and scheduling. The distinctive beauty of Yamhill Valley will intrigue groups of all sizes.

Yamhill Valley

Yamhill Valley is the home to several unique area festivals: UFO Festival, Carlton's Walk in the Park, Farmer's Markets, Art Walks, McMinnville Wine & Food Classic, International Pinot Noir Celebration and numerous wine events.

The Valley hosts the Evergreen Aviation & Space Museum and the famous "Spruce Goose" in McMinnville and The Allison Inn & Spa in Newberg.

The Yamhill Valley includes: Newberg, Dundee, McMinnville, Amity, Carlton, Yamhill, Lafayette and Sheridan, Dayton & Willamina.

Contact
Dan Shryock

Price
Our services are free. We also have business memberships available:
Supporting Membership: $200/year
Business Membership: $300/year
Sustaining Membership: $1,200/year

Quick Facts
- Yamhill Valley offers the largest concentration of wineries in the state.
- Yamhill Valley is diversified & the experience includes B & B's, fine dining, wineries, breweries, shopping & two of the largest tourist attractions in the state.
- Yamhill Valley Visitors Association provides itineraries for weddings, events, tours & destination travel.
- We represent the top restaurants in the area & are frequently featured in travel magazines.

Bravo! Member Since 2005

Notes

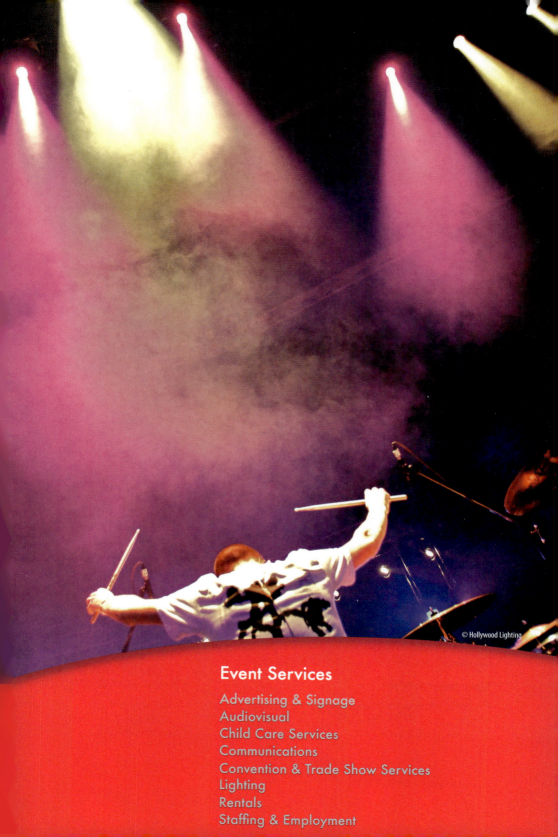

Event Services

Advertising & Signage
Audiovisual
Child Care Services
Communications
Convention & Trade Show Services
Lighting
Rentals
Staffing & Employment

About PosterGarden

Who we are:

Located in the Pearl District of Portland, Oregon, PosterGarden is an innovative, customer-focused leader in the portable trade show and event display products industry. Offering uniquely simple experiences, PosterGarden carries a full line of display products, including retractable banner stands, popup booths, tabletop displays, event tents and flags, and accessories. We also offer a comprehensive suite of graphic design services and pride ourselves on a stellar record of customer satisfaction.

Why we do it:

Thanks to our dedication to customer needs, PosterGarden knows what clients are looking for when it comes to trade show and event displays: simplicity, reliability and impact. Our products are high quality and easy to use, our design and printing services result in bold, colorful displays that catch the eye, and our trained project managers stay involved from a project's start to its finish. So why do we do it? Because we know exactly how.

Where we do what we do:

PosterGarden is located in the Pearl District of Portland, Oregon, at 630 Northwest 14th Avenue, 97209. We are also on the web at www.PosterGarden.com.

More information:

For more information about PosterGarden, please contact us at 1.800.707.0204 or visit us on the web at www.PosterGarden.com.

Contact

Laura Duffey

630 NW 14th Avenue
Portland, Oregon 97209
p. 503.297.9982
f. 503.297.9984
e. sales@PosterGarden.com
www.postergarden.com

Price
$99 – $5,000

Quick Facts

- Full-service creative portable trade show & event display company.
- Complete, easy-to-use display solutions: banner stands, popup displays, flooring, brochure racks, event tents & flags & more!
- PosterGarden specializes in lightweight, portable, easy-to-use displays.
- In-house graphic design services combine creativity and expertise.
- Skilled project managers provide top-notch service & attention to detail.
- We work with your deadline – there is no deadline too late.

Bravo! Member Since 2008

11516 SW Oak Creek Drive
Portland, Oregon 97219
p. 503.245.5300
f. 503.245.3250
e. steve@focalpointdigital.com
www.focalpointdigital.com

Rental Services

FocalPoint Digital provides rental projector services utilizing JVC D-ILA, Sanyo LCD and Sharp DLP technologies because they truly embody our goal of producing vastly superior graphic and video images for corporate and private events. From PowerPoint presentations to life-like High Definition video, JVC D-ILA delivers the best combination of brightness, resolution, contrast and color available anywhere.

For the event planner on a budget, our Sanyo LCD projectors represent the best value and enhanced flexibility solution available in an otherwise commodity rental marketplace. Sharp DLP technology brings great picture quality to a new level of convenience. When only the very best will do, call FocalPoint Digital.

We are poised to take any computer or video production feed from the client, extract every nuance of information and display it on 6 ft. to 30 ft. wide screens, front or rear, with uncompromising clarity and visual impact. We also rent a wide variety of screens, plasma panels and audio support equipment.

Client Benefits

Our company motto, Image is everything has become an axiom that says as much about our clients as the quality of the image itself. When communicating your special message, the back row should not be having difficulty reading the details, nor should the front row be subjected to a highly pixilated, artificial looking image. Better projection equipment is not a luxury. It is a reflection of the clients' reputation.

Unleash your creativity with video solutions from FocalPoint Digital!

Contact
Stephen Smith

Price
$100/day & up

Services
- Largest fleet of video projector rental equipment in the Portland Metro area.
- Video projection & audio support services for corporate & private events.
- High definition video solutions & flat screen plasma panel rentals for the most discriminating enthusiasts.
- A/V technical consulting for event & permanent installation applications.
- Create a large company impression on a small company budget.

"IMAGE IS EVERYTHING"

Our company motto, "Image is everything," has become an axiom that says as much about our clients as the quality of the image itself.

Audiovisual

17325 Banyan Lane
Lake Oswego, Oregon 97034
p. 503.422.3136
f. Call first
e. pj@rbvinc.com
www.reallybigvideo.com

About Really Big Video Inc.

Really Big Video Inc. provides event design, management, A/V equipment rental, production services, and technical labor to transform your ideas into reality. Whatever the size of the venue and number of attendees, Really Big Video handles the technical details to make your event run smoothly.

Really Big Video

Transform your event using gigantic video projection to create energy and excitement. We project directly on walls, floors, and building exteriors to create memorable experiences around your event.

Our Clients View

"A Big Card seemed like the only way to thank you for your Really Big Video projection at our 2009 Wild Splendor event. Wow! The images were so clear and impressive. Our biggest challenge is how to bring the experience of the land to people cooped up in a conference room without windows. The Big Video was the perfect way to do it!"

– Glenn Lamb, Exec. Director, Columbia Land Trust

Contact
Patrick (PJ) Harvey

Price
Varies by project
Call for information

Amenities
- Multi-screen/Widescreen Video Systems
- Large Format Video Projection
- Sound & Lighting Systems
- Graphics & Video Production
- Equipment Rental & Sales
- Technical Labor
- Scenic Design
- Event Staging

Architectural Projection Mapping

With some of the brightest projectors on the market today, we project full motion video directly on the outside of buildings. Using our architectural video mapping system we create content to highlight the features of the buildings exterior to attract attention and drive energy.

Creative Childcare Solutions, Inc.

Professional On-Site Childcare at Your Event or Hotel

p. 503.632.2271
c. 503.819.5554
e. michelle@munchkincare.com

www.munchkincare.com

About Creative Childcare Solutions

Our company provides professional on-site childcare for events and for hotel guests. We are not a nanny agency or babysitting service but a group of professional women who work with children in places like schools, daycare centers, preschools and as social workers. The types of events we have worked at include, but are not limited to, conferences, meetings, holiday parties, wedding ceremonies and receptions, large and small corporate events and for individual families staying in local hotels.

The Venues

We have worked in all the finer hotels in downtown Portland, as well as hotels outside the city limits: Skamania Lodge, Crowne Plaza, McMenamin's, Columbia Gorge Hotel, Timberline Lodge, Resort at the Mountain, Oregon Zoo, and many more. Our clients include 100's of brides and grooms, Nike, Intel, Tektronix, TAPS, Edward Jones, Lewis & Clark Law School, OHSU, Department of Human Services Clackamas County, and many, many more. Check our website for a more complete listing of venues and clients.

Contact
Michelle Davenport

Price
Based on groups' specific needs, call for quote

Services
- On-site childcare provided for your event.
- Individual hotel guest childcare provided for traveling clients.
- Professional, CPR & First Aid trained, criminal background checked caregivers.
- Commercial liability insurance.
- We bring all the necessary supplies to care for the children.
- Online registration available.

LENDING A HAND

We have been asked to provide childcare services for the children under 5-years old attending a very special event in Washington, D.C. every Memorial Day weekend. This group provides support for families who have lost a family member while training for or in a war.

7525 NE Ambassador Place
Suite M
Portland, Oregon 97220
p. 503.232.5600
f. 503.232.5601
e. jeff.Donaca@bearcom.com
www.Bearcom.com

Rental Program

For the times when you need daily, weekly, or monthly use of 2-way radio equipment, BearCom Rental is the answer. With the nation's largest fleet of equipment and the support of our experienced communications engineers, we can exceed your expectations.

Expert Assistance and Support

Along with reliable, quality equipment, you'll get something extra: BearCom's team of experts. We'll listen to your needs and design a system that meets your exact requirements to help your special event or project run smoothly, safely and profitably.

Service Provided

24-hour on-call service and support; our nationwide offices to assist you whenever your next event may be; free programming on our private carrier frequencies or on yours; delivery and pick-up available for a nominal fee. On-site demos available at no charge to determine the requirements per location.

Rental Equipment

BearCom's current inventory consists of over 20,000 portable and mobile radios and a large number of Nextel phones and cellular phones are available.

Contact
Jeff Donaca

Price
Varies based on service & rental

Equipment
- Portable & Mobile Radios
- Nextel 2-way/ Cellular Combination
- Cellular Phones
- Pagers
- Trunking Radios
- Repeaters
- Base Stations

Associations & Memberships
IAEE, MPI, ASAE, IFEA, ADME, TEAMS, NASC, PBA & POVA

ACCESSORIES
- Earpieces
- Radio Chargers
- Surveillance Kits
- Double-Muff Headsets
- Spare Batteries
- Lightweight Headsets
- Speaker Microphones
- Carrying Cases

Bravo! Member Since 2000

Convention & Trade Show Services

3720 NW Yeon Avenue
Portland, Oregon 97210
p. 503.228.6800
f. 503.228.6808
e. mbeyer@dwatradeshow.com
e. thagerup@dwatradeshow.com
www.dwatradeshow.com

Trade Show, Convention and Special Event Contractor

DWA is the leading general contractor in Portland and we have been servicing events in Oregon, Washington and California for over thirty years. Our knowledgeable staff has years of experience and "excellence in customer service" is our goal.

DWA has a large inventory of custom and standard rental items for your event. Our 65,000 square foot warehouse is centrally located in Northwest Portland and is 10 minutes from the Oregon Convention Center, Portland Expo Center, Rose Quarter and many other event facilities.

DWA Offers

- Floor plans & CAD design
- Convention & Trade Show decorating rentals
- Online exhibitor ordering
- Freight handling and storage
- Entrance units & Registration furnishings
- Eco friendly signs & banners

DWA is a proud recipient of Portland's Blue Works Business certification. This program certifies Portland businesses who participate in recycling, waste reduction, and sustainable purchasing practices.

DWA is a member of GMIC, Green Meeting Industry Council, whose mission is "Transforming the global meetings industry through sustainability".

Contact

Marc Beyer – Trade Shows
Tammy Hagerup – Special Events & Graphics

Serving Our Clients

- In business since 1977
- Very knowledgeable staff
- Leading the way in environmental sustainability

WHAT'S NEW

ECO FRIENDLY GRAPHICS!

DWA has invested in the future of our environment with the purchase of Mutoh's ValueJet 1608 hybrid printer which uses Mubio Ink. The ink is composed of 80% plant derived substances and contains no VOCs. The ink has also been recognized by the Environmental Protection Agency's Design for the Environment program. We print directly onto the most environmentally friendly substrates available such as cardboard, Fiberstone and biodegradable foamboards.

Please contact us at signs@dwatradeshow.com for information or quotes.

RecycleWorks Award Winner

Bravo! Member Since 1999

www.bravoevent.com

[**It's one of the thousands of colors we do very well**]

Your next event can leave a lighter footprint on our environment.

Call us at 503-232-9001 to find out about our low-energy event lighting solutions.

www.hollywoodlighting.biz

5251 SE McLoughlin Boulevard
Portland, Oregon 97202
p. 503.232.9001
p. 800.826.9881
f. 503.232.8505
e. production@hollywoodlighting.biz
www.hollywoodlighting.biz

About Hollywood Lighting Services

Hollywood Lighting Services is ready to help you excite, motivate, and inspire your audience! We offer an award-winning design team, a complete line of state-of-the-art lighting equipment, and attentive service throughout your production. We understand what our competitors don't; that effective event lighting is not just about the gear…anyone can rent you a light fixture! What sets Hollywood Lighting apart is our passion for creativity and exceptional service. Unlike "rental" suppliers, we strive to find meaningful ways to add value and quality to your event's objectives. Do you want to imprint your brand in the minds of the attendees? Light your products for the best possible booth ROI? Motivate your team? Transform a plain-jane space into an elegant gala? By utilizing our talented staff of lighting design professionals and the Northwest's widest selection of equipment, we will strive to assist you in creating a memorable event experience.

What's New at Hollywood Lighting

The event industry is becoming "greener." In response, we've added a host of exciting new low-energy light sources to our inventory, as part of our own Green Initiative. As a result, we can now offer a wide range of earth-friendly fixture options—featuring LED and HID technologies—for many of your lighting needs. And you won't have to sacrifice the appearance of your event: You can trust the creative experts at Hollywood Lighting Services to deliver great-looking AND greener lighting solutions every time. Call us at 1.800.826.9881 to find out how your next event can be greener!

Contact
Sales Department

Price
Call for pricing

Trust Us For:
- Stage & scenic lighting
- Digital scenery & projections
- Low-energy lighting alternatives
- On-stage entertainment
- Galas, weddings, & fundraisers
- Corporate events
- Exhibits & product displays
- Grand openings & new product rollouts
- Sporting events
- Festivals
- Branding events

EXPERT EVENT LIGHTING

For over 60 years, Hollywood Lighting has been the Pacific Northwest's trusted leader in event lighting design, production, rentals, and sales. Whether your event is large, small, or in-between; bring your lighting challenges to us!

See Page 82 under Event Design, Production & Décor.

Bravo! Member Since 1999

© Fireworks

15515 SE For Mor Court
Clackamas, Oregon 97015
p. 503.656.9587
f. 503.656.4170
e. info@barclayevents.com
www.barclayevents.com

About Barclay Event Rentals

Barclay Event Rentals is a family owned & operated business that prides itself on quality & unique inventory with outstanding customer service. We want to help make the vision of your special event a reality.

Tents, Tables and Chairs

Our tents and outdoor event decor help to make every event complete. We carry a variety of round, banquet, bistro and specialty tables to accommodate your every need, as well as 8 different chair selections.

Linens

We specialize in table linens. Our inventory in Basic colors, Satins, Satin Crush, Pintuck, Bengaline, Gingham, Organza, Lamour and many other fabrics is unmatched. We also carry chair covers in over 7 colors, Sashes, Table Runners, Aisle Runners, Napkins and Skirting. Custom linen sizes are also available.

China, Glassware, Flatware and Catering Equipment

We have over 8 different styles of china and chargers available. Thirty different glassware options and a variety of beverage service equipment, portable bars, food warmers, serving trays, punch bowls, and many other items.

Decorations

Please call and ask about our large glass vase & centerpiece inventory. Arbors, Columns, Garlands, Silk Trees, Pipe & Drape are just some of the items we carry in stock.

Contact

Linda Barclay
Robyn Franz

Price

Please call or visit our website for more details

Quick Facts

- Delivery, pick up and set up is available for a fee.
- Reservations are recommended.
- Please call with any questions you might have, our staff is happy to assist you.
- New and unique additions help to keep our inventory constantly expanding so bring your ideas.

A Nationwide Rental Furniture Resource for the Event Industry
p. 1.888.CORT.YES (267.8937)
e. dawn.turner@cort.com
www.CORTevents.com

A Fresh Perspective

Remember the first time you toured your favorite event venue? How inspired your were by the new space and the fresh perspective it gave you toward event and meeting planning? Gain a fresh perspective every time with CORT Event Furnishing's visionary product line – quality products that deliver style every time.

Let CORT help you ensure a memorable impact with the right rental furnishings. You can create a mood and personality within an event space that echoes your style and fosters a sense of inspired awe. CORT can help you enhance your image while reinforcing your branding and marketing strategy. Making sure your vision gets through loud and clear – giving your audience a fresh perspective after every event and meeting!

About CORT Event Furnishings

CORT's contemporary product collections provide flexible design options that spark creativity and rouse the imagination. Visit www.CORTevents.com to view our photo gallery and explore our catalog to see the entire CORT Event Furnishings collection. All CORT Event Furnishings products are available for CAD download through the online catalog, or contact a CORT Solutions Expert who will create customized CAD drawings to bring your designs to life.

CORT Event Furnishings is a nationwide provider of high-quality design-oriented rental furniture. Through our trusted solutions experts, we provides 24/7 service to answer the needs of event coordinators, meeting planners, and designers to help create events, meetings, and gala soirees. Get CORT and gain a fresh perspective.

Contact
Dawn Turner

Price
Please call for quote

Types of Events
- Sporting Events
- Movie Sets
- Exhibit or Display Houses
- Hotels
- Universities
- Weddings
- Parties
- Law Firms & Corporate Offices
- Conference Centers
- Convention Centers
- Special Event Facilities
- Corporate Meetings

AWARD WINNING
Event Solutions Spotlight Awards honored CORT with the Rental Company of the Year Award for 2007.

About Honey Bucket

Honey Bucket is the most experienced provider of portable sanitation services to Special Events in the Pacific Northwest. From the largest event with hundreds of units & on-site attendants, to a single unit for a wedding or company picnic, Honey Bucket is the right choice.

We take pride in our professional approach to Special Events. Our Honey Bucket name is "on the line" at each event & we expect attendees to have a pleasant experience when they use our units.

The "Event Planning Guide" on our website will help you determine the proper number of units, based on attendance, the length of the event & sanitary guidelines.

Honey Bucket continually adds new equipment to our extensive inventory & our units offer comfort, excellent design and appearance, & a variety of options. We only use our newest equipment for events.

You can go online to get a quote or information on products, event experience, & upcoming events. Or, you can call our Special Event experts who will be happy to help you with your specific needs.

Experience the CLEAR difference...

Contact

Terry Nelson

1685 McGilchrist Street SE
Salem, Oregon 97301

p. 800.966.2371

www.honeybucket.com

Price

Please call or visit us online for more information

Mention Bravo! for a 5% discount at time of your order

Services

- Experienced provider of portable sanitation services for events in the Pacific Northwest.
- On-site attendants available.
- Committed to providing the best planning, assistance, equipment, services & value.

Bravo! Member Since 2006

VISIT US ONLINE

You can go online to get a quote or information on products, event experience, upcoming events, Honey Bucket "fun stuff" and much, much more at
www.honeybucket.com

www.bravoevent.com

Peter Corvallis Productions
SINCE 1958

2204 N. Clark Avenue
Portland, Oregon 97227
p. 503.222.1664
f. 503.222.1047
e. alanna@petercorvallis.com
www.petercorvallis.com

About Peter Corvallis Productions
Distinguished for its exceptional service, Peter Corvallis Productions has provided quality tradition and experience in the event industry since 1958.

Event Coordination Service
Our event specialists will determine your event needs and apply our years of knowledge and expertise in planning, décor design and event layout. Lighting, sound and projection services are also available to complete your event.

Event Rental Inventory
As a full service event rental company our pledge is to grow our inventory according to our client needs. Visit our 100,000 sq. ft. warehouse to walk the aisles and view the thousands of theme décor items to enhance your next event.

Contact
Alanna Yellowbear

Price
Varies on size of event; call for quote

Rentals and Services
- Tent & canopy rentals
- Party rentals
- Linens & chair covers
- Catering items
- Theme décor
- Audio visual services & rentals
- Tradeshow decorating
- Event planning services

PROVIDES MORE THAN JUST QUALITY PRODUCTS.

Here is a list of rental equipment and the many services we offer to make your function run smoothly so you can enjoy your event along with your guests. Having an event will never be easier.

See page 75 under Event Design

Bravo! Member Since 1994

www.bravoevent.com

About West Coast Event Productions

West Coast Event Productions is the premier event planning, design and rental company servicing the Pacific Northwest and the west coast – from Portland and Seattle to Los Angeles and Las Vegas.

We are an inspired team of event planners, designers and technicians committed to developing innovative solutions for special events. Our comprehensive product line, creative design services and broad range of technical expertise have gained us recognition as one of the top ten event production companies nationwide. With four locations throughout the west coast, our 120,000 square feet of rental inventory consists of the most up-to-date and innovative products that the industry has to offer.

Whether planning a corporate gathering, personal celebration or wedding, you'll find an extensive and innovative range of services and products at your fingertips.

We invite you to come celebrate with us. Cheers!

Contact

Pat Smith
Elizabeth Hermann

1400 NW 15th Ave.
Portland Oregon, 97035

e. elizabeth@wcep.com

www.wcep.com

Price
Varies on service

Quick Facts

- Four locations & 30 years of experience: Portland, Bend, Las Vegas & Seattle.
- Services include: Event & Wedding Consulting, Design & Rentals.
- Over 120,000 square feet of rental inventory: linens, centerpieces & candles, china & glassware, tables & chairs, canopies & tents, staging & dance floors, props & life-size sets.
- Creative Design Services: rendering, fabrication, décor, theme development.
- Technical Services: audio visual, lighting & special effects, rigging & specialty trussing.

See page 77 under Event Design, Production & Décor

Bravo! Member Since 1996

www.bravoevent.com

EMERALD STAFFING
STRATEGIC STAFFING GROUP

About Emerald Staffing

Emerald Staffing is hired by a very unique group of corporations to separate those who excel at what they do from those of average skill. We believe strongly in front end agreements vs. tail end negotiations. Our tenured staff is available for your next project and is only a phone call away.

Your main focus is your business model, and what makes you a success in your marketplace. Let our experts guide you through the recruitment, screening and evaluation process allowing you to focus on mission-critical issues.

Our Commitment

Our entire staff is committed to total client satisfaction. We listen, respond and stand behind you! We value your business and know you will be pleased with our performance. Call today and see for yourself why Top Local and National Companies call Emerald first!

Contact
John Burton, Jr., CPC

101 South State Street
Suite 210F
Lake Oswego, Oregon 97034

p. 503.941.4788
f. 503.941.4799
e. johnjr@emeraldstaffing.com
www.emeraldstaffing.com

Price
Call for price

Quick Facts
- Established in 1978
- Boutique Staffing with Fortune 500 capabilities
- Online Skill Assessment
- Contract, contract-to-hire & direct placement

Bravo! Member Since 1988

Notes

Executive Gifts & Promotional Items

Advantage Graphics
BUSINESS PRINTING | PROMOTIONAL PRODUCTS

17400 SW Upper Boones Ferry Rd.
Portland, Oregon 97224
p. 503.684.2829
f. 503.684.0854
e. michael@advantagegraphics.com
www.advantagegraphics.com

About Advantage Graphics

Founded in 1979, Advantage Graphics is a single source provider of business printing and promotional products. We help companies and organizations develop brand awareness which in turn fosters sales growth, customer retention and employee pride. Our dedicated staff has a simple goal: to exceed our clients' expectations.

Our business printing division offers full service graphics – everything from a single 4-color banner to thousands of postcards that are printed with variable information.

From apparel to yo-yo's, our promotional products division will help make your next event or marketing campaign a resounding success. Our supply chain network includes over 4,300 suppliers, which means we will find the right product for you at the right price. Let our dedicated staff assist you with your next marketing campaign, golf tournament, tradeshow or special event.

Whats New

Go "green" with eco-friendly promotional items, and we're not just talking about recycled paper products. Ask us about bio-degradable pens, biodegradable bags and items made from recycled currency, newspaper, denim & rubber from tires. Even good quality headwear and apparel is now made with recyclable, re-purposed bio-degradable materials as well as corn, bamboo and organic materials.

Contact
Mike Klenz

Price
Please call for pricing

Quick Facts
- Embroidered Apparel
- Executive gifts
- Large format digital printing (banners, tradeshow booths)
- Special Events – tradeshows & golf tournaments

TESTIMONIALS:

"...not only do they provide great customer service, but they are great at suggesting products that always fit within our budget. They always seem to know what I am looking for even when I don't!" – Brent Whittaker, Oregon Golf Association

"Our association with Advantage Graphics has helped us advance the FCP brand name and make great impressions on customers, employees, and key partners with FCP."
– Steve Robinson, Fluid Connector Products, Inc.

"The best part about working with them is their willingness to always listen to my needs, my ideas and my input. For this reason every project we worked on has always come out better than anticipated." – Ryan Kline, Disdero Lumber Co.

Bravo! Member Since 2008

In Great Spirits

Executive Gifts & Promotional Items

2498 NW Schmidt Way, Suite 387
Beaverton, Oregon 97006
p. 503.213.3043
e. Sharona@InGreatSpirits.com
blog: ingreatspirits.wordpress.com
twitter: @ingreatspirits
www.InGreatSpirits.com

Client Appreciation Events

Want to stand out in today's market? Retain your best clients and show them how much you value their business by hosting a tasting for 10 to 100. Structured or free-flowing, this is an excellent way to reward your clients in a relaxed, no-pressure environment.

Corporate Morale-building

Tired of the same old team-building exercises? Strengthen the bonds within your company as you take a break after work to learn a little and laugh a lot. I offer entertaining, educational tastings, on-site or off, for small or large groups. Your "bored" room will never be the same!

In-Home or Venue-Based Private Tastings

These 90-minute events feature sumptuous, catered food and a lineup of wine, whisky, or sake, so you can taste and compare side-by-side. I will personally guide you and your guests as we discover the history, flavors, and charms of your favorite libation.

Contact
Sharona Tsubota

Price
$500 – $2,500

Amenities
- Memorable, customized corporate client appreciation events from 10–100 guests.
- Unique, private, in-home seminars and food pairing events from 6 – 30 guests.
- 13 years' experience sharing my knowledge of wine, whisky and sake.
- Variety of venues from resorts and hotels to restaurants, boardrooms, and private homes.
- No sales of wines or spirits at the events, so there is no pressure to buy anything – your clients just enjoy themselves and learn something.
- Many events feature catered food and crystal glassware.

Ramona's
Gift Baskets & NW Gourmet

p. 503.654.0446
f. 503.652.5929
e. Janelle@ramonasbaskets.com
www.ramonasbaskets.com

About Ramona's

For over 30 years we have delivered a great impression for our clients. Ramona's continues that tradition with our unique collection for gift baskets. Ramona's features award winning Northwest wines, microbrews, cheese, sausage, smoked salmon, fresh fruit, breakfast mixes, pastas, sauces, jams, coffee, tea and…you get the idea. At Ramona's we take great care in creating baskets brimming with gourmet foods and gifts that will be long remembered. We are sweet as can be with many varieties of the finest chocolates, cookies and confections that you have ever tasted. A basket full of delicate soaps, lotions, bubbles and candles can pamper and smooth or welcome a visitor to the northwest. We arrange and decorate each basket to fit the season, occasion and the recipient, and our style is one of a kind. Now and then you find customer service that goes above and beyond, well there's a reason Ramona's has been around for more than 30 years.

Contact
Janelle Meredith

Price
$25 and up

Quick Facts
Our most popular gift baskets:

- Wine Lover's Gourmet
- NW Brew Baskets
- Northwest Best
- Wild About Washington
- Snack Attack!

WHAT'S NEW
Our gifts can be hand delivered in the Vancouver – Greater Portland area or shipped around the world.

www.bravoevent.com

Show and Tell Cookies –
Who Knew Your Logo Tasted So Good!

When planning the next corporate event, trade show, company party, wedding or corporate gift (the possibilities are endless!).

Our custom cookies and favors are a great memento of your special event! We guarantee they will leave a lasting impression on your guests and clients!

We can take any logo, theme or text and put it on a delicious cookie that will stay fresh 2 – 3 weeks. All cookies are individually wrapped in cellophane bags.

Contact
Dawn Fisher

p. 503.699.1017
e. dawn@showandtellcookies.com

www.showandtellcookies.com

Price
$25 per dozen
Four dozen minimum

Quick Facts
- Logo cookies are a huge hit!

www.bravoevent.com

STARGAZER
Baskets & Blooms

9401 SE 32nd Avenue
Portland, Oregon 97222

p. 503.654.0446
f. 503.652.5929
e. shelly@stargazerbaskets.com

www.stargazerbaskets.com

About Stargazer Baskets & Blooms

Stargazer Baskets & Blooms combines the most scrumptious, aromatic and beautiful gourmet edibles, flowers and gifts into occasion-perfect gift baskets.

If we don't love it...the color, the fragrance, the packaging, the taste...you won't find it in our shop.

Each gift is custom made with careful attention to detail. We can create gifts that reflect your style and your brand and we are proficient in making sure that your gift will be remembered long after it was received.

We do all this while keeping your recipient and your budget in mind. All you need to do is give us a ring and one of our Corporate Gifting Consultants would be happy to meet with you to discuss your needs. Bonus! We arrive with yummy samples of our sweet & savory gourmet treats to try.

Contact
Janelle Meredith

Price
We will create within your budget

Quick Facts
We can help with:
- Hotel Amenities
- Corporate Events
- Trade Show Gifts
- Client Appreciation
- Holidays & Celebrations
- Employee Appreciation
- Annual Corporate Meetings
- Fundraisers

WHAT'S NEW
Last year, Stargazer Baskets & Blooms was named one of the Top 100 Gift Basket Companies in the country.

www.bravoevent.com

Golf Courses & Tournaments

10220 SE Causey Avenue
Happy Valley, Oregon 97086
p. 503.698.8616
f. 503.698.8060
e. joe@elventures.com
www.eaglelandingsite.com

Courses
Aerie at Eagle Landing has 27 holes of Executive Par 3 golf. Choose from our lower 9, upper 18 or the full 27 holes. It's a beautiful place to relax and enjoy the benefits of playing a shorter course that is still challenging and fun. It's also a great way to break up the work day by sneaking off for lunch and a quick round of golf. This course is ideal for the amateur golfer who needs a smaller course to learn the fundamentals and the avid golfer who enjoys the challenges of the short game. Eagle Landing also offers 36 holes of Miniature Golf surrounded by waterfalls, a meandering stream and beautiful landscaping. It's truly like no other course around. All of our courses are family friendly and a great location for fun, team building, picnics and parties!

Tournaments
Scramble, Shot-gun, Hole-in-One, you can do it all. Eagle Landing offers a great course where golfers of all skill levels can play in a tournament and have a great time. Whether it's Par 3 or Miniature Golf, tournaments are a great way to network and bring people together. Combine our Tent or ballroom to your golf tournament to create a wonderful event at Eagle Landing Golf Course.

Contact
Corporate Sales

Price
Please call for information

Quick Facts
- Open to the public 7 days a week
- Please call for seasonal hours
- 27 Holes Executive Par 3 Golf
- 36 Holes Miniature Golf
- Tournaments: Scramble, Shot Gun, Hole-in-One
- Club rentals available
- Golf Lessons – Individual, Junior or Group, with our experienced staff
- Nike, Titleist, TaylorMade & more items for sale in our Pro Shop
- Outdoor Tent for entertainment w/your golf event, 1,518 sq. ft.
- Indoor Ballrooms available, 2,453 sq. ft.
- Outdoor Bellevue Gardens, 7,000 sq. ft.

See page 95 under Event Sites

www.bravoevent.com

Golf Courses & Tournaments

CAMAS MEADOWS
GOLF CLUB

4105 NW Camas Meadows Drive
Camas, Washington 98607
p. 360.833.2000
f. 360.834.7075
e. jduce@camasmeadows.com
e. sweishaar@camasmeadows.com
www.camasmeadows.com

About Camas Meadows Golf Club

Camas Meadows Golf Club's par 72, 18-hole Championship Course combines incredible scenery with a unique, challenging design that will satisfy both beginning and accomplished golfers. Designed by architect Andy Raugust, the course has both narrow, tree-lined fairways and open fairways featuring grassy meadows and wetlands. Camas Meadows offers excellent practice facilities that are covered and heated and on-site golf instruction. The Club House is spacious and accommodating and is ideal for golf tournaments, banquets (indoor or outdoor) and meetings. Camas Meadows Golf Club was recently voted by the Portland Business Journal as the "Best Public Golf Course." Camas Meadows Golf Club...golf as nature intended.

Our goal at Camas Meadows Golf Club is to allow you to be a guest at your own event.

Our staff is experienced in handling groups of all sizes.

Contact
Jenny Duce
Stephanie Weishaar

Price
Call for Quotes

Quick Facts
- Professional scoring
- Golf cart with ParView Global positioning system
- GPS leader board
- Official scoreboard
- Driving range balls
- Bag drop services with driveway bag transport service
- Check in tables with linens
- Personalized cart signage & scorecards
- Placement of banners & sponsorship signs
- Roaming beverage carts for entire tournament
- Tees, towels, Camas Meadows ball markers & a divot repair tool in each cart
- Amplified announcement system
- Special tournament pricing for merchandise
- Four complimentary rounds of golf

See page 106 under Event & Meeting Sites

Bravo! Member Since 2007

www.bravoevent.com

LANGDON FARMS
GOLF CLUB

24377 NE Airport Road
Aurora, Oregon 97002
p. 503.678.GOLF (4653)
www.langdonfarms.com

About Langdon Farms Golf Club

Langdon Farms Golf Course is conveniently located 20 minutes south of Portland off I-5. The course is situated on several acres of pristine greens designed from the former farmland of the Langdon Family.

Designed by award winning architects, John Fought and Robert Cupp, the Club shares course architecture traditions with great courses from around the world. A commitment to superior playing conditions and excellent drainage makes Langdon Farms one of the best places to play every day of the year.

Types of Events

Sit-down and buffet dinners, cocktails and hors d'oeuvres, wine tastings, breakfast, lunch and dinner meetings, corporate parties, corporate golf tournaments, fund-raisers, barbeques, reunions, auctions, private parties and retreats.

Contact
Golf Outings
503.678.4734

Non-golf Outings
503.678.4723

Price
Varies on size & type of event

Quick Facts
- Ample FREE parking
- ADA: Fully accessible

Bravo! Member Since 2001

PUBLIC WELCOME
Langdon Farms Golf Club is open to the public. Call the Golf Shop for seasonal rates and to request a tee time.

See page 144 under Event & Meeting Sites

www.bravoevent.com

Golf Courses & Tournaments

About Persimmon Country Club

Our golf course is beautifully maintained to provide excellent play in scenic surroundings, and multiple sets of tees make it fun for golfers of all abilities. We'll also help you plan your food and beverage elements to perfectly complement your golf outing.

Whether you're a seasoned tournament chairperson or this is your first event, we'll help you plan and execute all event details to ensure that you and your participants enjoy a wonderful golf experience.

500 SE Butler Road
Gresham, Oregon 97080
p. 503.674.3233
f. 503.667.3885
e. groupsales@persimmoncc.com
www.persimmoncc.com

Contact
Jerilyn Walker

Price
Please call for pricing

Quick Facts
- Gresham Chamber of Commerce & POVA member
- Spectacular views of Mount Hood
- Complimentary self parking
- 30 minutes from downtown Portland

251

Bravo! Member Since 1995

See page 175 under Event & Meeting Sites

www.bravoevent.com

12930 Old Pumpkin Ridge Rd.
North Plains, Oregon 97133
p. 503.647.4747
e. dylan@pumpkinridge.com
www.pumpkinridge.com

About Pumpkin Ridge Golf Club

At Pumpkin Ridge Golf Club we pride ourselves on creating memorable, lasting events. Set on the edge of the beautiful Willamette Valley, yet convenient to downtown Portland, our Ghost Creek facility offers a gracious 18,000–square feet. clubhouse featuring dramatic architecture and an old Portland flavor. Your guests will delight in playing our championship course where golfing legends have made history.

Our Sunset Room is a spacious banquet facility with open beam ceilings, skylights, a generous deck and sweeping golf course views. Our expert catering and event staff promise to deliver culinary expertise and an event that far exceeds your expectations.

Contact
Dylan Campy

Price
Varies depending on size of tournament

Tournament Services
- Tournament pricing includes 18-hole green fees, carts & range balls.
- Tournaments & golf outings for both tee time & shotgun starts are available on the Ghost Creek Course at Pumpkin Ridge.
- Complete catering packages are available to meet all your needs.

See page 181 under Event & Meeting Sites

Bravo! Member Since 1998

4805 SW 229th Avenue
Aloha, Oregon 97007
p. 503.259.2008
f. 503.848.3825
e. ian.sperling@reservegolf.com
www.reservegolf.com

About The Reserve

The Reserve is a premier location for tournaments of all sizes. The conditioning and playability of the courses, as well as the functional nature of the clubhouse, enables group outings with players of mixed abilities to enjoy the day, whether in competition or playing to raise funds for charitable organizations. A tournament may request consecutive tee times for a group of 12 or more players. A deposit is due with the signed contract, and the remaining balance is due 30 days prior to the tournament. Groups may also purchase the course for a shotgun start; prices are based on a full field of 144 players.

Catering

The Reserve's in-house catering staff provides a variety of menu options; all dishes are prepared fresh on-site and served with impeccable care. From formal sit-down dinners to casual receptions, the choices encompass BBQs, continental breakfasts, box lunches and more.

Contact
Ian Sperling

Price
Please call for information

Quick Facts
- Tournament pricing includes 18-hole green fees, carts, a welcome gift for each player & range balls.
- Other services include golf clinics, group lessons & Swing Solutions analysis.

Bravo! Member Since 1997

See page 186 under Event & Meeting Sites

Golf Courses & Tournaments

5100 NW Neakahnie Avenue
Portland, Oregon 97229
p. 503.645.1115
f. 503.645.1755
e. theclubhouse2@rockcreekcc.com
www.rockcreekcountryclub.com

About Rock Creek Country Club

RCCC offers the finest in professional services, culinary delights, event planning and catering.

Enjoy a classic setting at our clubhouse and impressive 18-hole golf course. Relax and let Rock Creek Country Club ensure your event is a memorable affair.

Special Services

Rock Creek Country Club's experienced event planners can assist with all aspects of planning your event, whether at the club or off-premise at your business or facility. Our beautiful park-like setting makes us the perfect choice for your next special event.

RCCC offers extensive full service catering in our clubhouse as well as off-premise catering at your facility or business. Customized menus may be designed to make your event truly memorable.

Contact
Catering Department

Price
Price/fees vary according to menu selection & event size

Capacity
Up to 225 guests in our Banquet Room, Second Floor Banquet Room up to 100, Lower Floor up to 275, Seasonal Pavilion Tent up to 300; Clubhouse Bar & Grill up to 65.

Amenities
- Professional and courteous staff provided to ensure outstanding service.
- Full service, licensed bar available.
- 10' x 30' dance floor.
- 40' X 80' seasonal pavilion tent.
- Ample parking available.

TYPES OF EVENTS
Golf tournaments, manager retreats, holiday parties, conferences, seminars, auctions, receptions, outdoor and indoor ceremonies and rehearsal dinners.

See page 187 under Event & Meeting Sites

www.bravoevent.com

Skamania Lodge
Scenic Columbia River Gorge

1131 SW Skamania Lodge Way
P.O. Box 189
Stevenson, Washington 98648
p. 509.427.2541
p. 1.800.293.0418
e. skamaniares@destinationhotels.com
www.skamania.com

About the Skamania Lodge Golf Course

Not only will you find acres of breathtaking and tranquil views, you'll discover why our guests come back time and again to enjoy our beautiful Skamania Lodge Golf Course and the Waterleaf Spa & Fitness Center.

Our challenging year-round, 18-hole, par-70 golf course is beautifully tucked into the resort's 175 wooded acres. Our golf services include a driving range, practice bunker, chipping and putting greens. Our course also features a full-service golf shop, cart rentals and PGA Professionals to help assist you with your game.

The tournament schedule at Skamania Lodge Golf Course boasts over a dozen pleasurable, and well organized public golf tournaments a year. In addition, tournaments can be customized for private groups, wedding or special events.

Contact
Skamania Lodge Golf Course

Rates
- Rates vary seasonally
- Rental clubs are available
- Individual and annual golf passes are available

Dining
- Greenside Grille
- River Rock Lounge
- The Cascade Room

Awards & Accolades
- 2008 – 2009 Four Star Award, Best Places to Play Presented by Golf Digest Magazine.
- 2008 Best 25 Family Golf Resorts, Presented by Golf for Women Magazine.

See page 192 under Event & Meeting Sites and 292 under Resorts & Retreats

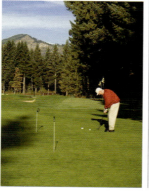

Bravo! Member Since 1995

Notes

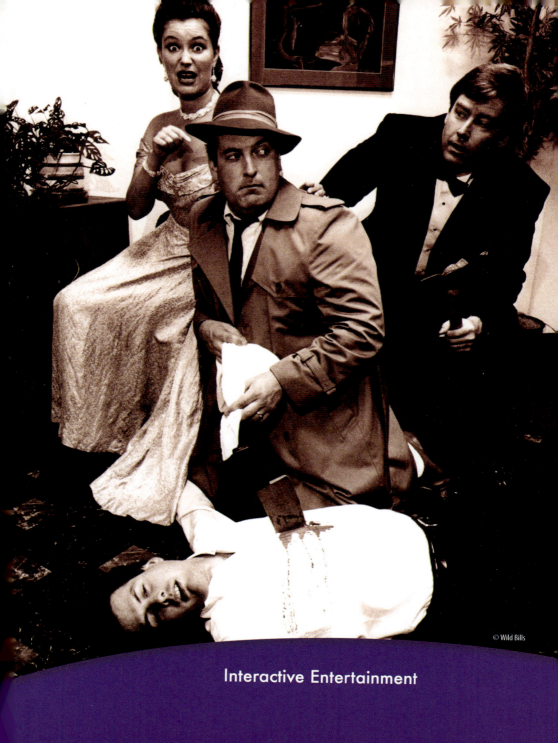

Interactive Entertainment

The Only Call You Need To Make For All Your Event And Entertainment Needs!

Want to create a fun event for your company, staff or customers and don't know where to begin? Call All About Fun! We can take care of all your event planning and entertainment needs with our huge selection of entertainment and event planning services.

Inflatable And Interactive Fun

Giant Slide, Mechanical Bull, Obstacle Course, Baja RC Race Track, Rock Wall, Virtual Reality, Lazer Tag, Sumo Wrestling, Bouncy Boxing, Gladiator Joust, Bungee Run, Cash Cube, Bounce Houses, Dunk Tank, Video Games, Pool Tables, Foosball, Dance Revolution, Air Hockey, Carnival Games, And Much More…

Casino Parties

Everyone loves a chance at "winning big" and "All About Fun" has great casino packages for whatever the occasion; holiday parties, fundraisers, client appreciation parties, managers retreats, grad parties, private parties, birthday parties, reunion events. Whether you're looking for Black Jack, Poker, Craps or Roulette; we have great equipment and professional dealers with lots of personality to make the event more fun.

DJ Services & Live Entertainment Options

Video Karaoke, Disc Jockey, Gameshows, Hypnotist, Comedy Shows, Magician, Tattoo Artist, Caricaturist, Face Painter.

Contact
Jason Hedges
p. 503.516.3878
www.allaboutfun.info

Price
Call for Quotes

Services
- Inflatables
- Interactive fun
- Casino parties
- DJ services
- Live entertainment

CALL "ALL ABOUT FUN!"
We can take care of all your event planning and entertainment needs with our huge selection of entertainment and event planning services.

See page 26 under Casino & Theme Parties and 259 under Interactive Entertainment

All About Fun

When you think Casino Parties, think All About Fun! At All About Fun our main focus is FUN! We want your guests to leave your party with a smile, so we've put together a staff of dealers that will engage your guests, teach them the game and show them how to "WIN BIG" in a FUN way your guests will remember. Whether the game of choice is Black Jack, Craps, Roulette or Texas Hold 'Em Poker, we've got the right mix of casino games for you.

Need a Great Fundraising Idea? The Casino Fundraiser!

If you've seen a drop in donations and need a big boost, host a Casino Fundraiser designed for your organization. A Casino Fundraiser is a great way to bring your donors together and get them excited about supporting your non-profit. We'll show you how you can maximize your receivables and keep your costs down, to make your fundraising event is a huge success.

Casino Parties Are Great For

Corporate mixers, employee appreciation events, birthdays, graduation parties, fundraisers, and holiday parties.

A Casino "Holiday" Party?

You bet! A Casino Party is one of the most popular entertainment choices for large and small holiday events. Whether you're entertaining 70 or 700, All About Fun will put the FUN in your party.

Contact
Jason Hedges

p. 503.516.3878

www.allaboutfun.info

Price
Call for Quotes

Services
- Casino Parties
- Inflatables & interactive games for company picnics.
- Live entertainment including game shows, comedy, hypnosis & magicians.
- Disc Jockeys & other music services.

CALL "ALL ABOUT FUN!"
We can take care of all your event planning and entertainment needs with our huge selection of entertainment and event planning services.

See page 26 under Casino & Theme Parties and 258 under Interactive Entertainment

Barbara Pikus Caricatures
Since 1994

A caricature is a moment in time that you can keep forever

Let me capture the best of who you are as a caricature at your next event. My drawings are always meant to make people feel good, and are a unique addition to any occasion, corporate or private. I can draw anyone, age is no object, from new-born babies to 99 years. I've drawn them all.

Many guests will be fascinated just watching me do my 5 minute drawings. At your next event, as an ice-breaker and inter-active entertainment, please include Barbara Pikus Caricatures.

Praise for Barbara's Caricatures

"Thank you once again for bringing your superb talents to our Company picnic. Our employees truly appreciated you as indicated by the long lines."
– Spirit Boosters, Spirit Mountain Casino

"Thank you so much for being a part of our recognition event at the Portland Art Museum. We received many compliments on your work and it was such a pleasure to have you there!"
– Wells Fargo Recognition Committee

Contact
Barbara Pikus
p. 503.238.4301
e. sketch@involved.com
www.barbarapikuscaricatures.com

Rates
Please call for pricing

Some Clients
- Art Institute of Portland
- Hewlett Packard
- Spirit Mountain Casino
- Sephora USA, Inc.
- Yoshida Group

Corporate & Private Events
- Parties
- Picnics
- Conventions
- Bar/Bat Mitzvahs
- Weddings

CARICATURES
Caricatures that capture the best of who you are.

See page 65 under Entertainers

Bravo! Member Since 2002

The Photo Booth without the Booth.....
Where Every Guest is the STAR at your Party!

Tonight Photo Booth is a mobile photo studio with a modern take on the retro photo booth experience. We take 4 shots 4 seconds apart. Your guests can either HAM IT UP or GLAM IT UP! Instant Prints for **everyone** in the shot. **Unlimited photos and onsite prints.**

Live Photographers: Ensure every shot is a winner.

Photo Souvenirs: The BEST Give Aways at ANY event! On Site Instant Printing allows EVERY GUEST an instant photo print, ensuring your event is memorable.

Creates Party Atmosphere: No more uncomfortable cocktail receptions. Fun and creative.

Instant Video Projection: Incorporate photos into event décor via large projection installations.

Branding: Custom Printed Logo backdrops, brand enhanced photo overlays and photo sleeves.

Themed Events: Printed Theme Photo backdrops and custom tailored prop kits accentuate your event theme. Hollywood and Red Carpet themes are our specialty.

Web Gallery: Public or password protected. All photos are online within 24hrs. Guests are able to download, reprint & share studio quality hi-res images.

Cutting Edge: Hollywood Lighting, and Professional Nikon Cameras.

High Capacity Printing System: Perfect for groups and events from 50-1,500 guests.

Locally Owned and Operated: Husband & Wife Team photograph each event.

PAPARAZZI TONIGHT Photo Booth.....where EVERY Guest is the STAR!
Reservations and Information 503.939.6097
www.paparazzitonight.com • info@paparazzitonight.com

See page 272 under Photobooth

www.bravoevent.com

Party Outfitters

With our unparalleled selection, we have what you need to create lasting memories!

"Your staff were a total joy to work with. They were very knowledgeable about their products, set up, safety and helping assure we were taken care of."

Party Outfitters Certification Program:

Our staff complete a 7-point certification program to ensure you the best possible event.

- Orientation
- Basic Training
- Safety
- CPR/First Aid
- Live Event Mentoring
- Leadership
- Customer Service

When quality, dependability, safety and experience count; call the pros at Party Outfitters.

You Relax. We'll do the work.

Delivered * Insured * L&I Certified * Full Staff

We Deliver Fun!

Call Now......Boost Morale!

Contact

Justin Patenaude

Seattle, Washington
& Portland, Oregon

p. 800.853.5867
f. 360.438.3614
e. justin@partyoutfitters.com

www.partyoutfitters.com

Party Outfitters... Your Corporate Event Specialists

- Company Picnics
- Team Building/Team Bonding
- Holiday Parties
- Tradeshows/Promotion
- Evening Socials
- Annual Conferences/Meetings
- Galas
- Product Launch/Grand Openings

TESTIMONIALS

See what our clients have to say, www.PartyOutfitters.com and click on the link. Updated weekly!

Bravo! Member Since 1996

15521 SE For Mor Court
Clackamas, Oregon 97015
p. 503.723.8300
f. 503.557.6263
e. info@portlandpartyworks.com
www.portlandpartyworks.com

About PartyWorks

PartyWorks has been at the forefront of new entertainment concepts and technologies since 1988. Such experience assures our customers that they are getting the best advice and service possible to guarantee their event is perfect! We are dedicated to bringing premium rides, games, entertainment and attractions to our client's special events, and pride ourselves in carrying one of the largest selections of interactive entertainment in the Northwest. Whether it's a backyard birthday bash or a company picnic for thousands, PartyWorks is your one-stop shop to get the job done right.

From Team Building, company picnics and church and school events, to fairs, festivals and special events, PartyWorks delivers! Our client list includes companies like the Trailblazers, Intel, Precision Castparts, Walt Disney, Nike, and thousands of schools, churches and special events throughout the West Coast!

Check out our website for a complete list of what we can do for you!

Contact
Sales Department

Price
Starting at $100

Services
- Full-service – delivered, staffed, insured.
- No event too large or too small!
- The Northwest's largest inventory of interactive entertainment.
- Activities for all ages.
- Complete event planning services.
- Best price guarantee.
- Additional services: clowns, face painters, DJ's, airbrush tattoos, game show packages, Karaoke, theme decorating and props & catering.

WHAT'S NEW
We've moved into our new 25,000 square foot warehouse in Clackamas, Oregon, and have expanded our inventory even more. Check out our website for all the new additions!

www.bravoevent.com

Interactive Entertainment

7901 SW Nimbus Avenue
Beaverton, Oregon 97008
p. 503.726.2121
f. 503.419.4494
e. sales@teamcasino.net
www.teamcasino.net

Team Casino – *Making Your Party a Winner!*

With Team Casino, you'll work with one experienced event planner from start to finish. We're always happy to meet and share ideas on creating a party your guests will talk about for years to come!

Team Casino's amazing personal service, tournament quality equipment & fun, friendly dealers really make the difference. We make the planning process easy for you, and produce a high-quality, professional atmosphere where anyone and everyone can have a good time!

Team Casino Parties Are Perfect For:

ANYTHING! Corporate events, Customer Appreciation, Conferences, Trade Shows, Company Picnics, Private Parties, Weddings, Birthdays, Anniversaries, Reunions, and of course:

Fundraisers!:

Our Fundraising bookie works personally to create the BEST fundraiser you've ever had.

Contact
Kristina Griffith

Price
Varies by size, date & location. No party too big or small! Always a free & immediate quote.

Quick Facts

- Casino Parties with Custom Funny Money!
- Texas Hold'em Tournaments.
- Night at the Derby Horseracing.
- Giant Screen Wii Tournaments.
- Arcade Games.
- Sports Lounge Games.
- D.J. & Music Services.
- Servicing locations in Oregon, Washington & Idaho.

WHAT'S NEW

Always be in the know! Follow @Team_Casino on Twitter & Facebook!

See page 27 under Casino & Theme Parties

Bravo! Member Since 2008

www.bravoevent.com

Interactive Entertainment

About Wild Bill's

More than 25 years entertaining corporate and non-profit clients with our unique interactive events. Casino nights, poker parties, murder mysteries and game shows are some of the exciting entertainment options available for your group.

Teambuilding

Since 1982, we have been creating custom teambuilding events for our corporate clients. Whether your group is small or large our professional staff is there every step of the way to make sure your event exceeds all expectations!

- Casino Tournaments
- Game Shows
- Murder Mysteries
- Treasure Hunts
- Rally's
- Field Games and races
- Survivor themes

13315 NE Airport Way
Portland, Oregon 97230
p. 503.224.0134
f. 503.224.0278
e. Shannon@wildbills.com
www.wildbills.com

Contact
Shannon Walker

Price
$300 to $30,000

Quick Facts
- Casino Parties
- Poker parties & tournaments
- Murder Mysteries
- Game shows
- Gaming equipment, supply rentals & sales
- 2,000 sq. ft. event space

265

Bravo! Member Since 1995

WHAT'S NEW

For more information please visit our website
www.wildbills.com

See page 28 under Casinos & Theme Parties & Event & Meeting Sites, 203

www.bravoevent.com

Notes

Invitations & Calligraphy

Alesia Zorn
calligraphy

Alesia Zorn Calligraphy
P.O. Box 12651
Portland, Oregon 97212
p. 503.287.3207
e. alesia@alesiazorn.com
www.alesiazorn.com

What our customers say:

"Thanks for your beautiful work on our envelopes. I know our constituents will appreciate it!"
– Andrea Rennie, All Classical 89.9

"Alesia has worked with Sisters Of The Road since 2006, supporting both our Auction with beautiful pieces of her artwork but also our planned giving program. Her work is beautiful, she is remarkably creative, inspired and talented. Further, she is reliable and timely, responding to requests for work with work that is impeccable. Alesia is also very fun to work with, with a great sense of humor, great communication and a warm and welcoming presence."
– Monica Beemer, Executive Director, Sisters Of The Road

"We exclusively refer Alesia to all our custom-invitation clients who desire traditional hand-lettering. She is the best!"
– Cherie Ronning, Uncommon Invites

Contact
Alesia Zorn

Price
Varies upon service requested

Amenities
- Calligrapher since 1996 serving all your hand lettering needs, such as:
- Invitation design
- Envelope addressing
- Name tags
- Certificate design
- Place cards and table markers
- Programs and menus
- Anything else you can dream up!

Bravo! Member Since 1996

WHAT'S NEW
Please visit my website and blog for the latest samples, news and trends

www.bravoevent.com

Uncommon Invites
800.676.3030 • uncommoninvites.com

Uncommon Invites specializes in complete services of custom invitation design to managing RSVPs.

We can create the printed pieces you need for your next company event – whether it is a sales & training meeting, a golf tournament, an employee retreat or a holiday celebration.

- Invitations & announcements
- Event posters & banners
- Holiday cards

We offer streamlined services that enable you to focus on the event and leave the time consuming details to us:

- Addressing & mailing
- RSVP receipt & guest list management
- Seating arrangement & place cards
- Event favors & gift bags

Contact
p. 800.676.3030
e. info@uncommoninvites.com
www.uncommoninvites.com

Price
Varies on product & design, please call for a complimentary consultation

Corporate Clients Include
- Multnomah Athletic Club
- Hybrid Moon Videography
- Embassy Suites
- Bravo! Publications, Inc.
- The Aerie
- The Vancouver Clinic
- The Portia Project
- Soiree
- Blush Bridal Consultation Group
- An Affair to Remember
- BBJ Linen
- The Grand Papery
- Encore Events
- Popp and Co. Catering
- Oregon Bride Magazine
- Dosha Salons

Bravo! Member Since 1992

Notes

Photographers

Photo Booth
Photography
Photography — Flip Book

The Photo Booth without the Booth.....
Where Every Guest is the STAR at your Party!

Paparazzi Tonight Photo Booth is a mobile photo studio with a modern take on the retro photo booth experience. We take 4 shots 4 seconds apart. Your guests can either HAM IT UP or GLAM IT UP! Instant Prints for **everyone** in the shot. **Unlimited photos and onsite prints.**

Live Photographers: Ensure every shot is a winner.

Photo Souvenirs: The BEST Giveaways at ANY event! On Site Instant Printing allows EVERY GUEST an instant photo print, ensuring your event is memorable.

Creates Party Atmosphere: No more uncomfortable cocktail receptions. Fun and creative.

Instant Video Projection: Incorporate photos into event décor via large projection installations.

Branding: Custom Printed Logo backdrops, brand enhanced photo overlays and photo sleeves.

Themed Events: Printed Theme Photo backdrops and custom tailored prop kits accentuate your event theme. Hollywood and Red Carpet themes are our specialty.

Web Gallery: Public or password protected. All photos are online within 24hrs. Guests are able to download, reprint & share studio quality hi-res images.

Cutting Edge: Hollywood Lighting, and Professional Nikon Cameras.

High Capacity Printing System: Perfect for groups and events from 50 – 1,500 guests.

Locally Owned and Operated: Husband & Wife Team photograph each event.

PAPARAZZI TONIGHT Photo Booth.....where EVERY Guest is the STAR!
Reservations and Information 503.939.6097
www.paparazzitonight.com • info@paparazzitonight.com

See page 261 under Interactive

www.bravoevent.com

Aden Photography & Video Productions
503 625-8900

travel PORTLAND

Style

Since 1968, Keith Aden Photography has been serving the greater Portland metro area. Over the years we have built a solid reputation for a professional, assertive and unobtrusive style that blends perfectly with your event. From international sales meetings to conventions, or political luncheons to company picnics, we can deliver the service that you expect. We are very detail–oriented and can tailor our services to fit your budget.

Someone Who Cares

Your choice of a photo or video professional is an important one. It reflects on your reputation as well as your company's reputation. We do not take that lightly! In fact, we put our good reputation on the line every time we take an assignment. And as a former purchasing manager for a national corporation, Keith also understands the needs of business. In short, it is our goal to make everyone look good!

Proud member of the Professional Photographers of America and Travel Portland.

Contact
Keith Aden

P.O. Box 1501
Lake Oswego, Oregon 97035

p. 503.625.8900
p. 877.230.0325
e. keith@adenphoto.com

www.adenphoto.com

Price
Tailored to fit your budget

Services
- Professional photography (digital, 4x5, medium format and 35mm).
- Event photography (digital or film).
- Video production/DVD (Professional 3-chip DV single or multi-camera coverage, non-linear or linear editing suites).
- Aerial photography.
- Brochures & postcards (design, photography & printing).
- Digital imaging services (prof. digital cameras).

PROFESSIONAL SERVICE FOR PROFESSIONAL PEOPLE

See page 325 under Videography

Bravo! Member Since 1990

Party Shots

360.694.6684   ajspartyshots.com

- Hollywood fashion lighting
- Ultra cool looking B&W's
- Everyone gets a copy!
- Live photographer
- Keepsake Coffee Table Album
- Up to 12 guests at a time!

www.bravoevent.com

Photography

275

Bryan Hoybook
photographer

Functional
Affordable
Professional

503.453.5239
bryanhoybook.com

www.bravoevent.com

Fliptography™

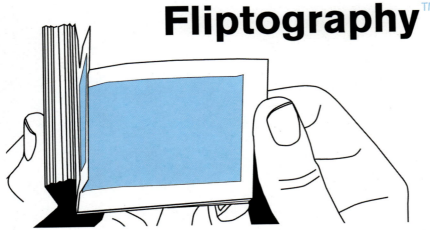

seven seconds of your life in a book™

Flip•to•gra•phy™: dance, get goofy, play-fight or kiss your date in front of a camera for seven seconds. In two minutes, have a 'video' flipbook of your performance in hand—right at your party!

Fliptography™ is a great way to make an event fun: invite your guests to turn a snippet of the party into a pocket-size take-home memory. Corporate clients often add a message or graphics on the cover to make a branded souvenir—quite possibly the coolest promotional item ever.

Fliptography™ has rapidly expanded to a twelve-person team since their Summer '08 debut. Since launch, they've traveled as far as Beverly Hills to help prominent businesses, non-profits and more than a few Fortune 500s stand out from the crowd.

Call today to learn how Fliptography™ can make you the coolest kid in school!

Contact
MJ Petroni
SE Portland Waterfront
p. 503.935.5340
e. 09events@fliptography.com
www.fliptography.net

Price
Starting at $300 per hour

Quick Facts
- Willamette Week "Best of Portland" Winner.
- Live on-site booth can produce over 90 flipbooks per hour.
- Professional custom covers, backdrops and in-book messages available for unique, 'sticky' branding.
- Extensive references, including Fortune 100 clients.
- Studio shots available for save-the-dates and promo products.
- National travel available at affordable rates.

WHAT'S NEW
Fliptography™ just opened a studio near the SE Portland Waterfront to complement their live on-site flipbook booth.

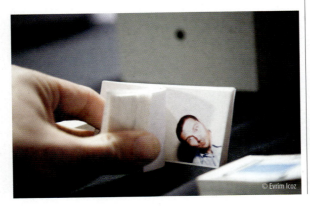
© Evrim Icoz

www.bravoevent.com

© Mt. Hood Meadows

Recreation, Attractions & Sports

Recreation, Attractions & Sports

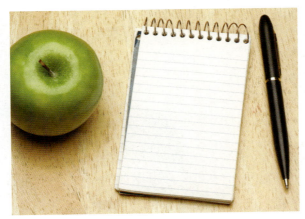

OREGON
sports · fitness · adventure

18120 SW Lower Boones Ferry Road
Tigard, Oregon 97224
p. 503.968.4519
f. 503.624.5497
e. jessica.demonte@clubsports.com
www.clubsports.com/oregon

ClubSport fitness resort is a private sports facility with an array of programs and amenities for individuals and families who are forging a healthy and active lifestyle.

This impressive 150,000 square foot complex offers members a complete range of state-of-the-art circuit training, free weights and cardiovascular equipment. A 5-court gymnasium hosts volleyball, basketball, badminton and the occasional dodge ball tournament. And for those that prefer group fitness, this club offers over 100 classes per week ranging from basic aerobic fitness classes to Zumba. In addition there is an outdoor aquatics center with a resort pool, waterslide, spa and cabana, a six-lane indoor lap pool, four racquetball and two squash courts; a juice bar, restaurant and an 11,000 square foot club-within-a-club for children under the age of 12.

One of the most impressive features of this club is the Rock Gym. It's the largest indoor rock climbing facility in Oregon and frequently used as the site for USCCA competitions. The gym features bouldering areas, as well as top roping and lead climbing routes. Classes are offered for climbers of all abilities with certified climbing instructors who are accomplished outdoor climbers.

ClubSport is ADA accessible.

Contact
Jessica DeMonte
Events Manager

Price
As low as $5.00 per person; call for rates & packages

Quick Facts
- 150,000 sq. ft. multi-purpose sports and fitness facility
- Indoor and outdoor swimming pools
- 45,000 square feet of indoor rock climbing
- 5 full size basketball courts
- Junior activities and on-site childcare
- State-of-the art fitness equipment

Bravo! Member Since 2000

See page 114 under Event & Meeting Sites and 309 under Team Building

www.bravoevent.com

29111 SW Town Center Loop West
Wilsonville, Oregon 97070
p. 503.685.5000
f. 503.685.9694
e. groupsales@fun-center.com
www.fun-center.com

Family Fun Center & Bullwinkle's Restaurant

When it comes to FUN…
we don't "Moose" around!

This amazing 6-acre amusement park is easily accessible off I-5 in Wilsonville, just 18 miles from Downtown Portland. The Family Fun Center & Bullwinkle's Restaurant has something for everyone – and is open year round for ANY event! Let us do all the work – while you take all the credit for your successful Company Picnic, Off-site Meeting or Training, Employee Incentive/Teambuilding Event, Graduation All-Nighter, Church Group Outing, Team Party, Holiday Party, Birthday Party…any event, the possibilities are endless!

Contact the Group Sales office today for your VIP tour of the Fun Park & Event Center. Our experienced Event Planners will assist in making your event the easiest event you've ever planned – and the most fun!

Contact
Special Events Director

Price
Prices vary per package

Capacity
Up to 3,000 people

Amenities
- Six acres of fun for ALL ages!
- Indoor & Outdoor Attractions operate year-round, rain or shine!
- 4,000 sq. ft. of Event Space/Meeting Rooms.
- Bullwinkle's Family Restaurant on-site.
- Great location for Company Picnics.
- Experienced Event Planners We put the pieces together for you!

ATTRACTIONS
- Go-Karts
- Lazer Tag
- Miniature Golf
- 28' Rock Wall
- Bumper Boats
- Batting Cages
- Sling Shot Bungee
- Max Flight Cyber Coaster
- Over 150 Arcade Games

See page 127 under
Event & Meeting Sites

Bravo! Member Since 1998

www.bravoevent.com

GRAPE ESCAPE
WINERY TOURS

About Grape Escape Winery Tours

We provide fun, personalized escapes to the Oregon Wine Country for team building events, special group occasions and corporate retreats. Whether you choose an Afternoon Escape, a Group Meeting in the wine country, or a Dinner Escape, we'll take care of all the details.

On the day of your escape, we'll greet you at your location. You'll begin to unwind as we take the scenic way to the wine country. Then throughout the day, we'll provide everything you need as you enjoy our wine country in an unhurried, relaxed style.

This winter, try our Holiday Escape, a novel way for your company to celebrate the season. We'll visit one or two nearby wineries (in Portland, or the wine country), and end with a festive dinner matched to wine. Yum.

To learn more about what we offer, take a look at our web site or give us a call. We'll guide you through the possibilities. Then once you select your escape, we'll take care of all the details, leaving you with nothing to do but anticipate a day of wine, food and fun.

Contact
Ralph Stinton

77 NE Holland Street
Portland, Oregon 97211
p. 503.283.3380
e. info@GrapeEscapeTours.com
www.GrapeEscapeTours.com

Price
Call for more information

Available Escapes
- Afternoon escape
- Full day escape
- Grape-r escape
- Dinner escape
- Holiday escape
- Urban escape
- Culinary escape
- Grape event
- In-house tasting

WHAT'S NEW
To learn more about what we offer, take a look at our web site or give us a call. We'll guide you through the possibilities.

See page 336 under Wine Tours

Bravo! Member Since 2003

www.bravoevent.com

MT. HOOD
MEADOWS
SKI RESORT

14040 Highway 35
35 miles South of Hood River
Mt. Hood, Oregon 97041
p. 503.659.1256
p. 800.ski.hood
e. george.evans@skihood.com
www.skihood.com

About Mt. Hood Meadows

Conveniently located just 65 miles east of Portland, Mt. Hood Meadows has the most diverse ski and snowboard terrain in Oregon. Our 11 chairlifts (including 5 high-speed quads), special programs, lodge facilities, Day Care Center, transportation options and friendly employees make Meadows the kind of place you will want to visit often.

Ski Hood

Our staff has extensive experience in hosting corporate events. Our professional banquet and catering staff offers an array of delicious menu items. We can also provide the meeting, conference and banquet amenities to which you are accustomed.

Mt. Hood Meadows has a truly magical ambiance. Majestic Mt. Hood framed by snow-covered trees in the winter and green meadows with wild flowers in the summer, provides the perfect atmosphere for your next event.

Contact
George Evans

Price
Prices vary, group rates available

Quick Facts
- The largest ski area on Mt. Hood.
- Professional ski & snowboard instructors.
- On hill event features
- Group rates available for groups of 15 or more.
- Discounts on lift tickets, rental equipment, group lessons & custom clinics available.
- Professional banquet & catering staff.

WHAT'S NEW
The "Uplift Special" provides a lift ticket and catered lunch for groups of 15 or more adults for just $59 (midweek, non-holiday) when arranged in advance. Those new to the sport in your group receive a beginner's special (beginner lift, lesson and equipment rentals) and lunch!

See page 164 under Event & Meeting Sites

Bravo! Member Since 1990

P.O. Box 280
Government Camp, Oregon 97028
p. 503.658.4385
f. 503.272.3554
e. knorton@skibowl.com
www.skibowl.com

Discover Mt. Hood Ski Bowl

Encompassed in over 1,000 acres and less than an hour drive from Portland, SKIBOWL provides the perfect backdrop for any group setting and features 20 hands-on attractions where you are in control. SKIBOWL offers something for all age groups, at affordable prices. Everyone will be able to experience unforgettable fun in the unique alpine environment offered only at Mt. Hood SKIBOWL.

Winter Activities

America's Largest Night Ski Area; 65 day runs, 34 night runs, 300 acres of outback terrain, snow tube tow and rentals, adventure park, terrain park, horse drawn sleigh rides, and snowmobile rentals.

Summer Activities

Over 20 mountain adventures offering fun for all ages where you are in control; including bungee trampoline, half-mile dual alpine slide, two scenic sky chairs, interpretive hiking trails, lift-assisted mountain bike park with 40 miles of trails, plus rentals and tours. We offer indy karts, disc and miniature golf, automated batting cages, zipline, free-fall bungee, kiddy jeeps and kiddy canoe rides, an indoor two story 2,400 sq. ft. play zone and more.

We can customize any package – from no-cost Company Day to closing the facility down exclusively for your company. Our professional and friendly staff knows just what it takes to make your event an unforgettable one.

Contact
Karen Norton

Price
Customized packages to fit any budget

Capacity
Up to 6,000 people (more with off-mountain shuttle)

Facility & Services
- Ample parking and free (east to west) shuttle on weekends.
- Two yurts, three day lodges & a historic mid-mountain Warming Hut.
- Tented picnic areas offer dining capabilities.
- Three full-service host/ no-host bars available.
- We customize any package to meet your needs & budget.

TYPES OF EVENTS
Company picnics, corporate events, meetings, team building, weddings, private parties, concerts, reunions and graduation parties.

See page 165 under Event & Meeting Sites

Sea to Summit Tours & Adventures

Based in Portland, Oregon, Sea to Summit provides visitors and locals a memorable experience in the beautiful Pacific Northwest.

Sea to Summit offers many activities including whitewater rafting, winery tours, brewery tours, sightseeing tours, personalized tours and much more. In the winter season, Sea to Summit is Portland's Premier Ski & Mountain Shuttle Service and is available seven days a week from Portland. Whether a corporate outing, a team building event or business guests visiting Oregon, Sea to Summit has activities and adventures to suit your groups interests and individuality.

Our knowledgeable guides and specialized 4x4 vehicles make Sea to Summit Tours & Adventures the most reliable service in any weather condition and for all destinations!

Simplify... make your reservation with Sea to Summit!

503.286.9333

www.seatosummit.net

Contact
Joshua Blaize
Portland, Oregon
p. 503.286.9333
e. seatosummit@qwest.net
www.seatosummit.net

Specializing In:
- Winery Tours
- Brewery Tours
- White Water Rafting Trips
- Sightseeing Tours
- Personalized Tours
- Ski Shuttles

Clients Include:
- Nordstrom
- Nike
- Adidas
- J.C. Penney
- REI
- Timberline Lodge
- Mt. Hood Meadows
- Intel, etc...

See page 320 under Transportation and 339 under Wine Tours

www.bravoevent.com

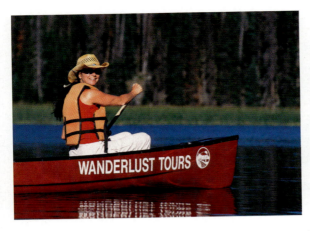

143 SW Cleveland Avenue
Bend, Oregon 97702

p. 800.258.0757
f. 541.383.4317
e. info@wanderlusttours.com
www.wanderlusttours.com

Wanderlust Tours

Wanderlust Tours offers half-day outings and teambuilding for corporate, associations and wedding groups. On our tours, you're enveloped in Central Oregon's most beautiful, natural and remote areas. Professional naturalist guides offer vibrant interpretation of Oregon's natural and cultural history. Wanderlust Tours, a family owned and operated business since 1993, was awarded the OSU Austin Excellence in Family Business Award in 2007, the Gene Leo Memorial Award given by Travel Oregon for excellence in outdoor recreation in 2005 and the Oregon Governor's Award for Tourism in 2000.

FivePine Lodge and Conference Center

32 craftsman cabins and lodge suites nestled in a pine forested meadow at the base of the Three Sisters mountains. All rooms are luxuriously appointed with a private deck or patio, fireplace, hand built furnishings, 42" plasma TV, waterfall soaking tub and Simmons very best super pillow top mattresses.

At FivePine, our wild flowered forest and blue sky set the ideal backdrop for your productive event. Cross the wood bridge to our Teresa Conference Center and you'll find meeting spaces in varying sizes and a staff dedicated to creating your perfect experience.

Contact
Dave Nissen

Price
$42 – $110 per person

Quick Facts
- Award winning, guided half-day tours.
- The best naturalist guides in Central Oregon.
- Transportation and all equipment provided.
- Custom tour, event planning and team-building activities available.
- No experience necessary, all ability levels and ages welcome!

Wanderlust Tours
- **Our summer offerings include:** canoeing, kayaking, caving, Brews and Views, Urban GPS Eco-Challenge and Volcano tours. Summer evenings we offer moonlight and starlight canoe plus Dinner Canoe Under the Stars tours.
- **Our winter offerings include:** daily snowshoeing and cave tours. Winter evenings we offer moonlight and starlight snowshoeing and Bonfire on the Snow.

Resorts & Retreats

Resorts & Retreats

20029 Highway 138 W.
Elkton, Oregon 97436

p. 541.584.2295
f. 541.584.2395
e. bigkranch@cascadeaccess.com
www.big-k.com

Big K Guest Ranch

We are an all-inclusive guest ranch that offers a place for everyone to enjoy the outdoors. From scenic float trips down the Umpqua River to horseback rides on our 2500 acre property to local wine tours, there is always something to do. You will love the home style meals that wait for you when you come off the river after catching more fish than you ever thought possible. Our professional fishing guides and friendly staff will give your an unforgettable experience on the Umpqua.

We are the perfect venue for a variety of events from corporate retreats to weekend getaways. With 20 private cabins and a full service log lodge we can accommodate groups as large as 300. Our dining room and adjoining conference room create a relaxing and productive environment for any group.

Our packages are fully customizable and tailored for your group or event. We work with you every step of the way.

Contact
Kathie Larson

Price
Call for customized pricing

Amenities

- Event/Conference Room (250 capacity)
- Full Service Restaurant
- 20 uniquely appointed cabins
- Recreational Room
- Guided Fishing on the Umpqua River
- Horseback Rides

See page 103 under
Event & Meeting Sites

www.bravoevent.com

Falcon's Crest Lodge
In Government Camp

Mt. Hood Vacations
38250 Pioneer Boulevard #607
Sandy, Oregon 97055
p. 503.686.8080
f. 503.622.0474
e. becca1st@gmail.com
www.FalconsCrestLodge.com

About Falcon's Crest Lodge

This amazing 5,700 sq. foot lodge, in the heart of Historic Government Camp, is walking distance to lifts, hiking trails and town. Craftsman style woodwork, granite counters and slate floors provide rustic charm and the luxury you desire. Falcon's Crest lets you relax in luxury and comfort.

Falcon's Crest sleeps 24 comfortably. There are 3 Deluxe King Master Suites with private baths and private decks and 1 Deluxe Family Suite that sleeps 4 with its own private sitting area and Jacuzzi tub. There are 2 bunk rooms, each sleeping 6, with full, private bathrooms. One even has its own 32-inch Satellite TV. Four families will feel right at home!

The Great Room has a custom Bar, the Dining Room a 15-foot log Family-Style table and your fully-equipped gourmet kitchen has a gas Viking 8-burner stove.

The Game Room has a Foosball Table, Air Hockey, Poker/Game Table and plenty of Board Games for the whole family.

Multiple large decks have great views of Mt. Hood and the night lights of Ski Bowl. At days end, relax in our new top-of-the-line 6-person Hot Tub. Falcon's Crest Lodge is how life is meant to be enjoyed!

Contact
Becca Niday

Price
$425 to $1,150 a night

Quick Facts
- Wireless Internet & Sirius Satellite Radio.
- Big screen- HDTV with Satellite, DVD & VCR, X-Box.
- Large laundry room with washer & two dryers.
- Slate foyer with convenient storage for ski gear.

Testimony
"This house is Heavenly! It is amazingly well-equipped & I LOVED the kitchen. The beds were the most comfortable I have ever slept in. The kids enjoyed the games and we all had a fantastic time. Everything about this home is excellent."
– Jeannie C.

"I just wanted to thank you again for all your help in making our stay at Government Camp so wonderful. Falcon's Crest was a dream! Hope we'll be able to visit again."
– Cathy O.

See page 15 under Accommodations

www.bravoevent.com

FIVE PINE
HEALTH ★ BALANCE ★ ADVENTURE

1021 Desperado Trail
Sisters, Oregon 97759
p. 541.549.5900
f. 541.549.5200
e. elena.mcmichaels@fivepinelodge.com
e. greg.willitts@fivepinelodge.com
www.fivepinelodge.com

Accommodations
Thirty-two classic craftsman cottage and lodge rooms nestled into a pine forested meadow at the base of the Three Sisters mountains. All rooms are luxuriously appointed with a private deck or patio, fireplace, hand built Amish furnishings, 42 inch plasma TV, waterfall soaking tub, and Simmons very best super pillow top mattresses.

Guest Amenities
Nightly wine reception at the lodge
Natural Energy Breakfast
Nightly Radio theatre at the lodge (winter)

Conference Center
At FivePine, our wild flowered forest and blue sky set the spirit of nature that becomes the backdrop for your productive event. Cross the wood bridge to our Teresa Conference Center and you'll find meeting spaces in varying sizes and a staff dedicated to creating your perfect experience.

Our Executive Chef will design a personalized menu of fresh and natural foods that will fill your soul.

Contact
Elena McMichaels

Capacity
Seated 240, stadium 350

Amenities
- 4800 sq. ft. Teresa Conference Center
- 4600 sq. ft. outdoor creek side meeting space
- 19,000 sq. ft. athletic club
- Innovative team building opportunities including rafting, caving, GPS eco tours & more
- Full service, in house catering
- State of the art audio visual
- Shibui spa
- Sisters movie house
- Three Creeks Brewing Company
- Pleiades fine dining restaurant
- Campus wide wireless Internet
- On site event coordinator

COME TAKE A TOUR

See page 129 under
Event & Meeting Sites

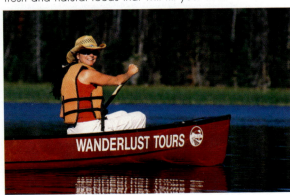

Bravo! Member Since 2006

www.bravoevent.com

Inn At Spanish Head
RESORT HOTEL

4009 SW Hwy 101
Lincoln City, Oregon 97367
p. 800.452.8127
f. 541.996.4089
e. kim@spanishhead.com
e. tonya@spanishhead.com
www.spanishhead.com

The Most Inspiring Meeting Facilities on the Oregon Coast

The Inn at Spanish Head Resort Hotel in Lincoln City is Oregon's only resort hotel <u>built right on the beach</u>. The Inn offers breathtaking views of the Pacific Ocean & easy access to the wonders of nature. As a smoke-free condominium hotel, each of the Inn's 120 guest rooms & all meeting rooms are oceanfront with floor-to-ceiling windows. A wide variety of suites, studios & bedrooms are available. Most have balconies & are equipped with a kitchen, kitchenette, or wet bar.

We can graciously accommodate groups from 10 to 150 people, complete with on-site catering & an experienced staff who take meticulous care of each detail. Elevators take you directly to the beach for mid-day breaks, barbecues or a nice walk to unwind at the end of the day.

Nearby there is exceptional hiking, golfing, fishing, tide pools, galleries & unique shops, a major casino and outlet shopping center.

Come & enjoy the Inn's excellent service & spectacular setting. It's the perfect combination to inspire your meeting, reward achievement or celebrate any occasion.

Contact
Kim Sparks, Dir. of Sales & Marketing

Tonya Weaver, Sr. Sales Manager

Price
Guest room rates vary by season & days of the week

Capacity
Up to 150

Amenities
- Five oceanfront meeting rooms featuring floor-to-ceiling windows & more than 3,500 square feet of space; wireless access in meeting & guest rooms.
- Two meeting rooms open directly to poolside & the beach offering opportunities for poolside receptions & bonfires.
- Heated outdoor pool, ocean view spa, saunas, recreation/exercise room, easy beach access.

ON-SITE OCEANVIEW RESTAURANT & BAR
Fathams Restaurant & Bar offers spectacular coast views, fresh seafood, juicy seak & other NW specialties.

See page 139 under Event & Meeting Sites

Bravo! Member Since 1996

2126 SW Halsey Street
Troutdale, Oregon 97060
p. 503.492.2777
p. 877.492.2777
e. salesed@mcmenamins.com
www.mcmenamins.com

About the Edgefield

Built as the county poor farm in 1911 at the mouth of the Columbia River Gorge and later used as an old folks' home, Edgefield was marked for demolition until the McMenamin brothers renovated the property in the mid-1990s. Today, this destination resort and national historic landmark offers over 100 guestrooms, along with indoor and outdoor meeting and event spaces that can accommodate up to 225 and include WiFi, original artwork and onsite catering. Or perhaps organize a golf tournament on one of our two par-3 courses. After your event, visit the fine-dining Black Rabbit Restaurant, the Power Station Pub, our many small bars, gardens, distillery, winery and tasting room, Ruby's Spa and soaking pool, movie theater and more! Photos, menus and room layouts available at *mcmenamins.com*.

Contact
Group Sales Office

Price
Food & beverage minimum; varies based on size of room & time of day

Capacity
Up to 200 guests seated
250 guests reception-style
300 guests reception-style available in summer

Amenities
- 114 guestrooms
- Restaurants & small bars
- Ruby's Spa & soaking pool
- Two par-3 golf courses
- Pool tables & shuffle board
- Movie Theater
- Brewery
- Winery
- Distillery
- WiFi

See page 151 under Event & Meeting Sites

Bravo! Member Since 1991

SEVENTH MOUNTAIN RESORT

18575 SW Century Drive
Bend, Oregon 97702
p. 800.452.6810 (reservations)
p. 541.382.8711
f. 541.382.3475
e. info@seventhmountain.com
www.seventhmountain.com

About Seventh Mountain Resort

Seventh Mountain Resort is in the heart of Central Oregon, on the Deschutes River, one of Oregon's premier whitewater rivers. The Seventh Mountain Resort is the closest lodging to Mt. Bachelor, Oregon's most celebrated ski and snowboard area.

The resort offers 240 condominium units with full kitchens, living areas, fireplaces and private decks.

With 11,000 square feet of meeting space indoors and outdoors, Seventh Mountain Resort can accommodate groups of 10 to 350 for meetings, conferences and retreats. We provide a comfortable natural setting in a relaxing atmosphere with the ability to escape into the Deschutes National Forest.

Seventh Mountain Resort is also a premier location for recreational activities from hiking and biking to horseback riding, we even offer on-site whitewater rafting. And for the golfers in the group, we are located right next door to one of central Oregon's finest golf courses, Widgi Creek.

Contact
Vanessa Berning

Price
Varies; please call

Capacity
Conference center – up to 250; individual breakout room; Mt. Bachelor Events Center – up to 400; outdoors – up to 1000

Amenities
- Closest resort to Mt. Bachelor, on the Deschutes River.
- Seasons, serving Pacific Northwest Cuisine, is open seven nights a week.
- In-house catering by Season's Restaurant.

NEWLY RENOVATED

We just finished a property wide renovation including 100 condos fully renovated, two new restaurants, 11,000 square feet of brand new meeting space, new guest arrivals building, fitness center, two year-round outdoor heated swimming pools and a new children's pool.

See page 191 under Event & Meeting Sites

Skamania Lodge
Scenic Columbia River Gorge

1131 SW Skamania Lodge Way
P.O. Box 189
Stevenson, Washington 98648

p. 509.427.2541
p. 1.800.293.0418
e. skamaniares@destination
   hotels.com
www.skamania.com

About the Skamania Lodge Golf Course

Not only will you find acres of breathtaking and tranquil views, you'll discover why our guests come back time and again to enjoy our beautiful Skamania Lodge Golf Course and the Waterleaf Spa & Fitness Center.

Our challenging year-round, 18-hole, par-70 golf course is beautifully tucked into the resort's 175 wooded acres. Our golf services include a driving range, practice bunker, chipping and putting greens. Our course also features a full-service golf shop, cart rentals and PGA Professionals to help assist you with your game.

The tournament schedule at Skamania Lodge Golf Course boasts over a dozen pleasurable, and well organized public golf tournaments a year. In addition, tournaments can be customized for private groups, wedding or special events.

Contact
Skamania Lodge Golf Course

Rates
- Rates vary seasonally
- Rental clubs are available
- Individual and annual golf passes are available

Dining
- Greenside Grille
- River Rock Lounge
- The Cascade Room

Awards & Accolades
- 2008 – 2009 Four Star Award, Best Places to Play Presented by Golf Digest Magazine.
- 2008 Best 25 Family Golf Resorts, Presented by Golf for Women Magazine.

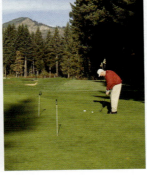

Bravo! Member Since 1995

See page 192 under Event & Meeting Sites and 255 under Golf Courses & Tournaments

www.bravoevent.com

SUNRIVER RESORT

57081 Meadow Road
Sunriver, Oregon 97707
p. 541.593.4605
f. 541.593.2742
e. weddings@sunriver-resort.com
www.sunriver-resort.com

About Sunriver Resort

Located near the breathtaking Cascade Mountain range, just 15 miles south of Bend, Oregon, Sunriver Resort offers a unique experience for all ages. A unique Northwest resort destination for all seasons that creates togetherness and memories among families and groups, Sunriver Resort provides unmatched activities and experiences in a serene, natural setting.

With more than 44,000 square feet of flexible meeting and banquet space, guests can choose from a wide variety of flexible indoor space featuring Northwest-style ambiance, or naturally gorgeous outdoor space, including the scenic Bachelor Lawn or the Great Hall Courtyard.

Whether planning a vacation, corporate meeting or a dream wedding, our state-of-the-art meeting facilities combined with the world-class recreation of Sunriver Resort will help execute your distinct vision with unrestricted flexibility and creativity that exceed your expectations.

Contact
Sunriver Catering Office

Price
Varies

Quick Facts
- Experienced professional staff to attend to every need.
- Custom weddings.
- Wedding packages are available for ease of planning.
- Multiple locations, both indoors and out, that can accommodate weddings and groups of all sizes.

See page 195 under
Event & Meeting Sites

www.bravoevent.com

SURFSAND resort
Cannon Beach, Oregon

148 West Gower
Cannon Beach, Oregon 97110
p. 503.436.2274
p. 1.800.797.4666
f. 503.436.2885
e. groups@t.com
www.surfsand.com

Located on the Pacific Ocean shores of Cannon Beach, Oregon, the Surfsand Resort is a premier northwest destination resort featuring spectacular views, unparalleled luxury and world-class amenities.

Rooms and suites, which feature breathtaking views of world famous Haystack Rock and Tillamook Lighthouse, offer the ultimate in comfort. Decorated in subtle earth tones inspired by the grandeur of the Pacific Ocean and nearby coastal forests, each room is carefully designed to enhance each guest's beach experience.

Indulge in the luxury of natural finishes and fine furnishings, including gas fireplaces, flat screen televisions with DVD players, iHome audio systems and wet bars in every room. Special touches include Tempur-Pedic mattresses, custom lighting, tile and wood work. Some rooms feature elegant ocean view jetted tubs, separated from the main room by a sliding shoji screen.

The resort provides stunning views of the rugged coastline for storm watching or enjoying the sunset. Our goal is to make the Surfsand Resort your beachfront home-away-from-home.

Contact
Group Events

Price
Call for pricing

Capacity
Seating for 200 guests

Amenities
- Full-service catering provided by The Wayfarer Restaurant & Lounge
- 32 inch flat-screen LCD televisions in all suites & 15 inch LCD televisions in all bathrooms
- Complimentary high-speed wireless internet
- Seasonal Beachfront Cabana Service
- Pet-free and pet friendly accommodations available

ON SITE FACILITIES
- Heated indoor pool and hot tub
- Comprehensive fitness center that features state-of-the-art workout equipment and cedar-lined saunas
- On-site massage rooms and services

See page 196 under Event & Meeting Sites

Bravo! Member Since 1998

About Timberline Lodge

Timberline Lodge is a year 'round historic lodge on Mt. Hood and considered by many as one of the most unique meeting venues in Oregon. As the "crown jewel" of the Cascades, The Lodge's inspirational art, craftsmanship, warmth and majesty make for memories that you and your attendees will always remember. Great outdoor opportunities available for groups interested in team-building activities.

With 60 rooms on-site as well as luxury condominiums available at The Lodge at Government Camp, you and your attendees can enjoy the convenience of your meetings, meals, reception and overnight accommodations together.

Banquet rooms have massive vaulted ceilings, timber beams, lofts, hand wrought iron, carved wood accents and soaring windows with spectacular views of Mt. Hood, and Mt. Jefferson.

Timberline Lodge is a masterpiece of mountain lodges located at the 6,000 feet level on the south side of Mt. Hood just an hour drive from Portland International Airport. The Lodge has all the amenities and services you would expect from a quality resort with a unique rustic elegance, yet a comfortable feel. In addition to meetings and conferences, Timberline is the perfect place for any special occasion.

Contact
Sales & Catering

Timberline, Oregon 97028
p. 503.272.3251
f. 503.272.3187
e. sales@timberlinelodge.com
www.timberlinelodge.com

Price
Starting at $20 per person

Capacity
Meetings for 10 to 300

Amenities
- One of the Greatest Historic Lodges in America.
- Just an hour from Portland & International Airport.
- Ullman Hall (2,400 sq.ft.) divisible with patio & mountain views.
- Barlow Room (1,500 sq.ft.) with original hewn wood interior.
- Raven's Nest (1,100 sq.ft.) with soaring ceilings, view & bar.
- Nationally recognized, on-premise food & beverage services. Award winning dining room & NW Wine Vault.
- Free WiFi in all lobbies & private meeting rooms.

See page 198 under Event & Meeting Sites

Bravo! Member Since 1993

Notes

p. 503.655.4775
e. designcorr@comcast.net
www.nsaoregon.net

Need a Speaker Who Will Really Deliver?

When you seek both education and entertainment. When you need to produce extraordinary results. When you must find experts who will thrill your audiences.

Contact the National Speakers Association – Oregon

www.nsaoregon.net

Our members are speaking, training, and consulting professionals who offer experience and expertise, delighting and enlightening audiences internationally.

Why NSA/Oregon?

• **Dependability and Quality:** NSA – Oregon members meet the stringent membership requirements of NSA. You can count on their professionalism and commitment.

• **Responsiveness:** Our speakers deliver material tailored to the needs of your group.

• **Savings:** Based locally, NSA – Oregon speakers offer national-caliber expertise with minimal – or no – travel expense.

• **Accessibility:** Our online directory indexes speakers by name and by topics.

Let NSA – Oregon be your premier resource for positively memorable customer-focused solutions and presentations. Whether your event is local or across the world, NSA – Oregon speakers, trainers and consultants will help you reach your goals successfully, every time.

Contact
Becky Klotz

Quick Facts

• Your perfect speaker is easy to locate. We can help you identify speakers at a range of fee levels to fit your budget.

• We have over 60 NSA – Oregon members as well as a cadre of emerging speaking professionals.

• Hear and see our members in action: Conveniently view them online at www.nsaoregon.net.

• National Speakers Association is the leading professional association for speakers, providing resources & education designed to advance the skills, integrity & value of its members & the speaking profession.

For information on how to become a professional speaker or reservations to a chapter event, contact:
Becky Klotz
p. 503.655.4775
e. designcorr@comcast.net

Bravo! Member Since 1996

5 Offenbach Place
Lake Oswego, Oregon 97035
p. 503.381.6585
f. 503.699.9366
e. christine@blackbeltbiz
solutions.com
www.blackbeltbizsolutions.com

About Christine Richards

What do you do when you're faced with virtually impossible obstacles? If you're Christine Richards, you study karate, apply what you learn in the dojo to the rest of your life, and build the career no one believed you could achieve. Today, a 1st degree black belt and 20-year business veteran, Christine brings gentle humor and engaging presence to keynotes and workshops that teach:

- Results-based sales, communication and business strategies you can implement quickly; combined with,
- Martial arts principles that empower audiences to develop the inner strength required for outward mastery.

Equip your audience to achieve more than they ever thought possible with:

Black Belt Selling: 5 Secrets to Double Your Sales Immediately. Give your sales numbers a good roundhouse kick in the pants—starting today!

Beyond Wishful Thinking: Achieve All You Can Imagine and More! Use the wisdom of Black Belt Masters and Christine's practical strategies to advance toward your goals with courage and strength.

Discover the Goddess Within: The Best is Yet to Come. Women, stop grappling with your age and start making the second half of your life the most powerful, creative, and dynamic time of all!

Call today to discuss other topics available or presentations tailored to fit your needs.

Contact
Christine Richards

Price
Varies

Services
- Keynote/Speaker
- Association Meetings
- Seminars
- Conference Breakouts
- Customized Training
- Retreats
- Coaching

Quick Facts
- Presentations to more than 30,000 people.
- Past President of Oregon National Speakers Assn.

"Christine really knocked it out of the park. She was great. Her smile sheet was a solid 5 out of 5—first time ever for a tough audience."

Carol Kelly, Ph.D.
Managing Director
e-Women Network

The Power of Laughter
by Gail Hand

MEMBER NSA
NATIONAL SPEAKERS ASSOCIATION

3439 NE Sandy Blvd #104
Portland, Oregon 97232
p. 503.284.2342
f. 503.296.2710
e. gail@gailhand.com
www.gailhand.com

About Gail Hand, The Power Of Laughter

Now a Corporate Speaker, Author and Sales Guru; Gail started her stand-up career in 1989 in San Francisco & has since toured over 1000 Companies, Universities & Associations in the U.S. & Canada. With her inspiring & motivational Power of Laughter programs including; leadership, sales, stress management, & diversity trainings; Gail has been a positive movement with companies, universities, & associations in North America. Along with her own YouTube channel, Gail is an avid photographer & blogger.

Experience

Gail is the owner of two prestigious companies, past President of the Oregon National Speakers Association, member of the International Federation of Speakers, & is even highlighted in Who's Who in Professional Speaking. Hand has been featured in numerous media from coast to coast including: ABC, CBS, NBC, AM Northwest, Curve Magazine, Women's Health & Fitness magazine, & most recently on iTunes! The media has highlighted her work producing Power of Laughter clubs in over 500 Companies, Universities, & Associations in the U.S.

Contact
Gail Hand, CLL

Price
Will trade for golf
(call for pricing)

Programs
- **The Power of Laughter** Seven Secrets to Living, and Laughing in a Changing World.
- **The Power of Laughter on the job** How to put Laughter to Work in the Workplace.
- **The Power of Generations** How to get the best performance working with different generations.
- **The Power of Laughter in Sales** 21 Secrets Guaranteed to make you Irresistible to Your Prospects.
- **Laughter Yoga** for Corporation, Associations or Special Events.

WHAT'S NEW
Gail's 2 new speaker's bureau websites:
InsightfulWomenSpeakers.com
InsightfulSpeakers.com
New Books:
The Power of Prospecting
The Power of Leadership

www.bravoevent.com

Speakers & Trainers

5225 SE Harney Drive
Portland, Oregon 97206
p. 503.869.0163
e. imagineyourreality@gmail.com
www.imagineyourreality.com

About Imagine Your Reality

Imagine Your Reality Business and Writing Coaching provides the following services:

Freelance editing and writing services – I do freelance editing and writing for newsletters, blogs, websites, articles, and books. Services range from proofing to copy writing to full content editing.

Coaching for writers who want to be published – Many writers don't realize that just writing a book isn't enough. I teach writers how to build effective marketing platforms to sell their books to publishers and their target market. The entire process is driven around showing writers how to take their writing to the next level of becoming a successful author.

Consulting for Businesses – I teach businesses how to automate their social media presence. I also teach business teams how to effectively work together in terms of each team member working toward his/her strength, while delegating weaknesses to people who are strong in those weaknesses. All of my business consulting is focused on showing businesses how to automate their processes so they can focus on their clients and having more time to enjoy life.

Public Speaking – I offer teleclasses, workshops, and key note speeches. Please see the section above for examples of what I speak on or visit www.imagineyourreality.wom/workshops.html.

Radio Show – I interview other speakers, authors, coaches, and business owners on my radio show. Contact me for more information.

Contact
Taylor Ellwood

Price
$150 one-on-one coaching, Fees vary for speaking engagements

Quick Facts
- I teach businesses how to automate their social media presence.
- I coach writers on how to market & publish their books.
- I offer freelance editing & writing services.
- I teach businesses how to focus on their strengths & delegate or automate their weaknesses in their business processes.

Workshops & Keynotes on the following subjects:
- Social Media Technology and its automation.
- How to be an Effective Networker.
- How to market & publish your book.
- How to play to your Strengths and Delegate your Weaknesses in your business.

301

www.bravoevent.com

Dawn Rasmussen's Contact Info
P.O. Box 20536
Portland, Oregon 97294
p. 503.539.3954
f. 504.408.4894
e. dawn@pathfindercareers.com
www.pathfindercareers.com

Secrets to Building Your Value Proposition

Money and jobs are tight. The stock market looks like a day at a theme park. The media warn of more layoffs. So what can a person do to make themselves and/or their companies as competitive as possible in an ever-crowded marketplace?

Dawn Rasmussen, president of Pathfinder Writing and Career Services, (and professional résumé writer and meeting planner) is a dynamic and engaging speaker who maps out how professional development helps develop personal market value, while at the same time showing companies how to position the professional credentials of their employees to capture new customers. Industry leadership and subject knowledge absolutely matters to target audiences… at a personal and corporate level!

Learn how to develop your unique value for target audiences while enhancing professional credentials with a specific, focused development plan benefiting companies and individuals alike. Having a clear definition of value and polished credentials can translate into profits and career advancement. Do you know what your brand is?

Contact
Dawn Rasmussen – CTP, CMP
Pathfinder Writing & Career Services

Price
$300 – $800

Quick Facts
- Develop a personal brand for what you deliver.
- Define your value to clients to stand out from the crowd.
- Map out how you can grow professionally to enhance your career.
- Make your company more competitive.

Member of Meeting Professionals International

WHAT'S NEW

Featured speaker at MPI-Oregon Chapter Cascadia Conference, 2009 MPI World Education Congress (Salt Lake City), and Oregon Speaker Showcase 2009. Proud member of MPI and the National Résumé Writer's Association.

Presentations with Pizzazz

Imagine an amazing experience that attendees will talk about and remember for years. This Schuh fits!

Shawna Schuh delivers with extraordinary storytelling, humor and excitement plus immediately usable authentic information. People take action after experiencing the Schuh and results are proven to be immediate and lasting.

Shawna addresses all issues relating to people skills from communication and presentation to questioning and closing. Her presentations are funny, energetic, powerful and packed with practical results driven information.

"Shawna tapped right into our key business points and the topics that are important to us plus it was Stimulating with a capital "S"!"

– Michalene Tomczyk, Customer Service Manager, Nike Golf

Bravo! Member Since 2008

Improve Your People Skills with our Inspirational Product Line

Contact
Shawna Schuh

24241 Highway 47
Gaston, Oregon 97119

p. 503.662.3044
p. 877.474.2962
e. Shawna@ShawnaSchuh.com
www.ShawnaSchuh.com

MEMBER NSA NATIONAL SPEAKERS ASSOCIATION

Quick Facts

- Holds the prestigious Certified Speaking Professional Designation (CSP) held by less than 8% of speakers worldwide & the first Oregonian to earn it.

- Ecstatic clients include: Nike, Nordstrom, US Bank, Spirit Mountain Casino & multiple industry clients across America.

- Repeat & referral clients account for 95% of business since 1995.

- Former co-host of a business show & constant contributor to media & print venues.

"World class presenter & perfect for our 600 members."

– Mike Walsh, President, High Performers International

www.bravoevent.com

Jathan Janove
training & consulting

MEMBER NSA — NATIONAL SPEAKERS ASSOCIATION

1311 NW Lovejoy Street
Suite 900
Portland, Oregon 97209
p. 503.226.1191
f. 503.226.0079
e. jj@aterwynne.com
www.jathanjanove.com

Jathan helps employers maximize employee performance while minimizing the risk of trouble. His 2nd book "The Star Profile: A Management Tool To Unleash Employee Potential" won a 2009 Gold Medal IPPY award in Business/Sales.

From his study of numerous failed workplace relationships and terminations, Jathan has developed a series of presentations and workshops centering on the lessons they offer. With stories, humor and interaction, he imparts to managers and HR professionals tools they can immediately implement.

Contact
Jathan Janove, JD

Quick Facts
- Workforce Productivity without Workplace Trouble
- Listed in the SHRM Recommended Speakers Directory
- Author and Employment Law Attorney with 25+ Years of Experience
- Training, Consulting, Coaching and Keynotes

Right Now COMMUNICATIONS

23240 NW Meier Road
Hillsboro, Oregon 97124
p. 503.705.8508
f. 503.647.2395
e. bburatti@easystreet.net
www.rightnowcommunications.com

Right Now Communications helps businesses and individuals do more and stress less. Its unique program, Extreme Time Management,™ shows you how to target your high return priorities and your truly vital tasks. Leaders are able to focus on moving the big goals forward, and staffs grow more efficient. Individuals find balance between their work and personal lives.

Founded by media executive Brenda Buratti, Right Now Communications provides keynote speeches and trainings to busy people everywhere.

Contact
Brenda Buratti

Quick Facts
- Time management & productivity
- Work-life balance for busy women
- Leading through change
- Media training from a pro

Speakers & Trainers

P.O. Box 1254
26801 SW Stafford Road
Wilsonville, Oregon 97070
p. 503.685.9426
c. 503.313.7962
f. 503.582.9149
e. sign@whirlwindpublishing.com
www.whirlwindpublishing.com

Kellie Grill "The Whirlwind Woman" is a motivational speaker, author, songwriter and the co-owner of Whirlwind Publishing. She speaks on happiness, positive attitude, overcoming obstacles, conquering fear and obtaining goals. She is on the board of directors for the National Speaker Association—Oregon Chapter as their Speaker Lab Coordinator and Secretary. Kellie's love story is "Send Me A Sign" and her audio book "Happiness Is Here — Simple Strategies for Staying Happy" is due out Oct '09.

Kellie is the mother of three children and has one granddaughter. She and her husband Dave live on a horse farm in Wilsonville Oregon called Whirlwind Ranch.

Bravo! Member Since 2008

Contact
Kellie Poulsen–Grill
"The Whirlwind Woman"

Quick Facts
Want your audiences happy, positive & productive in these uncertain times? Book Kellie Grill as the speaker for your next event — she will get the job done!

A portion of all book & speech proceeds go to breast cancer research.

MEMBER NSA
NATIONAL SPEAKERS ASSOCIATION

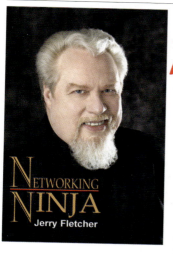

32475 Armitage Road
Wilsonville, Oregon 97070
p. 800.533.2893
p. 503.694.5849
f. 503 694-5177
e. Ninja@CenturyTel.net
www.NetworkingNinja.com

Since 1993 this enthusiastic pro has been speaking passionately about networking, marketing and building businesses, careers and lives of joy.

His Keynotes, Endnotes, Breakouts and Seminars can all be tailored to your meeting. Call today!

Contact
Jerry Fletcher, Networking Ninja

Price
Portland Metro Min. $5,000
Call for out of town pricing

Topics
- Trust-based Marketing
- Social Networking

What's New?

1/2 Day Fund-raising Seminar

www.bravoevent.com

Notes

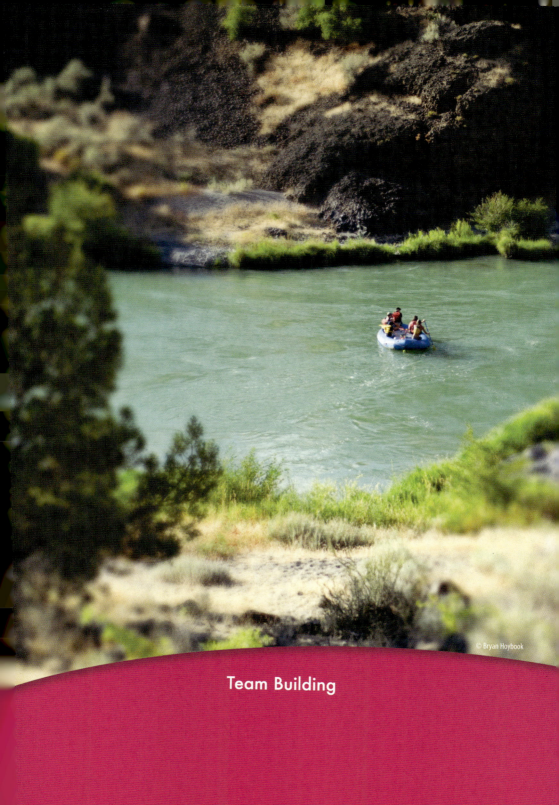

Team Building

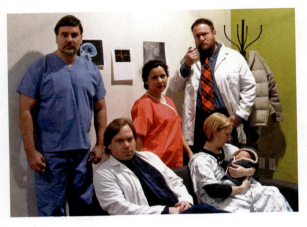

brainwaves
IMPROVISATIONAL COMEDY

650 SW Meadow Drive
Unit #214
Beaverton, Oregon 97006
p. 503.520.8928
e. info@brainwavesimprov.com
www.brainwavesimprov.com

About Brainwaves Improvisational Comedy

Brainwaves is a unique comedy ensemble that can make your next event a hilarious success! Made up entirely of professional comedic actors, Brainwaves plays corporate functions, colleges and special events all over the United States. Formed in 1986, they are pioneers of the West Coast improv scene. The cast has years of experience working together, which gives them what *The Oregonian* called, "An almost psychic connection on stage." The cast is adept at incorporating anything about life about your company or event into their show.

Additional Information

A Brainwaves show consists of fast paced scenes based entirely on suggestions from the audience. These may include a live-action soap opera based on the life of a favorite employee, the wit, wisdom and humor of a two-headed psychic and a plethora of scenes that involve the 'Wavers quick wits and zany characters. *The Oregonian* calls a Brainwaves show "Smart Fun!"

Brainwaves has headlined at numerous National Improv Festivals including Chicago, Ill. and Austin, TX. The group has performed for hundreds of corporate and college clients, including Nike, Intel, Columbia Sportswear, Creighton University, University of Oregon, METRO, St. Mary's Academy, and many more.

Contact
Daryl Olson
Tyler Hughs

Price
Average price for show in Portland Area: $1,500

Quick Facts
- Fast paced improvised comedy show ala "Whose Line Is It Anyway".
- Six very funny, professional comedic actors with credits in Film & TV.
- Performances can be any length, held in almost any venue & incorporate themes from your office/group.
- Portland's longest running improv group, celebrating more than 20 years of comedic life!

COME WATCH US
Brainwaves performs regularly for local audiences at The Shoebox Theater 2110 SE 10th Ave., Portland, Oregon.

See page 66 under Entertainers

Bravo! Member Since 1995

www.bravoevent.com

ClubSport
OREGON
sports • fitness • adventure

Team Building

18120 SW Lower Boones Ferry Road
Tigard, Oregon 97224
p. 503.968.4519
f. 503.624.5497
e. jessica.demonte@clubsports.com
www.clubsports.com/oregon

ClubSport fitness resort is a private sports facility with an array of programs and amenities for individuals and families who are forging a healthy and active lifestyle.

This impressive 150,000 square foot complex offers members a complete range of state-of-the-art circuit training, free weights and cardiovascular equipment. A 5-court gymnasium hosts volleyball, basketball, badminton and the occasional dodge ball tournament. And for those that prefer group fitness, this club offers over 100 classes per week ranging from basic aerobic fitness classes to Zumba. In addition there is an outdoor aquatics center with a resort pool, waterslide, spa and cabana, a six-lane indoor lap pool, four racquetball and two squash courts; a juice bar, restaurant and an 11,000 square foot club-within-a-club for children under the age of 12.

One of the most impressive features of this club is the Rock Gym. It's the largest indoor rock climbing facility in Oregon and frequently used as the site for USCCA competitions. The gym features bouldering areas, as well as top roping and lead climbing routes. Classes are offered for climbers of all abilities with certified climbing instructors who are accomplished outdoor climbers.

ClubSport is ADA accessible.

Contact
Jessica DeMonte
Events Manager

Price
As low as $5 per person; call for rates & packages

Quick Facts
- 150,000 sq. ft. multi-purpose sports and fitness facility
- Indoor and outdoor swimming pools
- 45,000 square feet of indoor rock climbing
- 5 full size basketball courts
- Junior activities and on-site childcare
- State-of-the art fitness equipment

See page 114 under Event & Meeting Sites and 278 under Recreation, Attractions & Sports

Bravo! Member Since 2000

www.bravoevent.com

ComedySportz Teambuilding

Since our first "improv. business" workshop with Apple Computer in San Jose in 1989, Patrick Short and the ComedySportz team have helped many businesses across the US bring joy, playfulness real communication to their workplaces.

Trust, focus, listening, confidence, awareness and making the other person look good: these are the tools that our professional improvisers use onstage to make people laugh. These are the same vital tools companies use "offstage" with clients, coworkers, and customers to succeed as a business.

ComedySportz is experiential training at its best – the soft skills they don't teach in most MBA programs. Our workshops are engaging, interactive, meaningful and entertaining. We showcase and analyze the elements that make improvisation successful, then provide empowering applications. Plus, our right-brained approach gives all attendees a memorable experience laughing as much as learning.

We offer small steps and big steps. Every program is customized to fit your objectives and your group – your group may be a large or small company, department, church, school, non-profit or association. Some of the areas we've covered are:

- Basic Team-Building, New Business Group, Post-Downsizing
- Team-Building for Multiple Worksite Groups
- Managing Change, Risk-Taking
- Communications, Customer Service
- Focus
- Meeting Kickoffs – Energize your big get-together
- Your idea – bring us a challenge – we'll construct a session or sessions that meet your issues head-on.

Office: 3308 E Burnside Street
Portland, Oregon 97214
Theater: 1963 NW Kearney Street
Portland, Oregon 97209
p. 503.236.8888
e. portland@comedysportz.com
www.portlandcomedy.com

Contact
Patrick Short

Price
Call for pricing

Quick Facts
- Established in Portland in 1993, more than 3,300 shows.
- Clean, fast-paced, tailored to your group & very funny.
- Public shows every weekend—check us out before you buy.
- We work with companies large & small, churches, schools, associations & any group gathering.
- ComedySportz is available 24 hours a day anywhere in the USA.

COMEDYSPORTZ
Let us design a workshop that fits your goals – we'll even help identify the goals!

Call us at 503.236.8888 or e-mail us at portland@comedysportz.com

See page 67 under Entertainers

20500 SW Old Highway 99
Centralia, Washington 98531
p. 360.347.0027
f. 360.273.8406
e. jpoole@greatwolf.com
www.greatwolf.com/
grandmound/waterpark

At Great Wolf, we understand it's more than just another meeting. It's your meeting and will be the event your attendees talk about and remember. Our Meeting Services team is ready and prepared. The logistics. The cuisine. The service. The technology. Perfect execution is our goal with each and every event. Our conference center features 12 separate rooms giving us the flexibility to accommodate events as small as 10 people and as grand as 1,050. There is a tastefully appointed pre-function area and a private registration counter to enhance your experience at Great Wolf Lodge, Grand Mound. From sales rallies and board meetings to team building events and product launches, Great Wolf adds a new dimension to your conference and meeting needs. When it is time to relax, our 60,000 square foot indoor waterpark, two full-service restaurants, Elements Spa Salon, Northern Lights Arcade and our proximity to beautiful golf courses and historic downtown Olympia makes it easy to see how Great Wolf Lodge creates excitement for all aspects of your event.

Contact
John Poole

Price
Please Inquire

Amenities
- State-of-the-art banquet rooms to accommodate groups of 10 – 1,050.
- Wireless high-speed internet available in every guest room.
- Full-service catering for all events.
- Close proximity to beautiful golf courses.
- Great Wolf's team of experienced meeting professionals.

See page 132 under
Event & Meeting Sites

www.bravoevent.com

Team Building

An Historic Oregon Ranch

7115 Holmes Road
Sisters, Oregon 97759
p. 541.923.1901
e. howdy@lhranch.com
www.lhranch.com

About Long Hollow Ranch

Long Hollow Ranch, Oregon's only working dude ranch, is nestled in between two rocky plateaus, with views of world famous Smith Rock to the East and the Cascade Mountains to the West. Long Hollow is the ideal setting for your unique western wedding or corporate retreat.

Our farm house, built in 1905, is the original headquarters for the Black Butte Land and Cattle Company. It features 5 bedrooms with private baths and a guest cottage perfect for the Bride and Groom.

At Long Hollow, we will assist you with all of your needs or simply step back and let you create the wedding of your dreams. You can plan a garden wedding, be adjacent to the farm house on the beautiful lawn, or be down at the barn, with high desert sunsets being our specialty.

If it is peace and tranquility you desire, then Long Hollow Ranch is your perfect combination, mixing the past and the present.

Contact
Dick & Shirley Bloomfeldt

Price
$200 – $10,000

Quick Facts
- 562 acre working dude ranch / Bed & Breakfast.
- Catering on site with our chef or caterer of your choosing.
- Weddings or corporate events up to 200.
- Historic barn, original farm house.
- 3 ponds for fishing and access to the Deschutes River; trail rides; cattle drives.
- Easy access to municipal airport and major airline carriers.

WHAT'S NEW
There is always something new at the ranch. In the fall of 2009 the corral was remodeled and the barn got old siding replaced with sustainable boards.

See page 147 under Event & Meeting Sites

Zoller's Outdoor Odysseys

p. 800.366.2004
e. MarkZ@ZooRaft.com
www.BeTheTeam.com
www.ZooRaft.com

About your Outdoor Odyssey with Zoller's

For three generations the Zoller's have entertained hundreds of thousands of guests from all points of the globe right here in the beautiful Columbia River Gorge. Headquartered on the shore of the White Salmon River, just east of Portland where founder Phil Zoller pioneered the first commercial rafting of the White Salmon River, Zoller's has set the benchmark for quality, safety and professionalism in all of the outdoor adventures.

Choose your Outdoor Odyssey!

Lava Tube Caving: Into the earth we descend through ancient lava caves created by the lava flows of the Mt. Adams and Indian Heaven wilderness. Zoller's "Cave Coaches" provide each participant with all of the needed caving tools to make this a unique and hard to match group event.

Whitewater Rafting: Want it wild? Need it mild? The Zoller's river team is ready to customize your experience and make you smile, ear to ear. Youngsters from age 6 to 90 have fun on the river with Zoller's year after year.

Team Geocaching: Hi-Tech treasure hunts for kids of all ages. With just a brief orientation by the Zoller's "GeoCoaches", your group will be on their way to solving mystery and finding treasure.

Contact
Mark Zoller

Price
Half day to full day
$55 – $120

Quick Facts
- Custom corporate outdoor activities for up to 150 guests.
- 90 minutes from Portland.
- Dutch Oven catering.
- Spacious riverside facility.
- The #1 day trip in the Pacific NW.
- The largest collection of veteran outdoor guides in the Pacific NW.
- Multi day/multi activity coordination.

Team Building

Bravo! Member Since 2003

Notes

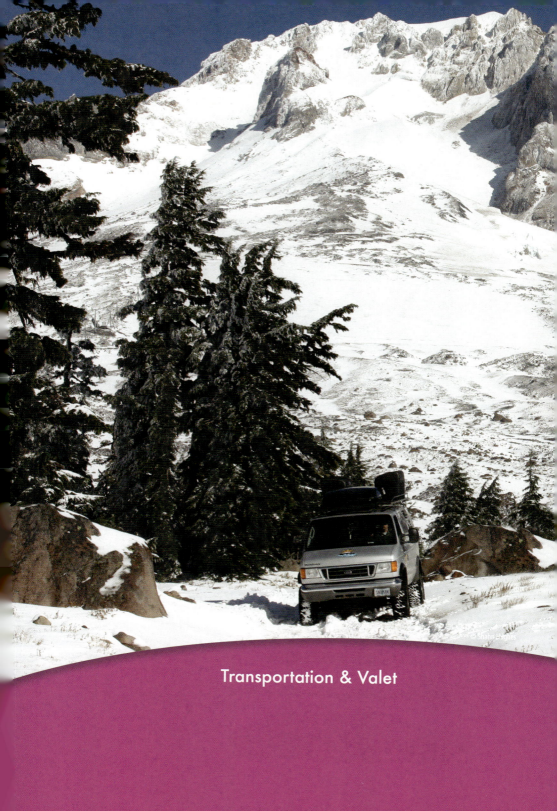

Transportation & Valet

All Star Limousine

p. 503.222.1704
f. 503.293.2094
e. limousine@aol.com
www.allstarlimo.biz

About All Star Limousine
Live life with opulence and elegance. View the beautiful city of Portland, Oregon from the privacy of your very own limousine. Whether it is your wedding, your prom or just a night out on the town, let All Star Limousine make your event a special ocassion.

Our Limousine Chauffeurs
Our chauffeurs are licensed professionals and each has been carefully screened. Each of our chauffeurs has many years of experience driving in the Portland area, which ensures prompt pick up and diligent routes. Your safety is our most prized concern.

All Limousines Are Equipped With the Following
- Color television
- Built-in ice chest
- Stereo System
- Beverage glasses & napkins
- Tinted windows
- Privacy partition

Certified & Founding Member of Limousine Owners and Operators of Oregon – Airport Approved

Contact
Roy Jay

Price
Quotes are for the Portland Metro area. Boundaries are:
- 1-5 Bridge – North
- Hillsboro, Oregon – West
- Wilsonville, Oregon – South
- Gresham, Oregon – East

Quick Facts
- Additional charges for out-of area transportation.
- Call for details & pricing.
- All limousines are non-smoking.
- All prices exclude 20% chauffeur tip; tip is based upon full price & is paid to chauffeur at the end of the run.
- Rates are billed in one hour increments only.
- Split time charge $50 per split times.

WHAT'S NEW
For reservations and more information pleae visit our web site at
www.allstarlimo.biz

Bravo! Member Since 2001

www.bravoevent.com

7219 NE 47th Avenue
Portland, Oregon 97218
p. 503.548.4480
p. 1.877.ECO.4PDX
f. 503.548.4821
e. info@ecoshuttle.net
www.ecoshuttle.net

Sustainable Transportation for any Occasion!

ecoShuttle provides sustainable transportation for any occasion! All of our vehicles are powered by 100% biodiesel but you won't smell french fries on board. We offer great amenities such as complimentary beverage packages and free mobile WiFi. You and your guests will feel like VIPs on our buses and vans!

What our customers are saying about us:

"I just wanted to express my thanks for the professional shuttle service we had last week. The driver was waiting upon our arrival, was friendly, and found our location without difficulty. I will definitely use ecoShuttle in the future. Keep up the phenomenal customer service. You truly are far above the rest!"
– Stacey Blunt

"It was really awesome we could use EcoShuttle…it made the trip go from being great to amazing."
– Caleb Coffman

Contact
Fiona Mitchell

Price Range for Service
Please call – rates vary depending on service type

Quick Facts
- Safe, reliable, & fun service so that you can have peace of mind.
- All services are customized to meet your unique needs.
- Our commitment to a clean, healthy environment makes it easy for you to reduce your carbon-footprint without changing your lifestyle.
- Excellent customer service from our friendly Reservation Specialists & our superb drivers – we'll give you an experience you'll want to repeat!
- Private PDX shuttle, weddings, wine tours, & more-we specialize in eco-friendly fun!

WHAT'S NEW
- Permitted for PDX pick-ups
- New vehicles & services added constantly-call for rates and availability

5319 SW Westgate Drive Suite 22
Portland, Oregon 97221
p. 503.244.4653
p. 800.778.6214
f. 503.244.6558
e. info@premierewinetours.com
www.premierewinetours.com

Premiere Transportation

Premiere is a local company with several vehicles that can handle your transportation needs for corporate shuttles, wine tours, Gorge tours, shuttle service for conventions, airport drop-offs, sporting events, casino trips, birthdays, and more.

We offer one-way transportation, in addition to hourly or day rates. Multiple vehicles can be booked for larger groups.

Our drivers are experienced, professionally trained and attired. Our fleet is well maintained, smoke-free and fully insured.

Luxury 12 passenger: 12 luxurious leather captain's chairs, flat screen LCD TV, DVD, CD, surround sound, MP3 input, game-systems input, refrigerator, coffee/hot water air-pots, tinted windows, privacy panel, AC, handicapped chair-lift and 7 ft x 6 ft rear storage.

Mini coaches: 14 passenger, generously sized! Passenger section features a wide aisle and 7 feet of interior head room in the vehicle that provides comfort and safety without sacrificing maneuverability. This small bus handles like a van and gets your guests to their destination in comfort and style. Cooler sized storage accessible to passengers.

Passenger vans: When a mini-van or car just isn't enough our 11 passenger provides ample, economical transportation for all of your needs. Front and rear AC, stereo, and comfortable cloth seating in 3 rows of seats.

Mini-vans: For smaller wine tours or shuttle needs a mini-van gets the job done! These are great for your more intimate shuttle needs or in venues where bigger vehicles won't work.

Bravo! Member Since 1995

Contact
Premiere Transportation

Price
Call for quotes

Services
- Experienced, professionally trained & attired drivers.
- One-way, hourly or day rates available.
- Please visit our website to view our fleet and view all of the services offered.

Memberships
- Travel Portland
- Washington County Visitors Association

See page 338 under Wine Tours

70+ Years of Offering Innovative Transportation Solutions!

Since our acquisition by Coach America in late 2004, the largest private motorcoach company in the US, we have undergone a complete face lift.

- NEW and Improved Fleet featuring 25 to 56 passenger coaches. Environmentally friendly Air conditioning systems, cleaner-burning, new-technology engines and now 100% powered by bio-diesel for a cleaner, greener environment!
- ADA–accessible coaches available in 26 to 52 passenger seating capacities.
- Experienced, well-trained professional drivers, some with as many as 40 years with Raz Transportation.
- 24/7 dispatch and maintenance departments to ensure the smooth operation of your trip and proper fleet maintenance.
- Charter Specialists with a combined 30 years of experience in providing outstanding and attentive customer service.

We understand the responsibility and importance of selecting the RIGHT transportation provider to ensure a safe, reliable, enjoyable and greener travel experience.

Well-trained and professional drivers, well-maintained deluxe & luxury motorcoaches, combined with 70+ years of experience and environmentally friendly vehicles, make Raz Transportation continues to be your BEST CHOICE in passenger transportation in the Northwest.

Contact
Raz Transportation
Gray Line of Portland,
A Coach America Company

11655 SW Pacific Highway
Portland, Oregon 97223-8629
p. 503.684.3322
p. 888.684.3322
f. 503.968.3223
e. sales@raztrans.com
www.raztrans.com

Group Sightseeing Tours
- Mount Hood Loop
- Columbia River Gorge
- Portland City Tour
- Mount St. Helens

WHAT'S NEW
The only private motorcoach company in the Northwest to use Bio-Diesel in all vehicles contributing to a cleaner, safer, environment.

Experience the DIFFERENCE at Raz Transportation and Gray Line of Portland!

Bravo! Member Since 1994

Sea to Summit Tours & Adventures

Based in Portland, Oregon, Sea to Summit provides visitors and locals a memorable experience in the beautiful Pacific Northwest.

Sea to Summit offers many activities including whitewater rafting, winery tours, brewery tours, sightseeing tours, personalized tours and much more. In the winter season, Sea to Summit is Portland's Premier Ski & Mountain Shuttle Service and is available seven days a week from Portland. Whether a corporate outing, a team building event or business guests visiting Oregon, Sea to Summit has activities and adventures to suit your groups interests and individuality.

Our knowledgeable guides and specialized 4x4 vehicles make Sea to Summit Tours & Adventures the most reliable service in any weather condition and for all destinations!

Simplify... make your reservation with Sea to Summit!

503.286.9333

www.seatosummit.net

Contact
Joshua Blaize

Portland, Oregon

p. 503.286.9333

e. seatosummit@qwest.net

www.seatosummit.net

Specializing In:
- Winery Tours
- Brewery Tours
- White Water Rafting Trips
- Sightseeing Tours
- Personalized Tours
- Ski Shuttles

Clients Include:
- Nordstrom
- Nike
- Adidas
- J.C. Penney
- REI
- Timberline Lodge
- Mt. Hood Meadows
- Intel, etc...

See page 283 under Recreation, Attractions & Sports and page 339 under Wine Tours

"World Class Transportation and Service"

VIP PDX can accommodate individuals, intimate groups, or events of up to 30 guests in luxury & style. For business or pleasure, VIP PDX offers first class fun in our executive party buses or choose our 'go anywhere' Land Rover or 7-series BMW for utmost in sophistication. Catering is available & special requests are always welcome. Our VIP staff is on site the duration of your event to ensure all your guest's needs are met. Our passion is customer service & exceeding your expectations.

Contact our friendly staff to customize your special event today & be sure to check out our website for further details!

VIP Coach Features

- Lounge Seating for 15 – 30
- 3 flat screen TV's & DVD/CD player
- iPod compatible sound system
- Spacious modern bathroom
- 2 beverages stations
- Professional driver
- VIP Host

Contact
Jennifer Berry

16869 SW 65th Avenue #238
Lake Oswego, Oregon 97035

p. 503.348.3233
f. 503.747.7202
e. info@vippdx.com
e. jennifer@vippdx.com
www.vippdx.com

Price
- Executive Cars $80 per hour
- Mini V starting at $130 per hour
- VIP Coach starting at $200 per hour
- Ask about seasonal specials

Ideal Transportation for:
- Corporate Events
- Wine Tours
- Sporting Events
- Golf Trips
- Brew Tours
- Ski/Snowboard Trips
- Holiday Parties

ABOUT VIP PDX

Try our new MINI V for up to 13 guests!
We are a locally owned and operated family business.

See page 340 under Wine Tours

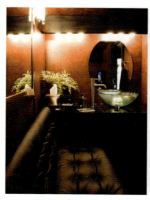

Bravo! Member Since 2007

Have You Thought About Parking?

Let us do the thinking for you! When planning for your next big event, selecting the right parking service will add a great first impression, as well as smooth, convenient parking accommodations.

Consider the unparalleled level of personalized service and professionalism that Premiere Valet Service has been providing Portland residents and restaurants for more than sixteen years. Superior guest service and responsiveness to our clients' needs are our preeminent themes. From the relaxed, comfortable initial consultation to the graciously assisted departure of your last guest, Premiere Valet Service will make the impression that you and your guests will notice and appreciate.

With our experience and knowledge, we have the ability to solve any parking problem. Insurance, claim checks, and signs are provided. All valets are trained, screened and field tested to ensure that you will receive only the finest service available.

Let Premiere Valet Service
enhance your wedding or event!
p. 503.244.7758

Contact
Private Event Coordinator

p. 503.244.7758
f. 503.244.6558
e. info@premierevalet.com
www.premierevalet.com

Price
Charges vary according to parking circumstances & time duration

Services
- Shuttle vans.
- Lot attendants.
- Light security.
- Parking Operations: Event parking & design, coning & signage, lot design, & use.
- Traffic Operations: Event traffic ingress & egress, street flagging, event traffic patterns, coning & signage.
- Coat check.

RESERVE EARLY
Please reserve your event date as far in advance as possible to ensure availability. A deposit of 50% of the total bill is required upon booking. Balance is due the day of the event.

Bravo! Member Since 1995

Videography

About A Hybrid Moon

In this competitive business climate, clear and powerful communication is vital.

A Hybrid Moon Video specializes in creating outstanding digital programming and delivering spectacular high quality products for corporate and broadcast clients. You'll be amazed at the ways you can enhance the power of your communications with customers, employees and the media.

Services

A Hybrid Moon produces the following types of video productions:

- Product Demonstrations
- Employee Recruitment & Orientation
- Corporate Identity Presentations
- Video Training and Tutorials
- Tradeshows & Conferences
- Seminar & Event Recording
- Standard Digital Conversion

Contact Us

Call us today and let us show you samples of our work. Even if you don't need our services today, it still pays to familiarize yourself with our company. We could be a valuable resource to you down the road.

Contact
Eric Newland
1321 NW 17th Avenue
Portland, Oregon 97209
p. 503.295.1991
e. eric@hybridmoon.com
www.hybridmoon.com

Price
Call for a price quote

Production Services
- Standard & high definition options
- Customized DVD & menu creation
- Photo montage & slideshow creation

TIP
"Do your homework! Meet the video artisan in person, and insist on watching several samples of finished product. A great video incorporates experience, talent, creativity and consistency."

Bravo! Member Since 1996

Aden
Photography & Video Productions
503 625-8900

travel PORTLAND

Videography

Style

Since 1968, Keith Aden Photography has been serving the greater Portland metro area. Over the years we have built a solid reputation for a professional, assertive and unobtrusive style that blends perfectly with your event. From international sales meetings to conventions, or political luncheons to company picnics, we can deliver the service that you expect. We are very detail-oriented and can tailor our services to fit your budget.

Someone Who Cares

Your choice of a photo or video professional is an important one. It reflects on your reputation as well as your company's reputation. We do not take that lightly! In fact, we put our good reputation on the line every time we take an assignment. And as a former purchasing manager for a national corporation, Keith also understands the needs of business. In short, it is our goal to make everyone look good!

Proud member of the Professional Photographers of America and Travel Portland.

Contact
Keith Aden

P.O. Box 1501
Lake Oswego, Oregon 97035
p. 503.625.8900
p. 877.230.0325
e. keith@adenphoto.com
www.adenphoto.com

Price
Tailored to fit your budget

Services
- Professional photography (digital, 4x5, medium format and 35mm).
- Event photography (digital or film).
- Video production/DVD (Professional 3-chip DV single or multi-camera coverage, non-linear or linear editing suites).
- Aerial photography.
- Brochures & postcards (design, photography & printing).
- Digital imaging services (prof. digital cameras).

PROFESSIONAL SERVICE FOR PROFESSIONAL PEOPLE

See page 273 under Photography

Bravo! Member Since 1990

Videography

JR Audio & Video provides one of the largest lists of services available in the state of Oregon for a Video Production Company. With 16 years of experience in areas such as Event and Commercial Filming, Video and Audio Editing, composing of original music, Tape and Film transfers to DVD, we can offer our clients a complete product from top to bottom.

We have basic and professional services for both consumers and businesses alike. Whether you're looking for a simple tape to DVD transfer, or you need a complete Video Production for TV, we can handle all your needs.

Unlike many video production companies, we use true Broadcast Cameras for all of our filming. The same cameras that we use for TV commercials we also use for weddings and events.

Services:
- Filming – TV Commercials, Events and Weddings
- Video & Audio Editing
- CD/DVD Duplication
- Tape to DVD (VHS, VHS-C, Betamax, Hi-8, Digital 8, Betacam, BetacamSP, Mini DV) and more
- Audio Tapes and Reels to CD
- Legal Video Services
- Format Conversions
- Web Video Streaming
- Creation of Training and Marketing Videos
- Voiceovers
- Power Point Conversions and Creation
- DVD Authoring
- Film to DVD (8mm and Super 8 film)

Contact
Jared Reck

618 Molalla Avenue
Oregon City, Oregon 97045
p. 503.607.0440
e. Jared.Reck@JRVideo-Services.com
www.JRVideo-Services.com

Price
$20 – $100,000

Clients
- Lile International
- CleaningCoach.com
- Hecht & Hecht Insurance
- Greg Moreland Magic
- Tradia

WHATS NEW
We are now a Microboards dealer. If you are interested in purchasing your own CD or DVD Duplicators we can provide the products including blank media. You can visit Microboards website for product details. A listing of products and services will be listed on our website soon.

www.bravoevent.com

matrix video

Creating your vision.

Certified Pro
Final Cut Pro, Level One

Video is absolutely the most effective way to captivate an audience and deliver your message! Let Matrix Video be your source for videography, editing, and production services. We take the time to understand our client's needs in order to produce a product that will exceed your expectations and make the most of your budget.

Services
- Videography & Editing
- Multi-Camera Shooting & Editing
- Live Events
- Web Videos
- Marketing & Promotional Videos
- Broadcast Commercials
- Product Demonstration Videos
- Educational & Training Videos
- Video & PowerPoint Integration
- Slideshows
- Custom DVD Authoring & Packaging
- Encoding, Compression, & Format Conversions

Testimonials

"First off, I can't tell you how much I LOVE the video. I thought it turned out great! Everyone who's seen it has agreed. Thanks for your flexibility!"

– Jason Ferrell, Capital One Brand Marketing

"Matrix Video did an amazing job at our three-day, multiple-location business event. They were flexible, easy to work with, and delivered an amazing video at a very competitive price. I can't say enough....I will absolutely use them again for my next event!"

– Angela Fontes, Chamberlain Research Consultants

Contact
Nicole Coon

23621 S Upper Highland Rd
Beavercreek, Oregon 97004
p. 503.913.0818
e. info@matrix-video.net
www.matrix-video.net

Price
Please contact for pricing

Quick Facts
- Apple Certified Pro Editor
- 4 time Telly Award Winner
- Competitive Rates
- Complimentary Consult

WHAT'S NEW

Is your Web-master or Marketing Director pulling double duty as your Videographer? If your videos are not turning out as well as you had hoped, or taking too long to finish, we can help! Matrix Video is now offering consulting services for your 'in-house' video team. We can help your team produce a better quality video with greater efficiency!

Videography

Video Media is your strategic partner in the integration of video into your marketing mix.

For everything from dynamic website video content and online seminars, to DVD collateral, electronic press kits, tradeshow videos, and sales training materials, we can help you produce intelligent video solutions that really get results.

Located in the heart of NW Portland, Video Media produces world-class productions to meet any aspect of your company's marketing or live event plan.

Take a moment to view our website or request a contact list of our long-standing happy clients, then give us a call for a custom quote. We will look forward to hearing from you soon.

Our services include, but are not limited to:

- Product/Software Demos
- Live Corporate Event Coverage
- On-Site Editing
- Trade Show Videos
- Customer Testimonials
- Voice Over/Script Writing

Contact
Dan Pred

2580 NW Upshur
Portland, Oregon 97210
p. 503.228.4060
f. 503.228.0619
e. dan@videomediaportland.com
www.videomediaportland.com

Price
Please call for custom quote

Quick Facts

- Oregon has the only state flag with 2 designs.
- Oregon has more ghost towns than any other state.
- If you carry an umbrella in Oregon, you're probably not a local.
- Video Media utilizes the latest technology to produce the most compelling video.

WHAT'S NEW
We've recently added a client lounge to our new HD editing suite and have fully redesigned our website where you can view our demo reel. Have a look.

Wineries & Custom Labeling

Wineries & Custom Labeling

CATHEDRAL RIDGE WINERY

4200 Post Canyon Drive
Hood River, Oregon 97031
p. 541.386.2882
p. 800.516.8710
f. 541.516.8710
e. crw@cathedralridgewinery.com
www.cathedralridgewinery.com

About Cathedral Ridge Vineyard

Whether it's one person or a wedding party of 250 people, we love to have people visit our winery and vineyard. Beautiful in virtually every season, you will be amazed by the views of Mt. Adams as you rest on the bench overlooking the vineyards and by Mt. Hood as you tour your way south through the vines. Our charming winery and gift house overlook manicured lawns and beautiful flower gardens, the perfect compliment to these stunning mountain views. Cathedral Ride exists to provide a perfect event for you and will extend every effort to refer you to appropriate suppliers for whatever you may require. Our friendly and knowledgeable hospitality team is here to help make your wedding or event the most special day of your life!

Types of events: Company meetings, holiday parties, corporate picnics, private lunches, anniversary parties, special event celebrations, Weddings, Weddings and receptions, rehearsal dinners, etc.

Contact
Event Coordinator

Price
Varies depending upon the day of the week & type of event.

Capacity
Up to 200 Guests

Amenities
- Outstanding full-service caterers for all types of events. We offer a list of both Hood River & Portland Caterers with outstanding references.
- We provide seating for 100 & tables to match.
- Staff is included in catering costs.
- We specialize in serving outstanding wines & also provide beer, water & soda as requested.
- Approximately 1200 square feet of dance floor
- Linens, china & glassware: Usually included in catering price.
- Ample free parking.
- All facilities are ADA accessible.

See page 109 under Event & Meeting Sites

www.bravoevent.com

ELK COVE
VINEYARDS

27751 NW Olson Road
Gaston, Oregon 97119
p. 503.985.7760
p. 877.ELKCOVE
f. 503.985.3525
e. info@elkcove.com
www.elkcove.com

About Elk Cove Vineyards

From atop a knoll with commanding views of premier vineyards and buttressing the scenic Oregon Coast Range, the Elk Cove facility is a superb site for that special event, yet only 45 minutes from downtown Portland.

The "Roosevelt Room", named after the herds of Roosevelt elk which roam the nearby mountains, will hold up to 150 people. With a full catering kitchen, Italian tiled floors, and a built-in dance floor, the Roosevelt Room's French doors open onto a full-length deck overlooking the vineyard and showcasing the marvelous spectacle that nature displays in one of Oregon's most picturesque locations.

Elk Cove is pleased to offer a wide range of wines, from our award-winning Pinot Gris (the 2005 was honored to be one of Wine Spectator magazine's top 100 wines of the year for 2007) to the much sought-after Pinot Noirs from our La Bohème vineyard, which have been served at two White House state dinners.

Contact
Hospitality Coordinator

Price
Please call for your customized quote

Quick Facts
- Available year round.
- Capacity up to 150.
- Roosevelt Room opens onto full length deck overlooking vineyards.
- Plenty of on-site parking.
- Utilize the vendors of your choice.
- Tables & chairs in Roosevelt Room included.

See page 124 under
Event & Meeting Sites

23269 NW Yungen Road
Hillsboro, Oregon 97124
p. 503.647.7596
e. info@helvetiawinery.com
www.helvetiawinery.com

Winery Tours And Events

Your country farm and winery experience just 25 minutes from downtown Portland and 10 minutes from high-tech Hillsboro. Our cozy, historic farmhouse, and the grounds surrounding it are available for wine tastings, private winemaker dinners, meetings, and picnics with a minimum wine purchase. Take a break from the business at hand and tour the Christmas tree farm, vineyards and winery. A perfect setting to learn about wine and winemaking in a relaxed and friendly atmosphere.

Wine Catering

Helvetia Winery will bring a variety of fine vintage wines from local vineyards, at special case prices, for wine tasting at your event in your location. An expert server will assist you and your guests in learning the finer points of Oregon wines, such as the importance of vintage, winemaking styles and aging.

Custom Labels

Your logo, your photo, a wine named after you: we can provide cases of wine with custom labels to serve at your event, or as gifts, mementos, motivational awards, and party favors.

"The north wind howls here every time it frosts. However, the grapes often ripen full and wonderful."

– Jakob Yungen writing to his Swiss relatives in 1917

Contact
John Platt

Price
Call for quotes

Quick Facts
- 25 minutes from downtown Portland.
- Enjoy a fine wine tasting with your offsite, dinner, party, meeting, wedding or any event.
- Custom labels for events, gifts, & souvenirs.

We're open every weekend from noon to five year-round. Come visit and see for yourself.

Bravo! Member Since 2001

www.bravoevent.com

9774 Highway 14 W
Goldendale, Washington 98620
p. 877.627.9445
f. 509.773.0586
e. joeg@maryhillwinery.com
www.maryhillwinery.com

About Maryhill Winery

Established in 1999 by Craig and Vicki Leuthold, Maryhill Winery is one of Washington state's largest family-owned wineries producing 80,000 cases annually. Located in the picturesque Columbia Gorge scenic area in Goldendale, Washington, the winery is perched on a bluff overlooking the Columbia River against the stunning backdrop of Mt. Hood. Nestled among rows of vines, Maryhill is a popular destination for picnics and special events, with an adjacent 4,000-seat outdoor amphitheatre that hosts a world-class summer concert series.

Maryhill's 3,000 sq. ft. tasting room draws more than 75,000 wine enthusiasts from around the globe each year, ranking among the top five most visited wineries in the state. Maryhill sources grapes from some of the most highly-regarded vineyards in the state to produce 23 varietals and 28 award-winning wines. Offering something for every palate, Maryhill's wines offer tremendous value with exceptional quality at accessible price points. For more information or to order wines online, visit www.maryhillwinery.com.

Contact
Joe Garoutte

Price
Fee is $6,500 & includes the following:

- Selection of sites
- Event Planner Assistance
- Day of event coordination
- 20 tables, 360 chairs

Quick Facts
- "2009 Washington Winery of the Year". – Winepress NW
- "Best Destination Winery". – Seattle Magazine
- Excellent caterers available for hire.
- Personalized Wine labels available for additional charge.
- Handicap accessible.

See page 150 under Event & Meeting Sites

Mt. Hood Winery

2882 Van Horn Drive
Hood River, Oregon 97031
p. 541.386.8333
f. 541.387.2578
e. linda@mthoodwinery.com
www.mthoodwinery.com

About Mt. Hood Winery

Mt. Hood Winery is conveniently located just 4 miles south of downtown Hood River off Highway 35. The newly completed lodge style Tasting Room opened in July of 2009.

Mt. Hood Winery is the perfect location for weddings, rehearsal dinners and receptions and meetings. With amazing views of Mt. Hood and Mt. Adams gatherings may be held indoors and out. If your event needs to be catered, we would be happy to arrange professional food service for you. The staff at Mt. Hood Winery is dedicated to providing exceptional service in making your event a success.

Contact
Linda Barber

Price
$250 to $5,000

Capacity
250

Amenities
- Estate grown and produced award winning wines.
- Family Owned Century Farm.
- Winery founded in 2002
- Stunning mountain and vineyard views.
- Brand new 2,500 sq. ft. Tasting Room.
- Conference room with surround sound and projection screen for presentations.
- Ample parking.

See page 166 under Event & Meeting Sites

www.bravoevent.com

Wine Tours

GRAPE ESCAPE WINERY TOURS

About Grape Escape Winery Tours

We provide fun, personalized escapes to the Oregon Wine Country for team building events, special group occasions and corporate retreats. Whether you choose an Afternoon Escape, a Group Meeting in the wine country, or a Dinner Escape, we'll take care of all the details.

On the day of your escape, we'll greet you at your location. You'll begin to unwind as we take the scenic way to the wine country. Then throughout the day, we'll provide everything you need as you enjoy our wine country in an unhurried, relaxed style.

This winter, try our Holiday Escape, a novel way for your company to celebrate the season. We'll visit one or two nearby wineries (in Portland, or the wine country), and end with a festive dinner matched to wine. Yum.

To learn more about what we offer, take a look at our web site or give us a call. We'll guide you through the possibilities. Then once you select your escape, we'll take care of all the details, leaving you with nothing to do but anticipate a day of wine, food and fun.

Contact
Ralph Stinton

77 NE Holland Street
Portland, Oregon 97211

p. 503.283.3380
e. info@GrapeEscapeTours.com
www.GrapeEscapeTours.com

Price
Call for more information

Available Escapes
- Mini-scape
- Multi-scape
- Afternoon escape
- Full day escape
- Dinner escape
- Holiday escape
- Urban escape
- Grape event
- In-house tasting
- Joinable tours

WHAT'S NEW
To learn more about what we offer, take a look at our web site or give us a call. We'll guide you through the possibilities.

See page 280 under Recreation, Attractions & Sports

Bravo! Member Since 2003

www.bravoevent.com

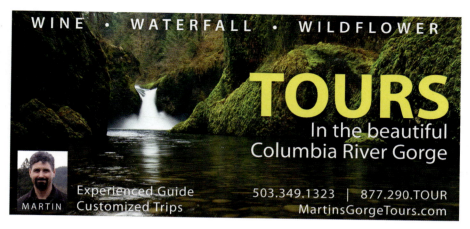

About Martin's Gorge Tours

Martin offers scenic tours for individuals, families, or groups. Discover the hidden attractions that make The Columbia River Gorge a National Scenic Area, from waterfalls to wildflowers to wineries. Most tours are available as half day, or full day excursions. Transportation, water and a snack are included. Service to hotels available by request. Just bring a windbreaker, comfortable shoes, your camera and a smile…leave your worries behind as we experience the natural beauty and explore the treasures of The Gorge.

Quick Facts

- Guided tours, shuttles, and charter services
- Wine, waterfall and wildflower tours (any combination).
- Charters and shuttles for weddings, reunions, birthdays, parties, field trips, and corporate events.
- Specializing in the Columbia River Gorge, and offering services to Portland & Vancouver, Mt. Hood, Mt. St. Helens, the Coast, and beyond.
- All dates available by advance reservation. Visa and MasterCard accepted.

Contact

Martin Hecht

P.O. Box 18177
Portland, Oregon 97218

p. 503.349.1323

e. Martin@MartinsGorgeTours.com

www.MartinsGorgeTours.com

Price range for shuttle and charter service

7 passenger vehicle at $69/hour, or 20 passenger coach at only $99/hour.

WHAT'S NEW

Special Offers are available based on availability: Wine Tours for only $69/person when reserving for 4 or more. Any 2 Tour Combinations for only $99/person.

Your company, organization, friends & family can take advantage of our group rate program to save 10% at the time of your booking. Group rates are available for groups of 10 (or more).

To request "Special" pricing, Call Martin at 877.290.TOUR (8687).

www.bravoevent.com

Wine Tours

Discover Oregon Wine Country!

The best way to experience Oregon wine is to go to the source. Whether you are new to wine tasting or know every winery in Oregon, you will appreciate the views, enjoy your guests, & savor each glass knowing Premiere Wine Tours is driving!

You & your guests will be picked up at your location & transported to Oregon's famous vineyards & boutique wineries for an afternoon of relaxation & fun! From a few hours to an all-day tour, we take care of all of the details.

- Do you know which wineries you'd like to visit? Great! We'll map the itinerary in a logical way to ensure you spend more time sniffing, swirling, & sipping wine. Additionally we will make the appointments at your preferred choices & negotiate tasting fees.

- If you're not sure what wineries to visit, don't worry! We can help you decide, map the itinerary, & make the appointments for your tour while negotiating tasting fees. Our only goal is to expose you to great wine & help acquaint you with Oregon's bounty.

5319 SW Westgate Drive, Suite 22
Portland, Oregon 97221
p. 503.244.4653
p. 800.778.6214
f. 503.244.6558
e. info@premierewinetours.com
www.premierewinetours.com

Contact
Premiere Wine Tours

Price
Call for quotes

Services
- Experienced, professionally trained & attired drivers.
- One-way, hourly or day rates available.
- Various sized vehicles to accommodate your number of guests & needs.
- Tour wine country for corporate retreats & team building, out of town guests, girlfriend getaways, anniversaries, birthdays, & more.

Memberships
- Travel Portland
- Washington County Visitor's Association

PREMIERE WINE TOURS
Please visit our website to view our fleet & view all of the services offered.
www.premierewinetours.com

See page 318 under Transportation

Bravo! Member Since 1995

www.bravoevent.com

Wine Tours

Sea to Summit Tours & Adventures

Based in Portland, Oregon, Sea to Summit provides visitors and locals a memorable experience in the beautiful Pacific Northwest.

Sea to Summit offers many activities including whitewater rafting, winery tours, brewery tours, sightseeing tours, personalized tours and much more. In the winter season, Sea to Summit is Portland's Premier Ski & Mountain Shuttle Service and is available seven days a week from Portland. Whether a corporate outing, a team building event or business guests visiting Oregon, Sea to Summit has activities and adventures to suit your groups interests and individuality.

Our knowledgeable guides and specialized 4x4 vehicles make Sea to Summit Tours & Adventures the most reliable service in any weather condition and for all destinations!

Simplify… make your reservation with Sea to Summit!

503.286.9333

www.seatosummit.net

Contact
Joshua Blaize

Portland, Oregon
p. 503.286.9333
e. seatosummit@qwest.net
www.seatosummit.net

Specializing In:
- Winery Tours
- Brewery Tours
- White Water Rafting Trips
- Sightseeing Tours
- Personalized Tours
- Ski Shuttles

Clients Include:
- Nordstrom
- Nike
- Adidas
- J.C. Penney
- REI
- Timberline Lodge
- Mt. Hood Meadows
- Intel, etc…

See page 283 under Recreation, Attractions & Sports and page 320 under Transportation

"World Class Transportation and Service"

VIP PDX can accommodate individuals, intimate groups, or events of up to 30 guests in luxury & style. Tour wine country year-round & leave the details to us. Enjoy the world-class wines of the Pacific Northwest. Savor Oregon's renowned pinot noir, chardonnay & many more. Sip between stops on our VIP Coach or Mini V & enjoy the countryside of the Willamette Valley. Pair your wine experience with fabulous catering or stop at your favorite restaurant. For business or pleasure, VIP PDX offers first class fun in our executive party buses or choose our 'go anywhere' Land Rover or 7-series BMW for utmost in sophistication.

Our passion is customer service & exceeding your expectations! Contact our friendly staff to customize your Vino Event today & be sure to check out our website for further details!

VIP Coach Features
- Lounge Seating for 15 – 30
- 3 flat screen TV's & DVD/CD player
- 2 beverage stations
- Spacious modern bathroom
- Professional driver
- VIP Host

Contact
Jennifer Berry

16869 SW 65th Avenue #238
Lake Oswego, Oregon 97035

p. 503.348.3233
f. 503.747.7202
e. info@vippdx.com
e. jennifer@vippdx.com

www.vippdx.com

Price
- Executive Cars $80 per hour
- All-inclusive wine tour starting at $60 per person
- Mini V starting at $130 per hour
- VIP Coach starting at $200 per hour
- Corporate Clients Enjoy 10% Off
- Ask about seasonal specials

Indulge in Wine Country...
- Corporate Wine Tours
- Customized Wine Tours
- Off-Road Wine Tours
- Couples & Intimate Groups

ABOUT VIP PDX
Try our new MINI V for up to 13 guests!
We are a locally owned and operated family business.

See page 321 under Transportation

Bravo! Member Since 2007

www.bravoevent.com

Central Oregon Businesses

Five Pine Lodge
1021 Desperado Trail
Sisters, Oregon 97759
p. 541.549.5900
e. elena@fivepinelodge.com
www.fivepinelodge.com
See pages 129, 288

McMenamins Old St. Francis School
700 NW Bond Street
Bend, Oregon 97701
p. 541.330.8567
e. salesbend@mcmenamins.com
www.mcmenamins.com
See page 155

Kah-Nee-Ta
P.O. Box 1240
Warmspring, Oregon 97761
p. 800.554.4SUN
e. sales@kahneeta.com
www.kahneeta.com
See pages 85, 141

Seventh Mountain Resort
18575 SW Century Drive
Bend, Oregon 97702
p. 541.452.6810
e. info@seventhmountain.com
www.seventhmountain.com
See pages 191, 291

Long Hollow Ranch
71105 Holmes Road
Sisters, Oregon 97759
p. 877.923.1901
e. howdy@lhranch.com
www.lhranch.com
See pages 147, 312

SunRiver Resort
57081 Meadow Road
Sunriver, Oregon 97707
p. 541.593.4605
e. weddings@sunriver-resort.com
www.sunriver-resort.com
See pages 195, 293

The Lodge at Suttle Lake
13300 Highway 20
Sisters, Oregon 97759
p. 541.595.2628
e. eventdirector@thelodgeatsuttlelake.com
www.thelodgeatsuttlelake.com
See page 146

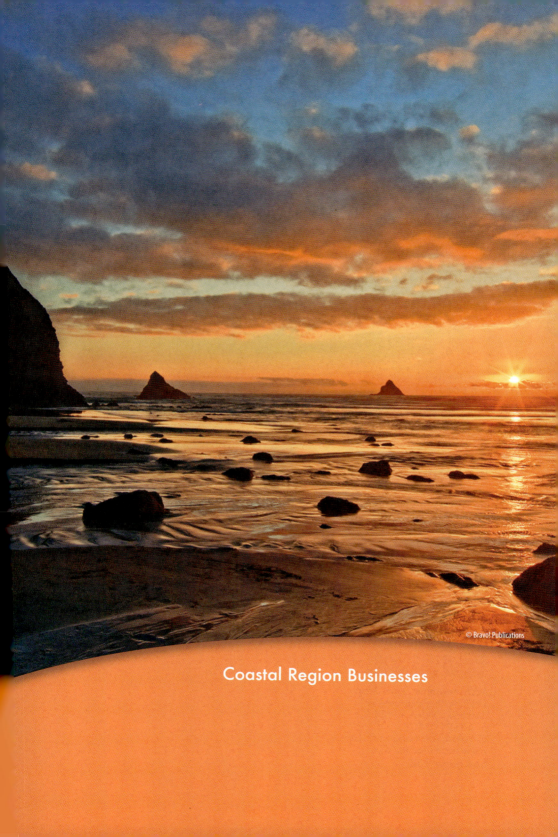

Coastal Region Businesses

Astoria-Warrenton Chamber of Commerce
P.O. Box 176, Astoria, Oregon 97103
p. 800.875.6807
e. reginawilkie@charter.net
www.oldoregon.com
See page 217

The Mill Casino
3201 Tremont Avenue
North Bend, Oregon 97459
p. 800.953.4800 ext. 2288
e. ldinovo@themillcasino.com
www.themillcasino.com
See pages 86, 160

The Banker's Suite

The Banker's Suite
1215 Duane St.
Astoria, Oregon 97103
p. 425.417.6512
e. bankerssuite@bluemars.com
www.thebankerssuite.com
See page 101

Pelican Brewpub
33180 Cape Kiwanda Drive
Pacific City, Oregon 97135
p. 503.965.3674
e. Events@pelicanbrewery.com
www.pelicanbrewery.com
See page 174

Inn at Spanish Head
4009 SW Hwy. 101
Lincoln City, Oregon 97367
p. 800.452.8127
e. kim@spanishhead.com
www.spanishhead.com
See pages 139, 289

Surfsand Resort
148 West Gower
Cannon Beach, Oregon 97110
p. 800.797.4666
e. groups@surfsand.com
www.surfsand.com
See pages 196, 294

McMenamins Sand Trap
1157 North Marion Avenue
Gearhart, Oregon 97138
p. 503.717.8502
e. salessandt@mcmenamins.com
www.mcmenamins.com
See page 156

Mt. Hood & Columbia River Gorge Businesses

A Majestic Mountain Retreat
38250 Pioneer Blvd. #602
Sandy, Oregon 97055
p. 503.686.8080
e. becca1st@gmail.com
www.amajesticmountainretreat.com
See page 12

Cathedral Ridge Winery
4200 Post Canyon
Hood River, Oregon 97031
p. 800.516.8710
e. crw@cathedralridgewinery.com
www.cathedralridgewinery.com
See pages 109, 330

Busy Bee Catering
P.O. Box 295
Welches, Oregon 97067
p. 503.622.6743
e. busybeecatering@hotmail.com
www.busybeecatering.com
See page 38

Columbia Cliff Villas
3880 Westcliff Drive
Hood River, Oregon 97031
p. 866.912.8366
e. info@columbiacliffvillas.com
www.columbiacliffvillas.com
See pages 13, 115

Bonneville Hotsprings Resort
1252 East Cascade Drive
North Bonneville, Washington 98639
p. 509.427.9718
e. groupsales@bhsr.us
See page 104

Columbia Gorge Hotel
400 Westcliff Drive
Hood River, Oregon 97031
p. 541.386.5566
e. kim.bosch@northp.com
www.columbiagorgehotel.com
See page 116

Carson Ridge Luxury Cabins
1261 Wind River Road,
Carson, Washington 98610
p. 877.816.7908
e. info@carsonridgecabins.com
www.carsonridgecabins.com
See page 108

Columbia River Adventure Cruises
110 SE Caruthers
Portland, Oregon 97214
p. 800.224.3901
e. sales@portlandspirit.com
www.portlandspirit.com
See pages 84, 117

www.bravoevent.com

Falcon's Crest Lodge
In Government Camp

Falcon's Crest Lodge – Mt. Hood Vacations
38250 Pioneer Blvd., #607
Sandy, Oregon 97055
p. 503.686.8080
www.mthoodrent.com
See pages 15, 287

Mt. Hood Bed and Breakfast
8885 Cooper Spur Road
Parkdale, Oregon 97041
p. 541.352.6858
e. mthoodbnb@gorge.net
www.mthoodbnb.com
See page 163

Gorge Crest Vineyards
P.O. Box 100
Underwood, Washington 98651
p. 509.493.2026
e. info@gorge.net
www.gorgecrest.com
See page 130

Mt. Hood Meadows
14040 Highway 35
Mt. Hood, Oregon 97041
p. 503.659.1256
e. george.evans@skihood.com
www.skihood.com
See pages 164, 281

Martin's Gorge Tours
P.O. Box 18177
Portland, Oregon 97218
p. 503.349.1323
e. martin@martinsgorgetours.com
www.martinsgorgetours.com
See page 337

Mt. Hood Ski Bowl
P.O. Box 280
Government Camp, Oregon 97028
p. 503.658.4385
e. knorton@skibowl.com
www.skibowl.com
See pages 165, 282

Maryhill Winery
9774 Highway 14 West
Goldendale, Washington 98620
p. 509.773.1976
e. joeg@maryhillwinery.com
www.maryhillwinery.com
See pages 150, 333

Mt. Hood Winery

Mt. Hood Winery
2882 Van Horn Drive
Hood River, Oregon 97031
p. 541.386.8333
e. linda@mthoodwinery.com
www.mthoodwinery.com
See pages 166, 334

Sea to Summit
Portland, Oregon 97217
p. 503.286.9333
e. seatosummit@qwest.net
www.seatosummit.net
See pages 283, 320, 339

Skamania Lodge
1311 SW Skamania Lodge Way
Stevenson, Washington 98648
p. 800.376.9116
e. slmeetings@destinationhotels.com
www.skamania.com
See pages 192, 255, 292

Timberline Lodge
Timberline, Oregon
p. 503.272.3251
e. sales@timberlinelodge.com
www.timberlinelodge.com
See pages 198, 295

Zoller's Outdoor Odyssey
1248 Highway 141
White Salmon, Washington 98672
p. 800.366.2004
e. markz@ZooRaft.com
See page 313

www.bravoevent.com

Southwest Washington Businesses

SW Washington Businesses

ALDERBROOK
RESORT & SPA

Alderbrook Resort & Spa
10 East Alderbrook Drive
Union, Washington 98592
p. 360.898.2200
e. sales@alderbrookresort.com
www.alderbrookresort.com
See page 97

Carson Ridge Luxury Cabins
1261 Wird River Road
Carson, Washington 98610
p. 877.816.7908
e. info@carsonridgecabins.com
www.carsonridgecabins.com
See page 108

Big Al's
16615 SE 18th St.
Vancouver, Washington 98683
360.944.6118
e. events@ILoveBigAls.com
www.ILoveBigAls.com
See page 102

Clark County Event Center
17402 NE Delfel Road
Ridgefield, Washington 98642
p. 360.397.6180
e. info@clarkcoeventcenter.com
www.clarkcoeventcenter.com
See page 112

Bonneville Hotsprings Resort
1252 East Cascade Drive
North Bonneville, Washington 98639
p. 509.427.9718
e. groupsales@bhsr.us
See page 104

David Cooley Band
p. 800.364.1522
e. info@davidcooleyband.com
www.davidcooleyband.com
See page 54

Camas Meadows Golf Club
4105 NW Camas Meadows Drive
Camas, Washington 98607
p. 360.833.2000
e. jduce@camasmeadows.com
www.camasmeadows.com
See pages 106, 249

Dippity Doodads
Chocolate Fountain Rentals

Dippity Doodads
8205 NE 91st Street
Vancouver, Washington 98662
p. 360.798.7395
e. shirley@dippitydoodads.com
www.dippitydoodads.com
See page 35

www.bravoevent.com

Gorge Crest Vineyard
P.O. Box 100
Underwood, Washington 98651
p. 509.493.2026
e. info@gorge.net
www.gorgecrest.com
See page 130

Maryhill Winery
9774 Highway 14 West
Goldendale, Washington 98620
p. 509.773.1976
e. joeg@maryhillwinery.com
www.maryhillwinery.com
See pages 150, 333

Great Wolf Lodge
20500 SW Old Highway 99
Centralia, Washington 98531
p. 360.273.7718
e. jpoole@greatwolf.com
www.greatwolf.com
See pages 132, 311

Maui Wowi
4001 NW 8th Circle
Camas, Washington 98607
p. 360.335.3180
e. tammythiemann@comcast.net
www.mauiwowiportland.com
See page 34

The Heathman Lodge

The Heathman Lodge
7801 NE Greenwood Drive
Vancouver, Washington 98662
p. 360.254.3100
maili.morrison@heathmanlodge.com
www.heathmanlodge.com
See page 134

Ramona's Gift Baskets
11504 SW Mill Plain Blvd Ste K
Vancouver, Washington 98684
p. 503.654.0446
e. janelle@ramonasbaskets.com
www.ramonabaskets.com
See page 244

JoFoody's Catering
1409 Broadway St
Vancouver, Washington 98663
p. 360.607.3281
e. jodell@jofoody.com
www.jofoody.com
See page 45

Skamania Lodge
Scenic Columbia River Gorge

Skamania Lodge
1311 SW Skamania Lodge Way
Stevenson, Washington 98648
p. 800.376.9116
e. slmeetings@destinationhotels.com
www.skamania.com
See page 192, 255, 292

Notes

Willamette Valley Businesses

Class Act Event Coordinators
Salem, Oregon
p. 503.371.8904
e. events@classactevents.net
www.classactevents.net
See page 211

Red Lion Hotel Salem
3301 Market Street NE
Salem, Oregon 97301
p. 503.370.7888
e. dos@redlionsalem.com
www.Redlion.com/salem
See page 185

Events at Copper Hill
3170 Commercial Street SE
Salem Oregon 97302
p. 503.373.3170
www.eventsatcopperhill.com
See page 125

Salem Conference Center
200 Commercial Street SE
Salem, Oregon 97301
p. 503.589.1700
e. dearly@salemconferencecenter.org
www.salemconferencecenter.org
See page 92

GOSGMP
P.O. Box 862
Salem, Oregon 97308
p. 503.378.2497
e. nancy.a.ahlbin@state.or.us
www.gosgmp.com
See page 220

Spirit Mountain Casino
27100 SW Salmon River Hwy
Grand Ronde, Oregon 97347
p. 800.760.7977 ext 3914
e. ashley.langley@spiritmtn.com
www.spiritmountain.com
See pages 87, 194

The Oregon Garden
879 W Main St.
Silverton, Oregon 97381
p. 503.874.6005
e. events@oregongarden.org
See page 169

Travel Salem
181 High St. SE
Salem, Oregon 97301
p. 503.581.4325
e. dmccune@travelsalem.com
www.travelsalem.com
See page 222

Yamhill Valley Busineses

5 Rock Ranch
23800 NW Flying M Road,
Yamhill, Oregon 97148
p. 503.662.5678
e. christy@5rockranch.com
www.5rockranch.com
See page 93

McMenamins – Hotel Oregon
310 NE Evans Street
McMinnville, OR 97128
p. 503.472.8427
e. salesoto@mcmenamins.com
www.mcmenamins.com
See page 153

ELK COVE
VINEYARDS

Elk Cove Vineyards
27751 NW Olson Road
Gaston, Oregon 97119
p. 503.985.7760
e. martha@elkcove.com
www.elkcove.com
See pages 124, 331

McMinnville Grand Ballroom
325 NE 3rd Street
McMinnville, Oregon 97128
p. 503.474.0264
e. info@mgballroom.com
www.mgballroom.com
See page 157

Evergreen Aviation Museum
500 NE Captain Michael King Smith Way
McMinnville, Oregon 97128
p. 503.434.4023
e. events@sprucegoose.org
www.evergreenmuseum.org
See page 126

Parrett Mountain Farm
10500 NE Parrett Mountain Road
Newberg, Oregon 97132
p. 503.625.6821
e. contact@parrettmountainfarm.com
www.parrettmountainfarm.com
See page 172

GRAPE ESCAPE
WINERY TOURS

Grape Escape
Oregon Wine Country Tours
p. 503.283.3380
e. info@GrapeEscapeTours.com
www.GrapeEscapeTours.com
See pages 280, 336

Certified Speaking Professional
877-474-2962
www.BusinessGraces.com

Shawna Schuh
24241 Highway 47
Gaston, Oregon 97119
p. 503.662.3044
e. shawna@shawnaschuh.com
www.ShawnaSchuh.com
See page 303

Windrose Conference & Meeting Center
809 W First St.
Newberg, Oregon 97132
p. 503.701.7273
e. lynn@windrosecenter.com
www.windrosecenter.com
See page 205

Yamhill Valley Visitors Association
P.O. Box 774
McMinnville, Oregon 97128
p. 503.883.7770
e. info@yamhillvalley.org
www.yamhillvalley.org
See Page 223

Notes

Index

INDEX

#
- 3 Leg Torso 52
- 5 Rock Ranch 93

A
- A Hybrid Moon 324
- A Majestic Mountain Retreat 12
- Accommodations 11
- Aarnegard's Premiere Catering 37
- Abernethy Center 94
- Aden Photography & Video Productions 273, 325
- Advantage Graphics 242
- Aerie at Eagle Landing, The 95, 248
- AJ's Party Shots 274
- Albertina's Restaurant & Shops 96
- Alderbrook Resort & Spa 97
- Alesia Zorn Calligraphy 268
- Alexander, Master of Marvels! 64
- All About Fun! 26, 258, 259
- All About Music Entertainment 60
- All Star Limousine 316
- Amadeus Manor 98
- Ambridge Event Center, The 99
- Andina 100
- Association of Catering & Event Planners 216
- Astoria-Warrenton Chamber of Commerce 217

B
- Banker's Suite, The 101
- Barbara Pikus Caricatures 65, 260
- Barclay Event Rentals 234
- BearCom Rental 230
- Bella Notte Events 210
- Big Al's 102
- Big K Guest Ranch, The 103, 286
- Black Belt Business Solutions 299
- Bonneville Hot Springs Resort and Spa 104
- Bouquets & Balloons 80
- Brainwaves Improvisational Comedy 66, 308
- Brenda Buratti 304
- Brian Odell Band, The 53
- Bridgeport Brewpub & Bakery 105
- Bryan Hoybook Photographer 275
- Business Journal, Portland 20
- Business Publications & Media 19
- Bust-A-Move DJ Services 61
- Busy Bee Catering 38

C
- Camas Meadows Golf Club .. 106, 249
- Caples House Museum 107
- Carson Ridge Luxury Cabins 108
- Casino & Theme Parties 25
- Catering At Its Best 39
- Catering Services 29
- Cathedral Ridge Winery 109, 330
- Central Oregon 341
- City of Hillsboro Parks & Recreation 110
- Clark County Event Center 112
- Class Act Event Coordinators 211
- Club Paesano-Cedarville Park 113
- ClubSport 114, 278, 309
- Coastal Region 343
- Columbia Cliff Villas 13, 115
- Columbia Gorge Hotel 116
- Columbia River Adventure Cruises & Marine Park 84, 117, 180
- ComedySportz 67, 310
- Cooper Spur Mt. Resort 118
- CORT Event Furnishings 235
- Courtyard by Marriott, Portland North Harbour 149
- Crave Catering 40
- Creative Childcare Solutions 229
- Crowne Plaza Downtown/Convention Center 14, 119
- Crystal Lilies 78
- Cultural Arts Center 120
- Curtis Frye 68
- Cusa Raz 347

D
- David Cooley Band 54
- Dawn Rasmussen 302
- DeAngelo's Catering 41
- Dippity DooDads 35
- Doll House Tea Room, The 121
- Doubletree Hotel Portland 122
- Drink Bar Events and Staffing 30
- Duo con Brio 72
- DWA Trade Show & Exposition Services . 231

E
- Eagle Landing 95, 248
- EcoShuttle 317
- Ecotrust Event Spaces 123
- Elephants Delicatessen 42
- Elk Cove Vineyards 124, 331
- Emerald Staffing 239
- Entertainment 51
- Espresso Arts Catering 31
- Espresso Elegance 32
- Espresso Volare 33
- Events at Copper Hill 125
- Event Design, Production & Décor 73
- Event & Meeting Sites 83
- Event Planners 209
- Event Professional Organizations 215
- Event Services 225
- Event Solutions 21
- Evergreen Aviation & Space Museum 126
- Executive Gifts & Promotional Items 241
- Expo Center 88, 89

www.bravoevent.com

F
Falcon's Crest Lodge 15, 287
Family Fun Center &
  Bullwinkle's Restaurant 127, 279
Fenouil 128
Fireworks Event Productions 212
FivePine 129, 288
Fliptography 276
FocalPoint Digital 227

G
Gail Hand, The Power Of Laughter .. 300
Golf Courses & Tournaments 247
Gorge Crest Vineyards 130
Greater Oregon Society of Government
  Meeting Professionals 220
Gourmet Productions 43
Grand Central Restaurant &
  Bowling Lounge 131
Grape Escape Winery Tours 280, 336
Great Wolf Lodge 132, 311
Grotto, The 133

H
Heathman Lodge, The 134
Helvetia Winery 332
Hilton Garden Inn
Portland Airport 16, 135
Holiday Inn Portland South/Wilsonville ... 136
Hollywood Lighting Services 82, 233
Holocene 137
Honey Bucket 236
Hula Halau 'Ohana Holo'oko'a 69
Hybrid Moon 324

I
Imagine Your Reality 301
In Great Spirits 243
Inn at Spanish Head Resort Hotel .. 139, 289
Interactive Entertainment 257
International Special Events Society 218
Invitations & Calligraphy 267

J
Jake's Catering 44, 140
Jathan Janove 304
Jerry Fletcher 305
Jo Foody's Catering 45
JR Audio & Video 326

K
Kah-Nee-Ta High Desert
  Resort & Casino 85, 141
Keizer Civic Center, City of 111
Kellie Poulsen-Grill 305
Kells Irish Restaurant and Pub 142

L
Lakeside Gardens 143
Langdon Farms Golf Club 144, 250
Lavish Floral 79
Lawrence Gallery 145
Lodge at Suttle Lake, The 146
Long Hollow Ranch 147, 312

M
Magic George 70
Majestic Inn and Spa 148
Martin's Gorge Tours 337
Maryhill Winery 150, 333
Matrix Video 327
Maui Wowi Coffees & Smoothies 34
McMenamins Edgefield 151, 290
McMenamins Grand Lodge 152
McMenamins Hotel Oregon 153
McMenamins Kennedy School 154
McMenamins Old St. Francis School 155
McMenamins Sand Trap 156
McMinnville Grand Ballroom 157
Meeting Professionals International
  Oregon Chapter 219
Meetings West 22
Melody Ballroom 158
Meriwether's Restaurant 159
Mill Casino, The 86, 160
Mittleman Jewish Community Center 161
Mobile Music Entertainment Services 62
Morton's, The Steakhouse 162
Mt. Hood Bed & Breakfast 163
Mt. Hood & Columbia River Gorge 345
Mt. Hood Meadows 164, 281
Mt. Hood SkiBowl 165, 282
Mt. Hood Winery 166, 334
Musica Melodia 71

N
National Speakers
  Association Oregon 298
Northwest Artist Management 58
Notes of Celebration 72

O
Old McDonald's Farm 167
OMSI 168
Oregon Business Magazine 23
Oregon Convention Center 90, 91
Oregon Garden, The 169
Oregon Historical Society 170
Oswego Lake House 171

P
Pacific Talent 59
Paparazzi Tonight 261, 272
Paradym Events 74
Parrett Mountain Living History Farm 172
Party Outfitters 262
Party Scoop, The 36
PartyWorks 263
Pathfinder Writing and Career Services ... 302
Patrick Lamb 55
Pazzo Ristorante 138
PCC – Portland Community College 173
Pearl Catering 46, 201
Pelican Pub & Brewery 174
Persimmon Country Club 175, 251
Peter Corvallis Productions 75, 237

www.bravoevent.com

PGE Park 176
Photographers 271
Pomeroy Farm 177
Portland Art Museum 178
Portland Business Journal 20
Portland Catering Company 47
Portland Classical Chinese Garden 179
Portland Expo Center 88, 89
Portland Spirit 84, 117, 180
PosterGarden 226
Power Of Laughter, The 300
Premiere Catering, Aarnegard's 37
Premiere Tours 318, 338
Premiere Valet Service 322
PRO DJs Oregon 63
Pumpkin Ridge Golf Club 181, 252

Q
Queen Anne Victorian Mansion.. 182

R
Rafati's Catering 48
Ramona's Gift Baskets 244
Raz Transportation 319
Really Big Video 228
Red Lion Hotel Portland
 Convention Center 17, 184
Red Lion Hotel On The River 183
Red Lion Hotel – Salem 185
Recreation, Attractions & Sports 277
Reserve Vineyards and Golf Club, The 186, 253
Residence Inn by Marriott Portland
 North Harbour 149
Resorts & Retreats 285
Right Now Communications 304
Rock Creek Country Club 187, 254
Royce's Prop Shop 76, 213

S
Salem Conference Center 92
Salty's 189
Scottish Rite Center, The 190
Sea to Summit Tours &
 Adventures 283, 320, 339
Seventh Mountain Resort 191, 291
Seymour Band 56
Shawna Schuh 303
Show and Tell Cookies 245
Skamania Lodge &
 Golf Course 192, 255, 292
Smart Meetings Media 24
Southpark Seafood Grill & Wine Bar 193
Southwest Washington 349
Speakers & Trainers 297
Spirit Mountain Casino 87, 194
Stargazer Baskets & Blooms 246
Still Pending 57

Successful Creations 214
Sunriver Resort 195, 293
Surfsand Resort 196, 294

T
Taylor Ellwood 301
Team Building 307
Team Casino 27, 264
Tiffany Center 197
Tim Alexander 64
Timberline Lodge 198, 295
Transportation & Valet 315
Travel Portland 221
Travel Salem 222
Treasury Ballroom, The 199
Tucci 200

U
Uncommon Invites 269
Urban Studio 46, 201

V
Vibrant Table 49
Videography 323
Video Media 328
Village Lake Conference in First Addition. 202
Vip PDX 321, 340

W
Wanderlust Tours 284
West Coast Event Productions 77, 238
Whirlwind Woman, The 305
Wild Bill's 28, 203, 265
Wilf's Restaurant & Bar 50, 204
Willamette Valley 353
Windrose Conference & Meeting Center . 205
Wineries & Custom Labeling 329
Wine Tours 335
World Forestry Center 206
World Trade Center Portland 207

Y
Yamhill Valley 355
Yamhill Valley Visitors Association.. 223

Z
Z-Axis Marketing/Networking Ninja 305
Zoller's Outdoor Odyssey 313

www.bravoevent.com

Notes

Notes

Notes

A special thank you to our vendors, planners, and partners who have supported Bravo! for over 20 years.

We look forward to continuing to provide you with the Northwest's most trusted name in event planning.

From all of us at Bravo! Publications, *Thank You!*